MINICOMPUTER SYSTEMS

Prentice-Hall

SERIES IN AUTOMATIC COMPUTATION

MINICOMPUTER SYSTEMS
ORGANIZATION
AND PROGRAMMING
(PDP-11)

RICHARD H. ECKHOUSE, JR.

Department of Computer and Information Sciences
University of Massachusetts

PRENTICE-HALL, INC.

ENGLEWOOD CLIFFS, NEW JERSEY

Library of Congress Cataloging in Publication Data

ECKHOUSE, RICHARD H.
  Minicomputer systems.

  (Prentice-Hall series in automatic computation)
  Bibliography
  Includes index.
  1. PDP-11 (Computer)—Programming. 2. Miniature
computers—Programming. I. Title.
QA76.8.P2E26   001.6'424   74-26619
ISBN 0-13-583906-8

10 9 8 7 6 5 4 3 2 1

Printed in the United States of America.

PRENTICE-HALL INTERNATIONAL, INC., *London*
PRENTICE-HALL OF AUSTRALIA PTY. LTD., *Sydney*
PRENTICE-HALL OF CANADA, LTD., *Toronto*
PRENTICE-HALL OF INDIA PRIVATE LIMITED, *New Delhi*
PRENTICE-HALL OF JAPAN, INC., *Tokyo*

CONTENTS

PREFACE

There is a certain fascination one feels when using a small, stand-alone computer. The fascination has to do with being in complete control of an entire computing system, knowing that there is nothing one cannot do, nothing one cannot try. I am sure that our computer pioneers, having developed and used the first machines, must have felt this way, and I know that the fascination still prevails among today's systems programmers.

Some might argue that the feeling I have described is nostalgic and not pertinent in today's world of closed shop computer operations. They would point out that the average computer user is quite satisfied programming in a high-level language. They would go on to describe these users as being primarily concerned with computer programming and very happy to ignore most aspects of computer hardware, software, and system design.

This book is not meant for the users just described, but rather for those whose fascination with computers has led them to want to understand the magic which surrounds the devices they have used. Such computer users (systems programmers, system designers, computer scientists, electrical engineers, application specialists) want to know something about computer organization and assembly language programming, and it is with them in mind that this book was fashioned.

My motivation in developing this book came as a consequence of having taught computer organization and assembly language programming to diverse groups of students using widely different computers. In all cases I strived to bring out the fundamental concepts in computer hardware and software, especially as these ideas effect the larger issue of computer systems and their organization. Having attempted various means for accomplishing my objective, I generally found that use of a real computer to illustrate the concepts presented was far preferable to use of a simulated machine.

Being widely available at relatively low cost, the small or minicomputer seemed to me to be the best choice for a real computer. Having features previously found only in larger systems (e.g., overlapped operations, interrupts, multiple registers, built-in multiply/divide, etc.), these small computers have gained widespread popularity and are to be found as an integral part of many systems. Thus these machines are well suited for a book, such as this, covering the area of computer organization and assembly language programming. I have assumed that readers of this book will have completed a basic course in a procedure-oriented language. Because of the prevalent use and the common knowledge of FORTRAN, I have chosen to use that language to illustrate many of my examples. Actually, the choice of a higher-level language (FORTRAN) to illustrate the same ideas in a lower-level (PAL-11) language serves to do more than merely exemplify one by the other. Programming fundamentals and techniques are largely independent of language implementation, and as a result, a variety of languages at various levels may be effectively used to illustrate new ideas. For the reader of this book, the result is that one can quite naturally develop the fundamental concepts of digital computers and programming while learning some of the details of PDP-11 programming.

The choice of the PDP-11 as the real machine was prompted by several reasons. These included (a) its popularity, (b) the large number of features available on the machine, and (c) the wide range of systems developed for this computer. I have attempted to present a concept and then illustrate it on the PDP-11, not vice versa. Thus I hope that people with no computer or with a different type of computer might be able to understand the concepts presented and be able to relate them to their own experience.

The book begins by discussing computer fundamentals quite independently of any specific machine. Topics in this section of the text include computing machines and computer organization, simple number systems and concepts, and logical operations and computer building blocks. Chapter 2 deals with programming fundamentals, including flowcharting and program coding, symbolic coding, registers and their uses, and the various addressing modes common to digital computers.

Chapter 3 discusses the organization and structure of the PDP-11. Examples illustrate how operations are performed on that computer. Chapter 4 deals with programming techniques, including position-independent programming, subroutines and coroutines, reentrancy and recursion, programming arithmetic operations, the representation of floating point numbers, and character handling.

Because of the importance of the representation of information within a computer, a separate chapter (Chapter 5) has been devoted to an introduction to data structures. Beginning with an understanding of FORTRAN arrays, the chapter not only discusses stacks, shelves, queues, lists, hashing, and packing techniques for the representation and storage of data, but it also illustrates these concepts with FORTRAN and assembly language programs or routines.

Being able to program a computer is of little value if there is no way of providing data and obtaining results from it. Thus Chapter 6 is devoted to

I/O programming and covers the subject from the basics to interrupt driven devices. Also included in the chapter is a description of the system software that is usually provided by the computer manufacturer to facilitate effective utilization of the I/O devices and to assist the programmer in writing programs which require input, output, or both. This last section leads quite nicely to the subject of the next chapter, system software.

Chapter 7 presents a brief description of the types of system software to be found on most small computers. Topics discussed include the functions of an editor, the flexibility of a macro assembler, the linking and loading process, and the facility of an on-line, dynamic debugging package.

One of the unusual features of this text is its treatment of operating systems (Chapter 8). After we have dealt with computer organization, assembly language programming, hardware features, and system software, this chapter serves to summarize and unify the ideas and concepts presented. First, we explain why an operating system is desirable. Second, a general-purpose system is conceived by considering what is needed and how it can be provided. Finally, having gained some insight into an operating system, the reader is then told about the various application areas which have been served by small computer system operating environments.

The last chapter of this book, Chapter 9, is devoted to the description of a modest multiprogramming system. This system is simple to understand and yet contains most of the ideas and concepts found in larger real-time operating systems supported by most small machine manufacturers. The system represents an applications environment, and the reader can learn, through the detailed analysis of its overall organization, how the basic system can be expanded for a particular application.

In order to help him remember what to do when, and also in order to clarify what has been presented, the reader is provided with many examples, successively difficult problems, and references for further study. The examples and problems are drawn from many sources, including the classroom projects which were developed in the course of preparing this book. Since some subjects may need further explanation, there are several appendices devoted to such topics as number systems, introductory concepts in logical operations, the operator's console, etc.

It is my intention that this introductory text serve as an educational stepping stone to more advanced topics in computer science. As a consequence, I have attempted to provide the reader with the necessary (and sufficient) skills required to further his understanding of computer systems. It is not my goal to teach the reader how to program and run a PDP-11 computer, although I expect that he will have acquired a good working knowledge of that machine. I do expect that as a result of using this text, the reader will become aware that he is learning something about the basic ideas of computer elements and the principles of computer systems organization.

As with all books, it is impossible to thank the myriad of people who helped make it possible. I have chosen to single out Professors Bob Taylor and John Greaves, and students Elliot Soloway, Al Klein, Ed Machado, and Steve Beckhardt for their helpful comments, Lynn Gilbert, Kathy Browne, and Mary Ann Rosenthal for their excellent typing assistance, and my wife Judy for her continuing support. Special thanks go to Gordon Bell, whose continued help has made this book possible.

Richard H. Eckhouse, Jr.

MINICOMPUTER SYSTEMS

1 COMPUTER FUNDAMENTALS

1.1. INTRODUCTION

During the past 25 years, the computer revolution has dramatically changed our world, and it promises to bring about even greater changes in the years ahead.

The general-purpose digital computers being built today are much faster, smaller, and more reliable and can be produced at lower cost than the earlier computers. New technologies, different architectures, and faster memories are having a great impact on the computer. But even more significant breakthroughs have come in the many new ways in which we have learned to use computers.

The first big electronic computers were usually employed as supercalculators to solve complex mathematical problems that had been impossible to attack before. In recent years, computer programmers have begun using computers for nonnumerical applications, such as control systems, communications, artificial intelligence, pattern recognition, and data handling and processing. In these operations, the computer system processes vast quantities of data at high speed.

1.1.1. The Computer Challenge

It has been said that a computer can be programmed to do any problem that can be defined. The key word here is "defined," which means that the solution of the problem can be broken down into a series of steps that can be written as a sequence of computer instructions. The definition of some problems, such as the translation of natural languages, has turned out to be very difficult. A few years ago it was thought that computer programs could be written to translate French into English, for example. As a matter of fact,

1

it is quite easy to translate a list of French words into English words with similar meanings. However, it is very difficult to translate sentences precisely because of the many shades of meaning associated with individual words and word combinations. For this reason, it is not practical to try to communicate with a computer using a conventional spoken language.

Although natural languages are impractical for computer use, programming languages, such as BASIC and FORTRAN, with their precisely defined structure and syntax, greatly simplify communication with a computer. Programming languages are problem-oriented and contain familiar words and expressions; thus, by using a programming language it is possible to learn to write programs after a relatively short training period. Since most computer manufacturers have adopted standard programming languages and implemented the use of these languages on their computers, a given program can be executed on a large number of computers. Small-computer programmers use FORTRAN for scientific and engineering problems and BASIC for shorter numerical calculations. Computer languages have been developed for programmed control of machine tools, computer typesetting, music composition, data acquisition, computer-aided instruction, and many other applications. It is likely that there will be many more new programming languages in the future. Each new language development will enable the user to more easily apply the power of the computer to his particular problem or task.

Who can be a programmer? In the early days of computer programming, most programmers were mathematicians. However, as this text illustrates, most programming requires only an elementary ability to handle arithmetic and logical operations. Perhaps the most basic requirement for programming is the ability to reason logically.

The rapid expansion of the computer field in the last decade has made the resources of the computer available to hundreds of thousands of people and has provided many new career opportunities.

1.1.2. Computer Applications

A computer, like any other machine, is used because it does certain tasks better and more efficiently than humans. Specifically, it can receive more information and process it faster than a human. Often, this speed means that weeks or months of pencil-and-paper work can be replaced by a method requiring only minutes of computer time. Therefore, computers are used when the time saved by using a computer offsets its cost. Further, because of its capacity to handle large volumes of data in a very short time, a computer may be the *only* means of resolving problems when time is limited. Because of the advantages of great speed and large capacity, computers are being used more and more in business, industry, and research. Most computer applications can be classified as either *business* uses, which usually rely upon the computer's capacity to store and quickly retrieve large amounts of information, or *scientific* uses, which require accuracy and speed in performing mathematical calculations. Both of these are performed on general-purpose computers. We shall now look at a few examples of computer applications.

Design problems. The computer is a very useful calculating tool for the design engineer. The wing design of a supersonic aircraft, for example, depends upon many factors. The designer describes each of these factors in the form of mathematical equations in a programming language. The computer can then be used to solve these equations.

Scientific and laboratory experiments. In scientific and laboratory experiments, computers are used to evaluate and store information from numerous types of electronic sensing devices. Computers are particularly useful in such systems as telemetry, where signals must be quickly recorded or they are lost. These applications require rapid and accurate processing for both fixed conditions and dynamic situations.

Process control. The computer is a useful tool for manufacturing and inspecting products automatically. A computer may be programmed to run and control milling machines, turret lathes, and many other machine tools with more rapid and accurate response than is possible for humans. It can be programmed to use special sensors to inspect a part as it is being made and adjust the machine tool as needed. If an incoming part is defective, the computer may be programmed to reject it and start the next part.

Training by simulation. It is often expensive, dangerous, and impractical to train a large group of men under actual conditions to fly a commercial airplane, control a satellite, or operate a space vehicle. A computer can simulate all these conditions for a trainee, respond to his actions, and report the results of the training. The trainee can receive many hours of on-the-job training without risk to himself, others, or the expensive equipment involved.

Applications such as these often require the processing of both analog and digital information. Analog information consists of continuous physical quantities that can be easily generated and controlled, such as electrical voltages or shaft rotations. Digital information, however, consists of discrete numerical values, which represent the variables of a problem. Normally, analog values are converted to equivalent digital values for arithmetic calculations to solve problems. Some computers, such as the LINC-8, combine the analog and digital characteristics in one computer system.

1.1.3. Computer Capabilities and Limitations

A computer is a machine and, like all machines, must be directed and controlled to perform a task. Until a program is prepared and stored in the computer's core memory, the computer "knows" absolutely nothing, not even how to receive input. No matter how good a computer may be, it must be "told" what to do. The usefulness of a computer cannot be fully realized, therefore, until the capabilities (and the limitations) of the computer are recognized.

1. *Repetitive operation:* a computer can perform similar operations thousands of times, without becoming bored, tired, or careless.

2. *Speed:* a computer processes information at enormous speeds, which are directly related to the ingenuity of the designer and the programmer. Modern computers can solve certain classes of problems millions of times faster than a skilled mathematician.

3. *Flexibility:* general-purpose computers may be programmed to solve many types of problems.

4. *Accuracy:* computers may be programmed to calculate answers with a desired level of accuracy as specified by the programmer.

5. *Intuition:* a computer has no intuition. A man may suddenly find the answers to a problem without working out the details, but a computer can only proceed as ordered.

The remainder of this chapter is devoted to the general organization of the computer and the manner in which it handles data. Included are the basic organization and structure of computing machines and the number systems used in programming, together with the arithmetic and logical operations of the computer. This information provides a necessary background for all who desire a basic appreciation of computers and their uses, and it is a prerequisite to machine- and assembly-language programming covered in subsequent chapters.

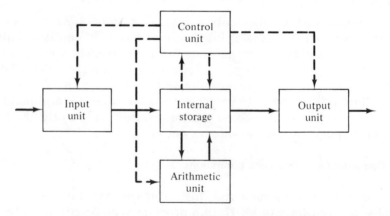

Fig. 1-1 General organization of a computer.

1.2. COMPUTING MACHINES AND COMPUTER ORGANIZATION

From an elementary standpoint, almost every general-purpose digital computer can be described as having the same basic structure. This structure is shown in Fig. 1-1.

1.2.1. Elements of the Basic Structure of a Computer

If a machine is to be called a computer, it must have the capability of performing some types of arithmetic operations. The element of a digital computer that meets this requirement is called the *arithmetic unit*. For the arithmetic unit to be able to do its required task, it must be told what to do; thus, a *control unit* is necessary.

Since mathematical operations are performed by the arithmetic unit, it may be necessary to store a partial answer while the unit is computing another part of the problem. This stored partial answer can then be used to solve other parts of the problem. It is also helpful for the control unit and arithmetic unit to have information immediately available for their use and for the use of other units within the computer. This requirement is met by the portion of the computer designated as the *memory* or *main storage unit*.

The prime purpose of a digital computer is to serve humans in some manner. To do this there must be a method of transmitting our wants to the computer and a means of receiving the results of the computer's calculations. The portions of the computer that carry out these functions are the *input and output (I/O) units*.

1.2.2. Arithmetic Unit

The *arithmetic unit* of a digital computer performs the actual work of computation and calculation. It carries out its job by the use of logic circuits. Modern computers use components called *integrated circuits*. Switches and relays were used previously, and were acceptable as far as their ability to perform computations was concerned. Modern computers, however, because of the speed desired, make use of smaller electronic components whenever possible.

1.2.3. Control Unit

The *control unit* of a digital computer is an administrative or switching section. It receives information entering the machine and decides how and when to perform operations. It tells the arithmetic unit what to do and where to get the necessary information. It knows when the arithmetic unit has completed a calculation, and it tells the arithmetic unit what to do with the results and what to do next.

The control unit itself decides what to tell the arithmetic unit to do by interpreting a set of instructions. This set of instructions for the control unit is called a *program* and is stored in the computer memory. The use of a stored program is one of the attributes that distinguish a computer from a calculator.

Having just performed the operation specified by the current instruction, the control unit must go to memory and fetch the next instruction to be executed. The location in memory where this instruction resides may be specified in one of two ways. First, the last instruction may specify the location. Second, and more commonly, a special *program counter* is used to hold the location in memory of the next instruction to be executed.

Regardless of the scheme used, however, the net result remains the same. Instructions are executed one at a time by the control unit in a sequence specified either as a part of the instructions themselves or by the program counter. These two schemes will become clearer when we consider the various computer instruction formats in Section 1.2.8.

1.2.4. Memory Unit

The *memory unit*, sometimes called the *main storage unit*, contains information for the control unit (instructions) and for the arithmetic unit (data). Sometimes external storage units, such as magnetic tapes and disks, are referred to as *secondary storage*; internal units, such as magnetic cores and semiconductor memories, are referred to as *primary storage*. The requirements of the internal storage units may vary greatly from computer to computer.

Memory is divided into sections called *locations* that can hold an element of data or an instruction. Storage in which each location can be specified and reached as easily as any other is referred to as *random-access* storage. The other type of storage is *sequential storage*, such as magnetic tape, in which case some locations (those at the beginning of the tape) are easier to reach than others (those at the end of the tape).

1.2.5. Input Unit

Input devices are used to supply the values needed by the computer and the instructions to tell the computer how to operate on the values. Input unit requirements vary greatly from machine to machine. A keyboard may be sufficient for a small computer. Computers that require faster input use punched cards for data inputs. Some systems utilize removable plugboards that can be prewired to perform certain instructions. Input may also be via punched paper tape or magnetic tape, two forms of input common in small computer systems.

1.2.6. Output Unit

Output devices record the results of the computer operations. These results may be recorded in a permanent form (e.g., as a printout on the teleprinter) or they may be used to initiate a physical action (e.g., to adjust a pressure-value setting). Many of the media used for input, such as paper tape, punched cards, and magnetic tape, can also be used for output.

1.2.7. Memory Organization

The memory of a computer is the repository of both instructions and data, which we shall refer to as the *information units to be processed*. Each information unit resides in a distinct location of the memory, and each location is capable of holding one such unit. There are two common organizational features of every memory:

1. Each information unit is the same size.

2. An information unit has a numbered value or address associated with it by which it may be referenced uniquely.

Such a memory location is characterized by two things:

1. An *address*, which has a numerical value associated with its relative position in memory.

2. The *contents*, which is a number that is physically stored at the particular location within memory.

It is important to understand the difference between the address (name) and the contents (information).

The size of an information unit may be one binary digit, called a *bit*; a collection of bits, called a *character* or *byte*; or an even larger unit called a *word*. When the computer is designed, the sizes are fixed and are based on the type of application to which the computer shall be put. For example, byte machines are most often used for administrative data processing, where the information to be processed includes names and English words besides numbers. On the other hand, word machines are most often used for scientific calculations, where large quantities of numbers are manipulated and accurate numerical results are desired.

The key difference among bit, character, and word machines is the size of the smallest addressable information unit. For a bit machine, it is one binary digit (i.e., a unit of information capable of representing either 0 or a 1). For a character machine, it is one character from the character set of that machine (i.e., a letter of the alphabet, a digit, or a special character). For a word machine, it is a numerical value from the range of permissible values that may be represented on a particular machine.

As we shall learn, words can often be subdivided into a fixed number of characters or digits. However, in a true word machine, we may reference only the collection, not the individual characters. Thus the subdivision is one of convenience in that it allows us to think of the word as "representing" the characters or digits. The representation is accomplished by "coding" the letters into unique combinations of binary digits. In Chapter 4 we shall see how this is typically done for small computers.

1.2.8. Addressing Schemes

In Fig. 1-1 there are two units, the arithmetic and control units, which when considered together form the *central processing unit (CPU)* of the computer. The job of the CPU is to fetch the next instruction to be executed from the memory, to fetch the operands necessary to carry out the instruction, and, finally, to execute the instruction. To perform these tasks, the CPU must be presented with instruction words that specify:

1. The operation code (e.g., ADD, SUBtract, MULtiply, etc.).

2. The addresses of the operands and resultant.

3. The address of the next instruction to be executed.

Since most arithmetic operations require two operands and a resultant, each instruction word will actually require four fields in total besides the operation code field. Figure 1-2 gives one possible layout for such an instruction form.

Operation code	Operand address 1	Operand address 2	Resultant address 3	Next instruction address

Fig. 1-2 Three-plus-one instruction format.

1.2.8.1. *Three-Plus-One-Address Machines*

Computers that utilize the instruction format shown in Fig. 1-2 are referred to as *three-plus-one (3+1) address machines*. Instructions for such a machine may be written symbolically as

$$\text{ADD, X, Y, Z, W}$$

representing the operation code   symbolic names for locations in memory meaning "add the contents of memory location X to the contents of memory location Y and place the results in memory location Z, taking the next instruction from memory location W." Adopting the convention that "(X)" means "the contents of memory location X," the words become unnecessary and the meaning of the symbolic ADD instruction may be expressed as

$$(Z) \leftarrow (X) + (Y)$$
$$\text{next instruction} \leftarrow (W)$$

where the arrow ($\leftarrow$) is read as "becomes" or "is set equal to." This form, which is used to describe the ADD instruction, is referred to as *infix notation*, where the operation to be performed is embedded between the operands to be operated on.

Let us now consider a sequence of computer instructions to calculate the FORTRAN expression:

$$A = (B * C) - (D * E)$$

where the instructions are to reside in consecutive memory locations I1: through I4:. Expressing this sequence of operations in both symbolic format and infix notation, we have

Symbolic Format	Infix Notation
I1: MUL B,C,T1,I2	I1: $(T1) \leftarrow (B)*(C)$; next instruction $\leftarrow (I2)$
I2: MUL D,E,T2,I3	I2: $(T2) \leftarrow (D)*(E)$; next instruction $\leftarrow (I3)$
I3: SUB T2,T1,A,I4	I3: $(A) \leftarrow (T1)-(T2)$; next instruction $\leftarrow (I4)$
I4: next instruction after sequence	I4: next instruction after sequence

where memory locations T1 and T2 represent temporary locations used to hold the intermediate arithmetic results. In the following sections we shall describe instructions using both the symbolic format and infix notation.

On closer examination, the instructions for this 3+1 address machine reveal two important things. First, although the example presented utilized consecutive memory locations for holding instruction words, there is no requirement within the structure of the machine for this to be so. Second, since there are three explicit addresses in each instruction, there is no need to have internal computer hardware for holding the results of an arithmetic operation. Thus each operation is complete in itself and is performed in one instruction cycle.

1.2.8.2. Three-Address Machines

Considering the first comment in the preceding paragraph, it seems worthwhile to question why sequential ordering of instructions into consecutive memory locations is not a requirement. Since most programs are written in a sequential fashion, it seems quite normal to expect a computer to execute the instructions sequentially, from one location to another. The answer, as it turns out, is really part of the historical development of computer memories. Before the era of magnetic core memories, where each memory location could be accessed randomly without any difference in access time, memories were definitely not random access, being made from mercury delay lines or magnetic drums. On these types of devices, the next sequential location was not, in general, as accessible as one somewhere else. As a result, a strictly sequential program would have executed more slowly than one that could minimize access time by specifying the next instruction location as the one most readily available (and not necessarily the next consecutive location). (A classical example of such a machine was the IBM 650, although it used 1+1 addressing rather than 3+1.)

But since random access memories do exist on most machines, the next instruction address is really not needed. Instead, a "pointer" called a *program counter (PC)* is maintained; it acts like a sliding arrow that always points to the next instruction to be executed. In reality, the PC is a hardware register that holds the address of the current instruction being executed and is updated to point to the next instruction when execution of the current one has been completed. [The CDC 6600 is an example of a computer that uses a P (program address counter register and executes three-register arithmetic instructions.]

Since an important cost factor in most machines is the memory, and the cost of memory is a function of the number of bits per word, it is clear that removing the next address field from each word and substituting one hardware register will effect a significant cost reduction. We may carry the savings further by removing one operand address field, resulting in a new, less costly machine called a *two-address machine*.

1.2.8.3. Two-Address Machines

The loss of the third operand address is not as drastic a move as it might seem. Often there is no need to place the resultant of an arithmetic operation in a different location. Instead, it is just as convenient to use the address of the second operand as both a source and a destination address. For example, let us consider the problem of moving the contents of location A to location B. In the case of the three-address machine it would be necessary to write an instruction such as

```
        ADD        A, ZERO, B                    (B) < (A) + 0
```

where memory location ZERO is assumed to contain a 0. For a two-address machine the instructions would be written as

```
        SUB        B, B                          (B) < (B) - (B)
        ADD        A, B                          (B) < (A) + (B)
```

but this instruction sequence occurs so often that it would be most useful to define a new instruction called *MOV* (for move), which would replace the two-instruction sequence with

```
MOV        A, B                          (B) < (A)
```

Since it is likely that there may be more instructions in a two-address machine than a three-address machine, and since large instruction sets tend to become unwieldly, it will be important to minimize the "may" as much as possible. To do so requires a careful consideration of each instruction and where it fits in the instruction set of the two-address machine. As a result we should not expect a simple carrying over of the three-instruction set to the two-instruction set machine (the MOV above is a case in point).

Both large and small computers have been designed to use two-address arithmetic. The PDP-11, the IBM 1620, the UNIVAC 1105, and the IBM System/360 are all machines that exhibit this architectural structure.

1.2.8.4.   One-Address Machines

To reduce costs even further, we may remove another operand field from the instruction word. As a result, the remaining address field must act as either a source or a destination address, and since most arithmetic operators must have two operands, it will be necessary to provide an implicit (part of the internal hardware) source/sink for the *one-address machine*. This implicit operand is called an *accumulator* and serves much the same purpose as the accumulator found in a desk calculator.

The arithmetic operations of the one-address machine will utilize the accumulator by adding to, subtracting from, and so on, the accumulator, since its use will be implicit in the execution of the instruction. In order to be able to initialize and save the values held in the accumulator, new instructions must be added to the one-address machine to *load the accumulator (LAC)* and *deposit the accumulator (DAC)* from or to memory.

A demonstration of the coding for the one-address machine is given below. Assuming the previously considered arithmetic calculation,

$$A = (B * C) - (D * E)$$

the code for the one-address machine might be

```
LAC     D          (ACC) < (D)
MUL     E          (ACC) < (ACC) * (E)
DAC     T1         (T1) < (ACC)
LAC     B          (ACC) < (B)
MUL     C          (ACC) < (ACC) * (C)
SUB     T1         (ACC) < (ACC) - (T1)
DAC     A          (A) < (ACC)
```

where T1 stands for a temporary location as before and ACC stands for the accumulator. The observant reader will note that if the second multiplication had not been performed first, an extra temporary location would have been needed along with extra DACs and LACs.

By far the most popular addressing scheme implemented has been the one-address architecture. The PDP-8, PDP-15, IBM 1130, IBM 7090, CDC 3600, and others are all examples of computers that utilize single-address instructions and accumulators.

1.2.8.5. *General Register Machines*

Once we have accepted the idea of a computer with an accumulator, it is easy enough to expand the concept to a machine with many accumulators. These accumulators serve as useful places to hold intermediate results once generated, so that the need for temporary memory locations diminishes. For example, on a two-accumulator machine with instructions "load accumulator 1" (LA1), "deposit accumulator 2" ($DA2$), "multiply contents of accumulator 1 by contents of specified memory location, leaving the results in accumulator 1" (MP1), and so on, the coding sequence for the FORTRAN expression $A = (B * C) - (D * E)$ might be

```
LA1      D              (ACC1) < (D)
MP1      E              (ACC1) < (ACC1) * (E)
LA2      B              (ACC2) < (B)
MP2      C              (ACC2) < (ACC2) * (C)
SB2      ACC1           (ACC2) < (ACC2) - (ACC1)
DA2      A               (A) < (ACC2)
```

Multiple accumulator machines are often referred to as *general register computers*. These computers utilize the registers not only to act as accumulators, but also to perform *indexing* on data items in an array, *looping* through a sequence of instructions a given number of times, and *pointing* to a particular place in memory. Thus we say that the registers may be used as accumulators, index registers, counters, and pointers.

Although the concept of general register computers has been developed from one-address machines, this should not be taken to imply that only such machines embody the idea. Rather, general register machines may be two- or even three-address machines with the general register(s) serving in place of a memory location as a given operand. For example, the PDP-11 (a two-address machine) can specify an ADD instruction to "add-to-register," "add-to-memory," or "add-to-register-to-register" as follows:

"Add-to-register":   ADD A, Reg $(Reg) \leftarrow (Reg) + (A)$
"Add-to-memory":   ADD Reg, A $(A) \leftarrow (A) + (Reg)$
"Add-register-to-register":   ADD Reg_1, Reg_2 $(Reg_1) \leftarrow (Reg_1) + (Reg_2)$

where "A" stands for a memory location and "Reg" stands for any of the eight general-purpose registers.

1.2.8.6.   Zero-Address Machines

At this point we may ask ourselves whether we can conceive of a machine with no addresses at all. The answer is yes, but a qualified yes. What is necessary is a mechanism that implicitly maintains the operands required for the standard arithmetic operations. This mechanism is called a *stack*.

A stack can be thought of as an ordered collection of memory locations (or registers, like the accumulator) with a top or first element, a second element, and so on. However, only the top element has to be accessible to perform all necessary stack/arithmetic operations.

Fetching the operands necessary for some arithmetic operations requires that a *POP* operation be performed on the stack. This operation takes the top element off the stack and moves every element up (toward the top of the stack) one position. Thus the second element becomes the first, the third the second, and so on. A complementary operation is *PUSH*, which places a new element in the stack, moving all old elements down one position. Figure 1-3 shows examples of PUSH and POP acting on an initially empty stack.

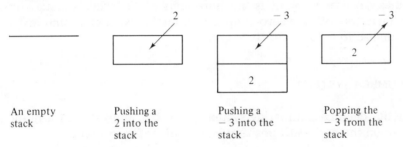

An empty stack	Pushing a 2 into the stack	Pushing a − 3 into the stack	Popping the − 3 from the stack

Fig. 1-3   PUSH and POP operations.

Arithmetic operations such as ADD can now be described as "POP first operand into adder, POP second operand, add operands, and PUSH resultant back into stack." Alternatively, the add may be described by using the previously defined parenthetical notation as follows:

$$(TS) + (TS\text{-}1) \rightarrow (TS\text{-}1) \ \& \ POP$$

where TS stands for top of stack. Such an add operation is shown by Fig. 1-4.

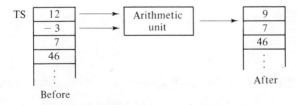

Fig. 1-4   Arithmetic stack operation.

How does such an operation execute the arithmetic equation

$$A = (B * C) - (D * E)?$$

A possible code sequence might be

```
PUSH    D
PUSH    E
MUL
PUSH    B
PUSH    C
MUL
SUB
POP     A
```

It is obvious that this is not truly a zero-address machine, since PUSH and POP require one operand. (After all, they are nothing more than the LAC and DAC instructions of the one-address machine!) Thus a zero-address machine does not have only zero-address instructions as part of the total instruction set, and so we are required to qualify our meaning of zero-address machines. A case in point is the Burroughs 5500. This is a stack machine which includes both the zero-address arithmetic instructions and instructions of the one-address load-and-store type.

1.3. NUMBER SYSTEMS

In the decimal numbering system (base 10), the value of a numeral depends upon the numeral's position in a number; for example,

$$
\begin{array}{rcl}
347 = 3 \times 100 & = & 300 \\
4 \times 10 & = & 40 \\
7 \times 1 & = & \underline{7} \\
& & 347
\end{array}
$$

The value of each position in a number is known as its *position coefficient*. It is also called the *digit-position weighting value, weighting value*, or simply the *weight*.

Utilizing the positional coefficients and weighting values, it is possible to express any weighted number system in the following generalized form:

$$X = x_n w_n + x_{n-1} w_{n-1} + \cdots + x_1 w_1 + x_0 w_0 + x_{-m} w_{-m}$$

where

$$w_i = r^i \text{ (i.e., } r^i = \text{ weighting values and } r = radix \text{ or } base)$$

$$0 \leqslant x_i \leqslant r - 1 \text{ (i.e., } x_i = \text{ positional coefficients)}$$

This formalism makes it clear that the largest value of a positional coefficient is always 1 less than the base value. For base 2 this means that the largest coefficient is 1; for base 10 it is a 9. Although this may seem intuitively obvious, it is not an uncommon mistake for the novice programmer (and even some old-timers) to write illegal numbers while coding programs (e.g., 10853 in base 8 or 102 in base 2).

Examples of writing the full formal expressions for weighted number systems are

$$132_{10} = 1 \times 10^2 + 3 \times 10^1 + 2 \times 10^0$$
$$= 1 \times 2^7 + 0 \times 2^6 + 0 \times 2^5 + 0 \times 2^4 + 0 \times 2^3$$
$$+ 1 \times 2^2 + 0 \times 2^1 + 0 \times 2^0$$
$$= 2 \times 8^2 + 0 \times 8^1 + 4 \times 8^0$$
$$= 8 \times 16^1 + 4 \times 16^0$$

In other words,

$$132_{10} = 10000100_2 = 204_8 = 84_{16}$$

It is interesting to note that although all examples have assumed a positive radix, negative radices are also possible. For example, assuming a radix of -3, the value 132_{10} may be expressed as

$$132_{10} = 2 \times (-3)^4 + 1 \times (-3)^3 + 0 \times (-3)^2 + 1 \times (-3)^1$$
$$+ 0 \times (-3)^0$$
$$= 21010_{-3}$$

It is even possible to conceive of nonweighted number systems (and such systems do exist, such as "Excess-3" and "2 out of 5"), but the discussion of such systems is beyond the scope of this book.

1.3.1. Representation of Computer Numbers[†]

Because of the inherent binary nature of computer components, modern digital computers are all based on the *binary number system*. However, no matter how convenient the binary system may be for computers, it is exceedingly cumbersome for human beings. Consequently, most computer programmers use base 8 or base 16 arithmetic instead, and leave it up to the various system components (assemblers, compilers, loaders, etc.) to convert such numbers to their binary equivalents.

[†]Appendix A provides a more detailed treatment of number systems for those readers who may need more than the brief summary presented here.

Base 8 or *octal* and base 16 or *hexadecimal* representations of binary numbers are not only convenient but also easily derived. The conversion simply requires the programmer to separate the binary number into 3-bit (octal) or 4-bit (hexadecimal) groups, starting from the *least significant digit (LSD)* and replacing each binary group with its equivalent. Thus, for the binary number 010011100001,

$$010 \ 011 \ 100 \ 001_2 \ = \ 2341_8$$
$$\uparrow$$
$$\text{LSD}$$

$$0100 \ 1110 \ 0001_2 \ = \ 4E1_{16}$$

This process is so naturally performed that most programmers can mentally convert visual representations of binary numbers (computer displays) to their octal (or hexadecimal) representation without consciously thinking about it.

1.3.2. Negative Numbers

For any base, there are three common ways to represent negative numbers. For example, negative binary numbers can be represented in (1) *sign-magnitude*, (2) *one's-complement*, or (3) *two's-complement* form. One might ask, therefore, which form a computer would use in performing arithmetic calculations.

In Appendix A, where the various representations of negative numbers are considered, sign-magnitude form is rejected in favor of complement form because it is more complex to add or subtract numbers using sign-magnitude arithmetic. Thus the choice of form for negative binary numbers is really between one's- and two's-complement representations. In reality, this choice boils down even further to the preference of the computer designer and the computer programmer.

Generation of one's-complement numbers is easier than generation of the two's-complement form. In addition, from the computer hardware point of view, it is more "uniform" to build a one's- than a two's-complement adder. On the other hand, the one's-complement notation allows for two representations of zero (e.g., both a positive and a negative zero):

$$000 \ 000 \quad \text{zero}$$

$$111 \ 111 \quad \text{minus zero in one's complement}$$

whereas only one zero exists in the two's-complement form:

$$
\begin{array}{rl}
000\ 000 & \text{zero} \\
111\ 111 & \text{one's complement} \\
+1 & \text{add one} \\
\hline
\textit{discarded } 1)\ 000\ 000 & \text{two's complement of zero}
\end{array}
$$

Mathematically speaking, it is not nice to have two representations for zero. As a result, most machines today use two's-complement notation to represent negative numbers.

1.4. BOOLEAN ALGEBRA AND LOGICAL FUNCTIONS

Although originally conceived as a means for dealing with certain classes of problems in symbolic logic, Boolean algebra is best known to computer programmers as a means for expressing logical relationships. Using the basic operators *AND*, *OR*, and *NOT*, the FORTRAN programmer is able to develop complex logical expressions that can be used both in logical assignment statements such as

```
LOGIC = 5 .LT. NUM .AND. .NOT. X
```

and in logical IF statements such as

```
IF (X .NE. Y .OR. Z) GO TO 10
```

On the other hand, one of the first uses of Boolean algebra as applied to computers was in the understanding of switching circuits. Using the postulates and theorems of Boolean algebra, one can express algebraically the way computer networks operate. Consequently, using only simple building blocks, complex circuits can be easily described, manipulated, and possibly simplified.

Although it is currently feasible to build a "computer on a chip," it is still worthwhile to consider the nature of simple logical circuits and computer elements. By doing so, some of the "magic" behind the operation of a computer is removed, and the user of the machine gains an appreciation for what is going on inside.

1.4.1. Simple Logical Circuits

In the description of simple logical circuits, the basic logical functions OR $(+)$, AND $(\cdot)$, XOR $(\oplus)$, and NOT $(\neg)$, which are presented in Appendix

B, can be represented graphically (as shown in Fig. 1-5) by the logic circuit symbols used in schematic drawings. The use of the small circle at the input

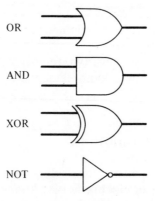

OR

AND

XOR

NOT

Fig. 1-5 Schematic representations of logic elements.

(or output) to a logic circuit symbol indicates that input (or output) is complemented. For example, the graphic representation of $F = A + \neg B$ is shown in Fig. 1-6.

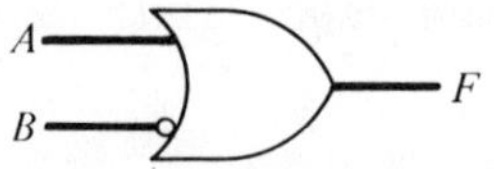

A

B

F

Fig. 1-6 Symbolic representation of $F = A + \neg B$.

To define the operation of a simple logical circuit it is necessary to define the meaning of both its inputs and its outputs. As described in Appendix B, there are two possible input/output states, conveniently referred to as 0 and 1: the state 0, which indicates that a relatively low electrical signal is present, and the state 1, which indicates that a relatively high signal is present. Graphically, these two states are shown in Fig. 1-7.

Signal

1

Time (t)

Signal

0

Time (t)

Fig. 1-7 Possible input/output states of a logic circuit.

If the signals being input to a logical circuit change with time, so might the output signal coming from it. For example, the representation of the function $F = A + \neg B$ given in Fig. 1-6 with time-varying input signals is shown in Fig. 1-8. Figure 1-9 shows the corresponding output signal.

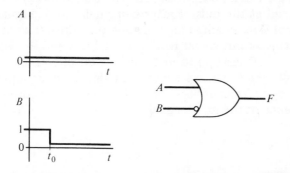

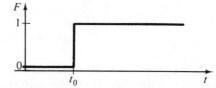

Fig. 1-8   Logic circuit with its inputs.

Fig. 1-9   Output signal for the circuit of Fig. 1-8.

The explanation of the output signal goes like this: Since the function F is 1 only when A is 1 or B is 0, and since A is always 0, then only when B becomes 0 at time t_0 does F become 1. The reader may infer from this description that changes in the state of the input signal causing changes in the state of the output signal are instantaneous; that is, there is no delay in the logical circuit itself. This may not be what actually happens; it is con-venient and perfectly acceptable for us to believe so, however.

Although it is possible with current technology to fabricate very com-plicated computer circuits (and soon whole computers) in one small package called a *chip*, it is very instructive to consider how computer circuits may be constructed from the simple logical building blocks described so far. How-ever, in order to use the building blocks to build computer circuits, one additional building block will be needed. This is a delay box:

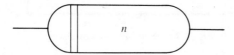

where things going in do not come out until after a delay of n units of time.

The delay building block when connected on itself, as shown in Fig. 1-10, forms a simple storage device. Given an initial 1 signal, the device will continue to produce a 1 as an output signal. The device works because the input signal is replicated at the output after being delayed one unit of time. Thus if the input signal is maintained high for one time unit, then at the same time it goes to low the output signal will be going high, and this signal can be fed back (through an OR circuit) to maintain the output signal. This circuit has a *feedback loop* which utilizes the output signal for its input so that once initiated it stores or "remembers" what has occurred without requiring the continued presence of the input signal.

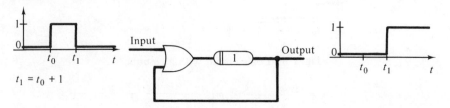

Fig. 1-10   Simple storage device.

The presence of an input signal serves to turn this storage device on, for example, to remember that a 1 signal once occurred. By adding another logic element in the feedback loop, it is possible to turn the storage device off. The circuit of Fig. 1-11 accomplishes just that, with the two input lines now labeled "set 1" and "set 0." As long as there is no set 0 signal, the AND

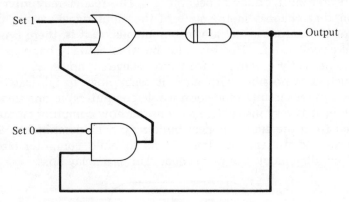

Fig. 1-11   Setable storage device.

element will pass the output signal through to the OR element. However, as soon as the set 0 signal becomes a 1, the output will no longer be passed through. A graph of the possible states for given set signals is shown in

Fig. 1-12. As before, the width of the set 0 and set 1 signals (often called *pulses*) are one time unit (e.g., $t_1 - t_0 = 1 = t_3 - t_2$).

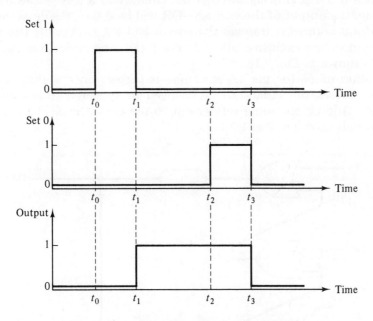

Fig. 1-12   Input/output states of Fig. 1-10.

Being able to set the circuit to 1 or 0 (called *set* and *reset*, for obvious reasons) is not enough. What is needed is the capability to reset it if it is set, or set it if it is not, without knowing or caring what the original state might

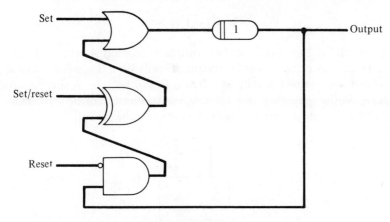

Fig. 1-13   Switchable storage device.

have been. To obtain this new capability, an exclusive-OR building block is added between the AND and OR blocks. This block acts as a "set/reset" line, since if a 1 is flowing through the circuit and a 1 is placed on the set/reset line, the output of the exclusive-OR will be 0 (i.e., the device is reset to 0); or if a 0 is flowing through the circuit and a 1 is presented to set/reset, the output of the exclusive-OR will be a 1 (i.e., the device is set to 1). This circuit is shown in Fig. 1-13.

Another name for the set/reset line is *trigger*, since the input signal to this line causes the circuit to be changed or triggered from one state to another. Adding one more refinement to the circuit, a NOT block, results in the circuit shown in Fig. 1-14.

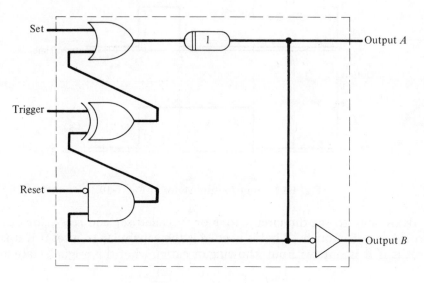

Fig. 1-14 Flip-flop.

The circuit of Fig. 1-14 has two outputs, labeled A and B. When output A is a 1 (e.g., the circuit is set), output B will be a 1. Alternatively, if the circuit is not set, output A will be a 0 and B will be a 1. A simple rotation of the figure, while painting out all the components inside the dashed lines (e.g., making it a black box), makes the circuit look as follows:

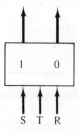

This is called a *flip-flop* or *RST flip-flop* and forms one of the most common circuit components in all computers.

1.4.2. Computer Elements

By connecting n flip-flops together and treating the collection as an *ordered* unit, it is possible to build a *register* capable of holding n bits of information. Operations may be performed on the register such as to "clear" it:

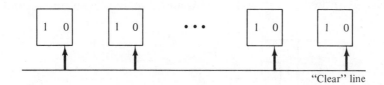

"Clear" line

(where the clear line serves to reset each flip-flop to the 0 state) and to transfer the contents from one register to another:

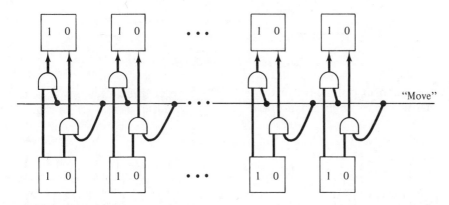

"Move"

Next, these registers may be combined with "adder circuits" in order to perform computer addition. An adder circuit in its simplest form must be capable of adding two inputs to produce a sum and a possible carry. Expressed in truth-table form:

Inputs		Outputs	
A	B	Sum	Carry
0	0	0	0
0	1	1	0
1	0	1	0
1	1	0	1

The logical equations for this binary arithmetic can be deduced as follows: The sum is 1 when A is 0 and B is 1, or when A is 1 and B is 0. The carry is 1 when both A and B are 1. Expressing this as a logical equation,

$$S = (\neg A \cdot B) + (A \cdot \neg B)$$
$$C = A \cdot B$$

Since these equations require only the AND, OR, and NOT building blocks already discussed, it is a simple matter to interconnect them to produce the adder circuit shown in Fig. 1-15. This adder suffers from one serious defect

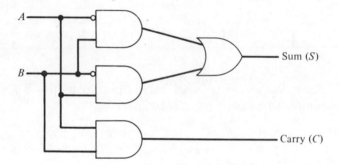

Fig. 1-15   Simple 1-bit adder.

—it can perform only 1-bit arithmetic. To correct this deficiency it is necessary to use n of them to perform n-bit arithmetic, as shown in Fig. 1-16.

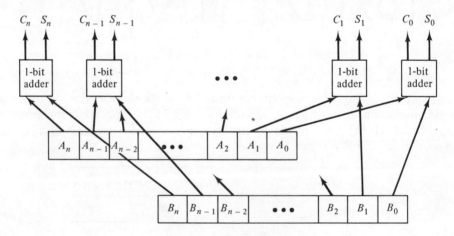

Fig. 1-16 n-bit adder.

However, what happens with the carries remains unclear. Obviously the carry from the preceding adder must participate in the adder to its left. Each adder thus must look as shown in Fig. 1-17. Such an adder is called

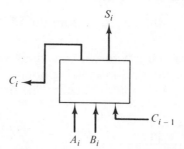

Fig. 1-17   Inputs/outputs of a full-adder.

a *full-adder*, in contrast to the *half-adder*, which does not account for the carry from the previous bit position. Another reason for these names is that a full-adder may be constructed from two half-adders, as shown in Fig. 1-18. (The development of the full-adder is left as an exercise for the reader.)

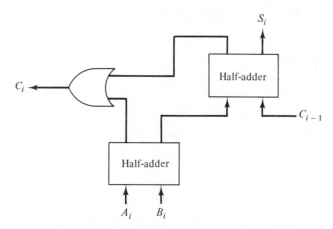

Fig. 1-18   Full-adder made up of two half-adders.

As developed, the full-adder is still a 1-bit adder. To add two n-bit numbers together requires n full-adders, or the switching of a single full-adder so that each of the bit pairs is added one at a time, in sequence. When the numbers are added a bit at a time, the circuit is called a *serial adder*; when all bits are added at once the circuit is called a *parallel adder*.

Most computer systems today have parallel adders and parallel data paths which allow for the simultaneous transfer of all bits within a computer word. For example, the sequence of operations for an "add" might be:

1. Move operand *A* (in register A) to the adders together with operand *B* (in register B), causing *A* and *B* to be added together.

2. Clear register B.

3. Move the resultant from the adders to the B register.

A computer circuit to perform these operations is shown in Fig. 1-19. The figure illustrates an interesting point: that there are two flows of information within a computer circuit. The first flow represents the data flow and is

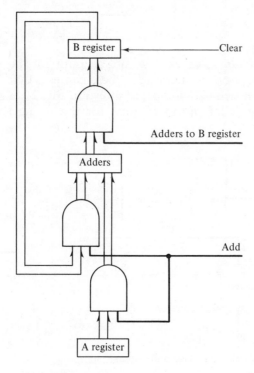

(Note: a double line means an *n*-bit transfer.)

Fig. 1-19 ADD circuit for
$(B) \leftarrow (A) + (B)$.

illustrated by the double lines in the picture. The second flow consists of the control signals which clear a register, cause an add to be performed, or set some data into a register. Although in both cases the actual flow is nothing more than electrical signals, the difference between them lies in their use. At the heart of a computer is the control unit, which is able to direct the sequence of operations to be performed. The control flow directs the operations performed on the data flow, causing (one hopes) meaningful results to be generated.

For the control unit to know what to do, control signals must be passed to it jointly from the instruction to be executed and from the results of the last calculation. The steps that the control unit performs are called *micro-instructions*, and usually several microinstructions will be executed by the control unit to execute one machine instruction.

1.4.3. Simple Computer Organization

By putting together all the circuits and techniques discussed so far, it is possible to describe a simple computer as shown in Fig. 1-20. The figure is meant to show the data flow of the computer without particular regard to the necessary *gates* (building blocks used to control the flow of the data). Besides the control unit, there is an *instruction register (IR)*, a *program counter (PC)*, the *adder circuit (ADDS)*, a *memory (MEM)*, and two *memory registers*, the *storage address register (SAR)* and the *storage buffer register (SBR)*. The SAR is necessary for "addressing" the memory, and the SBR is necessary for "buffering" a memory read or write, which often takes longer than one microinstruction.

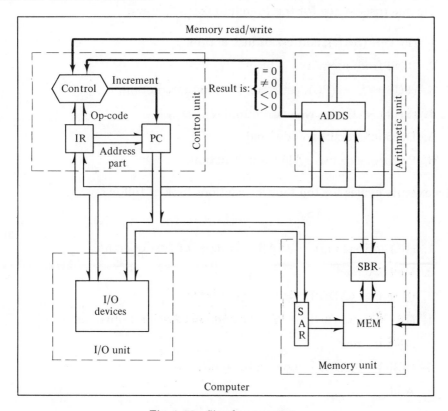

Fig. 1-20 Simple computer.

The computer is represented as a two-address machine and has instructions of the form

ADD	Address $_1$	Address $_2$

MOVE	Address $_1$	Address $_2$

TRANSFER ON ZERO	Not used	Address $_1$

To execute an instruction, it is necessary to fetch the instruction from memory and then, based on its operation code, perform the necessary microinstructions. The first half of this two-part cycle is called *I-fetch* and is the same for all instructions. The second half of the cycle is called *Execute* and depends on what instruction is being executed.

The microsequence for the I-fetch looks as follows:

1. (PC) → (SAR); address of instruction.

2. Read from memory.

3. (PC) + 1 → (PC); get ready for next instruction.

4. (SBR) → (IR); save instruction.

5. Decode operation code field.

6. Perform execute cycle for instruction.

The execute cycles for the four instructions look as follows:

ADD:

1. (IR) address part → (SAR); address of first operand.

2. Memory read.

3. (SBR) → (ADDS); first operand fetch.

4. (IR) address part$_2$ → (SAR); address of second operand.

5. Memory read.

6. (SBR) → (ADDS); second operand.

7. Add.

8. (ADDS) → (SBR); save results.

9. Memory write; SAR still contains resultant address.

10. Go to I-fetch.

MOVE:

1. (IR) address part$_1$ → (SAR); get first operand.

2. Memory read.

3. (IR) address part$_2$ → (SAR); store address.

4. Memory write; SBR contains operand.

5. Go to I-fetch

TRANSFER ON ZERO:

1. If "≠0" set by last arithmetic operation, go to I-fetch.

2. (IR) address part$_1$ → (PC).

3. Go to I-fetch.

Computers that allow the user or designer of the machine to alter or change the sequences of execution (called *microprograms*) are said to be *microprogrammable.* Instead of having a control unit that is wired to execute fixed sequences, these machines have "control memories" into which micro-sequences may be placed to alter the sequencing of the control unit and hence the basic structure of the machine.

EXERCISES

1. Write a sequence of instructions for a two-address machine, in both symbolic format and infix notation, to calculate the FORTRAN expression

$$A = (B * C) - (D * E)$$

2. Develop a set of instructions for a general register computer with a three-address instruction format. Use these instructions to calculate

$$R = (B/A) * C - (D + (E/F))$$

3. Write the truth table for the circuit shown in Fig. 1-6.

4. Suppose that the signals shown here are inputs to the circuit of Fig. 1-14. What are the outputs A and B for that circuit? *Note:* Each pulse is of unit width.

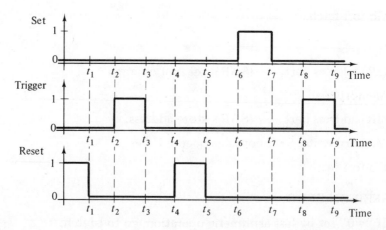

5. Develop a truth table for a full-adder. Write the logical equations using the truth table.

6. Using the simple computer of Fig. 1-20, develop a microsequence for a one-address instruction to load the accumulator from memory (LDA) of the form

LDA	Address

7. Compare and contrast the microsequences in control memory to the instruction sequences in the main memory. What differences, if any, are there between microprogramming and programming?

REFERENCES

For a different approach to the understanding of computer fundamentals, readers may wish to peruse through the earlier books by Gear (1969), Stone (1972), and Abrams and Stein (1973). Specified books on logical design [Phister (1959)], computer architecture [Foster (1970)], microprogramming [Husson (1970)], and system principles [Hellerman (1967)] may also be consulted, if the reader wishes a thorough in-depth treatment.

2 FUNDAMENTALS OF PROGRAMMING

The modern digital computer is capable of storing information, performing calculations, making decisions based on the results, and arriving at a final solution to a given problem. The computer cannot, however, perform these tasks without direction. Each step the computer is to perform must first be worked out by the programmer.

The programmer must write a program, which is a list of instructions for the computer to follow to arrive at a solution for a given problem. This list of instructions is based on a computational method, called an *algorithm*, used to solve the problem. The list of instructions is placed in the computer memory to activate the applicable circuitry so that the computer can process the problem.

2.1. PROGRAMMING PHASES

In order to solve a problem successfully with a computer, the programmer proceeds through six programming phases:

1. Definition of the problem to be solved.

2. Determination of the most feasible solution method.

3. Specification of the input data and output results.

4. Design and analysis of the solution—flowcharting, program documentation, and so on.

5. Coding the solution in the programming language.

6. Program checkout.

The *definition of the problem* is not always obvious. A great amount of time and energy can be wasted if the problem is not adequately defined. When the problem is to sum four numbers, no clarification is necessary. However, when the problem is to monitor and control a performance test for semiconductors, a precise definition of the problem is necessary before its solution can be attempted. The question that must be answered in this phase is: What precisely is the program to accomplish?

Determining the method to be followed is the second important phase in solving a problem with a computer. There are perhaps an infinite number of methods to solve a problem, and the selection of one method over another is often influenced by the computer system to be used. Having decided upon a method based on the definition of the problem and the capabilities of the computer system, the programmer must develop the method into a workable solution.

Somewhere between the process of determining the method and designing the solution to a computer problem, the programmer must consider and *specify the type and amount of information or data* that is involved. Because the data may have some implicit structure, or because they can be made to fit a well-defined structure, the programmer must consider the data very carefully when designing his program solution.

The programmer must *design and analyze the solution* by identifying the necessary steps to solve the problems and arranging them in a logical order, thus implementing the method. Flowcharting is a graphical means of representing the logical steps of the solution. The flowcharting technique is effective in providing an overview of the logical flow of a solution, thereby enabling further analysis and evaluation of alternative approaches.

Having designed the problem solution, the programmer begins *coding the solution in the programming language*. This phase is commonly called "programming" but is actually coding—and is only one part of the programming process. When the program has been coded and the program instructions have been stored in the computer memory, the problem can be solved. At this point, however, the programming process is rarely complete. There are very few programs written that function initially as expected. Whenever the program does not work properly, the programmer is forced to begin the sixth step of programming, that of checking out or "debugging" the program.

The *program checkout* phase requires the programmer to retrace the flow of the instructions methodically, step by step, to find any program errors that may exist. The programmer cannot tell a computer: "You know what I mean!", as he might say in daily life. The computer does not know what is meant until it is told, and once given a set of instructions, the computer follows them precisely. If needed instructions are left out or if coding is done incorrectly, the results may be surprising. These flaws, or "bugs" as they are often called, must be found and corrected. There are many approaches to finding bugs in a program; whatever the approach chosen, to be successful it must be organized and painstakingly methodical. Several techniques for debugging programs will be described later.

2.2. PROGRAM DOCUMENTATION

A simple problem to add three numbers together is solved in a few easily determined steps. A programmer could sit at his desk and write out three or four instructions for the computer to solve the problem. However, he probably could have added the same three numbers with paper and pencil in much less time than it took him to write the program. Thus the problems which the programmer is usually asked to solve are much more complex than the addition of three numbers, because the value of the computer is in the solution of problems that are inconvenient or time-consuming by human standards.

2.2.1. Flowcharting

When a more complex problem is to be solved by a computer, the program involves many steps, and writing it often becomes long and confusing. A method for solving a problem that is written in words and mathematical equations is extremely hard to follow, and coding computer instructions

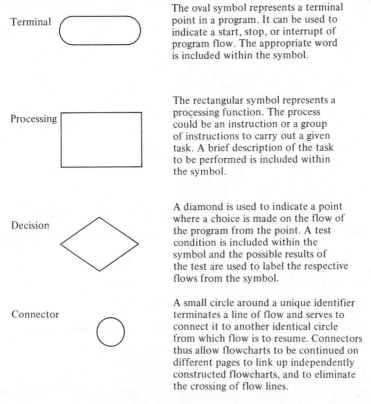

| Terminal | The oval symbol represents a terminal point in a program. It can be used to indicate a start, stop, or interrupt of program flow. The appropriate word is included within the symbol. |

Processing — The rectangular symbol represents a processing function. The process could be an instruction or a group of instructions to carry out a given task. A brief description of the task to be performed is included within the symbol.

Decision — A diamond is used to indicate a point where a choice is made on the flow of the program from the point. A test condition is included within the symbol and the possible results of the test are used to label the respective flows from the symbol.

Connector — A small circle around a unique identifier terminates a line of flow and serves to connect it to another identical circle from which flow is to resume. Connectors thus allow flowcharts to be continued on different pages to link up independently constructed flowcharts, and to eliminate the crossing of flow lines.

Fig. 2-1 Flowchart symbols.

from such a document would be equally difficult. A technique called *flow-charting* is used to simplify the writing of programs. A *flowchart* is a graphical representation of a given problem, indicating the logical sequence of operations that the computer is to perform. Having a diagram of the logical flow of a program is a tremendous advantage to the programmer when he is determining the method to be used for solving a problem, as well as when he writes the coded program instructions. In addition, the flowchart is often a valuable aid when the programmer checks the written program for errors.

The flowchart is basically a collection of boxes and lines. The boxes indicate what is to be done and the lines indicate the sequence of the boxes. The boxes are of various shapes which represent the action to be performed in the program. Figure 2-1 describes the various flowchart symbols as defined by ANSI/ISO symbol conventions.

Next, two examples of flowcharts are given. Example 1 adds three numbers together. Example 2 puts three numbers in increasing order.

Example 1: Straight-Line Programming

Example 1 is an illustration of straight-line programming. As Figure 2-2 shows, there is a straight-line progression through the processing steps with no change in course. The value of the expression $A + B + C$ is in location D when the program stops.

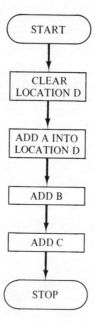

Fig. 2-2   Add three numbers.

Example 2: Program Branching

Example 2 is designed to arrange three numbers in increasing order (Fig. 2-3). The program must branch to interchange numbers that are out of

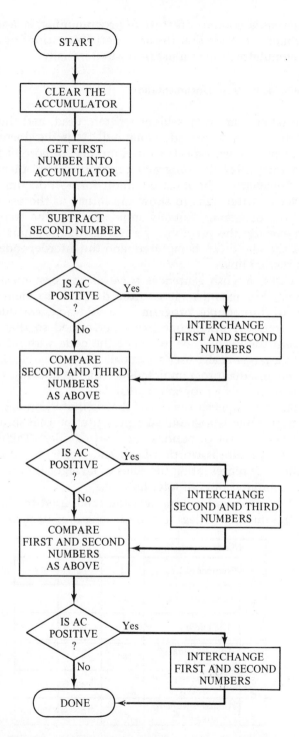

Fig. 2-3   Arrange three numbers in increasing order.

order. (Branching, a common feature of programming, is described in detail later in this chapter.) Note that the arithmetic operations of subtraction are done in an accumulator, which must be cleared initially.

2.2.2. Additional Methods for Documentation

Because programs are very seldom written, used, and then forgotten, it is important that they be well documented. It is the documentation that assists the next person who needs to use, modify, or correct those programs which live on long after the programmers who created them. A complete and accurate flowchart is the most common form of documentation. However, the flowchart often fails to show the intent of the programmer or the logic flow of the program. Equally important are the steps that must be performed to execute the program, the format of the input data items, the constraints of the algorithm being used, and the interdependencies that may exist among program units.

In many cases, English sentences serve as the best means for program documentation. For example, it is often desirable to include heading and dates as part of the source program. In addition, embedded comments logically block out the operations being performed so that the unfamiliar reader may learn the purpose or intent of the code without actually having to read it. On a larger scale, user's manuals serve to guide the nonprogrammer through the external program details so that he does not have to concern himself with why or how a program works.

An alternative to English sentences that is quite popular is the *decision table*. A decision table is a graphical representation that shows how a set of conditions relates to a set of actions for a set of rules. Taking advantage of the maxim that a picture is worth a thousand words, the decision table is a compact method for representing the rules of an algorithm without regard to any particular computer or computer language.

Figure 2-4 is an example of a decision table used to classify an animal according to the number of legs it has, the length of its neck, and the size of

	Characteristic	Rule		
Condition	Number of legs	4	4	2
	Length of neck	$> 4'$	$< 4'$	$< 4'$
	Small nose	Yes	No	Yes
Action	Animal is giraffe feed it	Hay		
	Animal is elephant feed it		Peanuts	
	Animal is woman feed it			Martini

Fig. 2-4 Example of a decision table.

its nose, so that it can be fed appropriately. Although this is a trivial example, it is important to note that decision tables are extremely useful for describing complex decision processes by programmers and nonprogrammers alike. Decision tables are easily constructed and modified, easily understood, and very compact in their representation of information.

Decision tables do, however, have two disadvantages associated with their use in writing programs. First, the translation from decision table to computer programming language is a complex task. Consequently, decision-table languages have been written that do not lay this burden on the programmer, but perform it for him. Second, decision tables are too powerful and hence very cumbersome when representing simple choice situations. Simple binary or tertiary flowchart decision boxes are preferable in that case. Because this text concentrates on an understanding of computers at a lower level than is found in a text that introduces programming in a higher-level language (e.g., FORTRAN), the disadvantages associated with decision tables generally preclude their use.

2.3. PROGRAM CODING

Binary numbers are the only language that the computer is able to understand. (For information on binary numbers, refer to Appendix A.) Numbers are stored in binary, and all arithmetic operations are in binary. What is more important to the programmer, however, is that for the computer to understand an instruction, it must be represented in binary. The computer cannot understand instructions that use English-language words. All instructions must be in the form of binary numbers (binary code).

2.3.1. Binary Coding

The computer uses a set of binary codes that it "understands" as instructions. In other words, the computer is designed and built to react to these binary numbers in a certain manner. These instructions have the same appearance as any other binary number; the computer can interpret the same binary configuration of 0s and 1s as data or as an instruction. The programmer tells the computer whether to interpret the binary configuration as an instruction or as data by the way in which the configuration is encountered in the program. Programmers seldom use the binary number system in actual practice. Instead, they substitute the octal (or hexadecimal) number system because it is easier for them to think in octal, the programs are more readable, and there is no loss of significance in doing so.

Coding a program in octal numbers, although an improvement upon binary coding, is nevertheless very inconvenient. The programmer must learn a complete set of octal numbers which have no logical connection with the operations they represent. The coding is difficult for the programmer when he is writing the program, and this difficulty is compounded when he is trying to debug or correct a program. There is no easy way to remember the correspondence between an octal number and a computer operation.

To simplify the process of writing or reading a program, each instruction is often represented by a simple two- to five-letter mnemonic symbol. These mnemonic symbols are considerably easier to relate to a computer operation because the letters often suggest the definition of the instruction. The programmer is now able to write a program in a language of letters and octal numbers that suggests the meaning of each instruction.

2.3.2. Programming Example

As most programmers quickly learn, the best way to learn programming is by example. It is instructive to hypothesize the following set of instructions in order to be able to write simple programs and illustrate important programming concepts. The hypothetical machine is the simple two-address machine of Chapter 1 and bears a strong resemblance to the PDP-11. However, actual consideration of the details of the PDP-11 are postponed until Chapter 3. For the moment our interest is in programming fundamentals. To this end it is useful to introduce the following basic instructions:

Operation	Mnemonic Form	Meaning
ADD	ADD 100,200	$(200) \leftarrow (200) + (100)$
MOVE	MOV 300,200	$(200) \leftarrow (300)$
JUMP (or TRANSFER)	JMP 400	$(PC) \leftarrow (400)$

Now a program to compute (and recompute!) the FORTRAN expression

$$D = A + B + C$$

could be described algorithmically by the flowchart shown in Fig. 2-5. Using

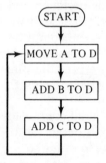

Fig. 2-5 Adding three numbers.

the flowchart, the following mnemonic program would continually compute D [†]:

---

†The instruction set lacks a stop or halt instruction!

Location	Content		Commentary
0	MOV	4,7	Move A to D.
1	ADD	5,7	Add B to D.
2	ADD	6,7	Add C to D.
3	JMP	0	Continue.
4	(value of A)		Real values
5	(value of B)		should be
6	(value of C)		substituted.
7	(resultant D)		Result.

The program starts at location 0 and ends at location 3. Locations 4 through 7 are used to hold data and must not be operated on as if they contained instructions. A memory reference instruction refers to a location by an ADDRESS; however, the instruction causes the computer to take some specified action with the CONTENTS of the location. Thus, although the address of a specific location in memory remains the same, the contents of the location are subject to change. In summary, a memory reference instruction uses an address value to refer to a memory location, and it operates on the number stored in the referenced location.

2.3.3. Stored Program Concept

The utilization of memory for holding both data and instructions is referred to as the *stored program concept*. Although it seems quite natural to use memory in this fashion, historically the first machines did not allow sharing memory, and it was not until the late 1940s that the idea was incorporated into computer systems by John von Neumann.

The impact of von Neumann's contribution was that it became possible to treat instructions as data, allowing arithmetic operations to be performed on the instructions. Even more importantly, it allowed for the rapid change in the order of instruction execution for both conditional and unconditional transfers. Thus the work of von Neumann is held as a major theoretical advance in computer design, and his name has been associated with the *stored program* or *von Neumann concept*.

2.3.4. Types of Instructions

There are four basic types of instructions which a computer understands. These instructions are arithmetic/logical, program control, internal data transmission, and input/output instructions. In *arithmetic/logical instruction* we can tell a computer to add, subtract, multiply, divide, or perform logical operations. (See Appendix B for information on logic.) Some computers, such as the PDP-11/05,[†] can only add and subtract, performing multiplica-

---

†Hereafter referred to simply as the PDP-11.

tion and division by repetitive addition or subtraction. Others, such as the IBM 1620, cannot even add, but have to look up arithmetic results from add and multiply tables stored in memory.

With the second type of instruction, *program control*, you can tell a computer in what order it is to add or subtract or perform any operation. In other words, you may instruct a computer to skip around from place to place; or jump over a sequence of instructions, as a result of arithmetic operations, because of some internal conditions, or simply because that is the way your program is written.

The third type of instruction, *internal data transmission*, allows for the movement of whole words or bytes as part of the internal data transmission required in most programs. In addition, this class of instructions includes the shift operations for adjusting the bits in a word.

The fourth and last type of instruction is *input or output instruction*. The input codes direct the control unit to transmit information available at some input device external to the system to specified locations in memory where it can be stored internally to the system. The output codes direct the transmission of information in the reverse direction. Additionally, control and status information may be passed to or collected from a device so as to determine its condition or change its state.

2.4. FUNCTION OF A SYMBOLIC ASSEMBLER

As we have stated, coding a machine language program in binary or octal is clearly a difficult task. It requires the programmer to remember both the machine language operation codes and the addresses of the instruction operands. By using mnemonic or memory assisting names for both *op codes* and operands, it is much easier to program and to read programs already written. This is so not only because the mnemonics are descriptive of the operation to be performed but also because the names of the operands can be chosen so as to suggest their use (e.g., SUMX, ABS, COUNT, etc.), in much the way that variable names are chosen in higher-level languages.

The clerical task of translating symbolic code to machine language is called the *assembly* process. This process is easily automated and done by the computer itself. A symbolic assembler is a translation program in the same sense that a FORTRAN compiler is. Both transform a *source language* into an *object language* (Fig. 2-6). One difference between an assembler and

Fig. 2-6 Translation of a program.

a compiler is found in the complexity of the source language. Assemblers usually perform a one-for-one transliteration of the symbolic source statements into machine language. Compilers operate on higher-level language statements, often producing many machine language statements from just one source statement.

In order to assemble a symbolic program, the assembly process requires three things:

1. Keeping track of instructions and where they are to reside in memory.

2. Keeping track of the symbols used and their values.

3. A translation technique for converting the op code and symbols into their machine language equivalents.

These requirements are facilitated by maintaining both a *location counter* and a *symbol table* within the assembler.

2.4.1. Location Counter

Most symbolic programs are written so as to be executed from successive memory locations. If the programmer assigned an absolute location to the first instruction, the assembler could be told to assign the next instructions to the following locations in order.

If we were to consider the assembler as a computing machine, then the *location counter (LC)* acts for the assembler as the *program counter (PC)* acts for the computer. The job of the LC is to keep track of where the next instruction or operand is to be placed in memory. As each symbolic instruction is translated, the value of the LC is updated to reflect the fact that the current location has been utilized.

2.4.2. Symbolic Addresses

The programmer does not know at the outset which locations he will use to hold initial values or constants or which locations to store results in. Therefore, he must arbitrarily assign symbolic names to the locations to which he must refer, and somehow assign address values for them.

Alternatively, the programmer may allow the assembler the job of assigning values. To do so requires that the programmer give a symbolic name for such a location. As each of these symbolic locations is encountered by the assembler,[†] the symbol is taken to be the *label* for the location which the

---

†The recognition of symbols as labels is facilitated by placing a special terminating character after the string of characters. As illustrated, the special character used here is a colon (e.g., A:).

symbol represents, and the value of the location counter is assigned to the symbol. In order to remember the values of all such symbols encountered, the assembler maintains a symbol table in which it records the octal value of all encountered symbol labels.

Using symbolic labels and instruction mnemonics, the previous program to calculate $D = A + B + C$ may be rewritten as follows, which is "readable" by both the programmer and the assembler:

Symbolic Label	Content	Commentary
LOOP:	MOV A,D	This code
	ADD B,D	forms the
	ADD C,D	sum of
	JMP LOOP	A, B, and C.
A:	(value of A)	
B:	(value of B)	
C:	(value of C)	
D:	0	

2.4.3. Assembly Language Process

The job of an assembly language programmer is to write in a symbolic language a *source program* (input) from which a machine language or *object program* (output) is to be produced. By using symbolic names and labels, the programmer is able to write a program that is relatively independent of all absolute memory references. Actually, the symbolic locations themselves are independent of location and the programmer is thus free to insert or delete such instructions at will.

In general, the assembler will accept the symbolic instructions and produce machine language statements on a one-for-one basis. Thus symbolic programming may be defined as a method wherein names, instructions, and symbols are used to write programs. The process of programming in assembly language is one of using declarative, imperative, and control statements for the purpose of specifying both what is to be produced and how it is to be produced.

The three basic types of assembly language statements are described as follows:

1. *Declarative:* used to control assignment of storage for various names, input/output, and working areas. These are not really instructions but rather reservations of space, definition of symbols, and assignments of contents to locations.

2. *Imperative:* these are the actual machine instructions as they appear in their symbolic form.

3. *Control:* instructions directed to the assembler to allow the programmer to have some control over portions of the assembly process.

2.5. SYMBOLIC PROGRAMMING EXAMPLE

The complete instruction set for a typical computer may have well over a hundred instructions in it. Trying to learn what each of these instructions does is a monumental task by itself, and coupled with a desire to be able to program the machine, it is rather formidable.

A better way to learn how to use a computer is to start with a basic instruction set. By choosing an appropriately small set, it is possible to systematize the learning process by concentrating on a more manageable set of instructions and concepts. With time and practice, these concepts will become second nature to the user, allowing for the easy introduction of new ideas and concepts.

2.5.1. Basic Operations

The three basic operations available on the hypothetical computer developed so far are MOV, ADD, and JMP. To this set we shall add the SUB instruction so as to be able to subtract the contents of the addressed memory locations from each other [e.g., SUB X,Y $=>(Y)\leftarrow(Y)-(X)$]. Another useful instruction is compare, CMP, which allows the programmer to compare two arithmetic values (e.g., CMP X,Y).

To be useful, the CMP instruction must somehow tell the computer, and ultimately the programmer, what the results of the compare operation were. When we look again at Fig. 1-20, we note a path from the arithmetic unit to the control unit which indicates that the last results generated were equal to, not equal to, greater than, or less than zero. Thus each time an ADD or a SUB operation occurs (or even a MOV, if the move is performed through the adder), the control unit is told that "the last result was . . . zero." In a similar fashion, the CMP operation can be expected to tell the control unit what the results were when the operands of the CMP instruction were compared (e.g., subtracted) and the arithmetic results discarded.

Just being able to tell the control unit that the last results were such and so is not enough, however. Some instructions that can take advantage of what the control unit knows are also needed. In particular, it is necessary to be able to control the execution of the program steps based on results generated in previous steps. For this reason, instructions that can jump or branch according to the last result generated must be included in the basic instruction set. These branch instructions are defined in Table 2-1, which lists both the old and the new instructions to be found in the basic instruction set.

Table 2-1 Basic instruction set.

Operation	Symbolic Form	Meaning
MOVE	MOV A,B	$(B) \leftarrow (A)$
ADD	ADD A,B	$(B) \leftarrow (B) + (A)$
SUBTRACT	SUB A,B	$(B) \leftarrow (B) - (A)$
COMPARE	CMF A,B	$(A) - (B)$
JUMP†	JMP X	$(PC) \leftarrow (X)$
BRANCH EQUAL ZERO	BEQ X	IF LAST OPERATION $\begin{cases} =0 \\ \neq 0 \\ \geq 0 \\ <0 \end{cases}$ THEN $(PC) \leftarrow (X)$
BRANCH NOT EQUAL ZERO	BNE X	
BRANCH IF PLUS	BPL X	
BRANCH IF MINUS	BMI X	
BRANCH ALWAYS†	BR X	$(PC) \leftarrow (X)$
HALT	HALT	machine stops

†The jump and branch-always instructions appear to perform the same function. In subsequent chapters we shall learn why they are different. In the meantime, either one may be used.

Given just these basic instructions, it is possible to solve the following problem: Add together the integers from 1 to N (where N is a variable). If N is equal to zero, the sum is to be zero. A flowchart of this problem appears in Fig. 2-7, and the corresponding symbolic code is as shown in

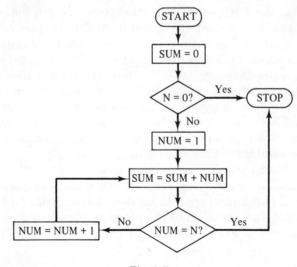

Fig. 2-7

Fig. 2-8. Since this symbolic program introduces many new ideas, several comments are in order.

```
; A PROGRAM TO COMPUTE THE SUM OF THE FIRST N INTEGERS
; 20 JULY 1973

N:         15                          ; VALUE OF N IN OCTAL
SUM:       0                           ; PLACE FOR SUM
START:     MOV      ZERO, SUM          ; INITIALIZE SUM
           CMP      ZERO, N            ; N=0?
           BEQ      STOP               ; IF YES, STOP
           MOV      ONE, NUM           ; INITIALIZE NUM
LOOP:      ADD      NUM, SUM           ; ADD NUM TO SUM
           CMP      N, NUM             ; TEST NUM=N?
           BEQ      STOP               ; DONE?
           ADD      ONE, NUM           ; INCREASE NUM
           BR       LOOP               ; CONTINUE
STOP:      HALT                        ; STOP HERE
ZERO:      0                           ; CONSTANT ZERO
ONE:       1                           ; CONSTANT ONE
NUM:       0                           ; PLACE FOR NUM
           . END    START              ; END OF ASSEMBLY PROGRAM



START:     MOV      ZERO, SUM
```

Fig. 2-8

First, labels in this program have been used:

1. To reserve memory locations, to attach symbol names to these locations, and to cause values to be stored.

2. To assign symbolic names to instructions so that transfer instructions may reference these lines of code.

3. To indicate the end of the program and to provide a starting instruction location for its execution (e.g.,.END   START).

Second, a new symbolic instruction called ".END" has been used. Since it is not a true machine language instruction, it is in the form of an op code but preceded by a period. As such, it is referred to as a *pseudo-op code*. It acts as a control statement for the assembler, informing it that this line is the last line to be assembled into machine code, and that, once translated, the program is to begin at the labeled instruction given as the operand of the .END statement. It is obviously equivalent to the END statement found in all FORTRAN programs.

Third, the example illustrates the use of comments and headings. Many times it is desired to include headings and dates to identify a program within the actual coding of the symbolic program. It is often helpful to add comments to simplify the reading of a symbolic program and to indicate the purpose of any less-than-obvious instruction. This example shows how comments and headings may be inserted simply by preceding any comments with a semicolon (;) so that the assembler recognizes them as such.

Fourth, the use of initializing statements can be found in the example. The statements include the initialization of the SUM:

```
START:   MOV      ZERO, SUM
```

and the initialization of NUM to 1. Although it is clearly possible to leave these statements out by simply attaching labels to words that are predefined at assembly time, initialization is preferable. The reason can be stated simply: A program that is *self-initializing* can be restarted any number of times, whereas one that is not must be reloaded into memory each time it is to be executed. Thus good programming includes proper initialization.

Fifth, and finally, it should be noted that the flowchart, as an expression of the algorithm or problem solution, does not specify what language will be used to write the program. The flowchart, therefore, should be planned to be language-independent so that it may be easily cast into any language. For example, the last program could have been written in FORTRAN as easily as it was written in assembly language, since the flowchart would be identical.

2.5.2. Symbolic Programming Conventions

Assembly language programming is similar to programming in any computer language. There are rigid rules that must be followed if the sentences (e.g., source statements) in the language are to be recognized by the assembler. Since both assemblers and compilers are language translators, it should not be surprising to find the rules for constructing sentences in assembly language similar to those found in FORTRAN.

Identifiers or *symbols* used in assembly language programs are made up of any sequence of letters (A, B, C, ..., Z) and digits, with the first character of the symbol a letter. For example, the mnemonic codes for the instructions defined so far are symbols for which the assembler retains their octal equivalents in a permanent symbol table. In general, *user-defined* symbols have a fixed maximum length, or else only the first few characters are considered and any additional characters are ignored. Examples of user-defined symbols include NUM, START, and ONE, which have been used in previous example programs.

Any sequence of digits forms a *number*. For programmer convenience, most assemblers will accept numbers that are in different bases, such as octal and decimal. However, if the assembler expects values in one base, say octal, it is necessary to indicate that a different base is being used by using a pseudo op such as .BASE or following the number with an identifying radix character such as a decimal point (e.g., 98. for decimal 98 in an octal assembler). Regardless of the base, each number and symbol written in the program must represent a binary value in order to be interpreted by the assembler.

Often there will be *special characters* in the assembler's character set to facilitate the recognition of labels, pseudo-ops, decimal values, comments, and so on. These characters include

$$. \quad \$ \quad : \quad = \quad \% \quad \# \quad @ \quad (\quad) \quad ; \quad " \quad ' \quad + \quad - \quad \& \quad !$$

plus the nonprinting space character, which does not have a graphic symbol but does affect the assembly process. These special characters are used to specify operations to be performed by the assembler upon the symbols or numbers appearing in programs. For example, the use of the colon after a label symbol has already been demonstrated.

Statement format up until now has been defined mainly by example. However, an assembler does have an assembly language format. For us, a symbolic line of code is composed of up to four fields, each field being either identified by its order of appearance or the special character used to terminate the last field. These fields are

```
LABEL    OPERATOR    OPERAND    COMMENT
```

The label and comment fields are optional. The operator and operand fields are interdependent—either may be omitted, depending on the contents of the other. An operand is that part of a statement which is operated on by the operator. Operands may be symbols, expressions, or numbers. When multiple operands appear within a statement, each must be separated from the next by a special character, such as a comma. The operand field is terminated by another special character when followed by a comment. For our purposes, a semicolon is used.

Rather than dictate a rigid format, an assembler that uses special characters to delimit fields allows for a *free-format layout* of assembler code. The statement format is thus controlled by the programmer, who may freely insert spaces. These spaces have no effect on the assembly process of the source program unless they are embedded within a symbol, number, or character string (to be discussed later); or are used as the operator field terminator. Thus they may be used to provide a neat, readable program. As an example, consider the statement:

```
LABEL:MOV(SP)+,TAG;POP VALUE OFF STACK
```

which, using formating characters, may be rewritten as

```
LABEL:    MOV      (SP)+,TAG        ;POP VALUE OFF STACK
```

which is much easier to read.

The characters and conventions present so far will be used throughout the remainder of this chapter so that we may be able to write programs and explain the common addressing methods found in most computers. The reader is reminded that these programs are written for a hypothetical machine, not a real one. However, in Chapter 3 the concepts will be tied to a PDP-11 computer so that they may be put into practice on a real machine.

2.6. ADDRESSING METHODS

One of the most common array problems that occurs in FORTRAN is the following program sequence to sum 50 elements in the integer array K:

```
          ISUM = 0
          DO 10 I = 1,50
   10     ISUM = ISUM + K(I)
```

The equivalent program in our assembly language could be[†]

```
   MOV     ZERO,ISUM      ; INITIALIZE SUM
   ADD     K,ISUM         ; ADD FIRST K VALUE
   ADD     K+1,ISUM       ; ADD SECOND K VALUE
   ADD     K+2,ISUM       ; ADD THIRD K VALUE


   ADD     K+49.,ISUM     ; NOTE DECIMAL 49
```

The solution assumes that the array K is loaded into consecutive words in memory, and the programmer has chosen to code the problem as a linear sequence of steps. It also illustrates what has been referred to as the programmer's "plus or minus 1 syndrome." This syndrome is exemplified by the question How many numbers are there between 19 and 27, inclusive? and by the usual and inaccurate answer, "8." Clearly, the computer programmer must remember to account for both end points.

In the problem being considered, there can arise a similar confusion: What is the actual address of the last element of the 50-word array—K + 49.,

---

†For the moment we shall ignore the definitions of the symbols ZERO, ISUM, and the array K.

or K + 50.? The answer as stated is correct, but it requires us to remember that when the first symbolic address is K + 0, the last address is "1 less" than the number of elements.

2.6.1. Address Modification

As any good FORTRAN programmer knows, the use of a *program loop*, in which a set of instructions is performed repeatedly, is common programming practice. Looping a program is one of the most powerful tools at the programmer's disposal. It enables him to perform similar operations many times using the same instructions, thus saving memory locations because he need not store the same instructions many times. Looping also makes a program more flexible because it is relatively easy to change the number of loops required for differing conditions by resetting a counter. It is good to remember that looping is little more than a jump to an earlier part of the program; however, the jump is usually dependent upon changing program conditions.

For the program at hand, the changing program conditions are program addresses. Each ADD instruction is similar to the last except that its operand value (array address) is 1 greater than its predecessor. Consequently, if we are to remake the linear program into a looping program, the address portion of the ADD instruction must be modified each time the program executes the instructions in the loop.

Earlier the von Neumann concept was discussed. One of the consequences of this concept was that a computer cannot distinguish between a number and an instruction. As applied to the problem at hand, it means that programs can operate on other programs, including themselves, so as to produce new programs. In particular, instructions in a program can be used to modify the operand or address portion of memory reference instructions.

Let us apply such *address modification* to the array problem on our computer. Dealing in specifics, we shall assume that the program resides in consecutive memory locations beginning at 1000, with the array K stored in locations 2000 and up, and ISUM equated to location 3000. Further, assume that an ADD operation has a numeric value of 10. Then having loaded memory with the program of Section 2-6, the octal contents would appear as:

Location	Contents		
1000	10	2000	3000
1001	10	2001	3000
1002	10	2002	3000
.		.	
.		.	
.		.	

The only difference in each instruction is the first address. It is conceivable to take the contents of location 1001, add 1 to the first address and produce as a result the contents of location 1002, e.g.,

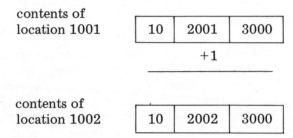

contents of
location 1001

| 10 | 2001 | 3000 |

$+1$

contents of
location 1002

| 10 | 2002 | 3000 |

A flowchart of what we want to do would look as shown in Fig. 2-9, and the program segment is

```
START:  MOV     ZERO,ISUM       ; INITIALIZE SUM
FIXUP:  ADD     K,ISUM          ; ADD IN ELEMENT OF ARRAY K
        CMP     FIXUP,LIMIT     ; DONE YET?
        BEQ     STOP            ; YES
        ADD     CONS,FIXUP      ; MODIFY ADDRESS
        BR      FIXUP           ; LOOP
STOP:   HALT                    ; STOP HERE
ZERO:   0                       ; CONSTANT ZERO
SUM     0                       ; RESULTANT SUM
CONS:   (A CONSTANT)            ; A SUITABLE VALUE OF ONE TO BE
                                ; ADDED TO THE INSTRUCTION AT FIXUP
LIMIT:  ADD     K+49.,ISUM      ; WHAT THE INSTRUCTION AT FIXUP LOOKS
                                ; LIKE AFTER IT HAS ADDED IN THE LAST
                                ; ARRAY ELEMENT
```

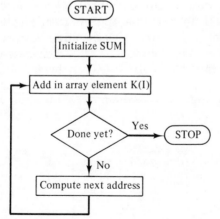

Fig. 2-9 Summing up the elements of the array K.

The reader can note several interesting points in this example. First, the instruction with label FIXUP is modified by adding a constant to the first operand of this instruction. This generates a new first address for the instruction so that the next time it is executed, the next element of the array K is added to ISUM. Second, the word labeled LIMIT contains a value that represents an instruction that will look like the instruction at FIXUP when it has been modified to add in the last element in the array K. Thus the CMP instruction is actually comparing two instruction values which are, in fact, represented by two numeric values. Third, although the program is *self-modifying*, it is not completely *self-initializing*. At the completion of its execution, the program will have modified the first operand address of the FIXUP instruction so that if the program is begun again, the results generated will be incorrect.

The use of address and instruction modification, although useful, should be discouraged. Several reasons for not doing so are: (1) such programs are often very difficult to debug, and (2) modern computing systems require treating instructions as pure, unmodified code because such programs may be protected, shared, handled more efficiently, and so on. However, in order to avoid using instruction modification, we shall need to take advantage of other features to be found on the computer.

2.6.2. General-Purpose Registers

Computer instruction sets are often more than sufficient in that they include instructions that duplicate other instructions in the same set. Nonetheless, these instructions do make programming easier and often increase machine resource utilization and efficiency.

One particular area in which the choice of specific computer instructions can have a very strong influence is in the area of operand addressing. By developing effective strategies for easily fetching elements of a simple data aggregate (i.e., the elements of a one-dimensional array or *vector*), the machine designer can significantly reduce the cost of programming and increase the speed of execution of programs. In particular, machine designers can add *general-purpose registers* to a computer so as to assist the programmer in operand addressing.

The previous example for summing the 50 elements in the array K is a prime candidate for using general-purpose registers for operand addressing. Actually, the registers may be used both as address accumulators, or more commonly, *index registers*, and as value accumulators.

When the general registers are used in index mode the final or *effective address (EA)* of the source and destination operands is calculated as the value of the operand or index word (X) plus the contents of the specified index register (R). The index word may be considered to be a signed, two's-complement value. As a result, the effective address for an indexed instruction is of the form

$$X + (R) = EA$$

where X may be a positive or negative value and an indexed ADD instruction may be written symbolically as

```
ADD      X(R), ISUM
```

Our hypothetical machine has two general-purpose registers, called R∅ and R1. Each register is capable of holding either an address or a data word, and either may be used for indexing.

2.6.3. Use of General-Purpose Registers

Usually the general registers are hardware registers, within the processor, which operate at high speeds and provide speed advantages when used for operating on frequently accessed variables. In our machine the registers may be used in all instructions as both accumulators and index registers.

Turning back to the flowchart of Fig. 2-5, a simple program sequence that uses the general-purpose registers to add three numbers together may be rewritten as

```
START:   MOV      A, R0          ; PUT A INTO R0
         ADD      B, R0          ; ADD IN B
         ADD      C, R0          ; ADD IN C
         MOV      R0, ANS        ; STORE ANSWER
         HALT
```

A better example can be found in the earlier problem of forming the sum of K(I) for I = 1,50. Using the general registers for indexing and accumulation, the program can be rewritten from the flowchart of Fig. 2-9 as given in Fig. 2-10.† Although this code sequence is longer than the earlier, self-modifying program, it does not modify the instructions and is self-initializing (e.g., R∅ starts at zero each time it is executed).

The program as shown uses R∅ as an accumulating register and R1 as an index register. After clearing both, it adds in elements of the array K by forming the effective address of the first operand from the contents of R1 and the base address K. Consequently, the effective addresses will be K, K+1, K+2, ..., K+49. The CMP instruction limits the looping since it compares the contents of R1 to the decimal value 49. As long as R1 < 49, the

---

†The careful reader will note that by using indexed addressing, the values being compared are no longer addresses but numeric offsets to a base address.

contents of R1 will be incremented by 1 and the loop repeated. When the
value of R1 reaches 50, the program stops.

```
           .
           .
           .
          MOV      ZERO, R0         ; SUM REGISTER
          MOV      ZERO, R1         ; COUNT REGISTER
LOOP:     ADD      K(R1), R0        ; ADD IN ELEMENT OF ARRAY K
          CMP      R1, D49          ; DONE?
          BPL      STOP             ; IF NOT, CONTINUE
          ADD      ONE, R1          ; GENERATE NEXT INDEX
          BR       LOOP             ; CONTINUE LOOP
           .
           .
           .
STOP:     HALT                      ; STOP HERE
ZERO:     0                         ; CONSTANT ZERO
ONE:      1                         ; CONSTANT ONE
D49:      49.                       ; DECIMAL CONSTANT 49
           .
           .
           .
```

Fig. 2-10

2.6.4. Immediate Mode

Before trying to continue the process of more effectively using our computer, a slight digression seems worthwhile. This digression concerns the use
of symbolic names to refer to frequently used constants in the program. For
example, an instruction utilizing the constant 2 might be of the form

```
          ADD      TWO, N
```

A more convenient way to specify that 2 was to be added to N, and one that
does not require a separate word to hold the constant TWO, would be to include the constant as part of the instruction. This change introduces a new
type of addressing, referred to as *immediate mode addressing*, which allows
the operand itself to be stored as the second or third word of the instruction.
For example, to add 2 to N, one could write

```
          ADD      #2, N
```

where the immediate mode is specified by preceding the number (or symbol)
by a "#" sign. It should be noted that immediate values being limited
by the size of the address field they replace can be no larger than the largest
address which the instruction can reference.

The immediate mode of addressing may be further illustrated by going
back to the array problem. This problem may be reprogrammed as follows:

```
        MOV     #49.,R1     ; INITIALIZE R1
        MOV     #0,R0       ; INITIALIZE SUM
LOOP:   ADD     K(R1),R0    ; ADD IN ELEMENT OF ARRAY K
        SUB     #1,R1       ; DECREMENT R1
        BPL     LOOP        ; LOOP AS LONG AS R1>=0
```

The total number of statements has been decreased. However, the decrease is a result of a new programming technique and not the result of immediate mode addressing. This technique recognizes the fact that the SUB instruction informs the control unit about the results of the last arithmetic operation just as the CMP instruction does. Thus by adding up the numbers in reverse order (last to first) and by allowing R1 to count down rather than up, it is unnecessary to use a CMP instruction. Instead, the program may simply test the N bit after each subtraction, continuing to loop as long as $R1 \geqslant 0$.

2.6.5. Autoindexing

Indexing occurs so often in computer programs that some machines have built-in hardware to index automatically by automatically incrementing or decrementing an index register during use.

The "autoincrement" and "autodecrement" addressing modes on our machine provide for the automatic stepping of an index register value through the sequential elements of a table of values or operands. This mode assumes the contents of the selected general register to be the address (sometimes called the *pointer*) of the operand. Thus the pointer is stepped through a series of addresses so that it always points to the next sequential element of a table.

In autodecrement mode, written as $-(R)$, the contents of the register are decremented *before* being used as the address of the operand. In autoincrement mode, written as $(R)+$, the contents of the register are incremented immediately *after* being used as the address of the operand. Unfortunately, autoincrementing and autodecrementing may not be combined with indexing (e.g., $\pm X(R)\pm$ is not a legal operand format). Thus the contents of the register must be an address, not an index over an address.

Turning our attention once again to the array problem, the program to solve the problem may now be written as

```
            .
            .
            .
        MOV     #0, R0          ; INITIALIZE SUM
        MOV     #K, R1          ; ADDRESS OF ARRAY K INTO R1
LOOP:   ADD     (R1)+, R0       ; ADD IN NEXT ELEMENT OF ARRAY K
        CMP     #K+49. , R1     ; DONE?
        BPL     LOOP            ; NO, CONTINUE
            .
            .
            .
```

which is one of the shortest solutions possible.

2.6.6. Indirect Addressing

An alternative to indexed addressing is *indirect addressing*, and while some computers have one mode of addressing or the other, our machine has both. This *deferred* mode of addressing may be used in conjunction with the other modes of addressing, such as register, indexed, or autoincrement, providing for a very sophisticated form of addressing.

Indirect addressing may be used in many ways. For example, it can assist the programmer in passing parameters to subroutines, as an alternative to utilizing index registers, for creating linked data structures, and so on. All these capabilities occur because indirect addressing specifies the "address of the address of the operand" (i.e., the address is indirectly specified) rather than the "address of the operand" directly.

Assembler syntax for indicating deferred addressing is "@" [or "( )" when this is not ambiguous] associated with the operand. As an example, the following program segment could be used to clear the contents of location HERE:

```
        MOV     #0, @INDR       ; CLEAR HERE INDIRECTLY
            .
            .
            .
INDR:   HERE                    ; CONTAINS ADDRESS OF HERE
            .
            .
            .
HERE:   ??                      ; LOCATION TO BE CLEARED
```

The operation of clearing a memory location may be applied to clearing an array of memory locations. The logical flow of operations to be performed is shown by the flowchart and accompanying program segment shown in Fig. 2-11. In this example the MOV statement is used to initialize R1 to the first address of the array A (e.g., since the first operand is #A, the address of A is placed in R1), so that the contents of R1 may be indirectly referenced.

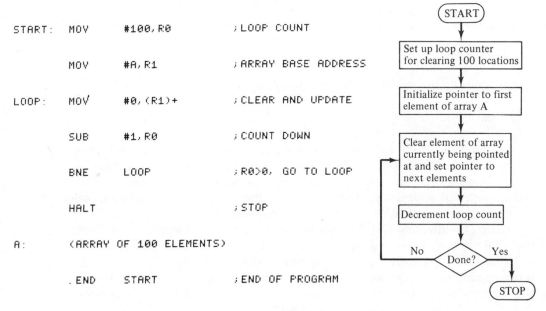

```
START:  MOV     #100, R0    ; LOOP COUNT

        MOV     #A, R1      ; ARRAY BASE ADDRESS

LOOP:   MOV     #0, (R1)+   ; CLEAR AND UPDATE

        SUB     #1, R0      ; COUNT DOWN

        BNE     LOOP        ; R0>0, GO TO LOOP

        HALT                ; STOP

A:      (ARRAY OF 100 ELEMENTS)

        .END    START       ; END OF PROGRAM
```

Fig. 2-11

Both examples just presented illustrated *single-level* indirect addressing. It is possible for a computer to utilize *multilevel* indirect addressing if the location indirectly addressed is itself the address of another location to be indirectly referenced. Multilevel indirectness requires that each location referenced have a bit which specifies whether this location is an address to be used directly or indirectly.

The choice of multilevel versus single-level indirectness is one based on user convenience and cost. On a short-word-length machine typified by today's small computers, where every bit must be utilized efficiently, multilevel indirect addressing is not provided. The reason is one of economics, in that as many bits as possible in the instruction word are used for directly addressing memory and, as a consequence, the indirect bit becomes a part of the instruction word rather than a part of the operand address.

Another point to be considered is that a computer which has both indexing and indirect addressing must specify which mode of addressing is performed first. Although it may seem that it does not really matter, there are reasons for performing indexing before indirectness, or vice versa.

In a computer that has a short word length, where it is not possible to address all of memory directly, indirect addressing is performed first. The reason is that the word used as an indirect address is generally larger than the address field of the instruction and can, therefore, address all of memory before being indexed. On the other hand, if all of memory can be referenced by an instruction, as on a long- or variable-instruction-length computer, it is more convenient to index first in order to facilitate such things as subroutine parameter passing. In Chapter 3, where we turn our attention to a real computer, we shall have to examine this point further.

EXERCISES

1. Rewrite the flowchart of Fig. 2-3 for a two-address computer.

2. Construct a flowchart to sum up all the positive values in the array K of 50 elements. Place the sum in symbolic location SUM.

3. Assembly languages often have what appear to be arbitrary restrictions. However, these restrictions make sense to the programmer who writes the assembler program for an assembly language in that they eliminate ambiguities, facilitate memory assignment, and so on. Below are listed some of these restrictions. In each case, give an explanation, from the point of view of the person writing a two-pass assembly, why they exist.

   a. Symbols must begin with a letter.

   b. Symbols cannot contain special characters (+, −, comma) or blanks.

   c. A symbol may not appear in the location field more than once in a program.

4. Write a program to add together all the *positive* numbers found in locations 3001, 3002, 3003, ... The number of numbers, N, is stored in location 3000 and $0 \leqslant N \leqslant 99$. If $N = 0$, the result should be zero. The sum of the numbers should be stored in location 2777.

5. Write a program to perform the equivalent FORTRAN program sequence for the integer arrays A, B, and C:

```
        DO 10   I=1,1000
   10        C(I) = A(I) + B(I)
```

6. Write a program to sort N numbers in place. Show that your program will work for all values of N such as $0 \leqslant N \leqslant 99$. Your solution should make use of index registers and should not result in a self-modifying program.

7. Suppose that a computer has 4096 words of memory addressed from octal location 0 to 7777, and one index register A. If the effective address for an indexed instruction is EA = X + (R), then if (R) = 0 and the desired EA = 7777, what is the value of X?

8. Given the same computer as for Exercise 6 but that this time (R) = 7777 and the desired EA = 0, what is the value of X?

9. Rewrite the program segment in Section 2.6.5 so that it uses autodecrementing rather than autoincrementing.

10. In a computer with both indexing and indirect addressing, it is important to know which is done first when an indexed indirect instruction is encountered. Explain why the order is so important by considering machines that will handle both short (say 12 bits) and long (say 36 bits) instruction words.

11. In a machine that has both immediate and indirect addressing, what is the meaning of an indirect-immediate reference?

12. Given *one* level of indirectness *or* index registers, which do you think is preferable and why?

13. Assume that we have a fixed-word-length, signed-magnitude, decimal, two-address machine with full addressing mode capabilities for both instruction addresses (i.e., immediate; direct and indirect). The symbolic instruction format is such that either address expression can be followed by a $ symbol to indicate immediate addressing, a # symbol to indicate indirect addressing, or neither symbol to indicate direct addressing. Among the instruction set for this machine are the following operations and their interpretations:

ADD	A1,A2	(A1)+(A3) to A1
SUB	A1,A2	(A1)−(A2) to A1
JGT	A1,A2	if (A1)>(A2) skip next instruction
JZE	A1,A2	if (A1)=0 jump to A2

where A1 and A2 are address expressions and include any addressing mode symbols that may be present. Assume, further, the following initial conditions for address symbols:

Symbol	Memory Location	Contents
A	0	2
B	1	1
	2	0
	3	−1
	4	3
C	5	4
D	6	5

State, for each of the following, the effect of executing the instruction or sequence of instructions; that is, what, if anything, has changed in memory? (For example, executing ADD A,B changes the contents of memory location 0 to 3.) Assume that the initial conditions apply for each question.

a. SUB A,A

b. ADD B,5$

c. SUB B+2,C#

d. JGT A$,B#

    ADD A#,B+3#

e. JZE 2#,*+2

    SUB D#,B+1$

REFERENCES

The purpose of this chapter was to develop programming concepts and fundamentals without unnecessarily tying them down to a particular computer. This approach has been taken by Abrams and Stein (1973), Walker (1972), Flores (1966), and Mauer (1968). Although still general in tone, books by Stone (1972), Gear (1969), and Katzan (1971) have tied their presentations to particular machines. Hopefully, the intent and style of presentation of this makes it possible to take a particular user's reference manual and relate the characteristics of a given computer to the topics being presented. Chapter 3, in fact, does this for the PDP-11; for those readers who are interested in this machine, the *PDP-11 Processor Handbook* can be used to reinforce the concepts being discussed.

3

ORGANIZATION AND STRUCTURE OF THE PDP-11

The PDP-11 is a high-speed, general-purpose digital computer that operates on 16-bit binary numbers. It is a variable-address parallel machine using two's-complement arithmetic. It is composed of the five basic computer units that were discussed in Chapter 1. The components of the five units and their interrelationships are shown in Fig. 3-1.

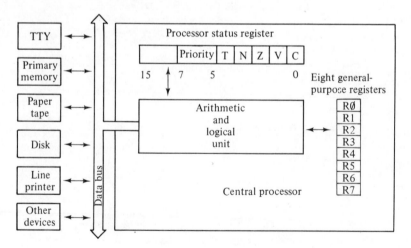

Fig. 3-1 PDP-11 system block diagram.

3.1. BLOCK STRUCTURE OF THE PDP-11

Since the five units are not clearly delineated in the figure, it will be instructive to discuss the block structure of this machine.

3.1.1. Input and Output Units

Typical input and output units are shown in Fig. 3-1. The connection between the central processing unit (CPU) and the input and output devices is through the *data bus*. This common bus represents a collection of wires that carry information signals between the devices connected to it. Because the bus is capable of carrying many signals simultaneously (such as all 16-bits of a memory word), it is represented by a wide line in Fig. 3-1.

The common data bus of Fig. 3-1 can be likened to a common highway for computer data flow. Any input or output device, or the CPU, may place information onto the highway, and conversely, any of them may take information from it. The common bus thus provides an efficient and effective means for passing information between the functional units connected to it.

The data bus of the PDP-11, more properly referred to as the UNIBUS, allows all input and output units to connect to and communicate with each other, as well as the central processor and the memory. Since all system elements communicate with each other in identical fashion via the UNIBUS, the input and output units have the same easy access with each other as the processor and memory have with them. And, since the UNIBUS is capable of accepting any number of external devices, new options (e.g., expanded memory or additional input and output devices) can be simply plugged in as they become available.

With bidirectional and asynchronous communications on the UNIBUS, devices can send, receive, and exchange data independently without central processor intervention. For example, a cathode ray tube (CRT) display can refresh itself from a disk file while the central processor unit (CPU) attends to other tasks. Because it is asynchronous, the UNIBUS is compatible with devices operating over a wide range of speeds.

Device communications on the UNIBUS are interlocked. For each command issued by a "master" device, a response signal is received from a "slave," completing the data transfer. Device-to-device communication is completely independent of physical bus length and the response times of master and slave devices.

Many of the same devices connected to the UNIBUS may act as both an input and an output unit. The disk, for example, can be used to input information via the UNIBUS to the computer. Alternatively, the same device can accept processed information and store it as output. Thus the two units of input and output are very often joined and referred to as input/output (I/O). Chapter 6 describes the methods for transmitting data as either input or output, but for the present the reader can assume that the computer is able to accept information from devices such as those shown in the block diagram and to return output information to the devices. The PDP-11 console allows the programmer direct access to primary memory and the program counter, by setting a series of switches, as described in detail in Chapter 6 and Appendix E.

3.1.2. Arithmetic Unit

In the center of the block diagram for the PDP-11 can be found the arithmetic unit. This unit, as shown in the diagram, accepts data from the UNIBUS and from the eight general-purpose registers. It may transmit processed information to these units as well as to the status register. Since the PDP-11 uses a two-address instruction format for its arithmetic operations, there is no accumulator in this machine. Instead, results may be stored either in the memory unit or in the eight general-purpose registers.

3.1.3. Control Unit

Although the control unit is not explicitly shown in Fig. 3-1, its presence is implicitly indicated by the status registers, the eight general-purpose registers, and the UNIBUS. For example, general register 7 acts as the PDP-11's program counter, while the N, Z, V, and C bits in the status register maintain the state of the machine by monitoring the results of previous instructions.

The program counter is used by the PDP-11 control unit to record the locations in memory (addresses) of the instructions to be executed. The PC always contains the address of the next word of the instruction being executed or the address of the next instruction to be executed. Thus, whenever the processor uses the program counter to acquire a word from memory, the PC is always incremented by 2 since, as we shall see, word addresses are always even. When an instruction causing transfer of command to another portion of the stored program is encountered, the PC is set to the appropriate address. The PC must be initially set by input to specify the starting address of a program, but further actions are controlled by program instructions.

The use of a general register as the program counter is unique on the PDP-11. The flexibility in doing so leads to some interesting techniques for specifying relative and immediate addressing. The characteristics of using the program counter for operand addressing are discussed in greater detail later in this chapter and in Chapter 6.

The processor status register (PS) of the PDP-11 contains information about the results of the last operation performed. The register is subdivided into one-bit indicators called *condition codes (CC)*, which are set according to the final value produced by an arithmetic operation (e.g., MOV, ADD, SUB, and CMP). These indicators are therefore "remembered" until another arithmetic operation resets them. Examining these bits, we find that the Z-bit indicates that the last result was zero and the N-bit indicates that the last result was negative. The C- and V-bits have to do with results that generate carries and overflow, and we shall postpone their discussion, along with that of the T-bit and the meaning of priority, until Chapters 4 and 6.

It is important to stress the interrelation between the condition codes and the instruction set, since the former are so important to the operation of

the latter. For example, in Chapter 2 the technique of counting down while
looping through a sequence of instructions,

```
        MOV     #100,R0     ; NUMBER OF TIMES THROUGH LOOP
        MOV     #A,R1       ; ADDRESS OF FIRST ELEMENT IN ARRAY
LOOP:   MOV     #0,(R1)+    ; CLEAR ARRAY LOCATION
        SUB     #1,R0       ; SETS CONDITION CODES
        BNE     LOOP        ; LOOP UNTIL Z=1
          .
          .
          .
```

made it unnecessary to compare the loop count to zero, thus saving an
instruction. And since the condition codes are not reset by a branch instruction, multiple-way branches are possible using only one compare instruction.
Thus if X is a value between 1 and 3 inclusive, a three-way branch based on
the value of X could be easily coded:

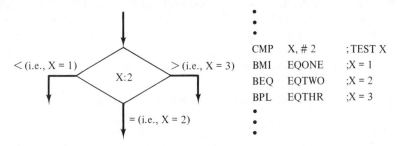

```
                                .
                                .
                                .
                        CMP     X, # 2      ; TEST X
< (i.e., X = 1)         BMI     EQONE       ;X = 1
                        BEQ     EQTWO       ;X = 2
            X:2
> (i.e., X = 3)         BPL     EQTHR       ;X = 3
                                .
= (i.e., X = 2)                 .
                                .
```

Not all the PDP-11 instructions affect the condition bits in the same
manner, however. Whereas the CMP instruction sets all the bits (N, Z, V, and
C) conditionally, the MOV instruction only sets the N- and Z-bits conditionally, while setting the V-bit unconditionally to 0 and not affecting the C-bit
at all. Appendix D, a brief summary of the complete instruction set for the
PDP-11, describes the operation of each instruction, including the effect on
the four condition codes N, Z, V, and C. As can be seen from the summary,
some apparently equivalent instructions, such as ADD#1, VALUE, and INC
VALUE (see Section 3.2.2 for a description of the single-operand instructions), do not affect the carry bit identically. Consequently, the knowledgeable programmer needs to pay particular attention to both the instruction
set and the condition codes it affects.

Another area of concern between the condition codes and the instruction
set is in the handling of conditional branches. There are two categories,
simple and signed, for the conditional branches in which individual condition
code bits and combinations of them are tested to decide whether or not the
branch is to be taken. The conditional instructions BEQ, BNE, BMI, and
BPL, discussed in Chapter 2, are all examples of simple conditional branches
that test a single bit (N or Z). The more complex signed conditional branches

will not be discussed until Chapter 4, however, since it is not until then that the concepts of carry and overflow are discussed. These topics are necessary for a complete understanding of this set of branches.

3.1.4. Memory Unit

The PDP-11 basic memory unit consists of 4096 16-bit words of memory. The memory unit may be expanded in units of 4096 words up to a maximum of 28,672 words, although the programmer can directly address 32,768 word locations. The memory can be viewed as a series of locations, with a number (address) assigned to each location.

Because PDP-11 memories and instructions are designed to accommodate both 16-bit words and 8-bit half-words, called *bytes*, the total number of addresses does not correspond to the number of words. Every word contains 2 bytes, so a 4096-word block contains 8192 byte locations. Consecutive words are therefore found in *even*-numbered addresses. Looking back at the hypothetical machine of Chapter 2, we can now see one important difference between it and the PDP-11—that word addresses will always be even values. Thus consecutive instructions will fall into consecutive *even* addresses, and operand addressing depends on *even*-numbered values being used as address pointers.

A PDP-11 word is divided into a high byte and a low byte as follows:

Low bytes are stored at even-numbered memory locations and high bytes at odd-numbered memory locations. Thus it is convenient for the programmer to view the PDP-11 memory as shown in Fig. 3-2.

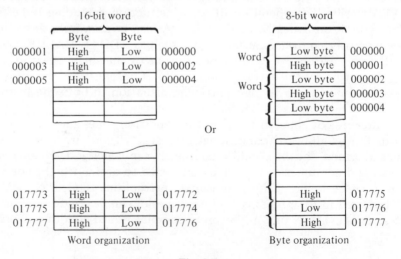

Fig. 3-2

Certain memory locations have been reserved for system use. These locations include addresses from 0 to 370_8 and the top 4096 word addresses (from 770000_8 up). The use of these locations is described in Chapter 6.

3.2. INSTRUCTION FORMAT

Data stored in memory must be accessed and manipulated. This data handling is defined by a PDP-11 instruction, which usually specifies:

    1. The function to be performed (i.e., the operation code).

    2. A general-purpose register to be used when locating the source and/or destination operand.

    3. An addressing mode (to specify how the selected register(s) is/are to be used).

The size of each field is very important in that it determines many of the external machine characteristics (e.g., how many registers, how much memory may be referenced directly, how many distinct op codes will exist). Of particular importance to the PDP-11 programmer is the instruction format and addressing techniques used by this computer. Unlike many small computers where the programmer may only address some small portion of memory such as 256 (an 8-bit address field) or 4096 (a 12-bit address field) words, the PDP-11 allows the programmer to address all of memory directly. In addition, addressing may be immediate, direct, indirect, indexed, and autoindexed in combination with the eight general-purpose registers. The result is a very general (and initially overwhelming) addressing structure which includes *relative addressing* (i.e., addresses that are determined in relation to the current value of the program counter) that can be utilized for writing programs that are not dependent on where they reside in memory (this topic will be discussed further in Chapter 4). Since a large portion of the data handled by a computer is usually structured (in character strings, in arrays, in lists, etc.), the computer must be designed to handle such data efficiently and flexibly. One of the functions of the general-purpose registers is to assist the programmer by functioning

    1. As accumulators in which the data to be manipulated reside.

    2. As pointers to the data rather than as data accumulators.

    3. As indices that describe the relative location of a data item in a table or a list.

The use of the registers for both data manipulation and address calculation leads to a variable-length instruction format for the PDP-11. For example, if registers alone are used to specify the data source or sink, only one memory word is needed to hold the instruction (op code plus source and destination operands). However, when registers are used as pointers to memory, as indices, as part of memory referencing instructions, and so on, two or three memory words may be needed to hold the basic instruction parts [op code, mode, register used, and addressing field(s)]. These additional words are used to address all 32,767 words (e.g., 2^{15} words) or 65,536 bytes (e.g., 2^{16} bytes), where all 16-bits are necessary to provide full byte addressing.

Since instructions may be one, two, or three words long, the PDP-11 is described as a *variable-instruction-length processor*. The format of its instructions determines how the programmer is to specify the addressing mode. The PDP-11 has four instruction formats.

3.2.1. Operate Group

The instruction format for the operate group is

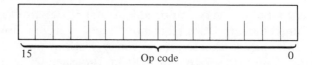

All bits of the instruction word are part of the op code, and all instructions in this group are one word long. The lone example of this group presented so far is HALT, which has the octal code of 000000_8 (the reader should note that when a 16-bit group is divided into 3-bit groups, or octal digits, the leading digit is actually only 1 bit long).

3.2.2. Single-Operand Group

The instruction format for the first word of all single-operand instructions (such as clear, increment, test) is

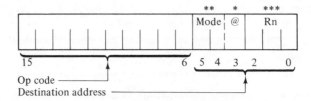

* Specifies direct or indirect address
** Specifies how register will be used
*** Specifies one of 8 general purpose registers

Bits 15 through 6 specify the operation code that defines the type of instruction to be executed. Bits 5 through 0 form a six-bit field called the *destination address field*. This consists of two subfields:

1. Bits 0–2 specify which of the eight general-purpose registers is to be referenced by this instruction word.

2. Bits 4 and 5 specify how the selected register will be used (address mode). Bit 3 indicates direct or deferred (indirect) addressing.

Depending on the addressing mode specified in bits 3–5, single-operand instructions may be one or two words in length. The second word holds a 16-bit address or data constant which is used to form the effective operand for the specified instruction. Table 3-1 is a subset of the single-operand instructions to be found in the PDP-11.

Table 3-1   Single-operand instructions.

Operation	Symbolic Form	Meaning
CLEAR	CLR R∅	(R ∅) ← 0
COMPLEMENT	COM VALUE	(VALUE) ← ˜(VALUE)
INCREMENT	INC VALUE	(VALUE) ← (VALUE) + 1
DECREMENT	DEC X(R2)	((R2)+ X) ← ((R2) + X) — 1
NEGATE	NEG R∅	(R ∅) ← —(R ∅)
TEST	TST —(R1)	((R1) — 2) — 0
JUMP	JMP HERE	(PC) ← HERE
SWAP BYTES†	SWAP AB	$(AB)_{15-8} \leftarrow (AB)_{7-0}$
		$(AB)_{7-0} \leftarrow (AB)_{15-8}$

†The subscript notation $(AB)_{15-8}$ is used to show that only some of the bits (e.g., 15–8) are to be swapped, not all of them.

3.2.2.1.   Examples of Single-Operand Instructions

As a consequence of the PDP-11's flexible addressing structure, there are eight modes associated with a single-operand instruction. For example, the single-word instruction

Symbolic	Instruction Octal Code	Description
INC R3	005203	Increment R3 by 1

can be represented as

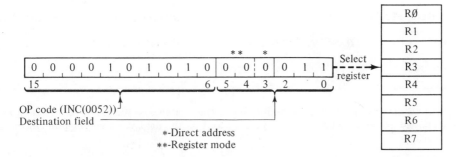

OP code (INC(0052))
Destination field
*-Direct address
**-Register mode

This is called *register mode*; the register contains the operand. If in this example register R3 contained a 5, then the before and after values of R3 can be depicted as

BEFORE   AFTER

R3 | 000005 | R3 | 000006 |

When the register contains the address of the operand (i.e., the register acts as a pointer), it can be automatically incremented (autoincrement mode) or decremented (autodecrement mode). In either case the contents of the registers are stepped to address the next sequential location. Two single-operand single-word examples are as shown in Table 3-2. The reader will note that autodecrementing is performed before using the register as a pointer, whereas autoincrementing is after pointer use.

Table 3-2

	Symbolic	Instruction Octal Code	Description
	INC (R5)+	005225	Use contents of R5 as the address of the operand. Increment the selected operand by 1 and then increment the contents of R5 by 2.†

BEFORE ADDRESS SPACE		REGISTER	AFTER ADDRESS SPACE		REGISTER
20000	005225	R5 030000	20000	005225	R5 030002
30000	123455		30000	123456	

	INC −(R3)	005243	The contents of R3 are decremented by 2† and used as the address of the operand. The operand is then increased by 1.

BEFORE ADDRESS SPACE		REGISTER	AFTER ADDRESS SPACE		REGISTER
1000	005243	R3 017776		005243	R3 017774
17774	000000		17774	000001	

†In autoincrement or autodecrement mode the contents of the specified register must be increased or decreased by *2* so as to guarantee that the next word will be pointed to by the register.

The last example of direct register use demonstrates indexing. In index mode, the contents of the selected register and an index word following the instruction word are summed to form the address of the operand. Since a 16-bit index word is needed to form the effective address, two words are necessary to hold this form of a single-operand instruction; see Table 3-3.

Table 3-3

Symbolic	Instruction Octal Code	Description
INC 200(R4)	005264 000200	The address of the operand is determined by adding 200 to the contents of R4. The location so specified is then incremented by 1.

	BEFORE ADDRESS SPACE	REGISTER		AFTER ADDRESS SPACE	REGISTER
1020	005264	R4 001000	1020	005264	001000
1022	000200		1022	000200	
1024			1024		
		1000 +200 1200			
1200	123455		1200	123456	

Table 3-4 summarizes the four basic modes used with direct addressing:

Table 3-4   Direct modes.

Binary Code	Name	Assembler Syntax	Function
000	Register	Rn	Register contains operand.
010	Autoincrement	(Rn)+	Register is used as a pointer to sequential data, then incremented.
100	Autodecrement	−(Rn)	Register is decremented and then used as a pointer.
110	Index	X(Rn)	Value X is added to (Rn) to produce address of operand. Neither X nor (Rn) is modified.

When bit 3 of the instruction is set, indirect addressing is specified and the four basic modes become deferred modes. In the register deferred mode, the contents of the selected register are taken as the address of the operand. In the three other deferred modes, the contents of the register specify the address of the operand rather than the operand itself.

To indicate deferred addressing, assembler syntax calls for prefacing the register operand(s) by an "@" sign or for parenthesizing the register when this is not ambiguous. Since each deferred mode is similar to its basic counterpart, separate descriptions of each deferred mode are not necessary. However, Tables 3-5, 3-6, 3-7, and 3-8 illustrate the four deferred modes.

Table 3-5 Register deferred mode.

Symbolic	Instruction Octal Code	Description
INC @R5	005215	Increment by 1 the contents of the location specified by R5.

	BEFORE ADDRESS SPACE		REGISTER		AFTER ADDRESS SPACE		REGISTER
1700	000100	R5	001700	1700	000101	R5	001700

Table 3-6 Autoincrement deferred mode.

Symbolic	Instruction Octal Code	Description
INC @(R2)+	005232	The contents of R2 are used as the address of the address of the operand which is increased by 1; then the contents of R2 are incremented by 2.

	BEFORE ADDRESS SPACE		REGISTER		AFTER ADDRESS SPACE		REGISTER
1010	000025	R2	010300	1010	000026	R2	010302
10300	001010			10300	001010		

Table 3-7 Autodecrement deferred mode.

Symbolic	Instruction Octal Code	Description
COM @−(R∅)	005150	The contents of R∅ are decremented by 2 and then used as the address of the operand. The operand is one's-complemented (i.e., logically complemented).

BEFORE ADDRESS SPACE		REGISTER		AFTER ADDRESS SPACE		REGISTER
10100	012345	R∅	010776	10100	165432	R∅ 010774
10774	010100			10774	010100	

Table 3-8 Index deferred mode.

Symbolic	Instruction Octal Code	Description
INC @1000(R2)	005272 001000	1000 and the contents of R2 are summed to produce the address of the address of the operand, which is incremented by 1.

BEFORE ADDRESS SPACE		REGISTER		AFTER ADDRESS SPACE		REGISTER
1050	007777	R2	000100	1050	010000	R2 000100
1100	001050			1100	001050	

1000
+100
1100

Table 3-9 summarizes the same four basic modes, this time with indirect addressing.

Table 3-9

Binary Code	Name	Assembler Syntax	Function
001	Register Deferred	@Rn or (Rn)	Register contains the address of the operand.
011	Autoincrement Deferred	@(Rn)+	Register is first used as a pointer to a word containing the address of the operand, then incremented (always by 2, even for byte instructions).
101	Autodecrement Deferred	@—(Rn)	Register is decremented (always by 2, even for byte instructions) and then used as a pointer to a word containing the address of the operand.
111	Index Deferred	@X(Rn)	Value X (stored in a word following the instruction) and (Rn) are added and the sum is used as a pointer to a word containing the address of the operand. Neither X nor (Rn) is modified.

For either direct or deferred addressing, the mode bits determine the actual number of words in the instruction (e.g., one or two). Only when indexing is performed is the actual instruction two words long.

3.2.3. Double-Operand Group

Operations that imply two operands (such as add, subtract, move, and compare) are handled by instructions that specify two addresses. The first operand is called the *source operand*, the second the *destination operand*. Bit assignments in the source and destination address fields may specify different modes and different registers. The instruction format for the first word of the double-operand instruction is as follows:

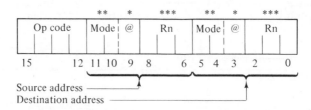

* Direct/deferred bit for source and destination address
** Specifies how selected registers are to be used
*** Specifies a general register

The source address field is used to select the source operand, the first operand. The destination is used similarly, and locates the second operand

and the result. For example, the instruction ADD A,B adds the contents (source operand) of location A to the contents (destination operand) of location B. After execution, B will contain the result of the addition and the contents of A will be unchanged.

3.2.3.1. Examples of Double-Operand Instructions

Since the meaning of the mode bits is the same for the double-operand group as for the single-operand group, instructions are also of variable length, being one, two, or three words long. Similarly, the calculation of the *effective address* of the operands is the same as for the single-operand group. For example, a two-word ADD instruction with one operand being indexed and the other register deferred would be as shown in Table 3-10.

Table 3-10

Symbolic	Instruction Octal Code	Description
ADD 30(R2),(R1)	066211 000030	30 and the contents of R2 are summed to produce the address of the source operand, the contents of which are added to the operand addressed by R1.

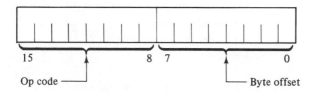

3.2.4. Conditional Branch Group

The branch instructions (BEQ, BNE, BPL, BMI, and BR, as specified in Table 2-1) are one-word instructions with the format

The high byte contains the op code and the low byte contains an 8-bit signed offset (7 bits plus sign), which specifies the branch address relative to the PC. The hardware calculates the branch address as follows:

1. Extend the sign of the offset through bits 8–15.

2. Multiply the result by 2. This creates a word offset rather than a byte offset.

3. Add the result to the PC to form the final branch address.

The assembler performs the reverse operation to form the byte offset from the specified address (denoted as E). It is important to remember that when the offset is added to the PC, the PC is pointing to the word following the branch instruction; hence the factor -2 in the calculation

$$\text{byte offset} = (E-PC)/2 \text{ (truncated to 8 bits)}$$

Since PC $= .+2$, then

$$\text{byte offset} = (E-\cdot-2)/2 \text{ (truncated to 8 bits)}$$

The 8-bit offset allows branching in the backward direction by 200_8 words (400_8 bytes) from the current PC, and in the forward direction by 177_8 words (376_8 bytes) from the current PC.

An illustration of relative branching can be found in the following program segment in Table 3-11.

Table 3-11

Location	Symbolic	Octal
100	HERE: INC R3	005203
.	.	
.	.	
.	.	
150	BR HERE	000753

The byte offset is calculated as follows, using 16-bit arithmetic:

$$
\begin{array}{lrr}
\text{branch address} & = & 100 \\
\text{current location} & = & 150 \\
\hline
\text{difference} & = & 177730 \\
\text{less two} & = & 2 \\
\hline
& & 177726 \\
\text{halved} & = & 077753 \\
\text{truncated to 8 bits} & = & 353
\end{array}
$$

and the branch instruction becomes

$$000400 + 353 \quad = 000753$$

When truncating a 16-bit word into an 8-bit byte, one has to be careful, since the octal representation does not correspond to byte boundaries. In the preceding example the 16-bit quantity 077753 would appear in binary as

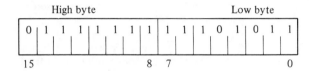

The value of the high byte is 177; the value of the low byte is 353. Thus the reader is cautioned against simply dividing a 16-bit value into two parts (e.g., 077 and 753 for the given value), because the result generated is not correct.

3.3. USE OF THE PC AS A GENERAL REGISTER

Although register 7 is a general-purpose register, it doubles in function as the PC for the PDP-11. Whenever the processor uses the PC to acquire a word from memory, the PC is automatically incremented by 2 to contain the address of the next word of the instruction being executed or the address of the next instruction to be executed. (When the program uses the PC to locate byte data, the PC is still incremented by 2.)

The PC responds to all the standard PDP-11 addressing modes. However, there are four of these modes with which the PC can provide advantages for handling *position-independent code* (see Chapter 4) and unstructured data. When regarding the PC, these modes are termed immediate, absolute (or immediate deferred), relative, and relative deferred, and are summarized in Table 3-12.

Table 3-12

Binary Code	Name	Assembler Syntax	Function
010	Immediate	#n	Operand follows instruction.
011	Absolute	@#A	Absolute address follows instructions.
110	Relative	A	Address of A, relative to the instruction, follows the instruction.
111	Relative Deferred	@A	Address of location containing address of A, relative to the instruction, follows the instruction.

The reader should remember that the special-effect modes are the same as modes described earlier, but the general register selected is R7, the program counter.

Examples of the various special forms of addressing are given in Table 3-13.

Table 3-13 Immediate addressing mode.

Symbolic	Instruction Octal Code	Description
ADD #10 R∅	062700 000010	The value of 10 is located in the second word of the instruction and is added to the contents of R∅.

BEFORE ADDRESS SPACE		REGISTER		AFTER ADDRESS SPACE		REGISTER
1020	062700	R0	000020	1020	062700	R0	000030
1022	000010	PC	001020	1022	000010	PC	001024
1024				1024			

Table 3-14 Absolute addressing mode.

Symbolic	Instruction Octal Code	Description
CLR @#1100	005037 001100	Clear the contents of location 1100.

BEFORE ADDRESS SPACE				AFTER ADDRESS SPACE		
20	005037			20	005037	
22	001100	PC	000020	22	001100	PC	000024
				24		
1100	177777			1100	000000	
1102				1102		

Note that just before this instruction is fetched and executed, the PC points to the first word of the instruction. The processor fetches the first word and increments the PC by 2. The source operand mode is 27 (autoincrement of PC); thus the PC is used as a pointer to fetch the operand (the second word of the instruction) before being incremented by 2 to point to the next instruction. (See Table 3-14.)

This mode is the equivalent of immediate deferred or autoincrement deferred using the PC. The contents of the location following the instruction are taken as the address of the operand. Immediate data are interpreted as an absolute address (i.e., an address that remains constant no matter where in memory the assembled instruction is executed). See Table 3-15.

Table 3-15   Relative addressing mode.

Symbolic	Instruction Octal Code	Description
INC A	005267 000054	To increment location A, contents of memory location immediately following instruction word are added to (PC) to produce address A. Contents of A are increased by 1.

BEFORE
ADDRESS SPACE

1020	005267
1022	000054
1024	
1026	
1100	000000

PC 001020

1024
+ 54
1100

AFTER
ADDRESS SPACE

1020	0005267
1022	000054
1024	
1026	
1100	000001

PC 001024

This mode is assembled as index mode using R7. The base of the address calculation, which is stored in the second or third word of the instruction, is not the address of the operand, but the number which when added to the (PC) becomes the address of the operand. See Table 3-16.

This mode is similar to the relative mode, except that the second word of the instruction, when added to the PC, contains the address of the address of the operand rather than the address of the operand.

Table 3-16 Relative deferred addressing mode.

Symbolic	Instruction Octal Code	Description
CLR @A	005077 000020	Add second word of instruction to PC to produce address of address of operand. Clear operand.

BEFORE
ADDRESS SPACE

AFTER
ADDRESS SPACE

1020	005037			1020	005037		
1022	000020	PC	001020	1022	000020	PC	001024
1024				1024			
		1024 +20 1044					
1044	010100			1044	010100		
10100	100001			10100	000000		

One point is worth special mention and concerns absolute/relative addressing. The point is that relative mode is the *normal* mode for memory references written in PAL-11, the symbolic assembler for the PDP-11. This occurs because every single- and double-operand instruction must reference a general register. As a result, when the programmer writes

```
CLR     100
MOV     X, Y
```

the base of the address calculation, which is stored in the second or third word of the instruction, is not the address of the operand. Rather, it is the number which when added to the PC becomes the address of the operand. Thus the base is X − PC, where X = actual address. The operation is explained as follows.

If the statement MOV 100,R3 is assembled at location 20, the assembled code is

Location 20:   0 1 6 7 0 3
Location 22:   0 0 0 0 5 4

The processor fetches the MOV instruction and adds 2 to the PC so that it points to location 22. The source operand mode is 67, that is, indexed by the PC. To pick up the base, the processor fetches the word pointed to by the PC and adds 2 to the PC. The PC now points to location 24. To calculate the address of the source operand, the base is added to the designated register. That is, base + PC = 54 + 24 = 100, the operand address.

Since the assembler considers . as the address of the first word of the instruction, an equivalent statement would be

```
MOV      100-. -4(PC), R3
```

This mode is called *relative* because the operand address is calculated relative to the current PC. The base is the distance (in bytes) between the operand and the current PC. If the operator and its operand are moved in memory so that the distance between the operator and data remains constant, the instruction will operate correctly. (By definition, branch instructions are also relative address instructions and can, therefore, be used in a position-independent fashion.)

Because the operand address is relative to the current PC, it is not a simple task to initialize instruction operands. Thus on machines such as the PDP-11 where the normal addressing mode is relative, self-modifying programs are much more difficult to write in self-initializing form and are therefore to be avoided.

Another aspect of relative mode addressing is the meaning of both immediate and absolute addressing modes in the PDP-11 computer. Immediate mode becomes equivalent to using autoincrement mode with the PC, while absolute mode is the equivalent of immediate deferred, or autoincrement deferred, mode using the PC. The value of using such relatively addressed operands will be found in Chapter 4, which begins with position-independent programming.

3.4. PAL-11 ASSEMBLER

Having learned about the varied forms of addressing on the PDP-11, the reader can appreciate why machine language programming in octal was not discussed in Chapter 2. However, it is instructive now to present a symbolic program complete with its octal code. But first we must consider a few additional characteristics of PAL-11 (*Program Assembly Language* for the PDP-11's Absolute Assembly) besides those presented in Chapter 2.

In PAL-11 the period (.) is the symbol for the assembly location counter. When used in the operand field of an instruction, it represents the address of the first word of the instruction. When used in the operand field of an assembler directive, it represents the address of the current byte or word. For example,

```
A:   MOV    #., R∅    ;.Refers to location A,
                      ;i.e., the address of the MOV
                      ;instruction
```

At the beginning of each assembly pass (see Section 5.4), the assembler sets the location counter to zero. Normally, consecutive memory locations are assigned to each byte/word of object code generated. However, the location where the object code is stored may be changed by a direct assignment altering the location counter.

A *direct assignment statement* associates a symbol with a value. When a direct assignment statement defines a symbol for the first time, that symbol is entered into the assembler's symbol table and the specified value is associated with it. A symbol may be redefined by assigning a new value to a previously defined symbol. The newly assigned value will replace the previous value assigned to the symbol. The general format for a direct assignment is

$$symbol = expression$$

One use for direct assignment is to assign the location counter an initial value (e.g., . = 1000). Another use is in equating commonly used values or expressions to symbolic names, increasing the information content of the program.

The decimal point, or period, is interpreted by the assembler in several ways. Used by itself it represents the value of the current location counter. As such it may be used both to initialize the LC (e.g., . = 1000) and to act as an operand of an instruction. For example, the instruction BR .−4 causes the computer to execute the instruction two words (or four half-words) preceding this instruction.

A common mistake would be to write BR .−2 in order to jump back two instructions. The error occurs because (1) the PDP-11 is both half-word and word addressable, and (2) PDP-11 instructions occupy one, two, or three PDP-11 words. Thus the use of "." for calculating branch addresses is a tricky business until the novice programmer is sure just how many words (or bytes) are to be skipped. Consequently, the use of offset addressing is to be discouraged very strongly!

The second use of the period can be found in its association with *assembler directives* or pseudo ops, which direct the assembly process and may generate data. One example of a pseudo op was the .END directive. Another is the .WORD directive.

The .WORD assembler directive may have one or more operands. Each operand is stored in a word of the object program. If there is more than one operand, they are stored in successive words. The operands may be any legally formed expressions. An operator field left blank will be interpreted as the .WORD directive if the operand field contains one or more expressions.

For example,

```
FIVE:   5
SIX:    .WORD   6
SEV:    .WORD   7,8
```

will assign the constants 5, 6, 7, and 8 to consecutive memory locations.

These characters and conventions will be used throughout the remainder of this text to code programs in PAL-11. Thus all examples given are real PDP-11 programs (or program segments) and may be assembled and executed on PDP-11 computers.

3.4.1. Sample Programs

Let us consider the array problem of Chapter 2 as flowcharted in Fig. 2-9. Since we had not concerned ourselves with the real PDP-11 and its variable-length instructions, it was easy to assume that each instruction required one word and that consecutive instructions occupied consecutive memory locations. As the contents of this chapter point out, that assumption was false and an actual assembly listing for the program looks as shown in Table 3-17. This listing shows two subtle changes over the program writ-

Table 3-17

Program Address	Program Contents	Label	Op Code	Operands	Comments
	001000		.=1000		; STARTING ADDR = 1000
001000	016767	START:	MOV	ZERO,ISUM	; INITIALIZE SUM
	000032				
	000032				
001006	066767	FIXUP:	ADD	K,ISUM	; ADD IN ELEMENT OF ARRAY K
	000034				
	000024				
001014	026767		CMP	FIXUP+2,LIMIT	; DONE YET?
	177770				
	000022				
001022	001404		BEQ	STOP	; YES
001024	066767		ADD	CONS,FIXUP+2	; MODIFY ADDRESS
	000012				
	177756				
001032	000765		BR	FIXUP	; LOOP
001034	000000	STOP:	HALT		; STOP HERE
001036	000000	ZERO:	.WORD	0	; CONSTANT ZERO
001040	000000	ISUM:	.WORD	0	; RESULTANT SUM
001042	000002	CONS:	.WORD	2	; CONS TO GENERATE NEXT ADDRESS
001044	000176	LIMIT:	.WORD	K—FIXUP—4+98.	; THE LAST REL ADDR GENERATED
001046		K			; THE ARRAY K
	001212		.=.+100.		; SAVE 100 DEC LOCS FOR ARRAY
	001000		.END	START	; END OF ASSEMBLY

ten for the hypothetical computer of Chapter 2. First, the instruction with label FIXUP is now modified by adding two to the second word of this three-word instruction (one word each is occupied by the op code, the source, and the destination operands). Two must be added since the array is stored in consecutive *words*, and it must be added to the second word, since this word contains the relative base address of the array K.

Second, the word labeled LIMIT contains a value that represents the address of the last element in the array K. This value is K—FIXUP—4+98., where K—FIXUP—4 represents the relative address generated for the initial instruction and the decimal 98 is "1 less" than the number of elements (i.e., it is given by $2*[N—1]$). Note then that the CMP instruction is actually comparing two address values that are, in fact, represented by two numerical values.

The reader is once again reminded that self-modifying programs, although useful, are not considered good programming practice. In this particular example, the program, once self-modified, cannot be rerun without resetting the second word of the instruction labeled FIXUP. And since relative addressing is used to specify the address of K, the initializing statement

```
MOV        #K, FIXUP+2
```

will *not* reestablish the instruction to its initial value.

The value of recoding this example was to show how real PDP-11 programs are assembled and what their object code looks like. Carrying this point one step further, the simplest version of the array problem is coded as shown in Table 3-18. Note that for the sake of brevity, the size of the array has been limited to 10 elements.

Table 3-18

Program Address	Program Contents	Label	Op Code	Operands	Comments
		;			THIS IS A PROGRAM TO SUM THE
		;			ELEMENTS OF THE ARRAY K. THE
		;			SUM IS LEFT IN R∅.
		;			R. ECKHOUSE OCTOBER 31, 1972
		;			
	000000		R∅=%0		; DEFINE R∅
	000001		R1=%1		; DEFINE R1
	001000		.=1000		; DEFINE STARTING ADDR
001000	005000	START:	CLR	R0	; INITIALIZE SUM
001002	012701		MOV	#K,R1	; ADDRESS OF K INOT R1
	001020				

Table 3-18 (continued)

Program Address	Program Contents	Label	Op Code	Operands	Comments
001006	062100	LOOP:	ADD	(R1)+,R∅	; ADD IN VALUE
001010	022701		CMP	#K+18.,R1	; DONE?
	001042				
001014	100374		BPL	LOOP	; NO, CONTINUE
001016	000000		HALT		; STOP
001020	000001	K:	1,2,3,4,5,6,7,10,11,12		
001022	000002				
001024	000003				
001026	000004				
001030	000005				
001032	000006				
001034	000007				
001036	000010				
001040	000011				
001042	000012				
	001000		.END	START	

EXERCISES

1. Assume that the following instruction begins in location 150 and show how PAL-11 would assemble it:

```
MOV     100,200
```

2. What change would occur in the assembled output if each of the addresses above were preceded by a # sign? A @ # sign pair?

3. Play assembler for the following instruction pair:

```
          .=26
DO:       ADD     R1,R2
          .=100
          BMI     DO
```

4. Using the format presented in this chapter to explain the different addressing modes, show how the instructions in Table 3-19 change the contents of certain memory locations (the BEFORE and AFTER address spaces). Assume that each instruction begins in location 1000 and that the initial contents of the registers and memory as given are the same for each.

Table 3-19

Instructions	Initial register and memory contents
a. CLR (R5)+	R0=0 R4=400
b. ADD (R2)+,R4	R2=200 R5=30000
	R3=1000
c. ADD −(R3),R0	A=2000 B=500
d. ADD 30(R2),20(R5)	(200)=1000
e. DEC @(R2)+	(230)=30000
f. ADD @1000(R2),R1	(500)=3000
g. MOV #10,R0	(776)=100
h. ADD @#1200,R5	(1000)=230
i. NEG A	(1200)=30020
j. SWAB @B	(3000)=123456
	(30020)=1000

5. Rewrite the array problem, as given in Chapter 2, using the general registers for indexing through the array elements.

6. In most machines, instruction sets are often redundant. For example, CLR is not absolutely essential on the PDP-11 since it already has a MOV instruction. The ADD instruction on the PDP-11 is another candidate for removal provided that one can show how its function can be performed by an "ADD-equivalent" sequence of other PDP-11 instructions. Give such an equivalent.

7. Explain why the "forward reference" (.=A−6) in the program segment here would present problems to the PAL assembler.

```
            . =A−6
            . WORD    0
    START:  MOV      #3, R0
    A:      CMP      R0, R1
            .
            .
            .
```

8. Do both the BR and JMP instructions use relative addressing through byte offsets? What, then, is the difference or similarity between the two instructions, and how would one be used where the other was not (could not be?)?

9. What are the contents of location A at the end of the following program written in PAL-11?

```
            . =200
            R1=%1
            R2=%2
    START:  MOV     #230, R1
            MOV     2(1), R2
            MOV     R1, B
            ADD     B, R2
            MOV     R2, A
            HALT
    B:      . WORD   0
    C:      . WORD   230, 20, 54
    A:      . WORD   0
            . END    START
```

10. The program in Exercise 9 is to be assembled starting at location 400. The final contents of A, however, must remain the same as in Exercise 9. What, if any, changes are required? Explain.

11. Add together all the numbers found in locations 2002, 2004, 2006, ... that are within the range of MIN to MAX. The values for MIN and MAX are located in location 2000 and $0 \leqslant N \leqslant 99$. If $N = 0$, the result should be zero. The sum of the numbers should be stored in location 1776. Note that there is no range associated with MIN and MAX; the actual values may be anything (positive or negative) within the range of acceptable numbers on the PDP-11.

12. Write a program to find the mode (most frequent value) of a set of N numbers. The numbers will be sorted (all numbers of equal value stored in sequential memory locations) but not ordered in ascending or descending order. Show that your program will work for all values of N in the range $0 \leqslant N \leqslant 99$.

REFERENCES

Since this chapter served to introduce the PDP-11, further readings can be found in the various Digital Equipment Corp. manuals describing this computer. These manuals include the *Processor Handbooks* for the PDP-11/10, PDP-11/20, PDP-11/40, and PDP-11/45 plus the *PDP-11 Paper Tape Software Programming Handbook*. The final test, however, of how well the material has been understood is found in the writing and running of actual computer programs. For this, the real thing is needed—a PDP-11 computer.

4 PROGRAMMING TECHNIQUES

Mastery of a basic instruction set is the first step in learning to program. The next step is to learn to use the instruction set to obtain correct results and to obtain them efficiently. This is best done by studying the following programming techniques. Examples, which should further familiarize the reader with the total instruction set and its use, are given to illustrate each technique.

4.1. POSITION-INDEPENDENT PROGRAMMING

Most programs written to run on a computer are written so as to occupy specified memory locations (e.g., the current location counter is used to define the location of the first instruction). Such programs are said to be absolute or *position-dependent programs*. However, it is sometimes desirable to have a standard program which is available to many different users. Since it will not be known a priori where the standard programs are to be loaded, it is necessary to be able to load the program into different areas of core and to run it there. There are several ways to do this:

1. Reassemble the program at the desired location.

2. Use a relocating loader which accepts specially coded binary from a relocatable assembler.

3. Have the program relocate itself after it is loaded.

4. Write a program that is *position-independent*.

On small machines, reassembly is often performed. When the required core is available, a relocating loader (usually called a *linking loader*) is preferable. It generally is not economical to have a program relocate itself, since hundreds or thousands of addresses may need adjustment. Writing position-independent code is usually not possible because of the structure of the addressing of the object machine. However, on the PDP-11, position-independent code (PIC) is possible.

PIC is achieved on the PDP-11 by using addressing modes which form an effective memory address relative to the program counter (PC). Thus, if an instruction and its object(s) are moved in such a way that the relative distance between them is not altered, the same offset relative to the PC can be used in all positions in memory. Thus PIC usually references locations relative to the current location. PIC programs may make absolute references as long as the locations referenced stay in the same place while the PIC program is relocated.

4.1.1. Position-Independent Modes

There are three position-independent modes or forms of instructions. They are:

1. *Branches*: the conditional branches, as well as the unconditional branch, BR, are position-independent, since the branch address is computed as an offset to the PC.

2. *Relative memory references*: any relative memory reference of the form

```
CLR     X
MOV     X, Y
BR      X
```

is position-independent because the assembler assembles it as an offset indexed by the PC. The offset is the difference between the referenced location and the PC. For example, assume that the instruction CLR 200 is at address 100:

Line Number	Address	Contents	Symbolic Instruction	Comments
1	000100	005067 000074	CLR 200	;FIRST WORD OF INSTRUCTION ;OFFSET=200−104

The offset is added to the PC. The PC contains 104, which is the address of the word following the offset (the second word of this two-word instruction). Note that although the form CLR X is position-independent, the form CLR @X is not. We may see this when we consider the following:

Line Number	Address	Contents	Label	Symbolic Instruction	Comments
1	001000	005077 000774	S:	CLR @X .	;CLEAR LOCATION A
2.	002000	003000	X:	.WORD A . .	;POINTER TO A
3.	003000	000000	A:	.WORD 0	

The contents of location X are used as the address of the operand, which is symbolically labeled A. The value stored at location X is the absolute address of the symbolic location A rather than the relative address or offset between location X and A. Thus, if all the code is relocated after assembly, the contents of location X must be altered to reflect the fact that location A now stands for a new absolute address.† If A, however, was the name associated with a fixed, absolute location, statements S and X could be relocated because now it is important for A to remain fixed. Thus the following code is position-independent:

Line Number	Address	Contents	Label	Symbolic Instruction	Comments
1		000036		A = 36	;FIXED ADDRESS OF 36
2	001000	005077 000774	S:	CLR @X . .	;CLEAR LOCATION A
3	002000	000036	X:	.WORD A	;POINTER TO A

3. *Immediate operands:* the assembler addressing form #X specifies immediate data; that is, the operand is in the instruction. Immediate data that are not addresses are position-independent, since they are a part of the instruction and are moved with the instruction. Consequently, a SUB #2,HERE is position-independent (since #2 is not an address), while MOV #A,ADRPTR is position-dependent if A is a symbolic address. This is so even though the operand is fetched, in both cases, using the PC in the autoincrement

---

†To verify this point the reader is encouraged to relocate the code, after assembly, into locations 4000, 5000, and 6000. By doing so he will discover that the contents of these locations are the same as for the original code and that the contents of location 5000 do not point to location 6000.

mode, since it is the quantity fetched that is being used rather than its form of addressing.

4.1.2. Absolute Modes

Any time a memory location or register is used as a pointer to data, the reference is absolute. If the referenced data remain always fixed in memory (e.g., an absolute memory location) independent of the position of the PIC, the absolute modes must be used.[†] Alternatively, if the data are relative to the position of the code, the absolute modes must not be used unless the pointers involved are modified. Restating this point in different words, if addressing is direct and relative, it is position-independent; if it is indirect and either relative or absolute, it is *not* position-independent. For example, the instruction

                    MOV   @#X, HERE

"move the contents of the word pointed to (indirectly referenced by) the PC (in this case absolute location X) to the word indexed relative to the PC (symbolically called HERE)" contains one operand that is referenced indirectly (X) and one operand that is referenced relatively (HERE). This instruction can be moved anywhere in memory as long as absolute location X stays the same, that is, it does not move with the instruction or program; otherwise it may not be.

The absolute modes are:

@X	Location X is a pointer.
@#X	The immediate word is a pointer.
(R)	The register is a pointer.
(R)+ and (R)	The register is a pointer.
@(R)+ and @—(R)	The register points to a pointer.
X(R) R≠6 or 7	The base, X, modified by (R), is the address of the operand.
@X(R)	The base, modified by (R), is a pointer.

The nondeferred index modes require a little clarification. As described in Chapter 3, the form X(7)[††] is the normal mode in which to reference memory and is a relative mode. Index mode, using a register, is also a relative mode and may be used conveniently in PIC. Basically, the register pointer points to a dynamic storage area, and the index mode is used to access data relative to the pointer. Once the pointer is set up, all data are referenced relative to the pointer.

[†]When PIC is not being written, references to fixed locations may be performed with either the absolute or relative forms.

[††]Recall that X(7) is equivalent to X(R7), which is equivalent to X(PC) where PC-R7.

4.1.3. Writing Automatic PIC

Automatic PIC is code that requires no alteration of addresses or pointers. Thus memory references are limited to relative modes unless the location referenced is fixed. In addition to the above rules, the following must be observed:

1. Start the program with .=0 to allow easy relocation using the absolute loader (see Chapter 7).

2. All location-setting statements must be of the form .=.±X or .= function of symbols within the PIC. For example, .=A+10, where A is a local label.

3. There must not be any absolute location-setting statements. This means that a block of PIC cannot set up specified core areas at load time with statements such as

```
. =340
. WORD     TRAPH, 340          ; PRE-LOAD 340, 342
```

The absolute loader, when it is relocating PIC, relocates all data by the load bias (see Chapter 7). Thus the data for the absolute location would be relocated to some other place. Such areas must be set at execution time:

```
MOV       #TRAPH, @#340     ; PUT ADDR IN ABS LOC 340
MOV       #340, @#342       ; AND ABS LOCATION 342
```

4.1.4. Writing Nonautomatic PIC

Often it is not possible or economical to write totally automated PIC. In these cases some relocation may be easily performed at execution time. Some of the required methods of solution are presented below. Basically, the methods operate by examining the PC to determine where the PIC is actually located. Then a relocation factor can be easily computed. In all examples it is assumed that the code is assembled at zero and has been relocated somewhere else by the absolute loader.

4.1.5. Setting Up Fixed Core Locations

Consider first the previous example to clear the contents of A indirectly. The pointer to A, contained in symbolic location X, must be changed if the code is to be relocated. The program segment in Fig. 4-1 recomputes the pointer value each time that it is executed. Thus the pointer value no longer depends on the value of the location counter at the time the program was assembled, but on the value of the PC where it is loaded.

```
         000000           R0=%0                    ;DEFINE R0
         000007           PC=%7                    ;DEFINE PC
000000   010700   S:      MOV     PC,R0            ;R0 = (ADDR OF S)+2
000002   062700           ADD     #A-S-2,R0        ;ADD IN OFFSET
         001776
000006   010067           MOV     R0,X             ;MOVE POINTER TO X
         000766
000012   005077           CLR     @X               ;CLEAR VALUE INDIRECTLY
         000762
000016   000000           HALT                     ;STOP
                          ;
                          ;
                          ;
         001000           . =. +760
001000   002000   X:      . WORD  A                ;POINTER TO A
                          ;
                          ;
                          ;
         002000           . =. +776
002000   000000   A:      . WORD  0                ;VALUE TO BE CLEARED
         000001           . END
```

Fig. 4-1

Now if this program is loaded into locations 4000 and higher, it should be clear that none of the program values is changed. This point could be shown pictorially by taking the Fig. 4-1 material, recopying it, but changing only the values in the leftmost column, the address column. Thus if one were to look in, say, location 4010, the contents would be 766 and the value found in location 5000 would be 2000 (i.e., neither value is changed).

Given that the program data have not changed, the question is: How does it work? The answer is that the offset $A-S-2$ is equivalent to $A-(S+2)$ and $S+2$ is the value of PC which is placed in R0 by the statement MOV PC,R0. At assembly time the offset value is $A-PC_0$, where $PC_0 = S+2$ and PC_0 is the PC that was assumed for the program when assembled beginning at location 0.

Later, after the program has been relocated, the move instruction will no longer store PC_0 in R0, but a new value, PC_n, which is the current value of PC for the executing program. However, the add instruction still adds in the immediate value $A-PC_0$, producing the final result in R0:

$$PC_n + (A-PC_0) = A+(PC_n-PC_0)$$

which is the desired value, since it yields the new absolute location of A [e.g., the assembled value of A plus the relocation factor (PC_n-PC_0)].

4.1.6. Relocating Pointers

If pointers must be used, they may be relocated as we have just shown. For example, assume that a list of data is to be accessed with the instruction

```
                    ADD        (R0)+, R1
```

The pointer to the list, list L, may be calculated at execution time as follows:

```
M:        MOV     PC, R0          ; GET CURRENT PC
          ADD     #L-M-2, R0      ; ADD OFFSET
```

Another variation is to gather all pointers into a table. The relocation factor may be calculated once and then applied to all pointers in the table in a loop. The program in Fig. 4-2 is an example of this technique. The reader should verify (Exercise 1 at the end of this chapter) that if this program is relocated so that if it begins in location 10000, the values in the pointer table, PTRTBL, will be 10000, 10020, and 10030.

```
           000000        R0=%0                     ; DEFINE R0
           000001        R1=%1                     ; DEFINE R1
           000002        R2=%2                     ; DEFINE R2
           000007        PC=%7                     ; DEFINE PC
000000 010700 X:   MOV     PC, R0         ; RELOCATE ALL ENTRIES IN PTRTBL
000002 162700      SUB     #X+2, R0       ; CALCULATE RELOCATION FACTOR
       000002
000006 012701      MOV     #PTRTBL, R1    ; GET AND RELOCATE A POINTER
       000030
000012 060001      ADD     R0, R1         ; TO PTRTBL
000014 012702      MOV     #TBLLEN, R2    ; GET LENGTH OF TABLE
       000003
000020 060021 LOOP:  ADD   R0, (R1)+      ; RELOCATE AN ENTRY
000022 005302      DEC     R2             ; COUNT DOWN
000024 001375      BNE     LOOP           ; BRANCH IF NOT DONE
000026 000000      HALT                   ; STOP WHEN DONE
       000003      TBLLEN=3               ; LENGTH OF TABLE
000030 000000 PTRTBL: .WORD  X, LOOP, PTRTBL
000032 000020
000034 000030
       000001        .END
```

Fig. 4-2

Care must be exercised when restarting a program that relocates a table of pointers. The restart procedure must not include the relocating again (i.e., the table must be relocated exactly once after each load).

4.2. JUMP INSTRUCTION

Although mentioned earlier, the JMP instruction has been overlooked somewhat up to now. The astute reader will, no doubt, recognize that the necessity of a jump instruction is dictated by the fact that the branch instructions, although relative, are incapable of branching more than 200 words in either a positive or a negative direction. Thus to branch from one end of memory to another, a jump instruction must be a part of the instruction set and must allow full-word addressing.

The jump instruction is indeed a part of the PDP-11 instruction set and belongs to the single-operand group. As a result, jumps may be relative, absolute, indirect, and indexed. This flexibility in determining the effective jump address is quite useful in solving a particular class of problems that occur in programming. This class is best illustrated by example.

4.2.1. Jump Table Problem

A common type of problem is one in which the input data represent a code for an action to be performed. For each code, the program is to take a certain action by executing a specified block of code. Such a problem would be coded in FORTRAN as

```
      .
      .
      .
READ, INDEX
GO TO (10,100,37,1150,...,7), INDEX
      .
      .
      .
```

In other words, based on the value of index, the program will go to the statement labeled 10, 100, 37, and so on.

The "computed GO TO" in FORTRAN must eventually be translated into machine language. One possibility in the language of the PDP-11 would be

```
              .
              .
              .
       READ     INDEX            ; A PSEUDO-INSTRUCTION
       MOV      INDEX, R1        ; PLACE IT IN R1
       DEC      R1               ; 0<=INDEX<=MAX-1
       ADD      R1, R1           ; FORM 2*INDEX
       JMP      @TABLE(R1)       ; INDIRECT JUMP
TABLE: .WORD    L10, L100, L37, L1150,..., L7
              .
              .
              .
```

The method used is called the *jump table method*, since it uses a table of addresses to jump to. The method works as follows:

1. The value of INDEX is obtained.

2. Since the range of INDEX is $1 \leqslant INDEX \leqslant$ maximum value, 1 is subtracted from the index so that its range is $0 \leqslant INDEX \leqslant max - 1$.

3. The value of index is doubled to take care of the fact that labels in the table are stored in even addresses; i.e., full words;

4. The address for the JMP instruction is utilized both as indexed and indirect, such that it points to an address to be jumped to in the table.

Although the jump instruction transfers control to the correct program label, it does not specify any way to come back. In the next section, where we shall consider subroutining, we shall see that a slight modification of the jump instructions allows for an orderly transfer of control, and a return, from one section of code to another.

4.3. SUBROUTINES

A good programming practice to get into is to separate large programs into smaller *subprograms*, which are easier to manage. These subprograms are activated either by a main program or by each other, allowing for the sharing of routines among the different programs and subprograms.

The saving in memory space resulting from having only one copy of the needed routine is a definite advantage. Equally important is the saving in time for the programmer, who needs to code the routine only once. However, in order to share common subprograms, there must be a mechanism to

1. Allow the transfer of control from one routine to another.

2. Pass values among the various routines.

The mechanism that accomplishes these requirements is called the *subroutine linkage* and is, in general, a combination of hardware features and software conventions.

The hardware features on the PDP-11 which assist in performing the subroutine linkage are the instructions JSR and RTS. These instructions are in the subroutine call and return group and have the following assembler form and instruction format[†]:

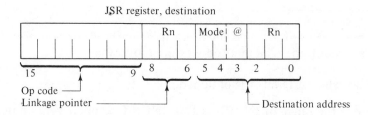

†Depending on the mode of addressing, one or two words are used for the JSR instruction.

RTS register

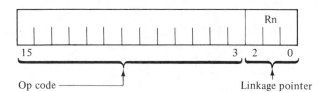

Both instructions make use of a "stack" mechanism similar to the stack mechanism described for zero-address machines in Section 1.2.8.6.

4.3.1. Stack

A *stack* is an area of memory set aside by the programmer for temporary storage or subroutine/interrupt service linkage. The instructions that facilitate stack handling (e.g., autoincrement and autodecrement) are useful features that may be found in low-cost computers. They allow a program to dynamically establish, modify, or delete a stack and items on it. The stack uses the *last-in, first-out* or *LIFO concept*; that is, various items may be added to a stack in sequential order and retrieved or deleted from the stack in reverse order (Fig. 4-3). On the PDP-11, a stack starts at the highest location reserved for it and expands linearly downward to the lowest address as items are added to the stack.

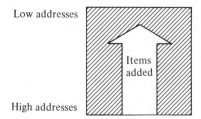

Fig. 4-3 Stack addresses.

The programmer does not need to keep track of the actual locations his data are being stacked into. This is done automatically through a *stack pointer*. To keep track of the last item added to the stack (or "where we are" in the stack), a general register always contains the memory address where the last item is stored in the stack. In the PDP-11 any register except register 7 (the PC) may be used as a stack pointer under program control; however, instructions associated with subroutine linkage and interrupt service automatically use register 6 (R6) as a hardware stack pointer. For this reason R6 is frequently referred to as the system *SP*.

Stacks in the PDP-11 may be maintained in either full-word or byte units. This is true for a stack pointed to by any register except R6, which must be organized in full-word units only. Byte stacks (Fig. 4-4) require instructions capable of operating on bytes rather than full words (byte handling is discussed in Section 4.6).

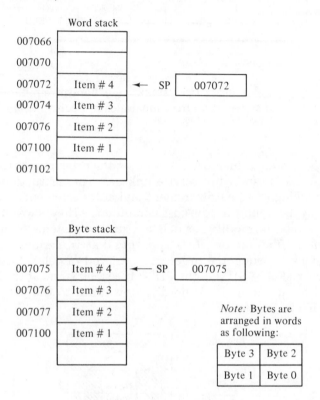

Fig. 4-4   Word and byte stacks.

Items are added to a stack using the autodecrement addressing mode with the appropriate pointer register. (See Chapter 2 for a description of the autoincrement/decrement modes.)

This operation is accomplished as follows:

```
MOV       SOURCE,-(SP)     ; MOVE SOURCE WORD ONTO THE STACK
```

or

```
MOVB      SOURCE,-(SP)     ; MOVE SOURCE BYTE ONTO THE STACK
```

This is called a "push" because data are "pushed onto the stack."

†See Section 4.6 for a discussion of byte instructions.

To remove an item from stack the autoincrement addressing mode with the appropriate SP is employed. This is accomplished in the following manner:

```
MOV      (SP)+,DEST      ;MOVE DESTINATION WORD OFF STACK
```

or

```
MOVB     (SP)+,DEST      ;MOVE DESTINATION BYTE OFF STACK
```

Removing an item from a stack is called a *pop*, for "popping from the stack." After an item has been popped, its stack location is considered free and available for other use. The stack pointer points to the last-used location, implying that the next (lower) location is free. Thus a stack may represent a pool of shareable temporary storage locations.

4.3.2. Subroutine Calls and Returns

When a JSR is executed, the contents of the linkage register are saved on the system R6 stack as if a MOV reg,—(SP) has been performed. Then the same register is loaded with the memory address following the JSR instruction (the contents of the current PC) and a jump is made to the entry location specified. The effect, then, of executing one JSR instruction is the same as simultaneously executing two MOVs and a JMP; for example,

```
                    MOV REG,-(SP)     ;PUSH REGISTER INTO THE STACK
   JSR   REG,SUBR   MOV PC,REG        ;PUT RETURN PC INTO REGISTER
                    JMP SUBR          ;JUMP TO SUBROUTINE
```

Figure 4-5 gives the "before" and after conditions when executing the subroutine instruction JSR R5,1064.

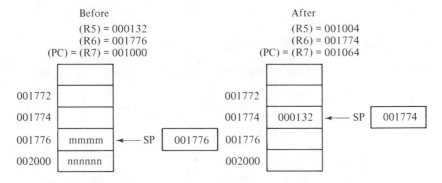

Fig. 4-5 JSR instruction.

In order to return from a subroutine, the RTS instruction is executed. It performs the inverse operation of the JSR, the unstacking and restoring of the saved register value, and the return of control to the instruction following the JSR instruction. The equivalent of an RTS is a concurrent MOV instruction pair:

```
RTS   REG        MOV REG,PC        ;RESTORE PC
                 MOV (SP)+,REG     ;RESTORE REGISTER
```

The use of a stack mechanism for subroutine calls and returns is particularly advantageous for two reasons. First, many JSR instructions can be executed without the need to provide any saving procedure for the linkage information, since all linkage information is automatically pushed into the stack in sequential order. Returns can simply be made by automatically popping this information from the stack in opposite order. Such linkage address bookkeeping is called automatic *nesting* of subroutine calls. This feature enables the programmer to construct fast, efficient linkages in an easy, flexible manner. It even permits a routine to be recalled or to call itself in those cases where this is meaningful (Sections 4.3.5 and 4.3.6). Other ramifications will appear after we examine the interrupt mechanism for the PDP-11 (Section 6.4).

The second advantage of the stack mechanism is found in its ease of use for saving and restoring registers. This case arises when a subroutine wants to use the general registers, but these registers were already in use by the calling program and must therefore be returned to it with their contents intact. The called subroutine (JSRPC, SUBR) could be written, then, as shown in Fig. 4-6.

```
SUBR:   MOV    R1,TEMPS        ;SAVE R1
        MOV    R2,TEMPS+2      ;SAVE R2
          .
          .
          .
        MOV    TEMPS+2,R2      ;RESTORE R2
        MOV    TEMPS,R1        ;RESTORE R1
        RTS    PC              ;RETURN
TEMPS:  .WORD  0,0,0,0,0,0,0   ;SAVE AREA
```

or using the stack as

```
SUBR:   MOV    R1,-(R6)        ;PUSH R1
        MOV    R2,-(R6)        ;PUSH R2
          .
          .
          .
        MOV    (R6)+,R2        ;POP R2
        MOV    (R6)+,R1        ;POP R1
        RTS    PC              ;RETURN
```

Fig. 4-6 Saving and restoring registers using the stack.

The second routine uses two fewer words per register save/restore and allows another routine to use the temporary stack storage at a latter point rather than permanently tying some memory locations (TEMPS) to a particular routine. This ability to share temporary storage in the form of a stack is a very economical way to save on memory usage, especially when the total amount of memory is limited.

The reader should note that the subroutine call JSR PC,SUBR is a legitimate form for a subroutine jump. The instruction does not utilize or stack any registers but the PC. On the other hand, the instruction JSR SP,SUBR, where SP = R6, is not normally considered a meaningful combination. Later, however, utilizing register 6 will be considered (see Section 4.3.7).

4.3.3. Argument Transmission

The JSR and RTS instructions handle the linkage problem for transferring control. What remains is the problem of passing arguments back and forth to the subroutine during its invocation. As it turns out, this is a fairly straightforward problem, and the real question becomes one of choosing one solution from the large number of ways for passing values.

A very simple-minded approach for argument transmission would be to agree ahead of time on the locations that might be used. For example, suppose that there exists a subroutine MUL which multiplies two 16-bit words together, producing a 32-bit result. The subroutine expects the multiplier and multiplicand to be placed in symbolic locations ARG1 and ARG2 respectively, and upon completion, the subroutine will leave the resultant in the same locations.

The subroutine linkage needed to set up, call, and save the generated results might look like:

```
MOV     X, ARG1          ; MULTIPLIER
MOV     Y, ARG2          ; MULTIPLICAND
JSR     PC, MUL          ; CALL MULTIPLY
MOV     ARG1, RSLT       ; SAVE THE TWO
MOV     ARG2, RSLT+2     ;   WORD RESULT
```

As an alternative to this linkage, one could use the registers for the subroutine arguments and write:

```
MOV     X, R1            ; MULTIPLIER
MOV     Y, R2            ; MULTIPLICAND
JSR     PC, MUL          ; CALL MULTIPLY
. . .
```

This last method, although acceptable, is somewhat restricted in that a maximum of six arguments could be transmitted, corresponding to the number of general registers available. As a result of this restriction, another alternative is used which makes use of the memory locations pointed to by the linkage register of the JSR instruction. Since this register points to the first word following the JSR instruction, it may be used as a pointer to the first word of a vector of arguments or argument addresses.

Considering the first case where the arguments follow the JSR instruction, the subroutine linkage would be of the form:

```
JSR     R0, MUL          ; CALL MULTIPLY
.WORD   XVALUE, YVALUE   ; ARGUMENTS
```

These arguments could be accessed using autoincrement mode:

```
MUL:    MOV     (R0)+, R1        ; GET MULTIPLIER
        MOV     (R0)+, R2        ; GET MULTIPLICAND
        .
        .
        .
        RTS     R0               ; RETURN
```

At the time of return, the value (address pointer) in R0 will have been incremented by 4 so that R0 contains the address of the next executable instruction following the JSR.

In the second case, where the addresses of the arguments follow the subroutine call, the linkage looks like

```
JSR     R0, MUL          ; CALL MULTIPLY
.WORD   XADDR, YADDR     ; ARGUMENTS
```

For this case, the values to be manipulated are fetched indirectly:

```
MUL:    MOV     @(R0)+, R1       ; FETCH MULTIPLIER
        MOV     @(R0)+, R2       ; FETCH MULTIPLICAND
        .
        .
        .
        RTS     R0               ; RETURN
```

Another method of transmitting arguments is to transmit only the address of the first item by placing this address in a general-purpose register. It is not necessary to have the actual argument list in the same general area as the subroutine call. Thus a subroutine can be called to work on data located anywhere in memory. In fact, in many cases, the operations performed by the subroutine can be applied directly to the data located on or pointed to by a stack (Fig. 4-7) without ever actually needing to move these data into the subroutine area.

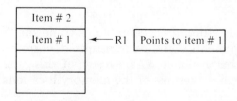

Fig. 4-7 Transmitting stacks as arguments.

Calling program:

```
     MOV      #POINTER, R1     ; SET UP POINTER
     JSR      PC, SUBR         ; CALL SUBROUTINE
```

Subroutine:

```
     ADD      (R1)+, (R1)      ; ADD ITEM #1 TO ITEM #2
                               ; PLACE RESULT IN ITEM #2. R1
                               ; POINTS TO ITEM #2 NOW.
     . . .
```

or

```
     ADD      (R1), 2(R1)      ; SAME EFFECT AS ABOVE EXCEPT
                               ; THAT R1 STILL POINTS TO
                               ; ITEM #1
     . . .
```

Given these many ways to pass arguments to a subroutine, it is worthwhile to ask, why have so many been presented and what is the rationale for presenting them all? The answer is that each method was presented as being somewhat "better" than the last, in that

1. Few registers were used to transmit arguments.

2. The number of parameters passed could be quite large.

3. The linkage mechanism was simplified to the point where only the address of the subroutine was needed to transfer control and pass parameters.

Point 3 requires some additional explanation. Since subroutines, like any other programs, may be written in position-independent code, it is possible to write and assemble them independently from the main program that uses them. The problem is filling in the appropriate address for the JSR instruction.

Filling in the address field in the JSR instruction is the job of the linking loader, since it can not only relocate PIC programs but also fill in subroutine addresses, i.e., *link* them together. The result is that a relocatable subroutine may be loaded anywhere in memory and be linked with one or more calling programs and/or subprograms. There will be only one copy of the routine, but it may be used in a repetitive manner by other programs located anywhere else in memory.

Another point not to be overlooked in recapping argument passing is the significant difference in the methods used. The first techniques presented used the simple method of passing a *value* to the subroutine. The later techniques passed the *address* of the value. The difference in these two techniques, *call by value* and *call by address*, can be quite important, as illustrated by the following FORTRAN-like program example:

```
PROGRAM TRICKY          SUBROUTINE SWAP(X,Y)
A=1.                    TEMP=X
B=2.                    X=Y
PRINT, A-B              Y=TEMP
CALL SWAP(1.,2.)        RETURN
A=1.                    END
B=2.
PRINT, A-B
END
```

If the real constants are passed in by value, both print statements will print out a −1. This occurs because subroutine SWAP interchanges the values that it has received, not the actual contents of the arguments themselves.

However, if the real constants are passed in by address, the two print statements will produce −1. and 1., respectively. In this case the subroutine SWAP references to real constants themselves, interchanging the actual argument values.

Higher-level language, such as FORTRAN, can pass parameters both by value and by address. Often the normal mode is by address, but when the argument is an expression, the address represents the location of the evaluated expression. Therefore, if one wished to call SWAP by value, it could be performed as

```
CALL SWAP(1.*1.,2.-0.)
```

causing the contents of the expressions, but not the constants themselves, to be switched.

These techniques for passing parameters are easy to understand at the assembly language level because the programmer can see exactly what method is being used. In higher-level languages, however, where the technique is not so transparent, interesting results can occur. Thus the knowledgeable higher-level language programmer must be aware of the techniques used if he is to avoid unusual or unexpected results.

4.3.4. Subroutine Register Usage

A subroutine, like any other program, will use the registers during its execution. As a result, the contents of the registers at the time that the subroutine is invoked may not be the same as when the subroutine returns. The sharing of these common resources (e.g., the registers) therefore dictates that on entry to the subroutine the registers be saved and, on exit, restored.

The responsibility for performing the save and restore function falls either on the calling routine or the called routine. Although arguments exist for making the calling program save the registers (since it need save only the ones in current use), it is more common for the subroutine itself to save and restore all registers used. On the PDP-11 the save and restore routine is greatly simplified by the use of a stack, as was illustrated in Fig. 4-6.

As pointed out previously, stacks grow downward in memory and are traditionally defined to occupy the memory space immediately preceding the program(s) that use them. One of the first things that any program which uses a stack (in particular one that executes a JSR) must do is to set the stack pointer up. For example, if SP (i.e., R6) is to be used, the program should begin with

```
                                  ; BEG IS THE FIRST
                                  ; INSTRUCTION OF THE PROGRAM
BEG:      MOV      PC, SP         ; SP=ADDR BEG+2
          TST      -(SP)          ; DECREMENT SP BY 2
                                  ; A PUSH ONTO THE STACK WILL
                                  ; STORE THE DATA AT BEG-2
```

This initialization routine is written in PIC form, and had it been assembled beginning at location 0 (.=0), the program could be easily relocated. The routine uses a programming trick to decrement the state: It uses the test instruction in autodecrement mode and ignores the setting of the condition codes. The alternative to using the TST instruction would be to SUB L2,SP, but this would require an extra instruction word.

4.3.5. Reentrancy

Further advantages of stack organization become apparent in complex situations which can arise in program systems that are engaged in the concurrent handling of several tasks. Such multitask program environments may range from relatively simple single-user applications which must manage an intermix of I/O service and background computation to large complex multiprogramming systems that manage a very intricate mixture of executive and multiuser programming situations. In all these applications there is a need for flexibility and time/memory economy. The use of the stack provides this economy and flexibility by providing a method for allowing many tasks to use a single copy of the same routine and a simple, unambiguous method for keeping track of complex program linkages.

The ability to share a single copy of a given program among users or tasks is called *reentrancy*. Reentrant program routines differ from ordinary subroutines in that it is unnecessary for reentrant routines to finish processing a given task before they can be used by another task. Multiple tasks can be in various stages of completion in the same routine at any time. Thus the situation shown in Fig. 4-8 may occur.

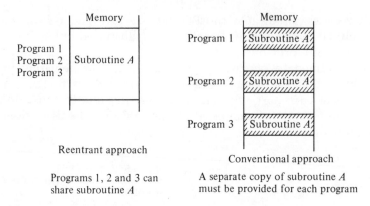

Fig. 4-8   Reentrant routines.

The chief programming distinction between a nonshareable routine and a reentrant routine is that the reentrant routine is composed solely of *pure code*; that is, it contains only instructions and constants. Thus a section of program code is reentrant (shareable) if and only if it is non-self-modifying; that is, no information within it is subject to modification. The philosophy behind pure code is actually not limited to reentrant routines. Any non-modifying program segment that has no temporary storage or data associated with it will be

1. Simpler to debug.

2. Read-only protectable (i.e., it can be kept in read-only memory).

3. Interruptable and restartable, besides being reentrant.

Using reentrant routines, control of a given routine may be shared as illustrated in Fig. 4-9.

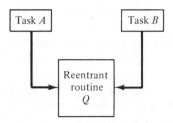

Fig. 4-9   Reentrant routine sharing.

1. Task A has requested processing by reentrant routine Q.

2. Task A temporarily relinquishes control of reentrant routine Q (i.e., is interrupted) before it finishes processing.

3. Task B starts processing in the same copy of reentrant routine Q.

4. Task B relinquishes control of reentrant routine Q at some point in its processing.

5. Task A regains control of reentrant routine Q and resumes processing from where it stopped.

The use of reentrant programming allows many tasks to share frequently used routines such as device service routines and ASCII-Binary conversion routines. In fact, in a multiuser system it is possible, for instance, to construct a reentrant FORTRAN compiler that can be used as a single copy by many user programs.

4.3.6. Recursion

It is often meaningful for a program segment to call itself. The ability to nest subroutine calls to the same subroutine is called *self-reentrancy* or *recursion*. The use of a stack organization permits easy unambiguous recursion. The technique of recursion is of great use to the mathematical analyst, as it also permits the evaluation of some otherwise noncomputable mathematical functions. This technique often permits very significant memory and speed economies in the linguistic operations of compilers and other higher-level software programs, as we shall illustrate.

A classical example of the technique of recursion can be found in computing N factorial ($N!$). Although

$$N! = N * (N - 1) * (N - 2)* \cdots *1$$

it is also true that

$$N! = N * (N - 1)!$$

$$1! = 1$$

Written in "pseudo-FORTRAN," a function for calculating $N!$ would look like:

```
        INTEGER FUNCTION FACT(N)
        IF (N .NE. 1) GO TO 1
        FACT=1
        RETURN
1       FACT=N*FAC(N-1)
        RETURN
        END
```

This code is pseudo-FORTRAN because it cannot actually be translated by most FORTRAN compilers; the problem is that the recursive call requires a stack capable of maintaining both the current values of FACT and the return pointers either to the function itself or its calling program. However, the function may be coded in PDP-11 assembly language in a simple fashion by taking advantage of its stack mechanism. Assuming that the value of N is in RO and the value of $N!$ is to be left in R1, the function FACT could be coded recursively as shown in Fig. 4-10.

```
FACT:   TST     R0              ; IS R0=0?
        BEQ     EXIT            ; YES
RET:    MOV     R0,-(SP)        ; SAVE N
        DEC     R0              ; TRY N-1
        JSR     PC,FACT         ; COMPUTE (N-1)!
        MOV     (SP)+,R1        ; FETCH FROM STACK
        JSR     PC,MUL          ; MULTIPLY VALUES
EXIT:   RTS     PC              ; RETURN
```

Fig. 4-10   Recursive coding of factorial function.

The program of Fig. 4-10 calls itself recursively by executing the JSR PC,FACT instruction. Each time it does so, it places both the current value of N and the return address (label RET) in the stack. When $N = 0$, the RTS instruction causes the return address to be popped off the stack. Next an N value is placed in R1, and a nonrecursive call is made to the MUL subroutine.

The subroutine multiply (MUL) uses the value of R1 to perform a multiplication of R1 by the value of an internal number (initially 1), held in MUL, which represents the partial product. This partial product is also left in R1.

Upon returning from the multiply subroutine, the program next encounters the RTS instruction again. Either the stack contains the return address of the calling program for FACT, or else another address-data pair of words generated by a recursive call on FACT. In the latter case, R1 is again loaded with an N value that is to be multiplied by the partial product being held locally in the MUL subroutine, and the above process is again repeated. Otherwise, the return to the calling program is performed, with $N!$ held in R1.

4.3.7. Coroutines

In some situations it happens that several program segments or routines are highly interactive. Control is passed back and forth between the routines, and each goes through a period of suspension before being resumed. Because the routines maintain a symmetric relationship to each other, they are called *coroutines*.

Basically, the coroutine idea is an extension of the subroutine concept. The difference between them is that a subroutine is subordinate to a larger calling program while the coroutine is not. Consequently, passing control is different for the two concepts.

When the calling program makes a call to a subroutine, it suspends itself and transfers control to the subroutine. The subroutine is entered at its beginning, performs its function, and terminates by passing control back to the calling program, which is thereupon resumed.

In passing control from one coroutine to another, execution begins in the newly activated routine where it last left off—not at the entrance to the routine. The flow of control passes back and forth between coroutines, and each time a coroutine gains control, its computational progress is advanced until it passes control on to another coroutine.

The PDP-11, with its hardware stack feature, can be easily programmed to implement a coroutine relationship between two interacting routines. Using a special case of the JSR instruction [i.e., JSR PC,@(R6)+], which exchanges the top element of the register 6 processor stack and the contents of the program counter (PC), the two routines may be permitted to swap program control and resume operation where they stopped, when recalled. This control swapping is illustrated in Fig. 4-11.

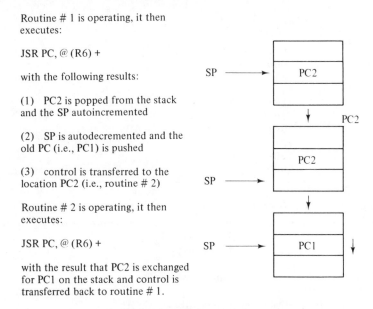

Routine # 1 is operating, it then executes:

JSR PC, @ (R6) +

with the following results:

(1) PC2 is popped from the stack and the SP autoincremented

(2) SP is autodecremented and the old PC (i.e., PC1) is pushed

(3) control is transferred to the location PC2 (i.e., routine # 2)

Routine # 2 is operating, it then executes:

JSR PC, @ (R6) +

with the result that PC2 is exchanged for PC1 on the stack and control is transferred back to routine # 1.

Fig. 4-11 Coroutine interaction.

The power of a coroutine structure is to be found in modern operating systems, a topic beyond the scope of this book. However, in Chapter 6 it is possible to demonstrate the use of coroutines for the double buffering of I/O while overlapping computation. The example presented in that chapter is elegant in its seeming simplicity, and yet it represents one of the most basic I/O operations to be performed in most operating systems.

4.4. CARRY AND OVERFLOW

In Chapter 1, where a discussion of binary and octal arithmetic was presented, one subject was intentionally left out, namely the problems of arithmetically manipulating large numbers which could conceivably exceed the arithmetic capability of the computer. For example, suppose that there exists a 4-bit two's-complement computer that can add or subtract. The range of numbers representable on such a machine is from $+7$ to -8, as shown in Table 4-1.

Table 4-1   Four-bit two's complement values.

Binary Value	Decimal Value
0111	+7
0110	+6
0101	+5
0100	+4
0011	+3
0010	+2
0001	+1
0000	0
1111	−1
1110	−2
1101	−3
1100	−4
1011	−5
1010	−6
1001	−7
1000	−8

To add the values 3 and 4, the binary arithmetic would look as follows:

$$
\begin{array}{ll}
3_{10} & 0011_2 \\
4_{10} & 0100_2 \\
\hline
7_{10} & 0111_2
\end{array}
$$

On the other hand, adding 3 and 5 results in a -8!

$$
\begin{array}{ll}
3_{10} & 0011_2 \\
5_{10} & 0101_2 \\
\hline
8_{10} & 1000_2 \Rightarrow -8
\end{array}
$$

The problem is that there is a *carry* into the sign position of the number, producing an incorrect result. The computer arithmetic is said to have generated an *overflow* condition in that the arithmetic results have spilled over into the *most significant bit (MSB)* position or sign position. However, because both the words *carry* and *overflow* have been used to describe the same phenomena, there tends to be some confusion over the exact meaning of the overflow and carry conditions that may be generated on two's—complement machines.

As the reader will soon see, the meaning of the carry and overflow conditions is truly different. In order to demonstrate their meaning and difference, an exact and consistent definition† of their generation will be given. The definition for an ADD operation†† is as follows:

1. CARRY: defined to be the carry out of the MSB position of the word.

2. OVERFLOW: defined to have occurred whenever both operands are of the same sign and the result generated is of an opposite sign.

The difference between CARRY and OVERFLOW is that CARRY is useful for *multiple-precision arithmetic*, while OVERFLOW is useful for determining whether or not the arithmetically generated results are correct.

To show the meaning of overflow and carry, examples using a 4-bit machine are presented in Table 4-2. Only for those cases where the overflow bit is set (i.e., when overflow occurs) are the results incorrect; the carry bit appears to have no significance at all.

Table 4-2 Setting of V- and C-bits for addition of 4-bit numbers.

Decimal	Binary	Carry from MSB	Unlike Signs	Setting of V	C	Results
1	0001					
+2	0010	no	no	0	0	correct
3	0011					
5	0101					
+6	0110	no	yes	1	0	incorrect
+11	1011					
−6	1010					
+7	0111	yes	no	0	1	correct
1	0001					
−6	1010					
−6	1010	yes	yes	1	1	incorrect
−12	0100					

---

†but not the only possible one

††It is important to note that this definition is for ADD. There is another definition for SUBtract.

The meaning of the carry bit becomes clear when double-precision arithmetic is performed. For this case, the two 4-bit words of the previous example are taken to represent an 8-bit double-precision value. The range of possible values for double precision is $127 \leqslant$ value $\leqslant -128$, since there are seven bits plus sign used to represent each unique value.

To perform double-precision arithmetic, the following algorithm is used:

1. Perform addition on the least significant 4-bits (*low-order word*).

2. Perform the addition on the most significant 4-bits (*high-order word*), adding in the carry bit if set.

3. The overflow last recorded (due to step 2) shows if the result is correct.

Table 4-3 gives several examples.

Table 4-3 Double-precision addition.

Decimal	Binary	First-Half Add		Second-Half Add		Results
		V	C	V	C	
49	0011 0001					
+50	0011 0010	0	0	0	0	correct
99	0110 0011					
53	0011 0101					
+70	0100 0110	1	0	0	0	correct
123	0111 1011					
60	0011 1100					
+70	0100 0110	0	1	1	0	incorrect
130	1000 0010					
26	0001 1010					
+26	0001 1010	1	1	0	0	correct
52	0011 0100					
−70	1011 1010					
−70	1011 1010	1	1	1	1	incorrect
−140	0111 0100					
−70	1011 1010					
80	0101 0000	0	0	0	1	correct
10	0000 1010					

The examples of Table 4-3 serve to make the significance of the carry bit clear—it propagates the carry from the addition of the least significant word into the addition of the most significant word. Additionally, the overflow bit should be ignored, except for the last addition, since in double-precision

arithmetic there is no sign bit associated with the least significant word!
Overflow into this bit position is therefore normal when performing double-
precision arithmetic.

Double- and multiple-precision arithmetic is common on minicomputers,
where the range of possible values is small due to the small word size. As a
result, special instructions are included to add or subtract the carry bits. On
the PDP-11 these instructions are as follows:

Operation	Symbolic Form	Meaning
ADD WITH CARRY	ADC X	$(X) \leftarrow (X) + (C)$
SUBTRACT WITH CARRY	SBC X	$(X) \leftarrow (X) - (C)$

where (C) = value of C condition code bit

If the C and V are to be useful to the programmer, they must be set as part
of the result of an arithmetic operation such as ADD, SUB, COM, or NEG,
as indeed they are on the PDP-11. Thus not only are the N and Z condition
bits affected by the result of an arithmetic operation, but so are the C and V
condition bits. For example, if one were to add two numbers,

```
            ADD     A, B
A:          .WORD   121354
B:          .WORD   134201
```

the erroneous result placed in B would be 055555, and the processor status
word would be set to 000003 (see Fig. 3-1 for a picture of the processor
status register). Additionally, some instructions, such as MOV, clear the
overflow or V-bit while setting the N- and Z-bits and not affecting the C-bit
at all. And since it may be necessary to set and clear any or all of the condition code bits directly, the following instructions are included in the PDP-
11 instruction set:

Operation	Symbolic Form	Meaning
CLEAR C BIT	CLC	$(C) \leftarrow 0$
CLEAR V BIT	CLV	$(V) \leftarrow 0$
CLEAR Z BIT	CLZ	$(Z) \leftarrow 0$
CLEAR N BIT	CLN	$(N) \leftarrow 0$
SET C BIT	SEC	$(C) \leftarrow 1$
SET V BIT	SEV	$(V) \leftarrow 1$
SET Z BIT	SEZ	$(Z) \leftarrow 1$
SET N BIT	SEN	$(N) \leftarrow 1$

The format of these instructions is as follows:

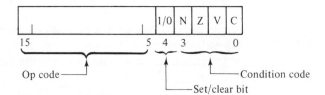

Selectable combinations of these bits may be cleared or set together. This is accomplished by "oring" the op codes together to form a combination (e.g., CLC!CLV, where ! is taken to mean "OR" by the assembler).

Taking advantage of the setting and clearing of the V- and C-bits by the ADD and NEG instructions, a double-precision add would be performed as

```
ADD      A0, B0      ; ADD LOW-ORDER PARTS
ADC      B1          ; ADD CARRY INTO HIGH-ORDER
ADD      A1, B1      ; ADD HIGH-ORDER PARTS
```

and a double-precision complement as

```
NEG      A1          ; 2'S COMPL HIGH-ORDER
NEG      A0          ; 2'S COMPL LOW-ORDER
SBC      A1          ; PROPAGATE CARRY
```

(The NEG instruction sets the carry to a 1 if the two's-complemented result is nonzero; otherwise it sets it to a zero.) The use of double- and multiple-precision arithmetic can be found in multiplying two single-precision values together, forming a double-precision result, and as part of floating-point arithmetic, to be discussed in Section 4.5.

4.4.1. Expanded Set of Branch Instructions

Another significant use of the carry and overflow condition bits is in *signed conditional branches*. Looking back at the conditional branches already considered (BEQ, BNE, BMI, and BPL), it may have occurred to the reader that other branch instructions, such as branch less than (BLT), branch less than or equal (BLE), branch greater than (BGT), and branch greater than or equal (BGE), would be quite useful to have. They do exist, but each of these branches uses the C- and V- as well as the N- and Z-bits, and up until now, it would not have been clear why.

The *unsigned* conditional branches (BEQ, BNE, BMI, and BPL) operate on all 16-bit numbers by treating the arithmetic sequence as highest value   177777

.

.

.

000001

lowest value   000000

On the other hand, the sequence of arithmetic values in signed, 16-bit, two's-complement arithmetic is

largest positive value   077777

.

.

.

smallest positive value $\underline{000000}$
smallest negative value   177777

.

.

.

largest negative value   100000

The difference between the two sequences is obvious; however, it is not clear why there should be a difference in conditional branches. A simple example will make the point clear.

Suppose that we wish to test the results of an instruction in which the operands are considered to be signed (two's-complement) values. For simplicity, let us again assume 4-bit arithmetic. Then if we were to compare a negative source (-7) to a position destination (7), the setting of the condition bits would be

$$
\begin{array}{rrl}
-7_{10} & 1001_2 & \text{with } Z = 0 \\
-7_{10} & -0111_2 & N = 0 \\
\hline
2_{10} & 0010_2 & C = 0 \\
& & V = 1
\end{array}
$$

The condition bits C and V are set according to the definition for a SUB operation:

1. CARRY: defined to be the borrow into the MSB position of the word.

2. OVERFLOW: defined to have occurred whenever the operands were of opposite signs and the result generated is of the same sign as the subtrahend (i.e., the source operand for a SUB operation and the destination operand for a CMP operation).

Then the instruction pair

```
CMP     #-7,#7
BMI     LESS
```

would not result in a branch (since $N = 0$). On the other hand, the pair

```
CMP     #-7,#7
BLT     LESS
```

would. The reason for the difference lies in the specification of which condition bits are to be tested. For the signed branches these are

Operation	Symbolic Form	Meaning
BRANCH LESS THAN	BLT X	$N \oplus V = 1$
BRANCH LESS THAN OR EQUAL	BLE X	$Z + (N \oplus V) = 1$
BRANCH GREATER THAN	BGT X	(PC)←X if $Z + (N \oplus V) = 0$
BRANCH GREATER THAN OR EQUAL	BGE X	$N \oplus V = 0$

In addition to the branches already discussed, there are several unsigned and simple conditional branches which are usefully introduced here. These are

Operation	Symbolic Form	Meaning
BRANCH IF HIGHER	BHI X	$C + V = 0$
BRANCH IF LOWER OR SAME	BLOS X	$C + Z = 0$
BRANCH IF CARRY CLEAR	BCC X	$C = 0$
BRANCH IF CARRY SET	BCS X	(PC)←X if $C = 1$
BRANCH IF OVERFLOW CLEAR	BVC X	$V = 0$
BRANCH IF OVERFLOW SET	BVS X	$V = 1$

Using the first four instructions, the programmer can test all two's-complement arithmetic results. Using the last six, he can test both unsigned arithmetic results and individual condition bits.

4.5. FIXED- AND FLOATING-POINT NUMBERS

Most higher-level languages allow for the representation of both *integer* (or *fixed-point*) numbers and *decimal* (or *floating-point*) numbers. Although a great many problems may be solved using integer arithmetic, such arithmetic becomes cumbersome when one attempts to use it to manipulate decimal values.

A floating-point number, like a fixed-point number, is a sequence of contiguous bits in memory which is interpreted as having two distinct parts, called the *fraction* and the *exponent*. For a binary computer, a floating-point number is expressed as

$$.nnnnnnn \times 2^{exponent}$$

and can be stored in a computer word:

exponent	fraction

Since the exponent and the fraction have a sign associated with them, it is necessary that some assignment of the bits in the computer word be made for these signs. For example, the first bit of each part of the computer word might be assigned as follows:

s	exponent	s	fraction

It is more common, however, to assign only one sign bit to a word. Thus a different representation is used. This representation assigns the MSB as the sign of the mantissa and divides the range of possible exponential values into two halves, one for negative exponents and one for positive exponents. We illustrate this technique as follows.

Suppose that the value 46.5_{10} is to be represented as a floating-point value in a 16-bit word-length machine. The bit assignments in the word look as follows:

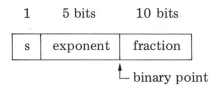

With the use of the base-conversion techniques presented in Chapter 1, the integer and fractional parts of the decimal number 46.5 are converted to octal and recombined to form the octal number 56.4. Expressing this octal value in binary, we obtain the result

$$46.5_{10} = 56.4_8 = .564 \times 8^2 = .101110100 \times 2^6$$

In order to express this binary result in floating-point format, it is necessary to divide the range of exponential values into two parts:

$$
\left.
\begin{array}{l}
11111_2 \\
\updownarrow \\
10000_2 \Rightarrow \\
\updownarrow \\
00000_2
\end{array}
\right\}
\quad
\begin{array}{l}
\text{positive exponents} \\
\text{zero exponent} \\
\text{negative exponents}
\end{array}
$$

A zero exponent is actually represented as 2^4 or 16, thereby attaching the name *excess-16 form* to this technique.

The value of 46.5_{10} now becomes a fraction of .101110100 and an exponent of $10000 + 110 = 10110$, and the number is represented as

0	10110	1011101000

The actual permissible values of floating-point numbers can be seen to range from a largest positive value of $.1777_8 \times 2^{17_8}$ (approximately 32,000) to a smallest positive value of $.1000 \times 2^{-20_8}$ (approximately .00001), with a corresponding range for negative values. The difference, then, between fixed and floating values is that, although the total range from largest positive value to largest negative value remains the same, floating-point values allow for the representation of fractional numbers. However, the cost of using floating-point values can be measured by the loss of bits used to represent the fraction (only 10 rather than 16, so that, given the same word size for representing both fixed- and floating-point values, the precision is less for floating point).

To increase the precision of floating-point values, it is necessary to go to a multiple-precision floating-point format. Two, three, or four words are used in this format to represent floating-point numbers. For example, using three words, a PDP-11 floating-point format is

3rd word	2nd word	1st word
exponent	s | high-order fraction	low-order fraction
15 0	15 0	15 0
location n + 4	location n + 2	location n

The 15-bit exponent allows for "excess 2^{15} form," and combined with a 31-bit fraction, the range of representable numbers certainly seems adequate.

When manipulating floating-point numbers it is often necessary to "align the exponents" before performing floating addition or subtraction. Thus, just as a human adds

$$
\begin{array}{rclcrcl}
15.75 & \times & 10^2 & \Rightarrow & 157.5 & \times & 10^1 \\
42.5 & \times & 10^1 & \Rightarrow & \underline{42.5} & \times & \underline{10^1} \\
20.0 & \times & 10^2 & \Leftarrow & 200.0 & \times & 10^1
\end{array}
$$

it is also necessary for the computer to scale the exponents in the floating-point number so that normal fixed-point arithmetic may be used to add or subtract values.

A problem arises when two values of nearly equal magnitude are subtracted. For example,

$$46.75_{10} = \boxed{\,0\;|\;10110\;|\;1011101100\,}$$

$$\underline{-46.50_{10}} = \boxed{\,0\;|\;10110\;|\;1011101000\,}$$

$$.25_{10} = \boxed{\,0\;|\;10110\;|\;0000000100\,}$$

The result generated is said to be *unnormalized*. The *normalized* form would be that form in which the first bit of the fraction is the complement of the sign bit. In the case above, this form is

$$.25_{10} = \boxed{\,0\;|\;01111\;|\;10000000000\,}$$

Normalized numbers are used for two reasons. First, they allow the largest number of bits to be used to represent a number, and, second, they simplify the process of performing floating-point operations.

There are two exceptions, however, to the form of a normalized number. First, the value zero is usually stored as an all-zero quantity. Second, negative powers of 2 are stored with a sign bit of 1 and a fractional part of 1000... (i.e., an MSB = 1). Thus, for a 16-bit floating-point representation, the values $-\frac{1}{2}$, -4, -1, and $-\frac{1}{8}$ would be stored as

$$-\frac{1}{2} = \boxed{\,1\;|\;10000\;|\;1000000000\,}$$

$$-4 = \boxed{\,1\;|\;10011\;|\;1000000000\,}$$

$$-1 = \boxed{\,1\;|\;10001\;|\;1000000000\,}$$

$$-\frac{1}{8} = \boxed{\,1\;|\;01110\;|\;1000000000\,}$$

The reader should not be confused by the exceptions for negative powers of 2. In a normalized floating-point number that is negative, the first bit of the fraction will be the complement of the sign bit. For example, the representation of -46.5_{10} is

$$-46.5 = \boxed{1} \boxed{10110} \boxed{010001100}$$

that is, it is the complement of the positive representation.

4.6. BYTE HANDLING AND CHARACTER CODES

The PDP-11 processor includes a full complement of instructions to manipulate byte operands. Since all PDP-11 addressing is byte-oriented, byte manipulation is straightforward and enables the PDP-11 to perform as either a word or a byte processor. With the exception of ADD and SUB, all single- and double-operand instructions may become byte instructions by simply attaching a B to their mnemonic operation code (e.g., MOVB, DECB).

The value of a byte-addressable computer lies not only in its ability to manipulate a quantity smaller than a word but also in its ability to manipulate a quantity that represents a character. The 8-bit bytes in the PDP-11 are able to represent 256 (2^8) different character codes, of which the 7-bit ASCII code is a subset. This subset (see Appendix C) forms the character set for the PDP-11 and allows for full character manipulation within it.

When one manipulates characters or bytes through byte operations, two things occur. First, byte operations in register mode access the low-order byte of the specified register. Second, byte instructions using autoincrement or autodecrement direct addressing cause the specified register to be modified by 1 to point to the next byte of data. As a result, a no-operation type of instruction to add 4 to a register might be

```
CMP      (R0)+, (R0)+
```

while the same instruction in byte mode,

```
CMPB     (R0)+, (R0)+
```

will only add 2 to the register.

To assist the programmer in byte and character manipulation, the PAL-11 assembler includes the .BYTE pseudo-op, similar to the .WORD pseudo-op, which stores 8-bit values in successive byte locations. In addition, the .ASCII pseudo-op is useful for assembling a string of ASCII characters into their byte representations while the .EVEN pseudo-op is used to force the current location counter to an even or word boundary value if it is odd.

When a character is preceded by an apostrophe, its value is that of the ASCII character value it represents. When it is preceded by a quotation mark, two ASCII characters are assigned the ASCII values of each of the characters to be used. Each value is stored in an 8-bit byte, and the bytes are combined to form a word. For example, "AB will store the ASCII value of A in the low-order (even) byte and the value of B in the high-order (odd) byte:

$$
\begin{array}{cccccc}
\text{high-order byte} & & | & & \text{low-order byte} \\
\end{array}
$$

B's value = 1   0   2 | 1   0   1   = A's value

0 100 001 0 01 000 001

0   4   1   1   0   1

"AB = 041101

To place the character representation of A in R0, the code would be

```
MOVB     #'A,R0
```

while to place the character string AB in R0, the code is

```
MOV      #"AB,R0
```

(Note carefully the use of the # sign; without it the character representation is used as an address!)

4.6.1. Logical Operations and Shifting

Although the word and byte instructions are useful for manipulating data at the word or byte level, it is still often necessary to manipulate bits within a word or a byte. The logical operations along with the shift and rotate instructions in the PDP-11 provide this capability.

The logical operations belong to the double-operand group and include BIS, BIC, and BIT for the setting, clearing, and testing of bits within a word. They are defined as follows:

Operation	Symbolic Form	Meaning
BIT SET	BIS X,Y	$(Y) \leftarrow (X) + (Y)$
BIT CLEAR	BIC X,Y	$(Y) \leftarrow \sim (X) \cdot (Y)$
BIT TEST	BIT X,Y	$(X) \cdot (Y)$

Since each of these instructions is performed in the central processor, each one affects the setting of the condition codes in the processor status register in the following manner:

1. The N- and Z-bits are set conditionally.

2. The V-bit is cleared.

3. The C-bit is not affected.

Within the PDP-11, all I/O devices have particular words set aside in memory as control and status registers. These registers have unique memory addresses and may be tested and set using the logical operations. For example, to test bits 15 and 7 in a status register (say STAT), one could write

```
        BIT     #100200,STAT    ;TEST BITS 15 AND 7
        BMI     BIT15           ;BIT 15 IS SET
        BNE     BIT7            ;BIT 7 IS SET
```

(The reader should note that if the BMI instruction is removed, the BNE becomes a test for both bits 15 and 7.)

The shift and rotate instructions belong to the single-operand group. The shift instructions perform one-bit arithmetic shifts either left or right, with the C-bit used as a register extender. Thus, for a left shift, the MSB is shifted into the C-bit, while all other bits are shifted left one position and the LSB is filled with a zero. The right shift is very much like the left shift except that the MSB is filled with a replication of the sign bit rather than a zero, and the LSB is shifted into the C-bit. In this way right shifts do not cause the sign to be changed if the number is negative, and right and left shifting may be thought of as a scaling of data by a factor of 2.

The arithmetic shift instructions can be shown pictorially as:

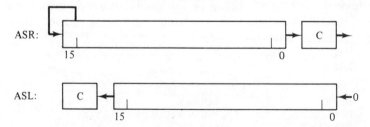

As expected, the N, Z, and C condition bits are set according to the result generated. The V-bit is set as the exclusive-OR of the N- and the C-bits.

The rotate instructions operate on their operands and the C-bit as if they formed a 17-bit "circular buffer." Thus on a rotate left, the MSB is shifted into the C-bit, the C-bit shifts into the LSB, and all other bits are shifted left one position. A rotate right is the inverse operation. Together, these instructions facilitate sequential bit testing and detailed bit manipulation.

The pictorial representation of the rotate instructions looks as follows:

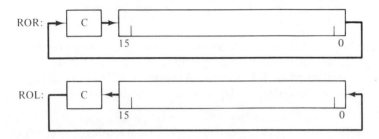

The setting of the condition bits for the rotate instructions follows the same rules as for the arithmetic shifts.

The four instructions are written as

Operation	Symbolic Form	Meaning
ARITHMETIC SHIFT RIGHT	ASR X	$(X_{14-0}) \leftarrow (X_{15-1}), (C) \leftarrow (X_0)$
ARITHMETIC SHIFT LEFT	ASL X	$(X_{15-1}) \leftarrow (X_{14-0}), (C) \leftarrow (X_{15})$
ROTATE RIGHT	ROR X	$(X_{14-0}) \leftarrow (X_{15-1}), (X_{15}) \leftarrow (C), (C) \leftarrow (X_0)$
ROTATE LEFT	ROL X	$(X_{15-1}) \leftarrow (X_{14-0}), (X_0) \leftarrow (C), (C) \leftarrow (X_{15})$

4.6.2. Internal and External Data Forms

In FORTRAN, the conversion of data from an external form to an internal form is handled by the format statement associated with a READ statement. The format associated with a WRITE statement assists in the reverse operation. Still, whether or not a programmer utilizes a higher-level language, there remains the necessity for external/internal conversion to be performed.

The problem can be stated more precisely in terms of a typical I/O operation utilizing the teletypewriter common to most minicomputers. If a user strikes the keys "3" and "5," he may believe that he has stored the octal value "35" in some memory word. On closer examination, it is clear that he has only stored two bytes which have the value 63_8 and 65_8, respectively. Clearly what is necessary is to perform the conversion from the teletypewriter-produced ASCII code to the internal value of 35_8. A subroutine to perform the conversion, assuming the ASCII character to be in R0 and the result in R1, might be

```
CONV:   BIC     #177770,R0      ;CLEAR ALL BUT LAST 3 BITS
        ASL     R1              ;SHIFT
        ASL     R1              ;  LEFT
        ASL     R1              ;     THREE
        BIS     R0,R1           ;"OR" IN R0
        RTS     PC              ;AND RETURN
```

Outputting to the teletypewriter presents the inverse problem. In this case the internal form must be converted to external ASCII. A subroutine to take a 16-bit word in R1 and store the six ASCII characters which represent the word in the buffer addressed by R2 could be written as

```
OUT:    MOV     #5,R0           ;LOOP COUNT
LOOP:   MOV     R1,-(SP)        ;COPY WORD INTO STACK
        BIC     #177770,@SP     ;ONE OCTAL VALUE
        ADD     #'0,@SP         ;CONVERT TO ASCII
        MOVB    (SP)+,-(R2)     ;STORE IN BUFFER
        ASR     R1              ;SHIFT
        ASR     R1              ;  RIGHT
        ASR     R1              ;     THREE
        DEC     R0              ;TEST IF DONE
        BNE     LOOP            ;NO, DO IT AGAIN
        BIC     #177776,R1      ;GET LAST BIT
        ADD     #'0,R1          ;CONVERT TO ASCII
        MOVB    R5,-(R2)        ;STORE IN BUFFER
        RTS     PC              ;DONE, RETURN
```

The use of "#'0" serves to add in the representation for ASCII zero, without requiring the programmer to know what it actually is.

These routines serve to convert the internal and external forms for use either by the computer or by the I/O device. The next subject to be covered is: How are the results transmitted to or from an I/O device so that it is possible for a human to communicate with a computer and vice versa? This is the subject of I/O programming to be covered in Chapter 6.

EXERCISES

1. Verify that the program of Section 4.1.6 does indeed perform the required relocation of all pointers in the pointer table.

2. Write a PIC program that clears all the memory below where the program is loaded (e.g., if the program is loaded in location 10000 and higher, it should clear locations 0–7777).

3. Write a subroutine to multiply two signed integer values together to produce a double-length integer result. The subroutine linkage will be of the form

```
MOV     #M1, R0      ; MULTIPLIER ADDRESS IN R0
MOV     #M2, R1      ; MULTIPLICAND ADDRESS IN R1
JSR     PC, MUL      ; CALL MULTIPLY
```

4. Write the multiply subroutine in PIC form so that it may be called by

```
JSR     R5, MUL
WORD    M1-ADDRESS, M2-ADDRESS
```

5. Write a mainline program to call the subroutine of Exercise 2 and execute it.

6. What are the differences in the definitions of overflow and carry when defined for subtraction?

7. Develop a table similar to Table 4-3 (i.e., use the same decimal values) for double-precision subtraction.

8. Represent 16,768 in both fixed-point and floating-point form for a 16-bit word computer with 10 bits for the fraction and 5 for the exponent.

9. Using a 16-bit word as defined above, show how a negative floating-point value can be formed directly without using the technique of complementation of the positive value.

10. Using the PDP-11 instruction set, write a subprogram to form the exclusive-OR of two values X and Y; that is, write a subprogram equivalent of the pseudo-instruction.

$$X \text{ OR } \quad X, Y$$

11. Given a string of ASCII characters stored in a byte stack pointed to by R0, write a subroutine to search for a "?" in the string. The search should be terminated when either a "?" character or a zero byte is found.

12. Write a program to translate the condition code instruction mnemonics (CLC, CLV, etc.) to their op-code equivalents. The instructions should be stored in arbitrary order in a table called INST, and their op-code equivalents should be placed in a table called OPS.

13. A main program fragment and subroutine are as follows:

```
R0=%0
R1=%1
SP=%6                                  . =2000
PC=%7                          SUB:    MOV     (R0)+, R1
. =1000                                DEC     R1
BEGIN:  MOV     PC, SP                 TST     R1
        TST     -(SP)                  BEQ     RETURN
        MOV     #1, R0                 JSR     R0, SUB
        JSR     R0, SUB                . WORD   1
        . WORD   3             RETURN: RTS     R0
```

a. Show the value of the stack pointer and the values in the processor stack before execution of the program. (*Note*: In this and in all succeeding parts, indicate that a quantity is unknown by filling in the symbol "?".)

b. Show the value of the stack pointer and the values in the processor stack just after execution of the MOV #1,R0 instruction in the main program.

c. Show the value of the stack pointer and the values in the processor stack *after each stack operation* (i.e., a push-down or a pop-up). Also indicate the address of each stack location used. Several blanks have been included below for your use; you may or may not need to use them all. Work from the left of the page.

d. Show the value of the stack pointer and the values in the processor stack upon completion of the execution of the main program fragment.

REFERENCES

Since position-independent coding is not very different from coding using a base register, the reader interested in this subject can read further in Stone (1972), Gear (1969), Abrams and Stein (1973), and Mauer (1968). These books also cover the subjects of subroutines and subroutine linkages. However, one should read Wegner (1968) and Ralston (1971) for coverage of the topics call-by-value, call-by-name, and call-by-address. Ralston is also a good source, as are the others, for a discussion of floating-point representation. Logical operations can be found in Hellerman (1967).

5 INTRODUCTION
TO DATA STRUCTURES

Up to this point, the reader's interest in the representation of information (e.g., programs and data) has been centered on how programs are represented, and how programs can manipulate *primitive* data elements (bits, bytes, words, registers, etc.). In this chapter that interest is explicitly directed toward data and the forms for representing data. In other words, the reader's interest is focused on those forms called *data structures*.

Data structures are of concern to the computer programmer for two reasons: (1) they play a key role in algorithm and hence program design, and (2) they limit and guide the process of problem specification and program coding. Since data structures are a means for the representation of information, they have a form both inside and outside a computer. For example, a decimal number has both a mathematical representation such as 0.465×10^2 and a computer floating—point form such as 0101101011101000. Indeed, the FORTRAN programmer spends a considerable amount of his time learning the various format specifications to be able to describe how the external-to-internal conversions (and vice versa) are to be performed by a running FORTRAN program.

A study of data structures is so fundamental a part of the study of algorithms and programming that all textbooks cover the subject implicitly if not explicitly. For example, the readers of this text have already considered the primitive data structures available to the PDP-11 programmer (bits, bytes, words, registers), and they have also delved into the representation and meaning of such data concepts as address, pointer, character, and stack. And in the more general context of information structures, the reader has been presented with the representations of computers and programs, including the transformation of symbolic information structures that constitute programs.

Now the reader's attention is focused on the construction and manipulation of somewhat more complex data structures; he should not be surprised to learn that the new data structures are based upon the more primitive ones already well understood. These new data types and structures (arrays, stacks, shelves, queues, circular buffers, lists, symbol tables, and so on) are nothing more than the combination of primitive data types to produce new aggregates of bits, bytes, words, and so on.

Good programming practice requires that the programmer carefully consider the form of his data so that he may create data structures that will be effectively and efficiently manipulated by his program. It is important that a new data structure be chosen carefully, since its use in a program may greatly affect the size and speed of execution of the program utilizing it. By considering some of the fundamental data structures that programmers use, the assembly language programmer will have a better understanding of what these data structures are and how they can be manipulated. A natural beginning is to start by considering a fundamental type, the array, with which every FORTRAN programmer is familiar.

5.1. ARRAYS

In its simplest form, the array is a *one-dimensional structure* that associates a collection of identical data types as members of a larger block identified by a single name. The array can be easily *mapped* from its external, conceptual representation into its internal form by assigning contiguous memory location to elements of the array. The choice of contiguous locations is clearly one of efficiency, since it allows elements of the array to be accessed through indexed addressing, as was seen by the example of Chapter 2.

Multidimensional arrays are also data structures commonly used by the FORTRAN programmer. The elements of such arrays are stored by columns in ascending order of storage location. An example is shown in Fig. 5-1 for

Element	Position	Element	Position
A(1,1,1)	0	A(1,2,1)	3
A(2,1,1)	1	A(2,2,1)	4
A(3,1,1)	2	A(3,2,1)	5

Element	Position	Element	Position
A(1,1,2)	6	A(1,2,2)	9
A(2,1,2)	7	A(2,2,2)	10
A(3,1,2)	8	A(3,2,2)	11

Fig. 5-1 Mapping of array A(3,2,2).

the three-dimensional array A(3,2,2). As shown in the figure, multidimensional arrays can be considered simple extensions of one-dimensional arrays. However, simple indexing cannot be performed in order to access individual array elements.

To find the location of an element in a three-dimensional array, an *address equation* must be used which describes the mapping of the three-dimensional array into the one-dimensional computer memory. For an array with dimensions $I \times J \times K$ the address of the particular element $A(i, j, k)$ is given by the equation

$$\text{address}[A(i, j, k)] = \text{address}[A(1, 1, 1)] + (i - 1) + I * (j - 1) + I * J * (k - 1)$$

This equation serves to transform the values given for the three indices into a *linear index* into the array storage area. Using the example shown in Fig. 5-1, the element $A(2, 1, 2)$ is seen to be in relative position 7 with respect to the first element of the array $A(1, 1, 1)$.

In its most general form, the address equation for an n-dimensional array $A(I, J, K, ..., N)$ is given by the rather complicated equation

$$\text{address}[A(i, j, k, ..., m, n)] = $$
$$\text{address}[A(1, 1, 1, ..., 1)] + (i - 1) + I * (J * (...M * (n - 1) + m - 1)...j - 1)$$

Although complicated, this equation serves to establish the fact that as the number of dimensions increases, so does the complexity of the address equation. Even for a three-dimensional array, the equation results in a three-term multiplication which represents a formidable task for a small computer that lacks multiplication hardware.

5.1.1. Simplified Array Address Calculation

When calculating array element addresses, two points must be considered. First, as mentioned above, the fewer the multiplications, the better. Second, address calculations are dynamic in that languages such as FORTRAN delay the evaluation of the address polynomial until the array element is actually required. These considerations lead to the following, often-used technique.

For each array defined as

$$\text{ARRAY} (K_1, K_2, ..., K_i) \qquad i = 1, 2, ..., m$$

where m specifies the dimensionality of the array, there is a corresponding *array descriptor block* (sometimes called a dope vector) which holds the infor-

Word 1	Type Size
Word 2	$N * K_1$ (0 if i = 1) i.e., one-dimensional
Word 3	$N * K_1 * K_2$ (0 if i = 1 or 2)
Word n	$N * K_1 * \ldots * K_{m-1}$ (0 if i = 1,2,..., n − 1)
Word n + 1	(address of first word of first element of array)†

Fig. 5-2 Array description or block.

mation given in Fig. 5-2, where SIZE $= N * K_1 * K_2 * \ldots * K_m$, and TYPE (the data type) and N (the number of words per element)† are specified as

Array Type	Type	N
INTEGER	0	1
REAL	1	2
DOUBLE PRECISION	2	4
COMPLEX	2	4
.	.	.
.	.	.
.	.	.

The information in the array descriptor block is made available to an execution-time subroutine which calculates the address of the first word (of a multiple-word) array element. Each call to this subroutine, AEAS, results in the evaluation of the address polynomial as follows:

If A is the address of the first word of the array element ARRAY $(k_1, \ldots, k_i)$ of the array ARRAY $(K_1, K_2, \ldots, K_i)$, and $1 \leqslant k_j \leqslant K_j$ for $j = 1$ to i, then the value of A is given by

$$A = \text{WD}(n + 1) + (k_1 - 1) * N + (k_2 + 1) * \text{WD2}$$
$$+ \cdots + (k_n - 1) * \text{WD}n$$

†In the small computer, where the number of bits per word is limited, it is usually necessary to use more than one word to represent a given quantity such as a floating-point value or a double-precision number.

where WD2, WD3, ... stand for the contents of words 2, 3, ... of the array descriptor block for the given array.

Now what is the value of using this technique? The answer is that it buys the user several advantages. First, it transforms the address polynomial into a simpler sum-of-products equation. Second, the number of terms in the equation grows linearly with the number of dimensions in the array. Third, it allows the translator to *bind* some of the multiplications (e.g., $N * K_1$, $N * K_1 * K_2$, ...) early and not make this part of the execution-time evaluation. And fourth, it presents a generalized data structure (the array descriptor block) which may be changed during execution time to allow the array to be *dynamically* allocated. Users of ALGOL recognize this last point as an important attribute of *block-structured languages*, which permit arrays to be variably dimensioned. In use, variably dimensioned and dynamically allocated arrays allow the programmer to make more effective use of the limited amounts of memory provided on small computers.

5.1.2. Example

Suppose that we wish to create an array M(3, 5, 7). In assembly language we would reserve room for the array and create the array descriptor block (shown in Fig. 5-2) as follows:

```
        TYPE=0                  ; ARRAY TYPE
        SIZE=151                ; SIZE OF ARRAY (OCTAL)
M:      . =. +SIZE+SIZE         ; STORAGE RESERVATION (TWO BYTES/WORD)
        TYPE+SIZE               ; FIRST ARRAY DESCRIPTOR BLOCK WORD
        3                       ; SECOND ADB WORD IN OCTAL
        17                      ; THIRD ADB WORD IN OCTAL
ADB:    M                       ; FOURTH ADB WORD--ADB ADDRESSED HERE
```

Access of any element of M(2, 3, 4) can be performed by the calculate *Array Element Address* Subroutine, which has the calling sequence:

```
        JSR     R0, AEAS        ; CALL SUBROUTINE
        ADB                     ; ADDRESS OF FOURTH WORD OF ADB
        2                       ; FIRST SUBSCRIPT
        3                       ; SECOND SUBSCRIPT
        4                       ; THIRD SUBSCRIPT
        0                       ; ARRAY ELEMENT ADDRESS
```

The subroutine to calculate the element address uses the register save (SAVE) and restore (REST) routines, has the logical flow shown in Fig. 5-3 and is coded as shown in Fig. 5-4.

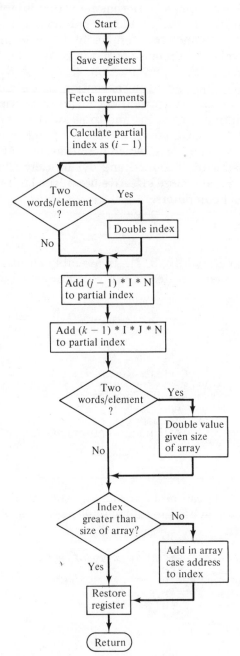

Fig. 5-3

```
AEAS:    JSR    PC, SAVE        ; SAVE R1-R5
         CLR    R1              ; HOLDS RELATIVE DISPLACEMENT
         MOV    (R0)+, R2       ; ARRAY DESCRIPTOR ADDRESS
         MOV    (R0)+, R3       ; FIRST SUBSCRIPT
         DEC    R3              ;  LESS ONE
         BLE    SKIP            ; IGNORE IF <=0
         MOV    -6(R2), R5      ; TYPE AND SIZE OF ARRAY
         BIC    #177777, R5     ; GET TYPE
         BEQ    NODBL           ; IF =0, THEN INTEGER
         ROL    R3              ; DOUBLE OTHERWISE
NODBL:   ADD    R3, R1          ; ADD TO RELATIVE DISP.
SKIP:    MOV    (R0)+, R3       ; SECOND SUBSCRIPT
         DEC    R3              ;  LESS ONE
         BLE    SKIP1           ; IGNORE IF <= 0
         MOV    -4(R2), R4      ; WORD 2 OF ADB
AGAIN:   ADD    R4, R1          ; ADD IT IN
         DEC    R3              ; DONE?
         BNE    AGAIN           ; NO
SKIP1:   MOV    (R0)+, R3       ; THIRD SUBSCRIPT
         DEC    R3              ;  LESS ONE
         BLE    TEST            ; IGNORE IF <= 0
         MOV    -2(R2), R4      ; WORD 3 OF ADB
TEST:    MOV    -6(R2), R4      ; BASE ADDRESS OF ADB
         BIC    #160000, R4     ; GET SIZE
         TST    R5              ; DO WE DOUBLE?
         BEQ    ARND            ; NO
         ROL    R1              ; TWO BYTES PER WORD
         MOV    (R2), (R0)      ; BASE ADDRESS OF ARRAY
         ADD    R1, (R0)        ; ADD IN INDEX
RET:     TST    (R0)+           ; ADD TWO TO R0
         JSR    PC, REST        ; RESTORE R1-R5
         RTS    PC              ; AND RETURN
```

Fig. 5-4

This subroutine thus calculates the actual address of the array element $A(i, j, k)$ by forming

$$A(i, j, k) = \underbrace{A(1, 1, 1)}_{\substack{\text{word 4 of} \\ ADB}} + \underbrace{N * (i - 1)}_{\substack{\text{word 1 of} \\ ADB}} + \underbrace{N * I * (j - 1)}_{\substack{\text{word 2 of} \\ ADB}} + \underbrace{N * I * J * (k - 1)}_{\substack{\text{word 3 of} \\ ADB}}$$

where

$$N = \text{number of words per element}$$
$$I, J, K = \text{maximum values of } i, j, k, \text{respectively}$$

Since some multiplications are required, either to double a value (e.g., when $N = 2$) or to form $(N * I) * (j - 1)$, the use of the rotate instruction or multiple additions, respectively, avoids the necessity of calling on a separate multiply subroutine.

Before returning to the caller, the subroutine checks to see if the relative address (or index) calculated is less than the given size of the array. If it is not, no array element address is returned. Otherwise the actual array address is returned. Since readability of the example was important, there are several possibilities for improving the subroutine (such as indice checking, array types different from INTEGER and REAL, better/tighter coding, but these are left to the reader.

5.2. STACKS, SHELVES, AND QUEUES

Because stack hardware is part of the PDP-11, the reader is already familiar with *push-down stacks*, or, more simply, stacks. Seen in the context of this chapter on data structures, a stack is nothing more than a special form of a one-dimensional array. As a matter of fact, most FORTRAN programmers have probably implemented the traditional *PUSH* and *POP* operations on a stack by writing the FORTRAN instructions shown in Fig. 5-5. As implemented, elements are not physically pushed or popped from the stack. Instead, a pointer is moved so that it always points to the most accessible or *top* element in the stack.

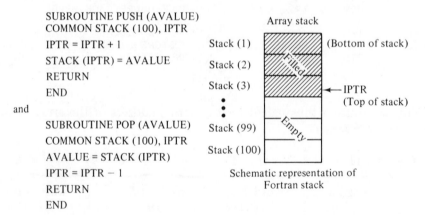

Fig. 5-5

We have already seen how stacks may be used for saving and restoring registers, for implementing automatic nesting of subroutine calls, and for writing recursive procedures. Stacks are also commonly found in language translators, where they aid in the process of compilation of arithmetic expression and code generation, and in operating systems, where they serve to keep a list of items in an order consistent with the need to know "which occurred last."

The growth of information on a stack is usually defined as being unidirectional. However, if it is possible to allow growth in two directions, then the basic stack structure can be transformed into a *shelf* or *double-ended queue*. On a computer such as the PDP-11, which implements stacks by use of register pointers, a shelf can be considered a stack with two pointers, one growing upward in memory and one growning downward.

Shelves have the additional property that when information is removed from a shelf, it is erased at the source. Thus, unlike a move or copy operation, a fetch operation on a shelf does not make a copy of what was on the shelf but rather represents the more intuitive notion about fetching and removing an item from some storage place.

Shelves can be implemented easily on the PDP-11 since it has both positive and negative autoindexing. However, because the autodecrementing and autoincrementing are done before and after the operand fetch, respectively, it is necessary to use the essentially null statements,

```
TST     -(R)
TST     (R)+
```

to keep the stack points in correct position.

There are four basic shelf operations—LSTORE (lower store), USTORE (upper store), LFETCH (lower fetch), and UFETCH (upper fetch)—and these are programmed as shown by the four routines in Fig. 5-6. A call on a shelf

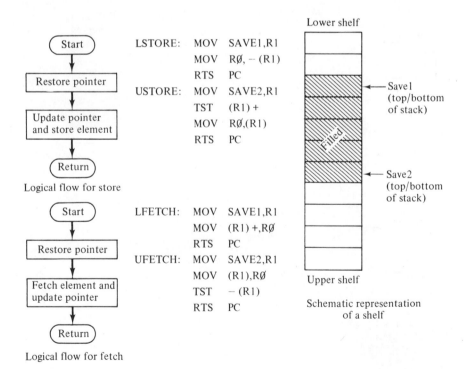

Fig. 5-6

subroutine presumes that either the value to be stored is in R0, or else the value to be fetched will be left in R0. As programmed, the fetch operation does not actually destroy the fetched information, but rather, like the stack operation it is, simply moves a stack pointer. Only when a new store is performed on that end of the shelf will the information be destroyed.

Shelves are quite useful in applications where a program may need to add or delete items at either end of a stack. The need to do so arises when these items are added to or removed from the shelf according to their order of importance. For example, a time-sharing system might service users in a round-robin fashion, taking each user to be served from one end of the shelf and returning him to the other end upon completion of his service request. However, some users may demand immediate service, and they would have to be added to the serving end of the shelf rather than the receiving end.

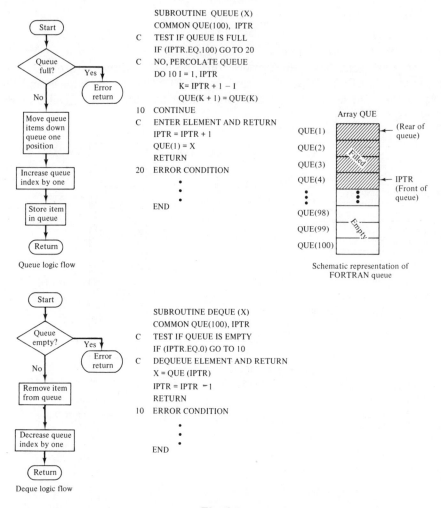

Fig. 5-7

When shelves are used so as to add on one end and to remove from the other, the characteristics of the shelf are changed significantly. Each item on a shelf becomes ordered with respect to its neighbors (the order being a function of when it was placed on the shelf), and it is not possible to remove items out of order. The ordering is known as *first in, first out (FIFO)*, and the data form taken by the shelf is called a *queue*. Like all other data structures discussed in this section, the queue is a special form of a one-dimensional array.

Although queues are not very complex data structures, one has to be careful about their implementation. For example, taking the simplistic approach of implementing a queue as a specialized form of a shelf can clearly lead to disaster. Instead, it is generally necessary to make a queue of a fixed size and to percolate all information through the queue. One question remains, however, and that is whether the items in the queue ought to actually percolate through the queue, or whether some pointers can be used to describe the percolation process.

Let us first consider items percolating through the queue. In FORTRAN, the queue and dequeue operations could be coded as shown in Fig. 5-7. The reader should note that the solution presented for implementing the queue not only moves all elements in the queue each time an add-to-queue is performed, but it also requires a pointer to keep track of where the queue ends in the 'static' array QUE.

Another approach to queue implementation can be found in the *circular buffer algorithm*. This technique allows the queue to be considered as if it were a cylindrical surface on which the highest addressed location is immediately followed by the lowest (such as the addresses on a disk). Logically the queue is pictured as shown in Fig. 5-8a, but physically the queue is actually as shown in Fig. 5-8b.

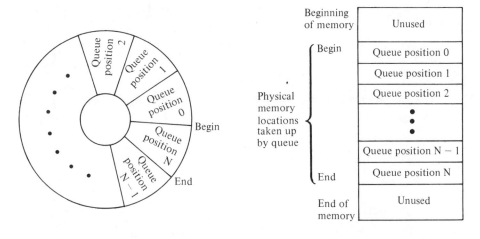

(a) Logical organization   (b) Physical organization

Fig. 5-8

Two pointers associated with the queue, BEGIN and END, are used to indicate the limits of the queue, while two others, IN and OUT, are used to indicate where the next item is to be placed in the queue and where the last item was taken from it, respectively. When IN = OUT, the queue is empty.

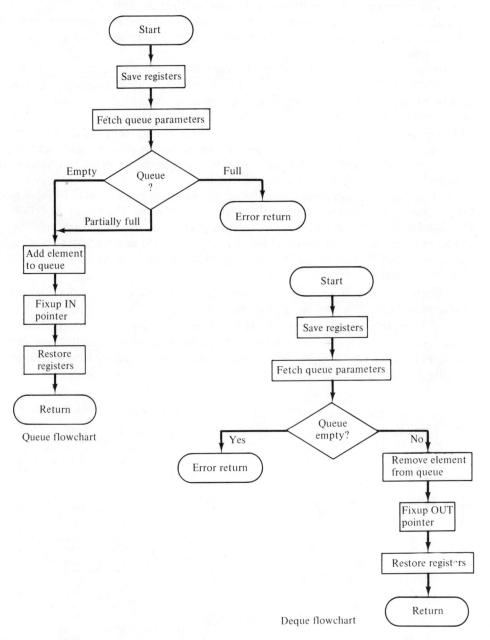

Fig. 5-9

This is the status of the queue initially. As an element is added to the queue, IN is advanced; correspondingly, as an element is removed from the queue, OUT is advanced. Thus when IN > OUT, the area from OUT to IN − 1 contains queued elements. And when OUT > IN, the area from OUT to END contains the first part of the queue and the area from BEGIN to IN − 1 contains the balance.

Queue and dequeue routines using the circular buffer algorithm can be flowcharted and coded as shown in Figs. 5-9 and 5-10. These routines assume that R0 holds the item entered on or removed from the queue, and that the routines are called by the instruction JSR PC,QUEUE or JSR PC,DEQUE.

```
QUE:       . = . +200            ; QUEUE SIZE=100 WORDS
BEGIN:     0                     ; START OF QUEUE
END:       200                   ; QUEUE LIMIT
IN:        0                     ; IN POINTER
OUT:       0                     ; OUT POINTER
QUEUE:     JSR      PC, SAVE     ; SAVE REGISTERS

           MOV      IN, R1       ; FETCH IN
           MOV      OUT, R2      ; FETCH OUT
           MOV      END, R3      ; FETCH END
           CMP      R1, R2       ; TEST IN : OUT
           BEQ      OKAY         ; IN = OUT
           BMI      INV          ; OUT > IN
           SUB      R1, R3       ; END - IN
           ADD      R2, R3       ; END - IN + OUT
           BGT      OKAY         ; TESTS OKAY
INV:       SUB      R2, R3       ; END - OUT
           ADD      R1, R3       ; END - OUT + IN
           BLE      ERROR1       ; QUEUE FULL
OKAY:      MOV      R0, QUE(R1)  ; PUT ELEMENT IN QUEUE
           TST      (R1)+        ; INCREMENT IN
           CMP      R1, END      ; AT END OF QUEUE?
           BMI      SAVE         ; NO
           CLR      R1           ; RESET IN (WRAP-AROUND)
STORE:     MOV      R1, IN       ; SAVE NEW IN POINTER
           JSR      PC, REST     ; RESTORE REGISTERS
           RTS      PC           ; RETURN
ERROR1:    . . .                 ; QUEUE FULL
           . . .                 ; ERROR RETURN
DEQUE:     JSR      PC, SAVE     ; SAVE REGISTERS
           MOV      IN, R1       ; FETCH IN
           MOV      OUT, R2      ; FETCH OUT
           SUB      R2, R1       ; QUEUE EMPTY?
           BEQ      ERROR2       ; YES
           MOV      QUE(R2), R0  ; TAKE ELEMENT OFF QUEUE
           TST      (R2)+        ; INCREMENT OUT
           CMP      R2, END      ; AT END OF QUEUE?
           BMI      STR          ; NO
           CLR      R2           ; RESET OUT
STR:       MOV      R2, OUT      ; SAVE NEW OUT POINTER
           JSR      PC, REST     ; RESTORE REGISTERS
           RTS      PC           ; RETURN
ERROR2:    . . .                 ; QUEUE EMPTY
           . . .                 ; ERROR RETURN
```

Fig. 5-10

Of the two routines, QUEUE is clearly the longer. The reason is simple; in testing for an empty queue, all one need do is check whether IN = OUT. However, when testing for full queue, two conditions may occur, as shown in Fig. 5-11. Either IN > OUT or OUT > IN.

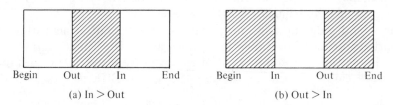

(a) In > Out   (b) Out > In

Note: Shaded area = current queue

Fig. 5-11 Possibilities for current filling of queue.

In the first case (Fig. 5-8a), as long as END − IN + OUT > 0, the queue is either empty or partially filled. On the second case (Fig. 5-8b), as long as END − OUT + IN > 0, the queue is only partially filled. The QUEUE routine must therefore determine which condition has occurred, and then test accordingly.

5.3. LISTS

Another commonly used data structure is the *list*. In its simplest form, a list may be conceived of as a one-dimensional array that need not occupy a block of adjoining memory locations. Instead, elements may reside any-where in memory and can be *linked* together, forming a linked list rather than a contiguous list. For example, a list structure representing this sentence might be

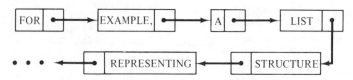

Except for the first and last elements, each element of a list has a *successor* and a *predecessor*. If the list is linked only to its successor, the list is called a *one-way list*. When doubly linked to both its successor and prede-cessor, such a list is called a *two-way list*.

Whether or not a list is one-way or two-way, there remains the problem of describing where a list begins, i.e., what the first element on the list is. This problem is resolved by using a special pointer, called the *head*, to point to the beginning of a list. As a matter of convenience, a second pointer, called the *tail*, is used to point to the end of a list. The tailpointer is not absolutely necessary because the link in the last element of a list is made to contain a special value, called *NIL*, which indicates that there is no successor element.

Lists are not constrained to one dimension, but like arrays may be multidimensional. An interesting two-dimensional list would be one that describes the FORTRAN expression

$$A = (B + C) * (D - E)$$

This expression can be represented by the following list structure:

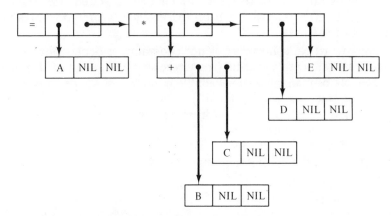

For each binary operator there are two links to the operands of the operator. In some cases the operands are simple variables; in others they are expressions. When traversing such a two-dimensional list, one has to have some way of recognizing the difference between list elements having the same physical representations. One method for doing so is to include descriptors, as part of the list structure, which characterize the list elements explicitly.

Whether one needs to manipulate one- or multidimensional lists, the basic list operations remain the same. These operations are: (1) create a list, (2) add an element to a list, (3) delete an element from a list, and (4) search for an element on a list. Thus when one is learning how these operations are performed, the simpler the list structure, the better.

Using the PDP-11 as the host machine, it will be easiest to consider a list element as a two-word pair. The first word will be the datum and the second will be the pointer to a successor list element. HEAD and TAIL will act as the special pointers to the beginning and end of the list. A NIL pointer will be represented by an all-zero value. Initially, then, an empty list will be indicated by

```
HEAD:    0
TAIL:    0
```

The function of a CREATE routine will be to zero out HEAD and TAIL:

```
CREATE: CLR     HEAD            ; NIL IN HEAD
        CLR     TAIL            ; NIL IN TAIL
        RTS     PC              ; RETURN
```

The next routine, ADD, must take a new list element and put it on the list. Two arguments needed by ADD are (1) the relative position on the list where the new element is to be placed, and (2) the new word pair to be added. The relative position is programmer-dependent with the following interpretation: If the value given is negative, the new element is added to the end of the list; if it is positive, the new element is added after the element specified by the given relative position (a zero is interpreted to mean add to the beginning of the list).

Obtaining word pairs, however, is not programmer-dependent. Instead, it is the job of an "allocate" routine (see Exercise 4 at the end of this chapter), which is capable of managing the available memory locations (those not used by the programmer or the "system"). Each time the allocate routine is called, it returns with either an address of a word pair or a flag indicating that no more word pairs are available.

Assuming that the programmer has utilized allocate and wishes to ADD an element to a list, the calling sequence to ADD might be

```
JSR     R0, ADD                 ; CALL ADD SUBROUTINE
(RELATIVE POSITION)             ; FIRST ARGUMENT FOR ADD
(WORD-PAIR ADDRESS)             ; SECOND ARGUMENT FOR ADD
```

and ADD would be as shown in Fig. 5-12.

```
ADD:     JSR    PC, SAVE        ; SAVE REGISTERS
         MOV    (R0)+, R1       ; RELATIVE POSITION
         MOV    (R0)+, R2       ; WORD-PAIR ADDRESS
         MOV    HEAD, R3        ; GET LIST POINTER
         TST    R1              ; NEGATIVE OR ZERO?
         BMI    END             ; ADD TO END
         BEQ    BEGIN           ; ADD TO BEGINNING
LOOP:    MOV    2(R3), R3       ; GET NEXT ELEMENT
         DEC    R1              ; ADD HERE?
         BNE    LOOP            ; NO
         MOV    R3, 2(R2)       ; SET UP LINK IN NEW ELEMENT
         MOV    R2, (R3)        ; AND OLD ELEMENT
RET:     JSR    PC, REST        ; RESTORE REGISTERS
         RTS    R0              ; RETURN
BEGIN:   MOV    R3, 2(R2)       ; LINK UP NEW ELEMENT
         MOV    R2, HEAD        ; FIX UP HEAD
         BR     RET             ; DONE
END:     MOV    TAIL, R3        ; GET TAIL
         MOV    2(R3), 2(R2)    ; LINK IN NEW ELEMENT
         MOV    R2, TAIL        ; FIX UP TAIL
         BR     RET             ; RETURN
```

Fig. 5-12

A picture of the ADD operation is shown in Fig. 5-13. The figures represent the list before and after the addition of an element to the middle of it.

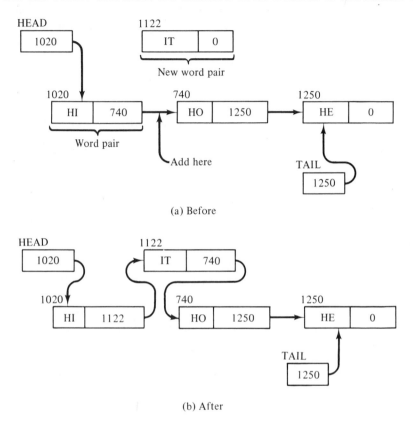

(a) Before

(b) After

Fig. 5-13　ADDing an element to a list.

Similar pictures could be drawn for adding an element to the beginning or end of the list. These pictures are left as reader exercises, as in the programming of the DELETE routine. The linkage to the DELETE routine would be

```
JSR      R0,DELETE          ;CALL DELETE SUBROUTINE
(RELATIVE POSITION)         ;FIRST ARGUMENT FOR DELETE
(WORD-PAIR ADDRESS)         ;SECOND ARGUMENT FOR DELETE
```

Complementary to the ADD process, the DELETE process requires the user to call a "free" routine which can return a word pair to the pool of available memory locations. Should the programmer not do so, there will be a continually diminishing supply of word pairs available and an increasing supply of unallocated and unavailable word pairs. As a result, when allocate runs out of word pairs, either the list processing stops, or someone has to perform a *garbage collection*, somehow picking up the unallocated word pairs.

Although the problems of garbage collection are not trivial, a technique may be given for simple lists. A simple list is one that does not have a closed path or loop in it, such as the following list:

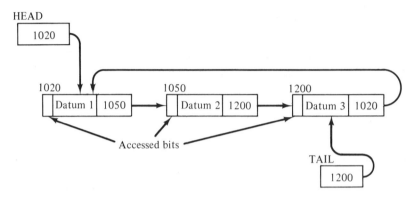

The garbage-collection technique to be used on simple lists requires that a bit, called the *accessed bit*, be reserved as part of each list element. Except during garbage collection, this bit is always 0. However, during garbage collection, every list is traversed, and as each element on the list is accessed, its accessed bit is set to 1. As a result of this operation, only those list elements that do not belong to any list will have an accessed bit of 0. These elements can be easily located (say by defining the accessed bit to be the sign bit and testing for nonnegative elements) and can be added to the list of free elements to be used once again. Garbage collection is not complete, however, until all accessed bits are reset back to 0.

Returning to the last problem for searching a list, let us consider the SEARCH routine. This routine is called by

```
JSR      R0, SEARCH          ; CALL SEARCH
(DATUM)                      ; DATUM TO BE LOCATED
(WORD-PAIR ADDRESS)          ; VALUE TO BE RETURNED
```

and could be programmed as shown in Fig. 5-14.

The SEARCH routine as written does a datum search, returning both the relative position and the word-pair address, if a match is found. Otherwise, no values are returned. Another form of the search routine might be to find the nth item on a list. For this case, the call to search would include the relative position rather than the datum. The perceptive reader will have

```
SEARCH:   JSR     PC, SAVE        ; SAVE REGISTERS
          MOV     (R0), R1        ; DATUM
          MOV     #1, R4          ; RELATIVE POSITION
          MOV     HEAD, R2        ; START OF LIST
          MOV     TAIL, R3        ; END OF LIST
LOOP:     CMP     R2, R3          ; EMPTY LIST OR NO MATCH
          BEQ     RET             ; NO HIT
          CMP     R1, (R2)        ; TEST FOR MATCH
          BEQ     FOUND           ; GOT A HIT
          MOV     2(R2), R2       ; NEXT ELEMENT
          INC     R4              ; ADD ONE TO RELATIVE POSITION
          BR      LOOP            ; AT END
FOUND:    MOV     R4, (R0)+               ; RETURN REL. POSITION
          MOV     R2, (R0)+       ; AND WORD-PAIR ADDRESS
RET:      JSR     PC, REST        ; RESTORE REGISTERS
          RTS     R0              ; RETURN
```

Fig. 5-14

recognized that this search function is already performed by the ADD routine and that only small changes are necessary to that routine in order to add this new search capability.

The significant advantage of list structures lies in the flexibility of manipulation as has been demonstrated. Additionally, lists are often more convenient data structures for the representation of nonnumeric information in the areas of artificial intelligence, pattern recognition, theorem proving, syntactic analysis, operating systems, and so on. Thus an understanding of list structures is fundamental to an understanding of the topics in these areas.

5.4. ASSEMBLY PROCESS

In a very meaningful sense, the assembly process is an example of the utilization of various data structures. The assembler accepts a program as data to be transformed into a machine language that can be executed on some computer. The transformation performed by the assembler is traditionally a two-step process whereby the program being assembled is passed through the assembler twice.

Figure 5-15 shows, in greatly simplified form, the basic operations of a *two-pass assembler*. At the heart of the assembly process, as seen in the figure, is the *symbol table*. The symbol table is also a data structure and provides a transformation between the symbols and the values they represent. Initially the symbol table may only include entries for each symbolic op code, but as user-defined symbols are encountered during the assembly process, the symbol table is expanded to include these new entries.

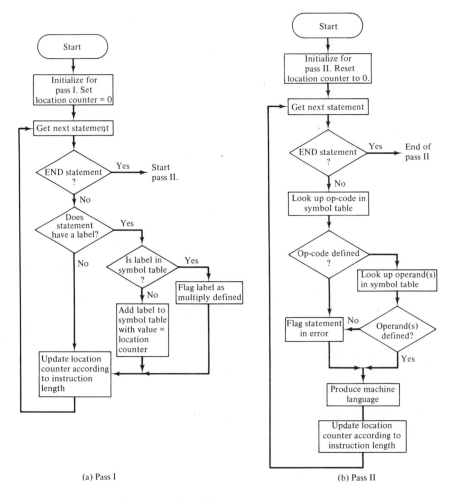

Fig. 5-15 Simplified two-pass assembler.

5.4.1. Symbol Table

Because the symbol table is scanned frequently (either to enter a new symbol or to retrieve the value of a previously defined one), the construction of the symbol table must be considered carefully. For example, since op codes will be referenced, in general, more frequently than user-defined symbols, and some op codes may be used more often than others, ordering the symbols can certainly reduce the search time required to locate symbols in the table.

If the symbol table is structured as either a one-dimensional array or a simple linked list, a linear search of the table for a particular symbol will require scanning about half the table. By preordering the table, this scan can be reduced somewhat, but it will still be on the average, fairly long. Consequently, another technique is often used which restructures the symbol table so as to avoid a linear search with its attendantly longer search time.

The technique used is that of *hashing* or *randomizing* the symbol being searched for into a pointer, and using the pointer as the address of the symbol's entry in the symbol table. The hashing thus acts as a mapping function which is easily performed and which (one hopes) maps each symbol into a unique entry in the table. For example, given symbols each 6 bytes in length, a simple hashing function might be to exclusive-OR the 6 bytes together. The hashed result could then be used as an index into a symbol table in much the same way that an index is used to specify a particular array element.

In FORTRAN, the process might be coded as

```
HINDEX = HASH(SYMBOL)
SYMVAL = SYMTBL(HINDEX)
```

where HASH is the hashing function and SYMTBL is the symbol-table array. In assembly language for the PDP-11 the hashing function could be coded as

```
HASHER:  MOV    #HINDEX,R0    ;MOVE HASH INDEX LOCATION INTO R0
         CLR    @R0           ;HINDEX=0
         MOV    #SYMB,R1      ;MOVE SYMBOL LOCATION INTO R1
HASH:    MOVB   @R1,-(SP)     ;STACK = EFFECTIVE BYTE
         BICB   @R0,@SP       ;STACK = -STACK . BYTE
         BICB   (R1)+,@R0     ;HINDEX = -HINDEX . BYTE
         BISB   (SP)+,@R0     ;HINDEX = HINDEX + STACK
         CMP    R1,#SYMB+5    ;ALL SIX BYTES USED
         BLE    HASH          ;NO, REITERATE PROCESS
```

The PDP-11 does not have an exclusive-OR operation. Instead, the programmer must make use of the relationship

$$A \oplus B = (\neg A \cdot B) + (A \cdot \neg B)$$

where $\neg A \cdot B$ is equivalent to a BIC operation. As shown, the routine actually forms, from the 6-byte symbol consisting of $B_0, B_1, B_2, B_3, B_4, B_5$, the hashed result

$$\text{HINDEX} = ((((((B_0 \oplus 0) \oplus B_1) \oplus B_2) \oplus B_3) \oplus B_4) \oplus B_5)$$

This hash value thus serves as an index into a symbol table consisting of 256 entries (e.g., 256 because HINDEX is a byte capable of $2^8 = 256$ bit combinations).

There are two apparent problems with this simple hashing technique; either the number of indices generated will be too small, or more than one symbol may map into the same hash index. Fortunately, both problems may be resolved using another simple technique. Instead of assuming the hashed symbol table to be a one-dimensional table, it is better to consider it two-dimensional such that for each prime entry or row (specified by the hash index) there are four columns in which to place the actual entry. Pictorially the situation looks as follows:

		Column		
Hindex	0	1	2	3
0	$entry_{0,0}$	$entry_{0,1}$	$entry_{0,2}$	$entry_{0,3}$
1	$entry_{1,0}$	$entry_{1,1}$	$entry_{1,2}$	$entry_{1,3}$
2	.	.		
.		.		
.	.	.		
.	.	.		
255	$entry_{255,0}$			

The two-dimensional scheme requires both that the hash index be computed and that a linear search be performed on each columnar entry until a match or an empty entry is found.

The two-dimensional approach has two drawbacks, however. First, since several entries may share the same hash index, the row entries must hold both the symbol itself and its value. Second, the approach must have allocated enough columns so that hashing conflicts may be uniquely resolved for a reasonable set of symbols. Should there be too few columns, and many symbols with the same hash index, the table will be sparsely filled; yet the assembler will be unable to add a new symbol to the table. Fortunately, this problem can be resolved by making each entry a list, adding list elements as needed.

As an alternative to using a two-dimensional table, there is the technique of adding a constant offset to the hash index each time a nonempty or non-match entry is found. This technique allows the table to be searched linearly after the hash index is computed, and attempts to fill the table to capacity. The algorithm for searching the table can be described as follows:

1. Calculate the hash index,

2. Test the entry for a match or an empty condition; if either, terminate search in success,

3. Add offset to hash index; check index to see if it points to an entry within the table; if it does not, go to step 5,

4. Check index to see if it is equal to the initial index (e.g., the index of the first entry in the table); if it is, terminate search in failure,

5. Subtract off table size from hash index; go to step 2.

As an example of such a search, consider a 16-element symbol table with an offset of 5 (must be relatively prime). Entries in the table have indices ranging from 0 to 15. If the hash index first computed was 2, the possible order of total entries searched would be

$$\{\,2,\,7,\,12,\,1,\,6,\,11,\,0\,\}$$

search terminates whenever
hash index computed $= 0$

5.4.2. Packed Entries in the Symbol Table

In almost all cases, one of the entries in the symbol table has to be the symbol itself. Since symbols may be several characters long, it is highly desirable to place as many characters in a word as possible. Having read about how a small computer, such as the PDP-11, packs 2 bytes or characters per word, the reader is probably convinced that the maximum number of characters per word is 2. Such is not the case.

Since the number of possible characters acceptable to a symbolic assembler is considerably less than 256 (i.e., 2^8), being more probably 36–40 (i.e., the 26 letters of the alphabet plus the 10 numerals and a few special symbols), it is quite conceivable to be able to pack three characters into a 16-bit word by using the formula

$$((C_1 \, * \, 50_8) \, + \, C_2) \, * \, 50_8 \, + \, C_3$$

where C_1, C_2, and C_3 are the three characters in converted or *Radix-50 format*. The relationship of Radix-50 format to ASCII is given by

	ASCII	Radix-50
Space	40	0
A–Z	101–132	1–32
$	44	33
.	56	34
Unused		35
0–9	60–71	36–47

Appendix C includes both the ASCII and Radix-50 octal codes. Using the tables, we can convert the six-character ASCII symbol,

	odd byte	even byte
word 1	131	123
word 2	102	115
word 3	114	117

$\equiv$ .ASCII   /SYMBOL/

occupying three words, into the Radix-50 format:

$$S = 073300$$
$$Y = 001750$$
$$M = 000015$$
$$\overline{075265} \equiv$$

word 1

075265
007344

word 2

$006200 = B$
$001130 = O$
$000014 = L$
$\overline{}$
$\equiv 007344$

which requires only two words and results in a significant saving in memory space.

There are two ways to write a Radix-50 format packing routine. One way would be to use a table of values for each character in each position as shown in Appendix C. A second would generate the final result by using the formula given earlier. A brief flowchart of this second method might be as shown in Fig. 5-16 and the program that utilizes this flowchart could be coded as shown in Fig. 5-17. The routine first extracts the RADIX-50 byte from the three-word pair. Next, the byte is shifted left three positions, effectively multiplying its value by 8. This partial result ($C_1 * 8_{10}$) is saved, and the byte is shifted twice more, resulting in a value of $C_1 * 32_{10}$. When the partial result is added in, the new partial result is

$$C_1 * 32_{10} + C_1 * 8_{10} = C_1 * 40_{10} = C_1 * 50_8$$

When the process is repeated for the second byte, the partial result is

$$((C_1 * 50_8) + C_2) * 50_8$$

to which C_3 may be added, giving the resultant triad. The conversion from ASCII to Radix-50, and the unpacking routine, are left as exercises for the reader.

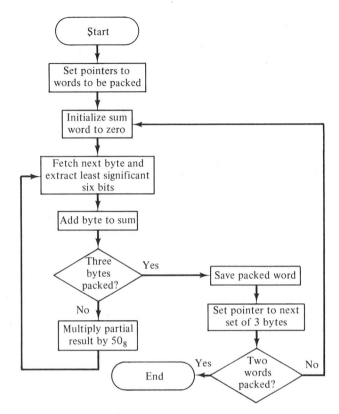

Fig. 5-16

```
PACKER: MOV    #SYMADR,R4      ; ADDRESS OF FIRST WORD TO BE PACKED
        MOV    #SYMADR+2,R5    ; ADDRESS OF SECOND WORD TO BE PACKED
        MOV    R4,R1           ; INITIALIZE R1
PACK:   CLR    R3              ; SUM=0
PACK1:  CLR    R2              ; R2=0
        MOVB   @R1,R2          ; GET CHARACTER
        BICB   #300,R2         ; CLEAR LEADING BITS
        ADD    R2,R3           ; SUM=SUM+TRANSLATED CHARACTER
        CLRB   (R1)+           ; CLEAR CHARACTER OUT
        CMP    R1,R5           ; IS R1<R5?
        BGE    PACK2           ; NOPE, TRIAD COMPLETED
        ASL    R3              ; SHIFT SUM
        ASL    R3              ;    LEFT 3
        ASL    R3              ;       BITS
        MOV    R3,-(SP)        ; SAVE PARTIAL RESULT
        ASL    R3              ; SHIFT SUM
        ASL    R3              ;    LEFT 2 BITS
        ADD    (SP)+,R3        ; SUM=SUM+PARTIAL RESULT
        BR     PACK1           ; PROCESS NEXT CHARACTER
PACK2:  MOV    R3,(R4)+        ; STORE RESULTANT TRIAD
        ADD    #3,R5           ; LAST WORD ADDRESS
        CMP    R5,#SYMADR+6    ; DONE?
        BLE    PACK            ; NOPE, REITERATE PACKING
```

Fig. 5-17

5.5. DATA STRUCTURES IN PRACTICE

In almost every facit of computing, data structures play an important role in the specification, design, and implementation of complete software systems. From the simple variable types found in higher-level languages (e.g., queues, multilevel lists), there exists a need to be able to represent information in a form that is convenient for use by both the programmer and the computer system. An example will make this point clear.

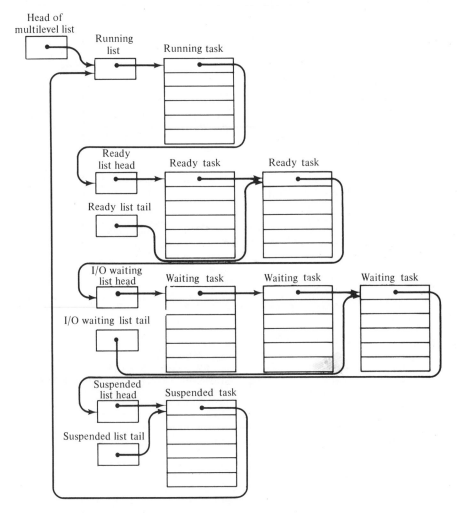

Fig. 5-18

Internal to any multiprogrammed computer system,[†] there is a queue of the tasks to be performed. Each entry in the queue may consist of several consecutive words to hold such things as (1) the task name, (2) task status, (3) task starting/restarting address, and (4) task invocation information. If tasks are grouped according to their status (e.g., running, ready, waiting for I/O, suspended), a multilevel list structure exists as shown in Fig. 5-18.

The multilevel list actually combines the features found not only in lists, but also tables, deques, queues, and stacks. For example, each task is described by a table and belongs to one of the four queues (e.g., running, ready, waiting, suspended). Since each queue has both a head and a tail pointer, task tables can be added and removed from either end; that is, the queue can be treated as a deque. But the deque can be used as a stack if items are added and removed from one end only, as might be the case when one program interrupts another and interrupted programs are stacked to await execution at a later time. Finally, the basic structure of the data form is that of a list, and it is the list structure which allows us to restructure the data so conveniently into what suits us.

EXERCISES

1. How must the calculate array element address subroutine be modified so as to correctly process all the array types given in the table on page 128?

2. Implement the FORTRAN QUEUE and DEQUE routines in PAL-11 assembly language. How do these routines compare to the routines coded using the circular buffer algorithm?

3. Write the DELETE routine as described on page 141.

4. Write the allocate and free routines described on pages 140 and 142.

5. Given a list of two-letter words, develop a sorting program to place the list in alphabetical order.

6. Rewrite ADD so that it may be called to perform a relative position search function.

7. Show how a list structure can be used to implement a queue.

8. What is a suitable offset for a 32-element symbol table using the hashing technique to search the table? Give a set of possible indices searched if the hash index first computed was 5.

9. Write an unpack routine for words in Radix-50 format.

[†]See Chapter 8 for a discussion of such a system.

REFERENCES

There are several good texts devoted to data structures, including Berztiss (1971), Brillinger and Cohen (1972), Flores (1970), and Johnson (1970). Of course, Knuth's book (1968) remains a classic and is one of the few texts that discusses data structures in the context of machine and assembly language programming. Stone (1972) also covers data structures, but most of his examples are in ALGOL. Since the trend is toward higher-level languages for creating and manipulating data structures, many indirect references to this subject can be found in the language manuals describing SNOBOL, LISP, COMIT, COBOL, PL/I, and so on.

6 I/O PROGRAMMING

Being able to program a computer to do calculations is of little use if there is no way of getting the results of calculations from the machine. Likewise, the programmer often must supply the computer with information to be processed. A programmer must, therefore, be provided with the means to transfer information between the computer and the peripheral devices that supply input or that serve as a means of output.

In order to perform an I/O function, the programmer must specify what the data are, where they are to go or come from, and how the I/O device is to be controlled. Depending on the small computer being utilized, the I/O function may require the CPU to wait until the I/O operation is complete, or the I/O function may allow the CPU to go on and process other functions while the operation is being performed. When the I/O function holds up the CPU, we say that the I/O operation is *interlocked* with the CPU. When both can be performed simultaneously, we say that I/O is *concurrent* with computation.

Concurrent operation is becoming the standard mode for most small computers. This mode takes several forms. In one form, the concurrent I/O function can operate on data words one at a time. During the operation, the data word is held temporarily in a special register, such as the accumulator.

In another form, the I/O function operates directly between memory and the I/O unit. This mode of operation requires a separate path [called a *direct memory access (DMA)* path] between the memory and the I/O unit. The DMA allows the I/O function to be performed with a minimum of dependency on the part of the CPU.

A third mode of operation allows a large block of I/O information to be passed between an I/O unit and the memory. As support for such *block transfers*, special registers are provided for holding a count of the number of words yet to be transferred, the current I/O unit and memory address of the data word being transferred, and the data. Once initiated by an I/O instruction, block transfers run concurrently and independently of the CPU until they are completed (i.e., the word count goes to zero or an addressing error occurs).

Whenever there is a DMA path as well as a CPU path to memory, conflicts may arise. Because the I/O requests for memory are time dependent, occur infrequently, and are of short duration, the I/O request is given preference over the CPU request. Such preferential treatment is called *cycle stealing* in that the I/O unit is granted memory cycles at the expense of the CPU.

It should be fairly obvious from this brief introduction that with the various possibilities, I/O programming is very machine dependent. The complexity of the I/O system determines the corresponding complexity of the I/O programming. On the PDP-11, the programming of I/O devices is extremely simple, and no new I/O instructions are necessary for dealing with input/output operations.

The key to the simplicity of I/O programming is the UNIBUS, described in Chapter 3. The UNIBUS permits a unified addressing structure in which control, status, and data registers for *peripheral* devices are *directly* addressed as memory locations. Therefore, all operations on these registers, such as transferring information into or out of them or manipulating data with them, are performed by normal memory reference instructions.

6.1. BASIC I/O PROGRAMMING AND OPERATIONS FOR THE PDP-11

The use of memory reference instructions on peripheral device registers greatly increases the flexibility of I/O programming. For example, information in a device register can be compared directly with a value and a branch made on the result:

```
CMPB    TKB,#'Y        ; IS CHARACTER = Y?
BEQ     YES            ; YES IT IS
```

In this case the program looks for a "Y" in the keyboard data buffer (TKB) and branches if it finds it. There is no need to transfer the information into an intermediate register for comparison.

When the character is of interest and is to be saved, a memory reference instruction can transfer the character into a user buffer in memory or to another peripheral device. The instruction

```
MOVB    PRB,LOC        ; SAVE CHARACTER IN MEMORY LOCATION "LOC"
```

transfers a character from the paper tape reader buffer (PRB) into a user-defined location.

Another aspect of I/O programming is that arithmetic operations may be performed on a peripheral device register that is used for both input and output. Thus there is no need to funnel all data transfers, arithmetic operations, and comparison through other words or general-purpose registers. Instead, the peripheral device register can itself be treated as an accumulator.

6.1.1. Device Registers

All peripheral devices are specified by a set of registers that are addressed as memory and manipulated as flexibly as an accumulator. For each device, there are two types of associated registers:

1. Control and status registers.

2. Data registers.

Each peripheral has one or more control and status registers (CSR's) that contain all the information necessary to communicate with that device. The general form shown here does not necessarily apply to every device, but is presented as a guide:

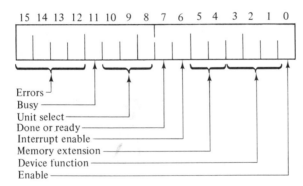

Many devices require less than 16 status bits. Other devices will require more than 16 bits and therefore will require additional status and control registers.

The bits in the control and status registers are generally assigned as follows:

Bit	Name	Description
15–12	Errors	Generally, there is an individual bit associated with a specific error. When more bits are required for errors, they can be obtained by expanding the error section in the word or by using another status word. Generally, bit 15 is the inclusive OR of all other error bits (if there is more than one). All errors are generally indicated by individual status bits.

11	Busy	Indicates that a step is being performed.
10–8	Unit Select	Some peripheral systems have more than one device per control. For example, a disk system can have multiple surfaces per control, and an analog-to-digital converter can have multiple channels. The unit bits select the proper surface or channel.
7	Done or Ready	The register can contain a DONE bit, a READY bit, or a DONE-BUSY pair of bits, depending on the device. These bits are set and cleared by the hardware, but may be queried by the program to determine the availability of the device.
6	Interrupt Enable	Independently programmable. If bit 6 is set, an interrupt will occur as a result of a function done or error condition.
5–4	Memory Extension	Will allow devices to use a full 18 bits to specify addresses on the bus.
3–1	Device Function Bits	Specify operations that a device is to perform. For example, a paper tape read function could be "read one character." An operation for a disk could be "read a block of words from memory and store them on the disk."
0	Enable	When set, this bit enables the device to perform the I/O device function.

Each device has at least one buffer register, besides the CSR registers, for temporarily storing data to be transferred into or out of the computer. The number and type of data registers is a function of the device. The paper tape reader and punch use single 8-bit data buffer registers. A disk would use 16-bit data registers and some devices may use two 16-bit registers for data buffers.

6.2. BASIC DEVICE FUNDAMENTALS

The two most basic peripheral devices commonly attached to a PDP-11 are the ASR-33 Teletype® and the DEC PC-11 high-speed paper tape unit. Actually, these two devices are really four units in that the teletypewriter keyboard/reader and printer/punch are two separate units, as are the paper tape reader and punch contained in the PC-11.

6.2.1. Teletype Keyboard/Reader

The teletype control contains an 8-bit buffer (TKB) which assembles and holds the code for the last character struck on the keyboard or read from the tape. Teletype characters from the keyboard/reader are received serially by the 8-bit shift register TKB. Upon program command, the contents of the TKB may be transferred in parallel to a memory location or a general register.

A character is read from the low-speed reader by setting the teletype reader enable bit, (RDR ENB), to a 1. This sets the busy bit (BUSY) to a 1. When a teletype character starts to enter, the control deenergizes a relay in the teletype unit to release the tape feed latch. When released, the latch mechanism stops tape motion only when a complete character has been sensed and before sensing of the next character is started. When the character is available in buffer (TKB), the busy bit (BUSY) is cleared and the done flag (DONE) is set. The keyboard must be read within 18 milliseconds of DONE to ensure that there is no loss of information.

Teletypewriter Keyboard/Reader Status Register (TKS):

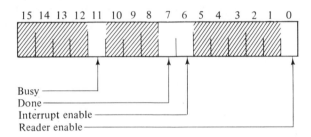

Bit	Name	Description
15–12		Not used.
11	Busy	Indicates that the teletype control is receiving a start bit or information bits. Cleared by INIT, set by start bit, cleared after reception of first halt bit. Read only.
10–8		Not used.
7	Done	Character available in buffer. Cleared by INIT, cleared by referencing data buffer, causes interrupt when INTR ENB = 1. Read only. Cleared when RDR ENB is set.
6	Reader Interrupt Enable (INTR ENB)	Interrupts Enable. Enables Error or Done to cause an interrupt. Cleared by INIT.
5–1		Not used.
0	Reader Enable (RDR ENB)	Enables reader (*not keyboard*) to read one character. Cleared by INIT; cleared when legitimate start bit is detected. Load only.

Teletypewriter Keyboard/Reader Buffer (TKB):

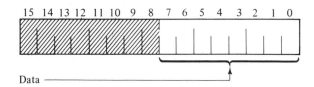

Bit	Name	Description
15–8		Not used.
7–0	Data	Holds character read. Cleared by start bit. Read only.

Any reference to TKB (as word or byte) or TKB + 1 clears DONE. The "unused" and "load only" bits are always read as zeros. Loading "unused" or "read only" bits has no effect on the bit position. The mnemonic "INIT" refers to the initialization signal issued by ON, POWER UP, console START, or RESET.

6.2.2. Teletype Printer/Punch

On program command, a character is sent in parallel from a memory location (or a general register) to the TPB for transmission to the teleprinter/punch unit. This transfer of information from the TPB into the teleprinter/punch unit is accomplished at the normal teletype rate and requires 100 milliseconds for completion. The READY flag in the teleprinter/punch indicates that the TPB is ready to receive a new character. A maintenance mode is provided which connects the TPB output to the TKB input so that the teletypewriter operation may be verified.

Teletypewriter Printer/Punch Status Register (TPS):

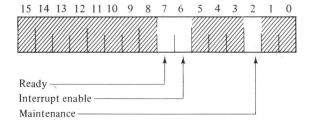

Bit	Name	Description
15–8		Not used.

7	Ready	Punch available. Set by INIT, cleared when buffer is loaded, set when punching complete. Caused interrupt if INTR ENB = 1. Read only.
6	Interrupt Enable (INTR ENB)	Enables READY to cause interrupt. Cleared by INIT.
5–3		Not used.
2	Maintenance	Maintenance function. Disables serial line input from teletype unit and enables serial output of punch to feed into reader buffer. Cleared by INIT.
1–0		Not used.

Teletypewriter Printer/Punch Buffer Register (TPB):

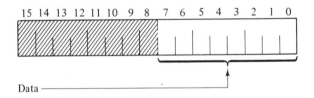

Bit	Name	Description
15–8		Not used.
7–0	Data	Holds character to be punched. Cleared by INIT. Load only.

Any instruction that could modify TPB as a byte or word clears READY and initiates punching. Other references to either byte or word have no effect on the punch.

The four addressable registers associated with the teletype may be read or loaded using any PDP-11 instruction that refers to their address. The address assignments for these registers are as follows:

Register	Address
TKS	177560
TKB	177562
TPS	177564
TPB	177566

When using PAL-11, a direct assignment is made (e.g., TKB = 177562) so that the device registers may be referenced symbolically.

6.2.3. Simple Programming Example

Since the teletype keyboard is treated as a separate unit from the printer, it is necessary to write a simple program to "echo" back to the printer a character typed on the keyboard. This program looks as follows:

```
        TKS=177560              ; DEFINE
        TKB=TKS+2               ; STATUS
        TPS=TKS+4               ; AND BUFFER
        TPB=TKS+6               ; REGISTERS
        =1000
ECHO:   INC     TKS            ; SET READER ENABLED
LOOP1:  TSTB    TKS            ; TEST FOR DONE
        BPL     LOOP1          ; GOES NEGATIVE WHEN SET
LOOP2:  TSTB    TPS            ; TEST PRINTER READY
        BPL     LOOP2          ; GOES NEGATIVE WHEN SET
        MOVB    TKB, TPB       ; MOVE CHARACTER
        BR      ECHO           ; LOOP AROUND AGAIN
        . END   START
```

The value of making the DONE bit line up with the byte boundary is clearly demonstrated in this example. Had it not been set up as the sign bit of the byte, it would have been necessary to copy the status register to a temporary location so that a bit test (BIT) could have been performed, followed by a branch on zero. Since this alternative, although possible, is not as "neat" as the TSTB, it illustrates once again the value of properly designing a computer at both the hardware and software levels.

The setting of the reader enable bit in this program is superfluous. However, by including the instruction to do so the program is generalized in that input is allowed to come from either the keyboard or the reader. Likewise, output can go to either the printer or the punch. All that is necessary is for the user to place a paper tape in the reader and set it to "start," or to turn on the punch, and these paper tape devices become operative (in parallel) with their counterparts (e.g., the keyboard or the printer). Consequently, this one program allows for any legitimate combination of teletype devices to be connected together.

6.2.4. More Complex Octal Dump Program

A programming tool frequently used by assembly language programmers is the *memory dump program*. This program aids the user who is developing or debugging programs by providing him with an octal copy of a program or portion of a program that resides in the computer's memory.

The program shown is a memory-to-teletypewriter octal dump routine and illustrates basic I/O programming utilizing the teleprinter. It also illustrates the use of position-independent coding. The need for PIC is dictated, of course, by the necessity of being able to load the dump routine anywhere in memory.

The program begins by typing an "A" character and waiting for the user to type in an octal starting location (up to five digits). The return key causes the program to respond with a line feed and an "N" character, signifying a program request for number of words to be dumped. The second return begins the dump:

```
A1000
N12

001000   010706   005746   112700   000015   004767   000142   112700   000012
001020   004767   000132
```

A flowchart of this program is shown in Fig. 6-1, and the actual program looks as shown in Fig. 6-2.

6.2.5. High-Speed Reader/Punch

The high-speed reader/punch consists of two units for reading and punching eight-hole perforated paper tape at, respectively, 300 characters per second and 60 characters per second. Each unit has its own status and buffer registers capable of controlling the transfer of one byte to or from the unit.

Data are recorded (punched) on paper tape by groups of holes arranged in a definite format along the length of the tape. The tape is divided into *channels*, which run the length of the tape, and into *columns*, which extend across the width of the tape as shown in Fig. 6-3.

The status register for the paper tape reader is almost identical in format to the status register for the teletypewriter keyboard/reader. The difference is found in the error bit, which is set by an "out of tape" or "off-line" condition.

Paper Tape Reader Status Register (PRS):

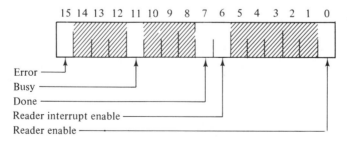

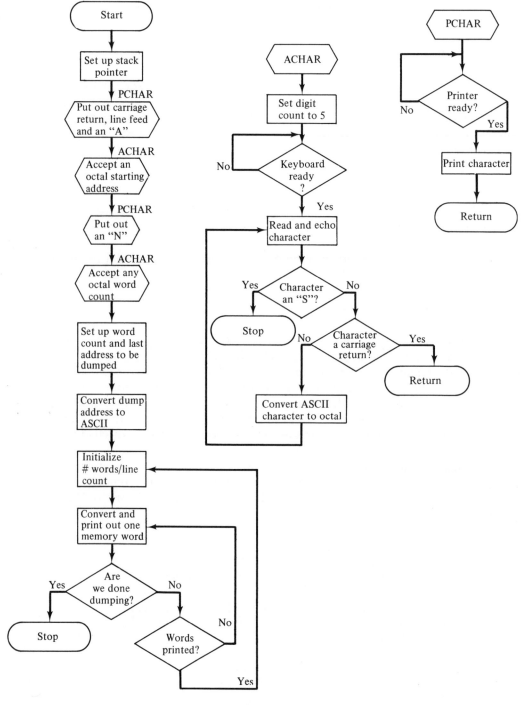

Fig. 6-1

```
;
;            EDUMP - AN OCTAL DUMP PROGRAM
;            WRITTEN BY ELLIOT SOLOWAY 6/1/72
;
;            INPUTS ARE N -- THE NUMBER OF WORDS
;                     AND A -- THE STARTING ADDRESS
;
;            OUTPUT IS THE STARTING MEMORY ADDRESS
;                     AND THE CONTENTS OF UP TO 8 WORDS
;                     OF MEMORY
;
             R0=%0
             R1=%1
             R2=%2
             R3=%3
             R4=%4
             R5=%5
             SP=%6
             PC=%7

             TKS=177560
             TKB=TKS+2
             TPS=TKS+4
             TPB=TKS+6

             CR=15
             LF=12

CORE:   MOV     PC,SP                  ;SET UP STACK POINTER
        TST     -(SP)
        MOVB    #CR,R0                 ;PRINT INITIAL CARRIAGE
        JSR     PC,PCHAR               ;RETURN AND
        MOVB    #LF,R0                 ;LINE FEED USING
        JSR     PC,PCHAR               ;PUT CHARACTER SUBROUTINE
ADDR:   MOVB    #'A,R0                 ;PRINT AN "A"
        JSR     PC,PCHAR
        JSR     PC,ACHAR               ;ACCEPT UP TO 5 OCTAL DIGITS AS ADDRESS
        MOV     R5,R1                  ;R1 CONTAINS START ADDRESS
        MOVB    #'N,R0                 ;PRINT AN N FOR NUMBER OF WORDS
        JSR     PC,PCHAR
        JSR     PC,ACHAR               ;ACCEPT <= 5 OCTAL DIGITS
        MOV     R5,R2                  ;FORM WORD COUNT NUMBER
        ADD     R5,R2                  ;TO BE DUMPED
        ADD     R1,R2                  ;FORM ENDING ADDRESS
        TST     -(R2)                  ;LESS TWO
LOOP1:  MOV     PC,R4                  ;SET UP RELATIVE ADDRESS
        ADD     #BUF-LOOP1-2+6,R4        ;OUTPUT BUFFER START ADDRESS
        MOV     #CR,R0                 ;RESET PRINTER
        JSR     PC,PCHAR               ;CARRIAGE
        MOV     #LF,R0                 ;FOR DUMP
        JSR     PC,PCHAR               ;INFORMATION
ARND:   MOV     R1,R0                  ;CONVERT THE DUMP ADDRESS
        JSR     PC,CNVRT2              ;TO ASCII CHARACTERS
        MOV     #8.,R3                 ;NUMBER OF WORDS DUMPED PER LINE
OCTAL:  MOV     PC,R4                  ;SET UP RELATIVE ADDRESS OF
        ADD     #BUF-OCTAL-2+6,R4        ;BUFFER
        JSR     PC,CNVRT1              ;PRINT ONE WORD
```

Fig. 6-2

```
        TST     (R1)+               ;NEXT ADDRESS TO BE DUMPED
        CMP     R2,R1               ;ARE WE DONE?
        BLT     FUDG                ;YES, PRINT A CR,LF
        MOVB    (R4)+,@#TPB         ;MOVE IT TO TELEPRINTER
COMP:   MOV     PC,R0               ;CALCULATE LAST BYTE ADDRESS
        ADD     #BUF-COMP+2+7,R0;   OF BUFFER
        CMP     R0,R4               ;ARE WE DONE?
        BGE     DUMP                ;NO, PRINT ANOTHER CHARACTER
        RTS     PC                  ;YES, RETURN
FUDG:   MOVB    #CR,R0              ;PUT OUT THE CR
        JSR     PC,PCHAR
        MOVB    #LF,R0              ;AND LF COMBINATION
        JSR     PC,PCHAR
        JSR     PC,PCHAR
        JMP     ADDR                ;RETURN
;
;       CONSTANTS AND DATA BUFFERS
;
FIVE:   .WORD   0
BUF:    .WORD   0
        .=.+4
        .ASCII  / /
CNT:    .WORD   0
        .END
```

Fig. 6-2   (cont.)

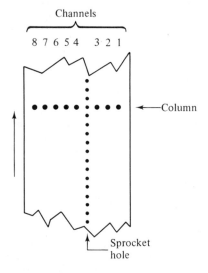

Fig. 6-3 Punched paper tape.

Bit	Name	Description
15	Error	Indicates one of three possible error conditions: no tape in the reader, reader is off-line, or reader has no power. Disables RDR ENB; causes interrupt if RDR INT ENB = 1.
14–12		Not used.
11	Busy	Indicates that a character is in the process of being read. Cleared by INIT, set by RDR ENB, cleared when character is available in buffer. Read only.
10–8		Not used.
7	Done	Character available in buffer. Cleared by INIT, set when character available, cleared by referencing reader buffer (PRB), cleared by setting RDR, ENG; causes interrupt when RDR INT ENB = 1. Read only.
6	Reader Interrupt Enable (RDR INT ENB)	Interrupts enable. Enables the error or done bits to cause an interrupt. Cleared by INIT.
5–1		Not used.
0	Reader Enable (RDR ENB)	Enables reader to fetch one character. Clears done, sets busy, and clears reader buffer (PRB). Operation of this bit is disabled if ERROR = 1; attempting to set it when ERROR = 1 will cause an immediate interrupt if RDR INT ENB = 1. Load only.

The paper tape punch unit behaves much like the teletypewriter keyboard/punch, only at a higher speed. It, too, like the paper tape reader, has an error bit which is set when the punch is "out of tape" or is "off-line."

Paper Tape Reader Buffer (PRB):

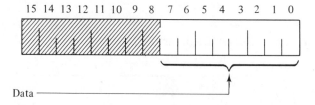

Data

Bit	Name	Description
15–8		Not used.
7–0	Data	Holds character to be read. Cleared by RDR ENB. Read only.

Note: Referencing either high byte or low byte or both bytes clears DONE. Referencing is any operation (read, load, test, compare).

Paper Tape Punch Status (PPS):

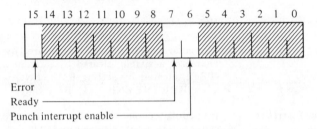

Bit	Name	Description
15	Error	Indicates one of two error conditions in punch: no tape in punch, or punch unit out of power. Causes interrupt if PUN INT ENB (or PPS) = 1.
14–8		Not used.
7	Ready	Ready to punch character. Set by INIT, cleared by loading data buffer (see note under PPB), set when punching complete. Causes interrupt when PUN INT ENB = 1. Read only.
6	Punch Interrupt Enable (PUN INT ENB)	Interrupts enable. Enables error or ready to cause interrupt. Cleared by INIT.
5–0		Not used.

Paper Tape Punch Buffer Register (PPB):

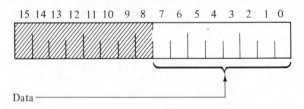

Bit	Name	Description
7-0	Data	Write only. Any instruction that could modify bits 7-0 of PPB clears Ready and initiates punching. An immediate interrupt will occur when punching is initiated if error = 1 and PUN INT ENB = 1.

6.3. INITIAL LOAD PROBLEM

When a computer is first received by the customer, its memory is usually in an unloaded state. With the exception of the hardware bootstrap option (discussed later), which may have been purchased with the system, the computer "knows" nothing, not even how to accept input. The problem is that in order to load memory with a user program, there must already be instructions in memory for loading the user program. This seeming contradiction is often compared to lifting oneself up by one's own bootstraps, and therefore gains the name of the *bootstrap* or *initial load problem.*

One possible solution to this apparent dilemma is to require the CPU to have some form of *deposit* mechanism which allows the user to deposit machine language instructions in specified memory locations. This mechanism includes a way of specifying both the data to be deposited and the address in memory of where it is to go.

The *software bootstrap* for the PDP-11 is a sequence of instructions for loading user programs. The bootstrap utilizes a special paper tape format and self-modification in order to work. The bootstrap loader source program is shown in Fig. 6-4. The starting address in the example denotes that the

```
        000001          R1=%1            ; USED FOR THE DEVICE ADDRESS
        000002          R2=%2            ; USED FOR THE LOAD ADDRESS DISPLACEMENT
        017400          LOAD=17400           ; DATA MAY BE LOADED NO LOWER
                                             ; THAN THIS
        017744          . =17744         ; START ADDRESS OF THE BOOTSTRAP LOADER
017744  016701 START:   MOV      DEVICE, R1      ; PICK UP DEVICE ADDRESS
        000026
017750  012702 LOOP:    MOV      #. -LOAD+2, R2  ; PICK UP ADDRESS DISPLACEMENT
        000352
017754  005211 ENABLE:  INC      @R1            ; ENABLE THE PAPER TAPE READER
017756  105711 WAIT:    TSTB     @R1            ; WAIT UNTIL FRAME
017760  100376          BPL      WAIT           ; IS AVAILABLE
017762  116162          MOVB     2(R1), LOAD(R2)  ; STORE FRAME READ FROM TAPE
        000002
        017400
017770  005267          INC      LOOP+2         ; INCREMENT LOAD ADDRESS
                                                ; DISPLACEMENT
        177756
017774  000765 BRNCH:   BR       LOOP           ; GO BACK AND READ MORE DATA
017776  000000 DEVICE:  0                       ; ADDR OF INPUT DEVICE
        000001          . END
```

Fig. 6-4

loader is to be loaded into memory bank zero (a 4K system). It is loaded by hand, using the deposit switch (see Appendix E), into the last 14_{10} memory words of the computer.

In operation, the bootstrap actually loads the data read into successive bytes located above the LOAD address. A sample tape input to load data starting at location 17600 and ending at 17742 would be

351
351
.
.
.
351 } leader

177 } lower byte of starting displacement − 1

.
.
. } date to be loaded

301
035
026
000 } byte equivalent to MOV DEVICE,R1

302
025
373 } byte equivalent to MOV #.LOAD+2,R2

XXX } address between 17600 and 17742 where loaded program begins

The necessity for the special leader is dictated by the need to be able to load an all-zero byte or blank tape. The bootstrap loader starts by loading the device status register address into R1 and 352_8 into R2. The next instruction indicates a read operation in the device and the next two instructions form a loop to wait for the read operation to be completed. When data are encountered, they are transferred to a location determined by the sum of the index word (177400) and the contents of R2.

Because R2 is initially 352_8, the first word is moved to location 177752, and it becomes the immediate data to set R2 in the next execution of the loop. These immediate data are then incremented by 1 and the program branches to the beginning of the loop.

The leader code, plus the increment, is equal in value to the data placed in R2 during the initialization; therefore, leader code has no effect on the loader program. Each time leader code is read, the processor executes the same loop and the program remains unmodified. The first code other than leader code, however, replaces the data to be loaded into R2 with some other value which acts as a pointer to the program starting location (loading address). Subsequent bytes are read not into the location of the immediate data but into consecutive core locations. The program will thus be read in byte by byte. The INC instruction which operates on the data for R2 puts data bytes in sequential locations and requires that the value of the leader code and the offset be 1 less than the desired value in R2.

The boot overlay code will overlay the first two instructions of the loader, because the last data byte is placed in the core location immediately preceding the loader. The first instruction is unchanged by the overlay, but the second instruction is changed to place the next byte read, jump offset, into the lower byte of the branch instruction. By changing the offset in this branch instruction, the loader can branch to the start of the loaded program or to any point within the program. The self-modification scheme used not only loads the data but also initializes the bootstrap code and forces a jump to an address 17XXX within the program just loaded.

The key requirement for a deposited bootstrap loader is that it be short in length. Clearly, as the bootstrap program becomes longer, its usefulness decreases as the frustration to deposit it in memory increases. Therefore, another technique is used to bootstrap in user programs.

The alternative technique is to add a *hardware* bootstrap loader to the CPU so that the hardware can perform the initial program load (IPL). The IPL is activated by pushing a "load" button on the CPU, causing a predefined instruction sequence to be executed. This instruction sequence includes both the command sequence for the input device and the specific memory locations into which information is to be placed.

The form that the hardware bootstrap mechanism takes varies from machine to machine. Examples include either reading a data record into memory and executing the first (or last) instruction word read in, or executing an instruction sequence held in read-only-memory (the PDP-11 uses an ROM) or on an alterable "dead-start" panel. Regardless of the method, the result is usually the same, the loading into memory of a short program sequence called the *absolute loader*.

In operation, the absolute loader is a *systems program* for reading input records that contain machine language instructions bound to absolute memory locations. Unlike the bootstrap loader, the absolute loader is capable of reading large amounts of information into various segments of memory. The format of the information is such that each record contains

1. A word count of the number of words in the record.

2. A load address where the first and subsequent words in the record are to be loaded.

3. The words to be loaded.

4. A transfer address for the absolute loader.

Both the absolute and bootstrap loaders are systems programs. Systems programs are those programs which of themselves do not produce useful results but rather aid the programmer in accomplishing his desired objective. Systems programs are written by systems programmers whose job is the support of the users of the system. Systems programs include such things as PAL-11 and EDUMP. Chapter 7 is devoted entirely to discussing the multitude of systems programs available to PDP-11 users.

6.4. TAPE AND DISK STORAGE UNITS

Many large-capacity storage devices may be connected to a small computer such as the PDP-11. Two such devices commonly found on this computer are the DECtape (capacity 147,968 words) and the DECdisk (capacity 65,536 words). Since these bulk storage devices require more elaborate programming and control, it is instructive to examine their characteristics and operation.

6.4.1. DECtape Operation

DECtapes consist of 10 tracks arranged in the format shown in Fig. 6-5. On a tape the first five tracks include the timing and mark tracks, plus three data tracks. The other five tracks are identical counterparts and serve to increase system reliability through redundant recording.

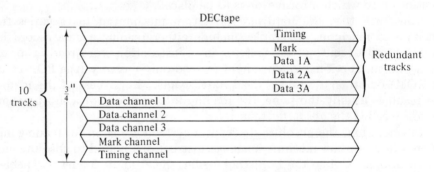

Fig. 6-5 DECtape format.

The timing and mark channels are recorded prior to all normal data reading and writing on the information channels. Information read from the mark channel is used during the reading and writing of data to indicate the beginning and ending of data blocks and to determine the functions to be performed by the system in each control mode. The data in one bit position of each track are referred to as a line or a character. Since six lines or characters make up a word, the tape can record 18-bit data words. Normally, the 2 extra bits are ignored.

A reel of DECtape is divided into three major areas: end zones, extension zones, and the information zones. The information area consists of blocks of data, containing 256 data words per block. Altogether there are 578 blocks of information (see Fig. 6-6).

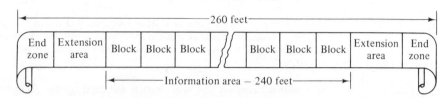

Fig. 6-6 DECtape block arrangement.

The blocks permit digital data to be partitioned into groups of words that are interrelated, at the same time reducing the amount of storage area that would be needed for addressing individual words. A simple example of such a group of words is a program. A program can be stored and retrieved from magnetic tape in a single block format because it is not necessary to be able to retrieve only a single word from the program. It is necessary, however, to be able to retrieve different programs that may not be related in any way. Thus each program can be stored in a different block on the tape.

Since DECtape is a fixed address system, the programmer need not know accurately where the tape has stopped. To locate a specific point on the tape he must only start the tape motion in the search mode. The address of the block currently passing over the head is read into the DECtape control and loaded into an interface register. Simultaneously, a flag is set and a program interrupt can occur. The program can then compare the block number found with the desired block address and tape motion continued or reversed accordingly.

All DECtape operations are handled by the controller through program instructions. The controller selects the transport, controls tape motion and direction, selects a read or write operation, and buffers data transferred.

The controller can select any one of eight commands that control operation of the DECtape system. When the system is operated on-line, these commands are used for reading or writing data on the tape and for controlling tape motion. The desired command is selected by the program, which sets or clears bits 03, 02, and 01 in the command register (TCCM) to specify an octal code representing the desired command.

The commands are as follows:

Octal Code	Mnemonic	Function
0	SAT	Stops all tape motion.
1	RNUM	Finds the mark track code that identifies the block number on the tape in the selected tape unit. Block number found is available in the data register (TCDT).
2	RDATA	Assembles one word of data at a time and transfers it directly to memory. Transfers continue until word count overflow, at which time data is read to the end of the current block and parity is checked.
3	RALL	Reads information on the tape that is not read by the RDATA function.
4	SST	Stops all tape motion in selected transport only.
5	WRTM†	Writes timing and mark track information on blank DECtape. Used for formatting new tape.
6	WDATA†	Writes data into the three data tracks. 16 bits of data are transferred directly from memory.
7	WALL†	Writes information on areas of tape not accessible to WDATA function.

†Switches on the DECtape unit itself must be set in order to prevent accidental overwriting on information already on the DECtape.

All software control of the DECtape system is performed by means of five device registers. They can be read or loaded using any PDP-11 instruction that refers to their address.

Register	Address
Control and Status Register (TCST)	777340
Command Register (TCCM)	777342
Word Count Register (TCWC)	777344
Bus Address Register (TCBA)	777346
Data Register (TCDT)	777350

The bit utilization for each of these registers is shown in Fig. 6-7.

Command register (TCCM):

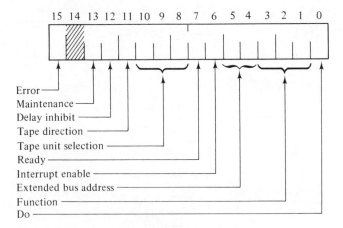

Error
Maintenance
Delay inhibit
Tape direction
Tape unit selection
Ready
Interrupt enable
Extended bus address
Function
Do

Control and status register (TCST):

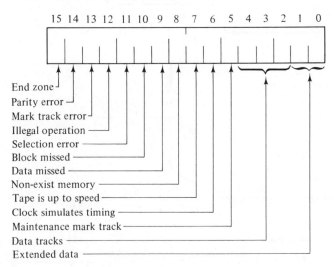

End zone
Parity error
Mark track error
Illegal operation
Selection error
Block missed
Data missed
Non-exist memory
Tape is up to speed
Clock simulates timing
Maintenance mark track
Data tracks
Extended data

Word count register (TCWC):

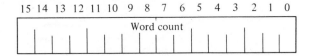

Fig. 6-7

Bus address register (TCBA):

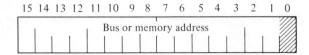

Data registers (TCDT):

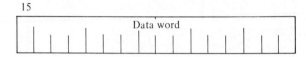

Fig. 6-7   (cont.)

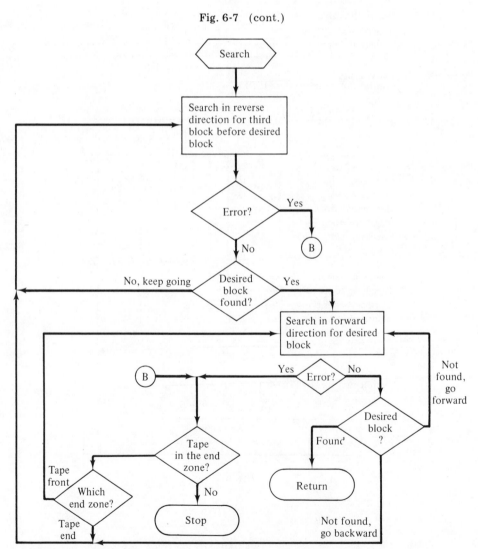

Fig. 6-8

6.4.2. Programming Examples

Because DECtapes are organized like disks, they are programmed in much the same fashion. Thus, before one can write in a specified block, the block must be located. A typical method to locate a block is to initiate tape motion and then search for the desired block in either the forward or reverse direction. The search consists of examining each block number as it is read and comparing it to the block number being sought. As soon as a match occurs, reading or writing to the located block may begin.

Although this procedure is relatively simple, several DECtape characteristics must be taken into consideration. First, before DECtapes can be read or written, they must be "up to speed." Thus it takes some time and hence some tape passed over the tape heads before the first block number will actually be read. Second, while waiting for a block number to read after start-up, the tape may be repositioned in the end zone. This error condition requires the tape motion to be reversed so that the tape may be searched in the opposite direction. Third, and finally, having found the desired block, reading or writing must be initiated shortly thereafter, or else the transfer will be unsuccessful and a tape error condition raised.

With these points in mind, it is possible to flowchart and code the search procedure as shown in Fig. 6-8. The routine to find a specified block (1) expects the block number wanted to be legitimate and in R0, and (2) finds the block while searching in the forward direction; see Fig. 6-9.

```
;DECTAPE SEARCH ROUTINE
;R0 CONTAINS DESIRED BLOCK NUMBER
;BLOCK FOUND IN FORWARD DIRECTION


        TCST=177340            ;CONTROL/STATUS REGISTER
        TCCM=TCST+2            ;COMMAND REGISTER
        TCDT=TCST+10          ;DATA REGISTER


SEARCH: MOV     R0,BWANT      ;SAVE BLOCK NUMBER
        SUB     #3,BWANT      ;OFFSET TO DESIRED BLOCK
        MOV     #4003,TCCM    ;READ BLOCK NUMBERS IN REVERSE DIR.
LOOP1:  BIT     #100200,TCCM  ;CHECK READY AND ERROR BITS
        BEQ     LOOP1         ;WAIT FOR READY
        BMI     ERROR         ;FOUND AN ERROR?
        SUB     TCDT,BWANT    ;CHECK BLOCK FOUND
        BLT     SEARCH        ;KEEP SEARCHING BACKWARDS
FORWRD: MOV     R0,BWANT      ;SAVE BLOCK NUMBER
        MOV     #3,TCCM       ;READ BLOCK NUMBERS IN FORWARD DIR.
LOOP2:  BIT     #100200,TCCM  ;CHECK READY AND ERROR BITS
        BEQ     LOOP2         ;WAIT FOR READY
        BMI     ERROR         ;HAVE AN ERROR?
        SUB     TCDT,BWANT    ;CHECK BLOCK FOUND
        BGT     FORWRD        ;BLOCK NUMBER TOO SMALL
        BLT     SEARCH        ;BLOCK NUMBER TOO BIG
        RTS     PC            ;RETURN WHEN BLOCK FOUND
ERROR:  TST     TCST          ;END ZONE ERROR?
        BMI     LOOP2         ;IF SO BRANCH
        HALT                  ;OTHERWISE HALT ON ERROR
```

Fig. 6-9

```
LOOP3:  BIT     #4000,TCCM      ; TEST DIRECTION
        BNE     FORWRD          ; IF REVERSE, SEARCH FORWARD
        BR      SEARCH          ; IF FORWARD, SEARCH REVERSE
BWANT:  0                       ; BLOCK NUMBER
```

Fig. 6-9   (cont.)

When a specified block has been searched for and found, the next thing to do is to transfer information from or to it. The routine shown in Fig. 6-10 uses the SEARCH subroutine to read 100 words from block 50 on DECtape unit 0. The program calls SEARCH, sets up the word count and buffer address, and then waits for the read to be completed. The reader should note that although blocks contain 256 data words, any number of words (up to 256) may be specified in the transfer operation.

```
        ; ROUTINE TO READ 100 WORDS FROM
        ; BLOCK 50, DECTAPE UNIT 0

        R0=%0                   ; REGISTER ZERO
        SP=%6                   ; STACK REGISTER
        PC=%7                   ; PROGRAM COUNTER
        TCCM=177342             ; COMMAND REGISTER
        TCWC=TCCM+2             ; WORD COUNT REGISTER
        TCBA=TCCM+4             ; BUS ADDRESS REGISTER

START:  MOV     PC,SP           ; INITIALIZE STACK
        TST     -(SP)           ;   POINTER
        MOV     #50,R0          ; BLOCK 50 TO BE
        JSR     PC,SEARCH       ;   SEARCHED FOR
        MOV     #-100,TCWC      ; COMPLEMENT OF WORD COUNT
        MOV     #BUFFER,TCBA    ; BUFFER ADDRESS
        MOV     #15,TCCM        ; READ DATA FORWARD DIRECTION
LOOP:   BIT     #100200,TCCM    ; CHECK ERROR AND READY
        BEQ     LOOP            ; WAIT FOR READY AND NO ERROR
        BMI     ERR             ; BRANCH ON ERROR



ERR:    HALT                    ; HALT ON ERROR
BUFFR:  .=.+200                 ; SAVE ROOM FOR BUFFER
        .END    START           ; END OF ASSEMBLY
```

Fig. 6-10

6.4.3. Disk Operation

Because of the differing requirements for disk storage, many storage alternatives are available to the small computer user. The choice of disk systems spans the range from fast access and fast storage to large storage and medium-access devices. For example, *fixed-head* disk systems are suited for swapping-type devices (e.g., those where the contents of memory and disk must be rapidly exchanged) and scientific applications where fast access and fast transfer are important. The *moving-head* systems are ideal for large storage requirements where fast access times are less vital.

Before discussing the programming of the disk devices, it is important to understand their basic operation. Generally, all disk devices are organized around flat magnetic surfaces, called *platters*, which look like pancakes. The surface is divided into concentric rings called *tracks* with each track subdivided into *sectors*. The sector is the smallest addressable unit and generally is capable of storing many computer words (e.g., 32 words per sector). Figure 6-11 shows such a disk organization.

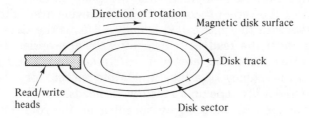

Fig. 6-11 Disk organization.

If the disk platter can be removed from the disk drive mechanism, and another platter used in its place, the removable surface becomes a *disk pack*. Disk packs may consist of one or more platters, with multiple surfaces being stacked vertically on the same shaft, as shown in Fig. 6-12. By logically grouping all the tracks at the same radius on each surface into a *cylinder*, more information is accessible as a unit, thereby effectively increasing the density of the system. However, since disk pack devices are manipulated in a similar fashion to simpler one-surface devices, it is sufficient to consider only the programming of devices typified by Fig. 6-11.

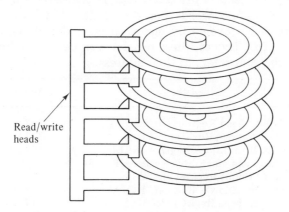

Fig. 6-12 Multisurface disk pack.

Reading or writing disk tracks and sectors can be accomplished in one of two ways. First, there can be one read/write head, which must be positioned over one track or another; this is the moving-head system, mentioned earlier. Second, there can be one read/write head per track, referred to earlier as a fixed-head disk system. The advantage of the fixed-head system is that there is no mechanical *seek time* associated with the physical positioning of the head over the appropriate track. Instead, there is a small electronic switching time required to select the appropriate head. The fixed-head system thus requires less time before the accessing of data, but there is a greater cost associated with it because more read/write heads are needed.

Regardless of the type of system, fixed or moving head, there is another delay associated with the disk called *latency*. This is the time it takes for a sector to pass under the read/write head after the appropriate head has been selected. Another name for latency is *rotational delay*, and in a sense it corresponds to the latency of a tape unit while waiting for a particular tape block to come under the tape unit's read/write heads.

Latency time can be reduced by speeding up the rotation of the disk. This also has the effect of passing more information by the read/write head in a given amount of time, thereby increasing the number of characters per second, or *transfer rate* of the device itself. Alternatively, the transfer rate may be increased by just putting more information on a track (e.g., increasing the *density* of information). All these factors, then, density, transfer rate, latency, seek time, fixed/moving head, number of disk surfaces, and so on, must be considered when selecting the appropriate disk system for a particular problem.

6.4.4 Programming a DECdisk

For simplicity we shall consider a fixed-head DECdisk which has 32 words per sector, 64 sectors per track, and 32 tracks per surface, providing a total capacity of 65,536 words per disk unit. Software control of this DECdisk system is performed by means of eight device registers. Like the registers of other I/O devices, these registers can be read or loaded using any PDP-11 instruction that refers to their address:

Register	Address
Look Ahead Register (RCLA)	777440
Disk Address Register (RCDA)	777442
Disk Error Status Register (RCER)	777444
Command and Status Register (RCCS)	777446
Word Count Register (RCWC)	777450
Current Address Register (RCCA)	777452
Maintenance Register (RCMN)	777454
Data Buffer Register (RCDB)	777456

The bit utilizations for these registers are shown in Fig. 6-13.

Look ahead register (RCLA):

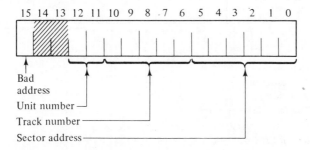

Disk address register (RCDA):

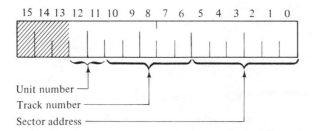

Disk error status register (RCER):

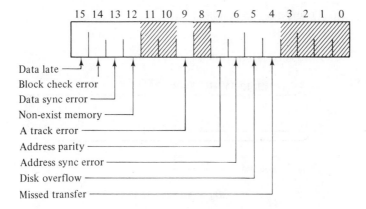

Fig. 6-13

Disk control and status register (RCCS):

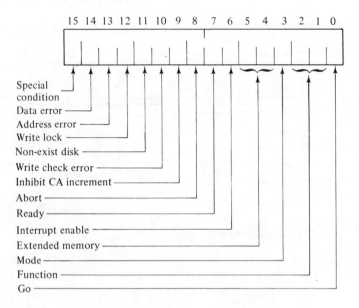

Word count register (RCWC):

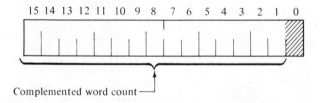

Current address register (RCCA):

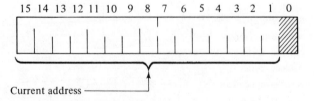

Fig. 6-13 (cont.)

Maintenance register (RCMN):

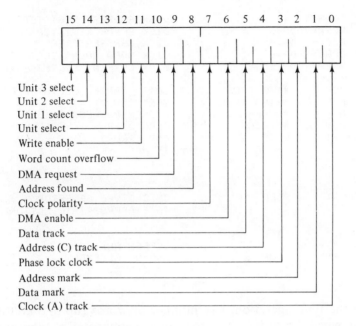

Data buffer register (RCDB):

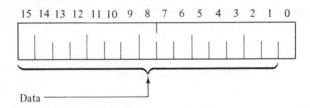

Fig. 6-13   (cont.)

Although there are more registers associated with the disk than with the tape unit, programming is easier because the search for a particular sector does not require us to start, stop, or reverse the direction of the disk. Instead, the disk rotates at a constant speed, and all that is necessary is for us to set up the sector address, word count, and buffer address and then wait for the transfer to occur. This sequence of operations can be programmed as shown in Fig. 6-14.

```
;PROGRAM TO READ 100 WORDS FROM
;DISK UNIT 0, TRACK 1, SECTOR 77

        RCDA=177442            ;DISK ADDRESS REGISTER
        RCER=RCDA+2            ;DISK ERROR REGISTER
        RCCS=RCDA+4            ;DISK CSR REGISTER
        RCWC=RCDA+6            ;DICK WORD COUNT REGISTER
        RCCA=RCDA+10           ;DICK CURRENT ADDRESS REGISTER

START:  MOV     #177,RCDA     ;UNIT, TRACK, SECTOR ADDRESS
        MOV     #-100,RCWA     ;WORD COUNT
        MOV     #BUFFR,RCCA    ;BUFFER ADDRESS
        MOV     #5,RCCS        ;READ DISK
        TST     RCCS           ;ANY ERROR?
        BMI     ERROR          ;IF NEG, YES
        .
        .
        .
ERROR:  TST     RCER           ;CHECK TYPE OF ERROR
        .                      ;TAKE APPROPRIATE ACTION
        .
        .
BUFFR:  .=.+200                ;BUFFER AREA
        .END    START          ;END OF ASSEMBLY
```

Fig. 6-14

As for the tape operation, any number of words (up to 65,536) may be transferred, since the disk address register is incremented automatically after each sector is transferred. This process continues both across tracks and even across disk units. Alternatively, if only a portion of the sector (less than 32 words) is desired, the word count register is set accordingly, and only that number of words is transferred to the buffer area.

6.5. PRIORITY INTERRUPT PROGRAMMING

The running time of programs using input and output routines is primarily made up of the time spent waiting for an I/O device to accept or transmit information. Specifically, this time is spent in testing or "polling" the status register of a device and waiting in a loop for a done condition:

```
TEST:   TSTB    TKS            ;TEST CSR
        BPL     TEST           ;WAIT FOR DONE
```

Such waiting loops waste a large amount of computer time. In those cases where the computer can be doing something else while waiting, the loops may be eliminated and useful routines included to take advantage of the waiting time. This sharing of a computer between two routines or tasks is accomplished through a program interrupt facility, which is standard on all PDP-11 series computers.

The value of an interrupt facility lies in the ability of the processor to respond automatically to conditions outside the system, or in the processor itself. Unusual conditions occurring at unknown times (such as I/O completion) can generate an interrupt and force the computer to execute an interrupt routine in response to the interrupting action. Thus the user need not poll or test for the occurrence of a condition after the execution of each instruction, but he may write interrupt routines in case they occur.

Basically, an interrupt is a subroutine jump executed by the hardware, as opposed to one written as an explicit software instruction. The interrupt occurs after the execution of an instruction (and before the I-fetch of the next instruction) and must inform the system of the cause of the interrupt. For example, when an interrupt occurs on some machines, an interrupt bit is set in an interrupt status register, indicating what condition raised the interrupt. At the same time, the CPU takes the address of the next instruction from a fixed interrupt location (possibly memory location zero) and begins execution of the interrupt analysis routine at that location.

6.5.1. Interrupt Linkages

Like subroutines, interrupts have linkage information so that a return to the interrupted program can be made. More information is actually necessary for an interrupt transfer than a subroutine transfer because of the random nature of interrupts. The complete machine state of the program immediately prior to the occurrence of the interrupt must be preserved in order to return to the program without any noticeable effects (i.e., was the previous operation zero or negative?). In this way the interrupt will be "invisible" to the interrupted program, since no information, only time, will be lost between the time the running program is interrupted and the time its execution is resumed.

6.5.2. Machine State During Interrupt

The complete machine state of the program immediately prior to the occurrence of the interrupt is generally held in a *processor status word (PSW)*. On computers with sufficiently long memory words, the PSW includes both the condition codes and the program counter. On minicomputers such as the PDP-11, it is necessary to subdivide the PSW into two or more words in order to maintain the *processor status (PS)* and the program counter (PC).

Using one or several words, the technique for handling the interrupt is to replace the current PSW with the interrupt PSW, saving the current PSW somewhere in memory. Diagrammatically this process is depicted in Fig. 6-15. The figure shows that two memory locations are required for the interrupt process, plus a register to hold the current PSW.

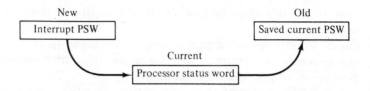

Fig. 6-15 Swapping processor status.

6.5.3. Stacking of Interrupts

One problem with this scheme is that all interrupts use the same swapping technique. Thus, should a second interrupt occur during the execution of the routine to service the first interrupt, the old PSW for the first interrupt will be overwritten and lost. To prevent this, it is necessary to *disable* further interrupts while the interrupt is being serviced. By allocating a bit in the PSW for interrupts enabled/disabled, it is a simple matter to have this bit on in the old PSW and off in the new PSW. Thus when the current PSW becomes the new PSW, interrupts are disabled. When a *return from interrupt (RTI)* occurs, the current PSW becomes the old or saved PSW and interrupts are once more enabled.

During the time in which interrupts are disabled, it is conceivable that other I/O conditions which would ordinarily cause an interrupt may occur. Instead of being allowed to cause an interrupt, these conditions are noted and held in the interrupt status register *(ISR)*. Consequently, when interrupts are enabled, they can cause an interrupt; this guarantees their eventual service.

The interrupt status register serves many purposes. First, it indicates which device has raised an interrupt condition. Second, it saves interruptable conditions during the time that interrupts are disabled. And third, it allows the programmer flexibility in deciding what device to service next after an interrupt has been raised. In particular, this flexibility allows the programmer to decide on the relative priorities of the various interrupts. In this way, under programmer control, when several interrupts occur simultaneously, the most critical interrupt may be serviced first.

Allowing the programmer to assign the priorities can lead to problems, however. For example, if a high-priority interrupt is raised when interrupts are disabled, there is no way the interrupt can be serviced until the interrupt analysis program is once again executed. Thus it becomes necessary to re-enable the interrupt mechanism during interrupt processing. To do so requires stacking the interrupt return information (the old PSW) and setting the interrupt enable bit. However, one problem connected with the priority of interrupting devices still remains.

6.5.4. Priority Interrupts

Once the interrupt enable bit is set, any device may interrupt. The program to analyze interrupts must therefore examine all the bits in the interrupt status register to choose the highest-priority interrupt to process. Clearly, all that is needed is to allow only higher-priority routines to cause new interrupts, since interrupts at the same or lower levels can wait to be serviced. Thus for programmer convenience, the priority can be built into the hardware and a *priority interrupt* scheme can assign devices to groups within a given priority level. Part of the PSW is used to hold the current priority level, and the loading of the PSW determines the value of the priority level.

Typical PSW and ISR words are shown in Fig. 6-16. These words could serve as the basis for a sophisticated interrupt scheme except for one thing. Although only higher-level priority interrupts are allowed to cause an interrupt, it still is the programmer's job to determine who caused the interrupt. A better scheme would be to let each priority group take its PSW from a different memory location. Thus when an interrupt occurred, it would be known a priori that only certain devices could have caused the interrupt.

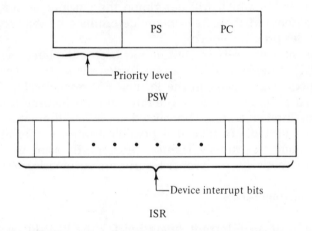

Fig. 6-16 Processor and interrupt status words.

6.5.5. Automatic Priority Interrupts

Carrying this idea to its logical conclusion, it should be possible for *each* device to have its own PSW. Thus, given 100 devices, there will be 100 new PSWs (and 100 old PSWs) pointing to 100 potentially different interrupt

service routines. Since each interrupt is uniquely identified, there is no need
to have an interrupt status register, and hence no interrupt analysis routine
is needed. The resultant savings in time and program space is absorbed, however, by the large number of PSW words that must be reserved in memory.

A modified version of this *automatic priority interrupt scheme* can be
found in the PDP-11. This computer uses two words, the processor status
word and the program counter, to hold all the machine state information (see
Fig. 3-1). Upon interrupt, the contents of the PC and the PS are automatically pushed onto the system stack maintained by the SP (register 6). The
effect is the same as if

```
MOV     PS,-(SP)        ; PUSH PROCESSOR STATUS
MOV     PC,-(SP)        ; AND PROGRAM COUNTER
```

had been executed.

The new contents of the PC and the PS are loaded from two preassigned
consecutive memory locations called an *interrupt vector*. The actual locations are chosen by the device interface designer and are located in low
memory addresses. The first word contains the interrupt service routine
address (the address of the new program sequence), and the second word
contains the new PS, which will determine the machine status and priority
level. The contents of these vectors are determined by the programmer and
may be set under program control.

After the interrupt service routine has been completed, an RTI (return
from interrupt) is performed. The two top words of the stack are automatically "popped" and placed in the PC and PS, respectively, thus resuming
the interrupted program. Because the interrupt mechanism utilizes the stack
automatically, interrupts may be nested in much the same manner that
subroutines are nested. In fact, it is possible to nest any arbitrary mixture
of subroutines and interrupts without confusion. By using the RTI and RTS
instructions, respectively, the proper returns are automatic.

6.5.6. Reader Interrupt Service

An example of an interrupt operation for the PDP-11 can be found in
the routine to read a block of characters from the paper tape reader to a
buffer as shown in Fig. 6-17. This code is written in a PIC format and includes setting up the interrupt vector (memory location 70) for the paper
tape reader. There are two separate routines. The first, beginning at label
INIT, initializes the buffer address pointer and word count in the interrupt
routines; then calculates the relocation factor from the offset PRSER-X-2
as follows:

If PC_0 is the PC that was assumed for the program when load at 0,
and if PC_n is the current real PC, the calculation is

$$PRSER - X - 2 + PC_n = PRSER - PC_0 + PC_n$$
$$= PRSER + (PC_n - PC_0)$$

since $(X + 2) = PC_0$. As a result, the relocation factor, $PC_n - PC_0$, is added to the assembled value of PRSER to produce the relocated value of PRSER.

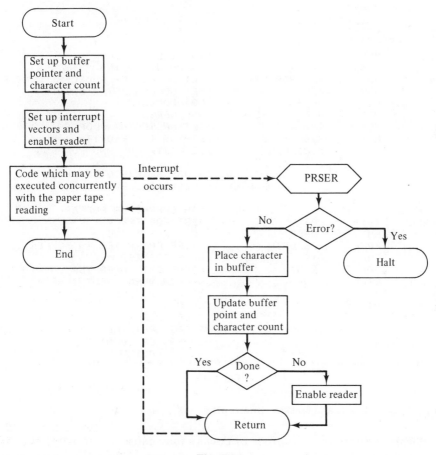

Fig. 6-17

Then it establishes the priority level for the reader and sets it to interrupt after a character has been read. This frees up the CPU so that other code may be executed while the buffer is being filled.

The second routine, the paper tape interrupt service routine, PRSER, is activated each time a character is received. Once activated, the routine stores the character in the buffer, updates the buffer pointer and word count, and resets the interrupt enable bit if more characters are to be read. The logical flow, then, of these two routines looks as shown in Fig. 6-17, and the code is as given in Fig. 6-18.

```
                    ; INTERRUPT DRIVEN ROUTINE TO
                    ; INPUT CHARACTERS FROM PAPER
                    ; TAPE READER

                    R0=%0                         ; DEFINE REGISTERS
                    SP=%6
                    PC=%7
                    PRS=177550                    ; DEFINE DEVICE
                    PRB=PRS+2                     ; REGISTERS

INIT:     MOV       PC, SP                        ; INITIALIZE STACK
          TST       -(SP)                         ; TO POINT TO INIT
          MOV       #BUFADR, PTR                  ; SET UP BUFFER ADDRESS POINTER
          MOV       #100, CRCNT                   ; SET UP CHARACTER COUNT
X:        MOV       PC, R0                        ; R0=ADDR(X+2)
          ADD       #PRSER-X-2, R0                ; ADD OFFSET
          MOV       R0, @#70                      ; SET UP VECTOR ADDRESS
          MOV       #200, @#72                    ; STATUS TO PRIORITY 4
          MOV       #101, PRS                     ; SET INTR ENB AND RDR ENB
          .
          .                     CODE WHICH MAY BE EXECUTED WHILE
          .                     BUFFER IS BEING FILLED
          .
BUFADR:   . =. +100                               ; 100 CHARACTER BUFFER
PRSER:    TST       PRS                           ; TEST FOR ERROR
          BMI       ERROR                         ; DO ERROR THING
          MOVB      PRB, @PTR                     ; STORE CHARACTER IN BUFFER
          INC       PTR                           ; BUMP POINTER
          DEC       CRCNT                         ; DECREMENT CHARACTER COUNT
          BEQ       DONE                          ; BRANCH WHEN INPUT DONE
          INC       PRS                           ; START UP READER
DONE:     RTI                                     ; RETURN
ERROR:    HALT                                    ; STOP ON ERROR
PTR:      0                                       ; BUFFER POINTER
CRCNT:    0                                       ; CHARACTER COUNTER
          . END     INIT                          ; END OF ASSEMBLY
```

Fig. 6-18

6.5.7. Priority Levels and Masking Interrupts

Within a group, any number of devices may cause an interrupt at a given priority level. Since it is conceivable that at any given time a programmer may wish to ignore some of the devices, the hardware usually includes a mechanism to mask interrupts from selected devices.

The PDP-11 uses a simple mechanism to mask device interrupts, by allowing the programmer to clear the interrupt enable bit in the device control and status register. Actually, the interrupt bit is automatically cleared each time the system is initialized (by pushing the START key or executing the RESET instruction) and must be set under program control. However, once set, the bit stays set until cleared.

Another approach to this problem is to use a *mask register*. This register contains a bit for each interruptable group (or bit in the ISR if one exists), and the hardware uses the mask bits by ANDing them to the interrupt bits. Only if the result is a 1 is the interrupt allowed to occur. In effect, the mask *disarms* certain specified interrupts. Still, the mask only disarms interrupts within a group and does not set up any priorities between interrupts or groups.

The need for priorities is demonstrated by the following example program. This program utilizes the teleprinter and the 60-cycle clock on the PDP-11. After being loaded and started, the program types out

```
WHAT TIME IS IT?
```

to which the user responds with a four-digit number. Thereafter, the program, utilizing clock interrupts every 1/60 of a second, keeps track of the time, responding with

```
AT THE BELL THE TIME WILL BE:   XX:XX:XX
```

every time a keyboard character is struck.

All three devices (keyboard, printer, and clock) are interrupt-driven. Thus while the printer is interrupting to fill its buffer, the clock can be interrupting to tick off another 1/60 of a second. However, the priority of the clock must be greater than that of the printer if ticks are not to be lost. (That this loss of ticks can actually occur can be demonstrated by changing the priority levels set near label NOFIX in the program.)

Priority level is, however, not simply a function of the device. Although each group or device has its own priority level, the running program also has a level. Thus each interrupt that causes an interrupt to occur can raise, lower, or maintain the current priority level of the running program. As a result, if an interrupt occurs at level 7, say, and the interrupt routine does not set the new level at 7, it is quite possible for the higher-level interrupt service routine to be constantly interrupted by lower-level devices. With this in mind, it can be seen that the processor priority level as maintained in the PS word acts as an I/O device interrupt mask.

The various vector addresses and priority levels for the teletype, high-speed reader/punch, and clock on the PDP-11 are as follows:

Device	Vector Address	Priority
Teletype keyboard	60	4
Teletype printer	64	4
High-speed reader	70	4
High-speed punch	74	4
Line clock	100	6

The example in Fig. 6-19 demonstrates the use of priority levels. In addition, it uses recursive programming, and it freely intermixes subroutine stacking with interrupt processing. It is therefore far from a trivial example of the power and flexibility of an interrupt facility on a small computer. A logical flow is included because it provides an overall picture of what the program does. Of particular interest is the clock interrupt routine, which calls on the clock increment subroutine in a recursive fashion.

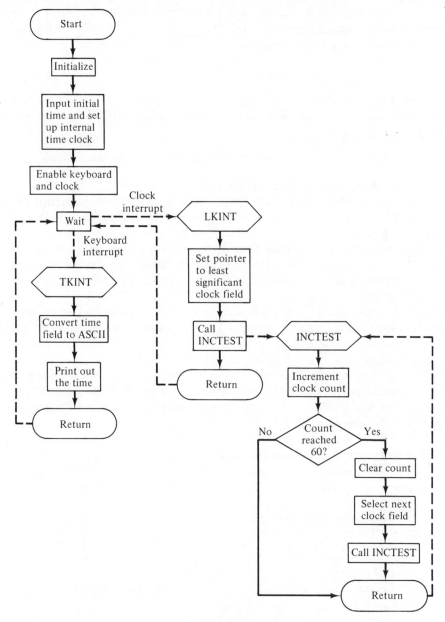

Fig. 6-19

```
                R0=%0
                R1=%1
                R2=%2
                R3=%3
                R4=%4
                SP=%6
                PC=%7
                ;
                TKCSR=177560
                TKDBR=177562
                TPCSR=177564
                TPDBR=177566
                LKCSR=177546
                ;
                .=1000
BEGIN:   MOV      #500,SP         ; INITIALIZE SP
         MOV      #M1,R2          ; ASK FOR
         MOV      #EM1,R3         ; THE TIME
         JSR      PC,DPR1         ; PRINT IT OUT
         MOV      #TIME,R2        ; ADDR OF TIME FIELD
         MOV      #4,R1           ; COUNT FOUR CHAR
         MOV      R2,R3           ; PRINT ADDRESSES
NEXTD:   INC      TKCSR           ; READ THE TIME
         TSTB     TKCSR           ; TEST FOR A CHARACTER
         BPL      -4              ; WAIT
         MOVB     TKDBR,(R2)      ; PUT IT IN TIME FIELD
         JSR      PC,DPR1         ; PRINT IT
         TSTB     (R3)+           ; NEXT BYTE
         DEC      R1              ; DECREASE COUNT
         BNE      NEXTD           ; KEEP GOING
         MOVB     TIME+1,HOURS    ; LSD OF HOURS
         BIC      #177700,HOURS   ; CLEAR PARITY
         SUB      #60,HOURS       ; CONVERT TO OCTAL
         BIC      #177700,TIME    ; CLEAR PARITY
NEXT:    CMPB     TIME,#61        ; ANY TENS?
         BLT      AROUND          ; NO
         ADD      #12,HOURS       ; INCREASE VALUE
         SUB      #1,TIME         ; DEC TENS COUNT
         BR       NEXT            ; ANYMORE?
AROUND:  MOVB     TIME+3,MIN      ; GET MINUTES LSD
         BIC      #177700,MIN     ; CLEAR PARITY
         SUB      #60,MIN         ; CONVERT TO OCTAL
         MOVB     TIME+2,R0       ; MUST CORRECT TENS
         BIC      #177700,R0      ; REMOVE PARITY
         MOV      #12,R1          ; ADD 10 DEC
         SUB      #61,R0          ; TEST FOR A ONE
         BMI      NOFIX           ; NO TENS
         BEQ      ADD             ; ONE TEN
MORE:    ADD      #12,R1          ; TRY AGAIN
         DEC      R0              ; COUNT THE TENS
         BNE      MORE            ; MORE?
ADD:     ADD      R1,MIN          ; ADD IN # OF TENS
NOFIX:   MOV      #300,62         ; LEVEL 4 INTERRUPT
         MOV      #TKINT,60       ; FOR THE TTY KBD
         MOV      #340,102        ; LEVEL 7 INTERRUPT
         MOV      #LKINT,100      ; FOR THE CLOCK
         MOV      #101,TKCSR      ; INIT KBD
         MOV      #100,LKCSR      ; AND CLOCK
AGAIN:   WAIT                     ; NOTHING TO DO
         BR       AGAIN           ; HANG IN THERE
```

Fig. 6-19 (cont.)

```
LKINT:    MOV      #MSEC,R0          ; ADDRESS OF LS FIELD
          JSR      PC,INCTEST        ; RECURSIVE CALL
          RTI                        ; CLOCK UPDATED
INCTEST:  INC      (R0)              ; ADD ONE
          CMP      (R0),#60.         ; REACHED LIMIT?
          BNE      RETURN            ; NO
          CLR      (R0)              ; RESET FIELD
          TST      -(R0)             ; ADDR OF NEXT FIELD
          JSR      PC,INCTEST        ; CALL ME AGAIN
RETURN:   RTS      PC                ; RETURN HOME
TKINT:    MOV      #M2,R2            ; PRINT OUT
          MOV      #EM2,R3           ; THE TIME
          JSR      PC,DPR1           ; MESSAGE
          MOV      #3,R3             ; NUMBER OF FIELDS
          MOV      #OUT,R2           ; OUTPUT AREA
          MOV      #HOURS,R4         ; FIRST FIELD ADDR
CNVRT:    CLR      R0                ; INITIALIZE
          MOV      (R4)+,R1          ; FIRST VALUE
LOOP:     CMP      R1,#12            ; ANY TENS?
          BLT      ADDUP             ; NO
          INC      R0                ; YES, COUNT
          SUB      #12,R1            ; DEC TENS
          BR       LOOP              ; DO IT AGAIN
ADDUP:    ADD      #60,R0            ; TENS IN ASCII
          MOVB     R0,(R2)+          ; STORE IT
          ADD      #60,R1            ; UNITS IN ASCII
          MOVB     R1,(R2)+          ; STORE IT
          TSTB     (R2)+             ; SKIP :
          DEC      R3                ; LOOP COUNT
          BNE      CNVRT             ; DO IT THREE TIMES
          MOV      #OUT,R2           ; READY
          MOV      #BELL,R3          ; TO PRINT
          MOV      #101,TKCSR        ; RDR ENB
          TST      TKDBR             ; CLEAR DONE BIT
          JSR      PC,DPR1           ; YES
          RTI                        ; DONE AT LAST
DPR1:     CMP      R2,R3             ; ARE WE DONE?
          BGT      DPR2              ; YES
          TSTB     TPCSR             ; READY TO PRINT?
          BPL      .-4               ; NO
          MOVB     (R2)+,TPDBR       ; PUT IN BUFFER
          BR       DPR1              ; NEXT CHARACTER
DPR2:     RTS      PC                ; RETURN
M1:       .BYTE    15,12             ; CR AND LF
          .ASCII   /WHAT TIME IS IT?/
EM1:      .BYTE    '
          .EVEN
TIME:     .BYTE    0,0,0,0           ; FOUR CHAR TIME
OUT:      .BYTE    0,0,':,0,0,':,0,0
BELL:     .BYTE    7                 ; STRIKE THE GONG
          .EVEN
HOURS:    .WORD    0
MIN:      .WORD    0
SEC:      .WORD    0
MSEC:     .WORD    0
M2:       .BYTE    15,12
          .ASCII   /AT THE BELL THE TIME WILL BE:/
EM2:      .BYTE    '
          .END     BEGIN
```

Fig. 6-19 (cont.)

To understand how the increment clock routine works, it is necessary to examine the stack after each call. Just after the line labeled LKINT is executed, the symbolic contents of the stack (and RØ) will be

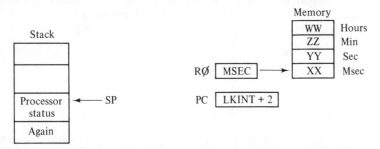

Now, when the subroutine INCTEST is called, the picture changes to

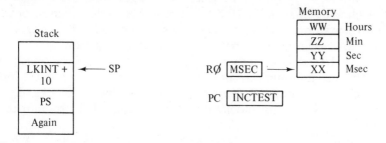

If the value in location MSEC is less than 59, it will be incremented by 1, a return made from the subroutine (e.g., the stack is popped) followed by a return from the interrupt routine (popping off the PC and PS from the stack); and the program will once again wait for an interrupt.

Suppose, however, that the value in location MSEC equals 59. In this case the increment subroutine will now set MSEC = 0, advance the pointer in R0 to point to the location SEC, and call the subroutines INCTEST recursively. At this point the picture looks as follows:

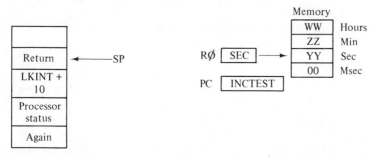

Again the value at the location pointed to by RØ is checked to see if it is 59. If it is, it is zeroed, RØ is advanced to point to the next most significant field, and the routine INCTEST is once again called recursively.

Alternatively, if the value pointed to by R∅ is less than 59, we have the case discussed previously, where the value pointed to by R0 is incremented and a subroutine return is made. Since the return causes the instruction following the subroutine call to be executed and this instruction is a return from subroutine, the stack is popped twice (or more) until the return from interrupt occurs, at which point the program waits for a new interrupt to occur. The actual unwinding of the recursive calls becomes quite simple, since it only serves to restore the stack.

6.6. BUFFERING AND BLOCKING

Although basic I/O units (teleprinter and paper tape reader/punch) operate on characters, characters per se are not exactly what the programmer wishes to input or output. Rather, I/O programming is concerned with strings of characters such as 10-digit numbers, people's names, octal representations of memory words, or lines of assembly code. In other words, the I/O consists of *blocks* of data that have a logical connection.

Since the I/O device does not perform I/O in a block fashion, it is generally the programmer's responsibility to *block* characters on input and *deblock* them on output. *Buffers*, which are contiguous blocks of memory, act as repositories for the blocks of data and allow the program to stream

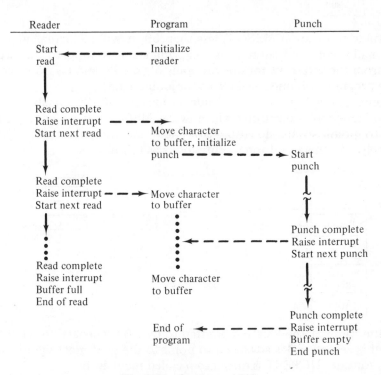

Fig. 6-20 Overlapped I/O.

data to or from an I/O unit at a rate consistent with the I/O device. Buffers are of particular use between two I/O devices with dissimilar I/O rates. For example, if the high-speed paper tape reader is six times faster than the high-speed paper tape punch, a buffer can be used to allow simultaneous input and output, provided, of course, that a full buffer terminates input and an empty buffer terminates output.

The overlap of input and output on the high-speed reader punch is shown in Fig. 6-20. Each device is running in interrupt mode at its maximum rate. Because the reader has a higher I/O transfer rate, it will finish first, followed by the punch routine emptying the buffer, and then by termination of the program.

6.6.1. Overlap of Computation and I/O Processing

Another use of buffers and blocking can be found in the overlap of computation and I/O processing. For this situation *double buffering* is used, so that while one buffer is being filled (or emptied), a second buffer is available to the running program. Actually, the number of buffers may be more than two, depending upon their rate of utilization by the program and the I/O device and upon the size of the buffers. In a *balanced system*, the buffer size and number is adjusted so that computation and I/O processing are 100 percent overlapped. When the computation is less than 100 percent, the system is said to be *I/O bound*. Correspondingly, when the system is *computation bound*, the I/O utilization is less than 100 percent.

Whether a system is one way or another depends on many things, including the computer configuration, economic considerations, system load, and so on. These considerations fall into the province of the systems programmer, who is concerned with operating systems design and performance.

6.7. INPUT/OUTPUT PROGRAMMING SYSTEMS

In order to facilitate effective utilization of I/O devices and to assist the user in writing his I/O code, most computer manufacturers provide their computer users with an *input/output programming system (IOPS)*. Such a system

1. Frees the programmer from the details of dealing directly with I/O devices.

2. Provides better I/O organization and service.

3. Facilitates I/O programming through simple assembly language macros.[†]

4. Provides conformity across various operating enviroments.

[†]Macros are discussed in Chapter 7.

In addition, the programmer can use an I/O programming system to allow

1. Asynchronous I/O service.

2. Concurrent (overlapped) I/O operation.

3. Device-independent programming.

4. Blocking and buffering.

I/O programming system macros fall into three categories. The first category includes the initializing commands. These commands initialize both the IOPS tables and the device interrupts, and assign unit numbers to system devices. In many respects these commands are similar to the assignment and open commands in FORTRAN, which relate a unit number to a device and open a file on the specified device.

The second category of commands includes all the actual data transfers, such as READ and WRITE. Finally, the third category includes the control commands, such as EOF, WAIT, and RESTART. The latter two categories include macro statements, which make reference to I/O buffers. I/O buffers are of the form

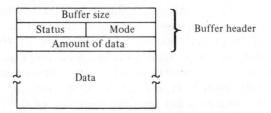

The size of the buffer is of interest to IOPS in that it cannot allow data to overflow the buffer. On the other hand, the amount of data is of concern to the programmer, since it tells him how much of the buffer is filled. For both IOPS and the programmer, the mode and status bits are necessary in order to describe the buffer contents (e.g., ASCII, binary, formatted, unformatted, packed, unpacked) and to indicate the status of the I/O operation (e.g., complete, EOF, checksum error, truncation upon buffer overflow).

6.7.1. Example

An example of the use of IOPS to provide a simple input–process–output sequence would include

1. The definition of a buffer.

2. The initialization of the system.

3. A read into the buffer.

4. A wait for the read to be completed.

5. The processing of the data read.

6. A write from the buffer.

This sequence might be coded using IOX (*input/output executive*) for the PDP-11:

```
START:  .RESET                      ;INITIALIZE IOX
        .READ    KBD,BUF,ASCII      ;READ INTO BUFFER
IDLE:   .WAITR   IDLE               ;WAIT TIL READ DONE

         .

        PROCESS BUFFER

         .

        .WRITE   PRT,BUF,ASCII      ;WRITE OUT BUFFER
        .END     START
```

The purpose of the macro instruction is to serve as a linkage to the I/O programming system. Thus each macro instruction results in a service call to IOX with the macro arguments being passed to IOX as a means of specifying what is to be done.

6.7.2. IOPS Linkage Problem

In a large computer system the expansion of a macro into a service routine linkage requires both a macro assembler and a linking loader. Since neither of these exist as part of the basic software supplied with a small computer system (although they may be available as part of advanced software systems), it becomes the programmer's responsibility to expand the macros into assembly language statements and to link up the program with IOPS.

The technique most often used to link programs with IOPS is through interrupt-producing machine instructions called *service calls (SVC)* or *I/O traps (IOT)*. These program-initiated interrupts are handled like I/O interrupts, and result in the replacement of the current PSW by a new PSW pointing to the I/O programming system. Such SVCs or IOTs have all the advantages of subroutine calls, including arguments passing (the old PC in the PSW points to the first word in the argument list); they also facilitate the functioning of the I/O programming system in that

1. It need not save the processor state (except for the register it uses).

2. It can operate at any priority level it wishes to.

3. It provides a direct linkage between the user program and IOPS through a fixed memory location.

The last point is clearly the most important. The trap instruction effectively does away with the need for a linking loader, since all IOPS calls will be through IOTs, which do not require direct linkage to IOPS. Instead, IOPS need only preload its trap vector so that all IOTs will cause a transfer of control to IOPS, at which point the reason for the IOPS call can be determined. In this regard an I/O trap is analogous to the single-level interrupt system already discussed.

6.7.3. Interrupts and Traps

It is worthwhile to digress for a moment and point out that interrupts and traps are not associated only with I/O instructions. Indeed, interrupts may be used to

1. Indicate program faults, such as addressing errors, illegal instruction errors, and abnormal arithmetic results.

2. Handle machine errors, including memory parity checks and automatically detected hardware malfunctions.

3. Flag external conditions, such as power failure and console key interruptions.

Additionally, since these interrupts cause a change in the current PSW, it is possible to utilize an interrupt-generating condition to change the *protection state* of the system.

For example, if I/O instructions are illegal in the *protected* or *user* state, they will cause an interrupt to be raised whenever the computer attempts to execute them. However, should the system be in the *unprotected* or *monitor* state, no interrupt will occur. Consequently, all I/O requests must be handled by an I/O programming system, which is activated by an SVC or IOT instruction that results in a change of state from protected to unprotected mode.

The monitor and user modes permit a structured environment by providing for two distinct states of system operation. Depending upon the state, full or limited memory addressing and instruction execution capabilities are permitted. By making the system state a bit in the PSW, a change of state can occur automatically, thus guaranteeing that all system capabilities may be made available to the interrupt service routine. In Chapter 8, where more advanced operating systems (such as multiprogrammed and time-sharing systems) are discussed, this concept of system state will be discussed more fully.

6.7.4. Programming of a Trap Instruction

Turning back to the use of an I/O programming system, it would be well to examine how such a system might be used on the PDP-11. The earlier macro program, although quite nice, just does not exist. Instead, the I/O executive IOX requires the same problem to be cast as shown in Fig. 6-21.

```
          RESET=2                    ; ASSIGN IOX COMMAND
          READ=11                    ; CODES
          WAITR=4
          WRITE=12
          KBD=0
          PRT=1
START:    IOT                        ; I/O TRAP INSTRUCTION
          . WORD    0                ; PERFORM NECESSARY
          . BYTE    RESET, 0         ; INITILAIZATION

          IOT                        ; TRAP TO IOX
          . WORD    BUF              ; SPECIFY BUFFER
          . BYTE    READ, KBD        ; AND KEYBOARD READ

IDLE:     IOT                        ; TRAP TO IOX
          . WORD    IDLE             ; JUMP TO IDLE
          . BYTE    WAITR, KBD       ; KBD READ IS FINISHED
              .
              .
              .
;         PROCESS BUFFER
              .
              .
              .
          IOT                        ; TRAP TO IOX
          . WORD    BUF              ; SPECIFY BUFFER
          . BYTE    WRITE, PRT       ; AND PRINTER WRITE

BUF:      100                        ; BUFFER SIZE (BYTES)
          0                          ; STATUS/MODE (ASCII)
          0                          ; IOX WILL FILL IN BYTE COUNT
          . =. +100                  ; RESERVE 100 BYTES
          . END     START
```

Fig. 6-21

An important point to notice is that since IOX processes buffers, interrupt handling is no longer at the character level but rather at the buffer (filled or empty) level. Since this is consistent with the units of information required (strings of digits, lines of input, etc.), the useability of IOX is clearly demonstrated.

6.7.5. Coroutine Example Utilizing IOX

In Chapter 4 it was mentioned that coroutines were used for I/O processing and represented one of the basic operations to be performed by modern operating systems. The example that follows demonstrates the use of coroutines in a double-buffer I/O scheme which overlaps I/O with computation, performing as follows:

$$\left.\begin{array}{l}\text{Write 01} \\ \text{Read I1} \\ \text{Process I2}\end{array}\right\} \text{concurrently} \qquad \left.\begin{array}{l}\text{Write 02} \\ \text{Read I2} \\ \text{Process I1}\end{array}\right\} \text{concurrently}$$

The reader should recall that the JSR PC, @(SP)+ always performs a jump to the address specified on top of the stack and replaces that address with the new return address. Thus each time the JSR at B is executed, it jumps to a different location; initially to A and thereafter to the location following the JSR executed prior to the one at B. All other JSR's jump to B+2 (Fig. 6-22). This code, although deceptively short, is a powerful and elegant solution for the programming of double-buffered I/O overlapped with computation. It clearly demonstrates the power and capability of the small computer, on which may be developed time-sharing, real-time, and communications-based systems.

EXERCISES

1. Write a program to type out the message "HELLO?" on the teleprinter.

2. Write a format subroutine for the teleprinter to tab-space the teleprinter carriage. The subroutine is entered with the number of spaces to be tabbed in register R0.

3. Write a program to read columns from the low-speed paper tape reader, punching out each column on the high-speed paper tape punch as three octal digits.

4. Write a subroutine that accepts one to six octal digits from the teleprinter and forms a 16-bit word in $R\emptyset$. As each character is typed, it should be echoed back to the teleprinter. Assume that the line is terminated with a carriage return and that your routine will insert a line feed.

5. Rewrite Exercise 3 to utilize interrupts.

6. Write an interrupt structured program to read 400 characters simultaneously from the high-speed reader, while punching and printing the first 100 characters read. Be careful to terminate the reading while allowing the slower printing and punching devices to complete.

7. Devise a scheme for measuring execution time used by a program. This scheme should be accurate to within 16.6 milliseconds.

8. Code Exercise 3 utilizing IOX.

9. Can Exercise 6 be coded using IOX?

10. Code the coroutine double-buffer example on page 200 so that it can duplicate a paper tape from the low-speed reader to the high-speed punch.

```
        SP=%6
        PC=%7
BEGIN:  (DO I/O RESETS, INITS, ETC.)
          .
          .
          .
        IOT                         ;READ INTO I1 TO START PROCESS
        .WORD   I1
        .BYTE   READ,INSLOT
        MOV     #A,-(SP)            ;INITIALIZE STACK FOR FIRST JSR
B:      JSR     PC,@(SP)+           ;DO I/O FOR O1 AND I1 OR O2 AND I2
          .
          .
          .
;       PERFORM PROCESSING
          .
          .
          .
        BR      B                   ;MORE I/O

;END OF MAIN LOOP

;I/O CO-ROUTINES FOLLOW

A:      IOT                         ;READ INTO I2
        .WORD   I2
        .BYTE   READ,INSLOT
          .
          .
          .
;       SET PARAMETERS TO PROCESS I1 AND O1
          .
          .
          .
        JSR     PC,@(SP)+           ;RETURN TO PROCESS AT B+2
        IOT                         ;WRITE FROM O1
        .WORD   O1
        .BYTE   WRITE,OUTSLT
        IOT                         ;READ INTO I1
        .WORD   I1
        .BYTE   READ,INSLOT
          .
          .
          .
;       SET PARAMETERS TO PROCESS I2 AND O2
          .
          .
          .
        JSR     PC,@(SP)+           ;RETURN TO PROCESS AT B+2
        IOT                         ;WRITE FROM O2
        .WORD   O2
        .BYTE   WRITE,OUTSLT
        BR      A                   ;READ INTO I2

        .END    BEGIN
```

Fig. 6-22

REFERENCES

I/O programming is very personal in the sense that each computer type has its own I/O instructions and hence I/O idiosyncracies. Books by Flores (1969), Hellerman (1967), and Foster (1970) discuss I/O from the conceptual level, making it more universal in flavor. Others, like this book, treat I/O as it is embodied in a particular machine. For the PDP-11 the best source is the *Peripherals and Interfacing Handbook*, which covers not only I/O devices but also UNIBUS extensions, communication interfaces, and data and control options.

7 SYSTEM SOFTWARE

A comprehensive package of system software accompanies each computer in use today, from the small minicomputer to the large number cruncher. These packages include programs and routines plus associated documentation which allow the programmer to write, edit, assemble, compile, debug, and run his programs, making the full data-processing capability of the computer immediately available.

System software represents the on-going process and continual efforts of system programmers to make the utilization of computers easier, more comprehensible, and less time-consuming than was possible before. Most systems are modular and open-ended, permitting the user to construct specified systems tailored to his particular environment. As such, they act as the buffers or interfaces between the user's needs and the hardware's capability.

We have introduced you previously to three software systems: the assembler, the I/O programming system, and the memory dump routine. Now your attention is directed to those other software systems that assist in the creation and execution of programs—the editor, the macro assembler, and the loader. In addition, since no nontrivial program or system is ever fully debugged or tested, it is worthwhile to conclude our investigation of system software with an examination of testing and debugging techniques.

7.1. EDITOR

The text editor is a powerful context-editing program used to create and modify symbolic source programs and other text material. By means of commands issued from the teleprinter, the editor can be used to create and delete characters, lines, or groups of lines which it maintains in its internal buffer.

Because the editor is on-line in most systems, response to commands is immediate and dynamic.

A good editor is both productive and cost-effective. In use it turns the teleprinter into a very sophisticated typewriter that assists the programmer in the normal "cut and paste" operation of putting a program together. As a result, the editor must not only allow for the insertion and deletion of characters and lines, but it must also be capable of locating symbols, making corrections, and reading or writing blocks of data.

Typical editor commands include the following:

1. INPUT: to enter a new string of characters.

2. DELETE: to delete a string of characters.

3. CHANGE: to replace one string of characters with another.

4. LOCATE: to find the first or nth occurrence of a character string.

5. PRINT: to print a string of characters.

6. VERIFY: to print out a string after it has been changed, or located.

7. READ: to fill the editor's internal buffer by reading a block of text from some peripheral device.

8. WRITE: to empty the internal buffer onto a peripheral device.

In addition, there are commands that have to do with the character or line pointer.

Associated with the internal buffer of the editor is a pointer that refers to the line or character in the buffer considered to be the current line or character. The current line or character is defined as the line or character that is being created or edited by the user.

Some editors operate only on lines, some only on characters; others operate on both. If the editor recognizes entire lines, it does so by defining a line to end with an especially significant character, such as a carriage return. In this way the editor may assume that each line begins with the character after the terminating carriage return in the last line and ends with the terminating carriage return for the current line.

Various editor requests are provided for moving the current location pointer. These requests include

1. BEGIN: to position the pointer at the beginning of the buffer.

2. END: to position the pointer at the end of the buffer.

3. NEXT: to position the pointer at the beginning of the next line.

4. LAST: to position the pointer at the beginning of the previous line.

5. FORW: to move the pointer forward one character position.

6. BACK: to move the pointer backward one character position.

In addition, editor commands, such as LOCATE, INPUT, DELETE, and so on, will cause the current location pointer to be repositioned.

There are two response modes in which the editor environment may operate. These are called "normal" and "brief" modes. The normal mode automatically types out each line that has been changed or searched for as the result of an editor request. The brief mode does not respond by typing the edited lines and thus requires the user to issue a verify command (for one line) or a print request (for several lines) in order to see the results of the last command(s).

The editor environment includes two modes of operation: the input and the command modes. The *input mode* specifies that all characters entered are to be treated as input until a special character is recognized as a request for a mode change. The *command mode* implies that the character strings entered are to be treated as requests to the editor.

The sophistication of the editor depends greatly on its operating environment. Large computer systems allow for maximum editor flexibility, including full or abbreviated commands, concatenation of command strings (macro statements), file manipulating requests, and sophisticated text editing. Small computers generally have very terse, one-letter commands, limited internal buffers, and rigid command formats. Nonetheless, even small computer editors allow sufficient flexibility for creating and modifying source programs.

7.1.1. Example of the Use of a Small Computer Editor

The editor for the PDP-11 is typical of the small computer editor. Requests are entered while the editor is in command mode (each line begins with the editor typing out an *), and they include

1. B: equivalent to BEGIN.

2. ±nA: equivalent to NEXT or LAST depending on the sign. n specifies the number of lines.

3. ±nJ: like A but for characters (e.g., equivalent to FORW and BACK).

4. I: equivalent to INPUT.

5. ±nC: to replace n characters before (−) or after (+) the current pointer position (e.g., equivalent to CHANGE).

6. ±nL: equivalent to PRINT but ±n lines from the current pointer.

This subset of editor commands may be used to write the trivial program given in Fig. 7-1. In the example, the editor is assumed to be running and all nonprinting characters are not shown (e.g., carriage return, tab, line feed). Additionally, the right-hand comments have been added for the sake of readability:

```
*I
        R0=%0                                    USER PLACES EDITOR
        R1=%1                                    IN INPUT MODE AND TYPES IN
        MOV       #1,R0                          LINES OF INPUT.
        CLR       R1
        CMP       R0,R1
        .END      START

                                                 A LINE-FEED TERMINATES
                                         INPUT MODE.

*B                                       POSITION POINTER AT BEGINNING.

*2A                                      ADVANCE 2 LINES.

*1L                                      PRINT THE CURRENT LINE.
        MOV       #1,RO

*I                                       BACK TO INPUT MODE.

START:                                   AND ADD A LABEL.

*0A                                               TO REPOSITION THE POINTER
                                         TO THE BEGINNING OF THE LINE.

*1L                                      THE LINE IS LISTED.

START:  MOV       #1,R0

*15J                                     THE CHARACTER O IS TO
*1C                                      BE CHANGED TO A 0.

0

*0A                                      THE POINTER IS REPOSITIONED.

*1L                                      AND THE LINE IS PRINTED OUT.

START:  MOV       #1,R0
```

Fig. 7-1

Although far from exhaustive, this example demonstrates how a small computer editor might work.

7.2. MACRO ASSEMBLERS

The reader has already read how a basic symbolic assembler makes machine language programming easier, faster, and more efficient. In addition, the reader has been presented with the need for and advantage of pseudo-operation instructions for directing the actions of the assembler. Now we shall discuss the advanced features of a macro instruction generator, which is a part of an expanded or *macro assembler*. Note that the keyword is "expanded," since the macro assembler contains all the features normally found in a symbolic assembler plus those necessary to handle macro instruction generation. Thus MACRO-11, the macro assembler for the PDP-11, is a superset of PAL-11, the symbolic assembler, and users of MACRO-11 may write programs that are identical to the programs that they would write for PAL-11.

One of the features of a macro-instruction generator is that it permits easy handling of recursive instruction sequences utilizing the simple technique of parameterization. The generator allows the programmer to create new language elements in order to be able to adapt the assembler to his specific programming applications. In addition, macros may be called inside macros, nested to multiple levels, and redefined within the program.

At this point it might be well to define just what a macro is rather than only what it can do. Very specifically, a macro is an "open routine" which is defined in a formal sequence of coded instructions and, when called or evoked, results in the replacement of the macro call by the actual body of code that it represents. The use of a macro statement does not result in saving memory locations but rather in saving programmer time.

For example, when a program is being written, it often happens that certain coding sequences are repeated several times, with only the arguments changed. It would be convenient if the entire repeated sequence could be generated by a single statement. To accomplish this it is first necessary to define the coding sequence with dummy parameters as a macro instruction, referring to the macro name along with a list of real arguments that will replace the dummy parameters and generate the desired sequence.

Macros must be defined before they may be used. The way to define a macro is to bound the sequence of symbolic instructions with the pseudo-ops .MACRO and .ENDM. For example,

```
. MACRO   MAC  ◄──── ─── Macro name
LINE1 ⎫
LINE2 ⎬  ◄──────── ─── Macro body
LINE3 ⎭
. ENDM
```

With each macro call (macro order), the macro body is substituted in place of the macro name:

```
                              ADD     A, B
ADD     A, B                  MOV     B, A
MOV     B, A                  LINE1
MAC          ═══════════►     LINE2
MOV     C, B                  LINE3
                              MOV     C, B
```

This replacement process occurs essentially before assembly and can be conceived of as a character-string substitution.

Since the programmer may wish to use the same macro bit on different data, macro calls include argument transmission. Thus, if a programmer desires to define a macro instruction "add byte" (ADDB), the following macro definition would suffice:

```
        . MACRO    ADDB, X, Y
        MOV       R0, TEMP1        ; SAVE R0
        MOV       R1, TEMP2        ; SAVE R1
        MOVB      X, R0            ; PUTS FIRST BYTE IN R0
        MOVB      Y, R1            ; PUTS SECOND BYTE IN R1
        ADD       R0, R1           ; FORMS RESULT
        MOVB      R1, Y            ; PLACE RESULT IN Y
        MOV       TEMP1, R0        ; RESTORE R0
        MOV       TEMP2, R1        ; AND R1
        BR        TEMP2+2          ; BRANCH AROUND
TEMP1:  . WORD    0                ; TEMP LOCATIONS
TEMP2:  . WORD    0
        . ENDM
```

7.2.1. Location and Created Symbols

Although it may not have been necessary, the macro body of the preceding example preserved the contents of registers R0 and R1. In doing so, the macro definition developed a serious problem. Each time the macro is called, the symbols TEMP1 and TEMP2 will be redefined, resulting in an assembly error message.

There are, fortunately, two ways out of this dilemma:

1. Parameterize the temporary locations, leaving their definition up to the programmer; for example,

```
        . MACRO    ADDB, X, Y, TEMP1, TEMP2
        MOV        R0, TEMP1
```

2. Allow the programmer to inform the assembler that certain symbols are known only to the macro and should be replaced by the macro assembler with a *created* symbol, which will be unique for each call of the macro:

```
        . MACRO    ROR6, A, ?B
        MOV        #6, R0          ; SHIFT COUNT
B :     ROR        · A             ; ROTATE
        DEC        R0              ; DECREMENT COUNT
        BNE        B               ; LOOP IF NOT DONE
        . ENDM
```

which generates the following code when called:

```
                               ( MOV    #6, R0
                       64$:   |  ROR    SUM
    ROR6    SUM               {  DEC    R0
                               ( BNE    64$


                               ( MOV    #6, R0
                       65$:   |  ROR    VALUE
    ROR6    VALUE             {  DEC    R0
                               ( BNE    65$
```

Created symbols are always local symbols between 64$ and 127$. The local symbols are created by the macro assembler in numerical order and are generated only when there is no real argument being substituted in place of the dummy argument in the macro definition. If a real argument is specified in the macro call, the generation of a local symbol is inhibited and normal replacement is performed.

7.2.2. Nesting of Macros

Macros may be nested; that is, macros may be defined within other macros. For ease of discussion, levels are assigned to nested macros. The outermost macros (those defined directly) are called *first-level macros*. Macros defined within first-level macros are called *second-level macros*; and so on. For example,

```
. MACRO   LEVEL1, A, B                              )
ADD       A, B                                      |
. MACRO   LEVEL2, C, D                       )      |
SUB       C, D                               |      |
. MACRO   LEVEL3, E, F   )                    }      }
ADD       E, F           |                   | Level | Level
ADD       F, F           } Level 3   Level 2 |   2   |   1
. ENDM                   )                   |      |
CLR       C                                  |      |
. ENDM                                       )      |
CLR       A                                         |
. ENDM                                              )
```

At the beginning of the macro processing only first-level macros are defined and may be called in the normal manner. Second- and higher-level macros will not yet be defined. However, when a first-level macro is called, all its second-level macros become defined. Thereafter, the level of definition is irrelevant and macros at either level may be called in the normal manner. Of course, higher-level macros will not be defined until the lower-level macros containing them have been called.

Using the last example, the following would occur:

Call		Expansion		Comments
LEVEL1	X,Y	ADD CLR	X,Y X	Causes LEVEL2 to be defined.
LEVEL2	I,J	SUB CLR	I,J I	Causes LEVEL3 to be defined.
LEVEL3	Y,I	ADD ADD	Y,I I,I	

If a call to LEVEL3 were made before LEVEL2 defined it, an error would result, since the code expansion would be undefined.

7.2.3. Macro Calls Within Macro Definitions

The body of a macro definition may contain calls for other macros which have not yet been defined. However, the embedded calls must be defined before a call is issued to the macro which contains the embedded call.

As an example, we consider the macro called SWITCH, which transfers the contents of buffer A to buffer B and vice versa:

```
    .MACRO   SWITCH, A, B, TEMP, N
    COPY     A, TEMP, N
    COPY     B, A, N
    .ENDM

    .MACRO   COPY, FROM, TO, COUNT, ?L
    MOV      COUNT, R0
L:  MOV      FROM, TO
    DEC      R0
    BNE      L
    .ENDM
```

7.2.4. Recursive Calls

Although it is legal for a macro definition to contain an embedded call to itself, care must be taken to ensure that the recursive macro expansion will eventually terminate. Somehow the assembler must be told that a condition has been detected and that the recursive definition may now stop. The technique used to accomplish this is the conditional assembly statement, although such statements may be used for things other than recursive macro definitions.

7.2.4.1. Conditional Assembly

Conditional assembly directives are most often used to assemble certain parts of a source program on an optional basis. The instruction is of the form

.IF   cond, argument(s)

where **cond** represents a conditional that

1. Tests the value of an argument expression; or

2. Tests the assembly environment; or

3. Determines the attributes of a single symbol or address expression; or

4. Tests the value of character strings.

If the condition is satisfied, that part of the source program starting with the statement immediately following the conditional statement, and including the statements up to the .ENDC (end conditional) assembly directive, are assembled. However, if the condition is not satisfied, the code is not assembled.

Conditional statements may be nested. For each .IF statement there must be a termination .ENDC statement. If the outermost .IF is not satisfied, the entire group is not assembled. If the first .IF is satisfied, the following code is assembled. However, if an inner .IF is encountered, its condition is tested, and the code given in Table 7-1 is assembled only if the second .IF is satisfied. Logically, nested .IF statements are like AND circuits. If the first, second, and third are satisfied, the code that follows the third nested .IF statement ia assembled.

Table 7-1 Conditional assembly directives.

Type	Pseudo-op	Condition
Comparand	.IF EQ	argument $= 0$
	.IF NE	argument $\neq 0$
	.IF GT	argument > 0
	.IF GE	argument $\geqslant 0$
	.IF LT	argument < 0
	.IF LE	argument $\leqslant 0$
Environment	.IF B	Is macro-type argument[†] blank (i.e., missing)?
	.IF NB	Is macro-type argument[†] not blank (i.e., present)?
Attribute	.IF DF	Is argument symbol defined?
	.IF NDF	Is argument symbol undefined?
Character String	.IF IDN	Are two macro-type arguments[†] identical?
	.IF DIF	Are two macro-type arguments[†] different?

[†]A macro-type argument is one enclosed in angle brackets (e.g., $\langle A,B,C \rangle$). Such arguments allow expressions to be treated as single terms.

1. The code generator should put out a BR instruction if the relative distance for the branch is 255 bytes or less. Otherwise, a JMP is generated. The conditional code is

```
.MACRO   BRJUMP,LOOP
.IF      DF,LOOP
.IF      LT,255-.-LOOP
BR       LOOP
.ENDC
JMP      LOOP
.ENDC
.ENDM
```

(The .IF DF is necessary since LOOP may be a forward-referenced label.)

2. Code may be saved when using the previously defined ADDB macro when two or more such macros are used in the same program, since TEMP1 and TEMP2 need only be defined once.

```
        .MACRO   ADDB,A,B
        MOV      R0,TEMP1
        MOV      R1,TEMP2
        MOVB     A,R0
        MOVB     B,R1
        ADD      R0,R1
        MOVB     R1,B
        MOV      TEMP1,R0
        MOV      TEMP2,R1
        .IF      NDF,SW
        SW=1
        BR       .+6
TEMP1:  .WORD    0
TEMP2:  .WORD    0
        .ENDC
        .ENDM
```

3. The conditional assembly code may be used to terminate macro recursion.

```
        A=0
SUM:    .MACRO   X,Y
        ADD      X,Y
        A=A+1
        .IF      NE,A-3
        SUM      X,Y
        .ENDC
        .ENDM
```

7.2.5. Repeat Blocks, Concatenation, and Numeric Arguments

Occasionally it is useful to duplicate a block of code a number of times in line with other source codes. This is performed by creating a repeat block of the form

```
. REPT    EXPR
      .
      .
      .
. ENDR
```

where expr is any legal expression controlling the number of times the block of code is assembled. For example, to generate a table of ASCII characters, the .REPT could be used as follows:

```
A='A
. REPT    26
. BYTE    A
A=A+1
. ENDR
```

The repeat pseudo-op can also be usefully combined with two other macro features. The first is concatenation. This feature allows the apostrophe or single quote (') character to operate as a legal separating character such that when the ' precedes and/or follows a dummy argument, the ' is removed and substitution of the real argument occurs at that point.

The second feature is the capability of passing a symbolic argument as a numeric string. Such an argument is preceded by the unary operator backslash (\) and is treated as a number. Combining these features, we get the following interesting example:

```
B=0
. MACRO    INC, A, B
CNT        A, \B
B=B+1
. ENDM

       . MACRO    CNT, A, B
A'B:   . ASCII    /B/
       . ENDM
```

This macro pair, when called by

```
. REPT    5
INC       X, B
. ENDR
```

results in the following macro expansion:

```
X0:    . ASCII    /0/
X1:    . ASCII    /1/
X2:    . ASCII    /2/
X3:    . ASCII    /3/
X4:    . ASCII    /4/
```

The two macros are necessary because the dummy value of B cannot be updated in the CNT macro. This is because the ASCII characters representing the number are inserted in the macro expansion. Thus in the CNT macro, the number passed is treated as a string argument.

7.2.6. System Macros

In any macro assembler there can be found a *system macro* facility. This facility allows the user to access a set of macros that have been predefined for programmer convenience. The system macros are called like any other macro but result in a search of some system library to find the requested definition.

Most often the purpose of calling a system macro is not merely that of substituting a macro body for a macro call. Instead, the macro calls are treated more as subroutine calls on the system to perform such functions as I/O reads and writes, register saving and restoring, and other specialized functions, including using a real time clock or returning control to the monitor after completion of a user program.

Typical system macro calls look as follows:

```
. READ     PAR1, PAR2


. WRITE    PAR3, PAR4
```

where PAR1, PAR2, ... are parameters associated with the macro call. The actual expansion of the macro looks as follows:

```
MOV      #PAR1, -(SP)
MOV      #PAR2, -(SP)
EMT      4


MOV      #PAR3, -(SP)
MOV      #PAR4, -(SP)
EMT      2
```

On the PDP-11, the *EMT (emulator trap) instruction* serves as a call to the system monitor. Thus the effect of making a read/write macro call is the stacking of parameters and the turning over of control to the monitor, which can subsequently invoke the I/O programming system to process the request.

7.2.7. Power of the Macro Assembler

Macro assemblers, which possess the features of nested definitions, conditional code generation, and recursive calls, provide a capability more powerful than a subroutine facility. The reason is that the macro assembler allows code generation at translation time so that the actual program generated fits the applications for which it was intended. Thus, unlike the subroutine, it does not require extensive testing of conditions that may occur at execution time because the code was generated to handle only those cases that were known to occur.

An example in the use of such macro assemblers can be found in system generators. System generators are parameterized macro programs that allow the user to define his particular operation environment as arguments to the program. The program may then be assembled, and produces as output machine language programs tailored to his installation. Such programs do not test to see how much memory or what options are available; instead, such information is already embedded in the operating environment code. As a result, instructions for testing memory size or whether or not a printer is available need never be executed.

Finally, a powerful use of macros can be found in totally parameterized macro programs. The instructions in such programs are either macro calls or macro definitions based entirely on previously defined macros. Thus the macro programmer need never know what the actual machine instructions are or what they are capable of doing. Indeed, the programmer need not know anything at all about the host computer, since the macro expansion is based on character strings and does not depend on the generated result.

A classic example of the use of such a macro-generation scheme can be found in the implementation of SNOBOL4 by its designers and users. This language is written as a macro-generation implementation and only requires that each macro be defined for the host computer. Once each macro is defined, the macros, along with the SNOBOL4 system, may be assembled into a running SNOBOL4 interpretor.

7.3. THE LOADER

The initial load problem was discussed in Chapter 6 in connection with the bootstrap loader. The bootstrap loader, although sufficient for loading short programs, was not general or flexible enough for loading long programs. Instead, that task falls on the *absolute loader*.

The absolute loader is a system program which enables the programmer to load his programs into any available memory locations, in any order. It is used to load programs that are in absolute binary (i.e., fixed to absolute memory locations) or PIC format. Having completed its task, the absolute loader will either halt or transfer control to the start of the newly loaded program.

The absolute loader is usually loaded by the bootstrap into the uppermost area of available memory. In this way it may be preserved across user or system program loads so that it can be available without reloading. Of course, when writing programs, the user must be aware of what memory locations the absolute loader (and the bootstrap if it resides in memory) occupies so that it will not be altered by his program(s).

An absolute program as seen by the absolute loader consists of one or more blocks of data. Each block may include

1. A start-of-block indicator.

2. A record count of the number of bytes, words, and so on, to be loaded.

3. A load address.

4. The information to be loaded.

5. A block checksum.

Although the first and last items are not absolutely necessary, they occur frequently in block requirements for small computer loaders.

The start of block indicator is used to indicate that a load block follows. In this way nonloader data may be mixed with loader information. For example, a small computer with only a teletype as a system I/O device may put both the assembly listing and the binary loader tape out to the teletype punch, and leave it up to the loader to separate the two.

The block checksum is used as error indicator for the loader. As each load record is generated by the assembler it is added (logically) to the checksum, which eventually becomes part of the load block. During normal program loading, the checksum is again computed, and if this new value does not agree with the block checksum of the block data, a load error is indicated and the loader halts. Thus the block checksum serves to guarantee that the load operation has been performed correctly.

The rest of the loader block fields are used as shown by the flowchart in Fig. 7-2. Note that the last load address may or may not be used as a transfer address upon completion of the load process. This decision depends on whether the assembly program terminated with a

ENO   LABEL

or simply an .END. One way of indicating this difference, which is used by the absolute loader for the PDP-11, is to make the load address even or odd, depending on its being a transfer address or not.

As an alternative to taking the load address from the load block, it should be possible to indicate the load address by use of the computer console switches. This capability allows PIC programs to be loaded in memory

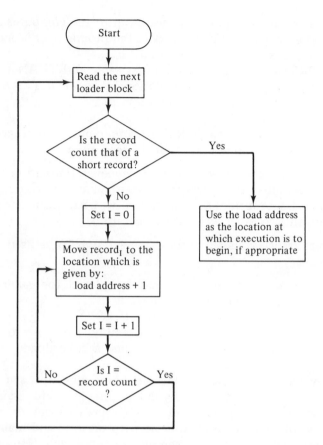

Fig. 7-2

locations different from the relative load addresses given in the load blocks. PIC programs are thereby *relocated* into new memory positions by the simple process of making the actual load address for each block be the sum of the two addresses provided.

7.3.1. Relocation of Programs

Relocation of PIC programs by the absolute loader turns out to be not only useful but necessary. For example, it allows the user to control the loading of the dump routine so that it may be placed in a location of memory that does not overlap the area to be dumped. More generally, such relocation of PIC programs makes it possible for the user to write separate PIC segments, which may be combined in memory to form one large program.

However, making the programmer write all his relocatable programs in PIC format is unduly restrictive. Instead, it seems much more sensible to leave the mechanical process of relocation up to the computer since it can easily handle the problem. Consequently, the programmer is encouraged to write all his programs in a relocatable form.

As the FORTRAN programmer knows, each FORTRAN program and subprogram requires a separate compilation by the FORTRAN translator. The following are advantages of this requirement:

1. Errors discovered in one FORTRAN program (or subprogram) require only that that program and not all others be recompiled.

2. Absolute addresses need not be assigned at translation time. Thus programs are prevented from arbitrarily overlaying each other. This flexibility also allows subroutines to change size without influencing the placement of other routines or affecting their operation.

3. Separate translations allow the same symbols to be used in different source programs.

4. Once translated, subroutines may be placed for general use in a *library* for future use without retranslation.

Fortunately, these advantages apply to assembly language programming as well, provided that a relocatable assembler and a linker/loader are available as system programs.

Up to now we have not really considered how subroutines are linked and loaded with their calling routines. By default, the absolute assembler would be used to assemble all programs and subprograms together, determining which portions of memory each routine is to occupy, and maintaining the subroutine entry addresses in the assembler's symbol table. However, should we have decided to assemble each routine separately, we would have been faced with the tasks of keeping track of what memory is to be allocated to which routine and what addresses need to be adjusted (e.g., the address portion of the

```
        JSR      REG, SUBR
```

instruction must be modified to point to the entry point of the subroutine).

The relocatable assembler and linker/loader mechanize this process for us in the following way. First, the assembler produces object code as if it were to be loaded starting at location zero. Second, the assembler flags each *relative* address and data word so that the linker/loader will know what parts of the program will be affected by relocation. Third, the assembler allows the programmer to declare certain symbols *global* symbols. A global symbol is either defined in a program (as a label or by direct assignment) or it is assumed to be defined in some other separately assembled program. In the first case the global is called an *entry symbol*; in the second case it is called an *external symbol*.

7.3.2. Linking and Loading

As the start of the linking and loading process, the linker/loader receives the following information from the relocatable assembler:

1. Object code.

2. Relocation information about the individual fields in the object code.

3. Relative assembly address of the first instruction or datum in the load module.

4. Global entry point and external reference symbols.

5. Length of the load module.

This information assists the linker/loader in developing a *load map* detailing what programs have been loaded, how long they are, where they reside in memory, and what other programs they require. The linker/loader will attempt to load programs until all programs are loaded and no new ones are required, or programs are found to be missing.

Some programs may be part of a user or system library. Such libraries include already translated user routines and intrinsic functions such as SIN, COS, TAN, EXP, LOG, and so on. These programs must be located by the linker/loader through a *directory* which describes the routine, its entry points (some routines such as SIN and COS may share common code), what other routines this routine may need, the length of the routine, and where the routine is to be found. A typical load map and directory are shown in Fig. 7-3.

Load Map

Routines present	Memory address	Length	Routines required	Calling addresses
MAIN	150	1025		350
SUB1	1175	300	SIN	1220, 1345
			EXP	1415

Directory

Routine	Entry points	Called routines	Length	Physical location
SIN	SIN, COS	– –	268	Desk address
MATH	EXP, LOG SQRT	FLTPT, CLOG	500	Paper tape (external)

Fig. 7-3 Load map and directory.

The actual process of linking and loading is generally handled by one of two possible techniques. The first is called the *transfer vector method* and utilizes a technique similar to the jump table example presented in Chapter 4. By making each external routine call result in a transfer into a jump table, the loader can eventually fill in the address where the called routine has been loaded. Figure 7-4 shows how the assembler code for the PDP-11 could be used to produce relocatable code that includes a jump table to the called routines MUL and DIV. After loading, these table entries will contain jump instructions to the actual starting locations for MUL and DIV.

Assembler code		Relocatable output			Program in memory (with MUL at 200, DIV at 300)		
		0	MUL:	0	100	JMP	200
.GLOBL	MUL,DIV	2	DIV:	0	102	JMP	300
ADD	A,B	4	ADD	50,52	104	ADD	150,152
JSR	PC,MUL	12	JSR	PC,0	112	JSR	PC,100
SUB	B,C	16	SUB	52,54	116	SUB	152,154
JSR	PC,DIV	24	JSR	PC,2	124	JSR	PC,102
JSR	PC,MUL	30	JSR	PC,0	130	JSR	PC,100
	•		•			•	
	•		•			•	
	•		•			•	

Fig. 7-4   Loading process using the transfer vector technique.

The linking loader method attempts to avoid the one level of indirectness of the transfer vector technique. It therefore creates a linked list of all calls to the external routine and preserves this list until such time as the relative load address of the external routine is known. At that time, the linking loader traverses the linked list, building up direct calls to the external routine(s).

Figure 7-5 shows the same PDP-11 code being linked and loaded as in Fig. 7-4, except that the linking loader technique is used in the figure. The relocatable output of the assembler includes a linked list of all references to the same external routine, with the list terminating in a null [shown by a dash (-) in the figure].

The basic difference between these two techniques is that the transfer vector method resolves links during loading, while the linking loader does it before loading. The output of the linker part of the linking loader is, therefore, one complete load module, which is loaded by the relocatable loader part.

Assembler code			Relocatable output		Program in memory (with MUL at 200, DIV at 300)		
			MUL	L24			
.GLOBL	MUL,DIV		DIV	L20			
ADD	A,B	0	ADD	44,46	100	ADD	144,146
JSR	PC,MUL	6	JSR	PC,—	106	JSR	PC,200
SUB	B,C	12	SUB	46,50	112	SUB	146,150
JSR	PC,DIV	20	JSR	PC,—	120	JSR	PC,300
JSR	PC,MUL	24	JSR	PC,L6	124	JSR	PC,200
•		•			•		
•		•			•		
•		•			•		

Fig. 7-5 Loading process using linking loader technique.

In either case, the results are the same:

1. Object modules are relocated and assigned absolute addresses.

2. Different modules are linked together and global symbols are correlated between those modules which define them and those which use them.

3. A load map is produced, displaying the assigned absolute addresses.

thus allowing the programmer to assemble his program and subprograms separately.

7.4. DEBUGGING TECHNIQUES

One of the maxims of programming seems to be that no program of any degree of complexity will run correctly the first time it is executed. The problem is that a symbolic program can be assembled correctly and still contain logical errors, that is, errors that cause the program to do something other than what is intended. Although the assembler can check for and detect syntactic errors, it cannot detect logical errors. Consequently, logical errors are usually detected only when the program is run on a computer.

Determining whether or not a program has a logical error is sometimes difficult in itself. A computer is generally used to solve the kinds of problems that require involved calculations, which preclude knowing much about the answers generated. As a result, only when answers are grossly incorrect is the programmer sure that a logical error exists. When seemingly small errors or results that cannot be measured against known values appear, the programmer is faced with the difficult task of deciding whether or not his program is indeed incorrect. And given a large, complicated program, the programmer may not be able to test all conceivable cases that could be generated, thus causing him to accept on faith that his program does work, until proved wrong!

Assuming that a logical error is known to exist, the problem becomes that of determining its cause. Several techniques for this are available:

1. Taking a memory dump of all locations that affect the results.

2. Using the console switches and lights to monitor program execution.

3. Tracing the program as it is executed.

4. Producing intermediate output as the results are generated.

Taking a memory dump, although often helpful, is both static and after the fact. By the time the dump is taken, the error may have caused all pertinent information, including itself, to be altered or eliminated.

Alternatively, the programmer, having the machine to himself, may use the console switches to examine specific locations while stepping through the program instruction by instruction. Besides the difficulty in both interpreting binary console displays and translating them into symbolic expressions related to the user's program listing, this technique is extremely time-consuming and very tiring. A better technique would be to place a halt in the program just before the section of code which is to be checked so that the magnitude of the operation may be reduced. Of course, this requires the programmer to know where to place the halt.

A better technique would be to let the computer print out the program instructions and results as they are being interpreted by some trace program. This, too, is a time-consuming process, but only on the part of the computer, since the programmer need not be present while the trace is being run. Some computers, the PDP-11, for example, even have a T-bit in the processor status word to assist in tracing instructions. This bit, when set, causes a processor trap at the end of each instruction execution, greatly facilitating the tracing process.

If computer time is a matter of concern, the programmer is faced with having to trace only selected variables or locations. Either a trace routine is used, or the programmer himself generates intermediate output which indicates that a certain variable has changed value or a specific location has been branched to or referenced.

The programmer can, of course, while sitting at his desk using the program assembly listing, mentally execute his program. This method is frequently used with very short programs, but only with very short ones.

Human memory cannot retain every step and instruction in even a fairly short program; it cannot match a computer memory.

What is needed to debug a user program conveniently and accurately is a service program that will assume the tasks the programmer would have to perform if he used the console switches, took a memory dump, and/or selectively traced his program. Such a facility is known as a *dynamic debugging program (DDP)*.

On a small computer, the DDP takes the form of a conversational system program. It provides the user with a convenient means for debugging and closely monitoring the operation of their programs. In fact, the DDP acts both as a program supervisor and as a binary editor.

Through commands issued to the DDP via the teletype, the user is able to: (1) start a program, (2) suspend its execution at predetermined points, (3) examine and modify the contents of memory words and registers, and (4) make additions and corrections to the running program using either symbolic or octal code. Commands are of the following forms:

1. OPEN: to examine and/or modify contents.

2. CLOSE: to go on to another OPEN or DDP operation.

3. MODE: to establish the type of in or out modes of operation.

4. BREAKPOINT: to suspend the execution of the program at a predetermined point.

5. SEARCH: to search for a particular occurrence of a bit pattern (e.g., an address, a constant, or an instruction).

6. LIMIT: to establish the limits (memory addresses) of the search.

7. BEGIN: to start execution of the user program at a specified location.

8. PROCEED: to continue execution after a breakpoint interruption.

Like all other system programs discussed in this chapter, the sophistication of the dynamic debugging program depends on its operating environment.

7.4.1. Example of a Debugging Session

ODT-11 (On-line Debugging Technique) for the PDP-11 is typical of a small-computer dynamic debugging program. Like the PDP-11 editor, ODT has a command mode that is indicated by an asterisk being printed out by the system. Basic commands include

1. n/: opens word n.

2. cr : a carriage return to close an open location.

3. n;G: begins execution at location n.

4. n;B: sets a breakpoint at location n.

5. ;P: proceeds from a breakpoint.

6. $n/: opens register n.

Given the following trivial assembly language program

```
        .=1000
        R0=%0
        R1=%1
START:  MOV     #1,R0
        CLR     R1
        CMP     R0,R1
        HALT
        .END
```

(no label follows .END, since ODT will begin execution of the program), then using ODT-11, the following dialogue may be had (comments have been added for readability):

```
*1004/005001                            EXAMINE THE CLR INSTRUCTION.

*$1/000000 123456                       CHANGE THE CONTENTS OF R1.

*1004;B                                 PLACE BREAKPOINTS AT
*1010;B                                 LOCATIONS 1004 AND 1010.

*1000;G                                 BEGIN EXECUTION AT START.

B0;001004                               BREAKPOINT OCCURS.

*$0/000001                              CHECK R0 AND R1
*$1/123456                              AND THEN
*;P                                     PROCEED.

B1;001010                               NEXT BREAKPOINT.

*$1/000000                              CHECK R0 AND
*$0/000001                              AND R1 AGAIN.
```

Although this example is rather brief, it does give the reader some idea of what a dynamic debugging program does. When faced with a typical small computer, with its often-limited number of display lights and means for examining memory or processor registers, the programmer quickly seizes the opportunity to use a DDP rather than probe memory and measure program progress through the console.

7.5. OPERATING ENVIRONMENTS

Having dealt with computers, including their organization and programming, we should now consider their operating environment. After all, from the user's point of view, the purpose of the computer is to assist the user in the mechanics of solving problems. Thus the operating environment greatly influences how the user is able to solve his problems. This subject forms the content of Chapter 8.

EXERCISES

1. What are the differences between an editor used for program creation and one used for manuscript creation? What types of commands might you find in one or the other?

2. Using the PDP-11 program editor as an example, list its good and bad features. Then give a suggested remedy for each of its bad features.

3. Expand the macro call

   ```
   SWITCH   BUF1, BUF2, SPARE, 10
   ```

   for the macro definition given above.

4. Rewrite the macro definitions for SWITCH so that the intermediate storage array TEMP need only be one word long.

5. Define the macro BSS X which is to reserve a block of storage locations X bytes long.

6. Develop a macro that can perform multiplication through recursive calls to the macro body, which performs shifting and adding.

7. Write a program to implement the absolute loader function as flowcharted in Fig. 7-2.

8. What features are missing from ODT-11 as described in the text? Describe a method for implementing them.

9. What difference is there between an on-line debugging package and a continuous trace program?

10. Develop a procedure for implementing a dynamic dump routine which produces a selective dump of specified memory and register contents upon call, without affecting the results of the running program that calls it.

REFERENCES

One of the best references for text editing can be found in the survey article by Van Dam and Rice (1971). Of course, for a particular system, one should read the appropriate manual, such as the PDP-11 *Edit-11 Text Editor*. Similarly, the manuals *Macro-11 Assembler*, *ODT-11R Debugging Program*, and *Link-11 Linker and Libr-11 Librarian* cover the topics of macros, outline debugging, and linking/loading for the PDP-11. However, the books by Gear (1969), Wegner (1968), and Stone (1972), as well as the survey by Kent (1969), are excellent treatments of macro assemblers, while the survey article by Presser and White (1972) is an equally well done presentation of linkers and loaders.

8 OPERATING SYSTEMS

Today it is inconceivable that a medium-to-large computer could exist without an operating system for its users. Indeed, even small or minicomputers can and do have sophisticated disk and tape operating systems as part of manufacturer-supplied software. For this reason, almost all programmers will, at one time or another, come face to face with an operating system environment.

Operating systems, if properly designed, exist for the users' convenience. They serve to bridge the gap between the needs of the user and the characteristics of the hardware. In this capacity, they directly assist the user in solving his problems through simplified programming and more efficient computer operation. However, to a large extent, the user never knows what the operating system is really doing. Instead, the user sees the system in terms of the services it provides for: program preparation, translation, execution, and debugging.

In order to understand what a computer system is all about, it is necessary to understand the system components and their organization. These components, computer hardware and software, were discussed in previous chapters. This chapter is thus concerned with the general job of organization as it is performed by the operating system. However, since our concern has been with small computer systems, we shall continue that interest as we take a look at rather specialized operating environments which exist for this class of machines. Because of the limited resources available, operating systems for small machines tend to be more constrained than for their larger computer system counterparts. Nonetheless, the same principals and concepts apply, the chief difference being that of the relative emphasis placed on the various system components.

8.1. VERY BASIC COMPUTER SYSTEMS

At the very least, every small computer comes complete with a paper tape system. In this environment, very reminiscent of the early days of computing, the input and output of programs and data are performed manually by the user via a paper tape reader and punch. The user communicates with, and receives printed output from, system and user programs through the teletypewriter device connected to the machine.

Even though the loading of programs is performed manually, a paper tape system normally contains a comprehensive software package of commonly used system programs which provide the user with complete facilities for writing, editing, translating, debugging, loading, and running his own programs. Since system programs have already been covered in Chapter 7 and earlier chapters, the reader is familiar with the capabilities of such a paper tape system.

Unless the reader has had the experience of using a paper tape system, he is not likely to realize how unsatisfactory and trying it can be. Operating such a basic system requires the user to take his coded program and manually perform the following operations:

1. Load and execute the paper tape editor.

2. Produce paper tape source programs using the editor.

3. Load and execute the paper tape assembler.

4. Translate the editor produced source program.

5. Load and execute the binary object program produced by the assembler.

6. Debug the program, repeating the first five steps as necessary.

Each step presumes that the software bootstrap and absolute loaders remain intact during successive program loads and executions. Unfortunately, this is not usually the case, and more often than not, the beginning programmer will load both loaders at one time or another.

Manual control of the operating environment is clearly inconvenient. It involves manipulating and maintaining numerous paper tape programming systems, and it results, in general, in the inefficient use of the hardware. Consequently, a more automatic level is desirable, and this level of control is found in the typical general-purpose disk operating system (DOS).

8.2. COMPONENTS OF A DISK OPERATING SYSTEM

The addition of a *secondary storage system device* (e.g., a disk) is what makes the disk operating system a comprehensive operating environment for both the development and execution of user programs. User programs and data, along with system programs, can all reside on the disk and other secondary storage devices, to be loaded into memory under program control. Instead of loading and reloading paper tapes, the DOS user can perform the same functions by issuing *commands* to the system. These commands not only provide user services (such as program loading) but also provide for efficient program and system management. Typical commands and their functions are shown in Table 8-1 for the PDP-11 disk operating system.

Table 8-1 System commands.

Command	Function
GET	Load a program
RUN	Load and begin a program
DUMP	Remove a program from memory
BEGIN	Start execution of a program
STOP	Halt the current program
CONTINUE	Resume execution of a halted program
END	End input from a device
LOGIN	Identify user to system
FINISH	Log off system
ASSIGN	Assign a physical device to a dataset

Commands, however, are only the outward manifestation of an operating system. To gain an understanding of how its functions and facilities are provided, it is necessary to consider the components of the system and their organization. Since one of the most important functions of an operating system is the effective management of its information structures (e.g., programs and data), it is important to understand the basic informational unit of the system. This unit is called a *file*.

8.2.1. Files—Organization and Access

A file is a collection of related records or data items treated as a unit. The word "file" is thus used in the general sense of "any collection of information items similar to one another in purpose, form, and content." For example, a program may be a file, just as a data structure (called a *dataset*) or even some system program such as an editor or assembler, may be. Unfortunately, the same word *file* is also generally applied to external storage media, such as disks and tapes, when what is really meant is *file-oriented devices*.

Each file-oriented peripheral device has a *file structure*, which represents the method of recording, linking, and cataloging data files. The file structure dictates the organization of the file on the device and the method of file access. This organizational structuring is important because a file can be effective for a user application only if it is designed to meet specific user requirements. Such factors as size, activity, and accessibility must be considered when determining the structure of a file.

The way in which a file is organized upon a storage media depends upon the way in which the user normally expects to create and later process it. Three methods that have been used are: (1) contiguous allocation, (2) linked list allocation, and (3) indexed allocation. Each of these methods is shown in Fig. 8-1.

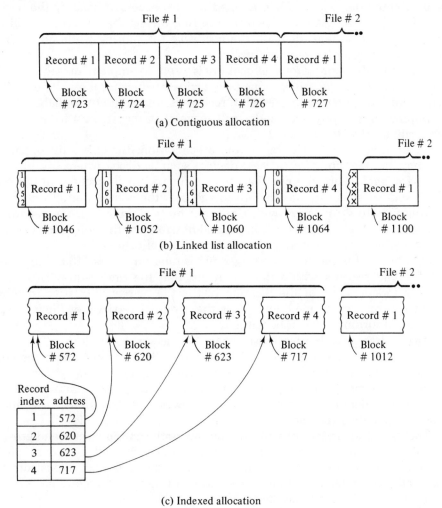

Fig. 8-1 File organization.

In the small computer system, file structure organization is not usually left up to the user but is predefined for the various peripheral devices.

Similarly, the method of access is system defined and is ultimately connected with the file structure. The most usual access technique involves *sequential access* to both the data file and the individual data records. This access method is characteristic of unidirectional devices, such as magnetic tape, although other devices, such as disks, may be organized so as to permit sequential access.

Sequential access is a storage retrieval technique in which a file and the records within it must be retrieved in the sequence in which they physically occur. Sequential access, when applied to the process of locating the beginning of a file or a data record within the file, means that the time required for such access is dependent on the necessity for waiting while nondesired files or records are processed in turn.

Traditionally, contiguous allocation is used to implement sequentially accessed files on sequentially organized devices such as magnetic tape. After each record is processed, the next record is immediately available, since positioning of the physical media will leave that record positioned at the read/write head of the device.

As an alternative to the sequential organization, the linked-list organization may be used for *direct-access devices* such as disks, where the time to search for and locate the next record is insignificant in processing the file. The linked-list structure has the advantage over the contiguous allocation of allowing files to grow larger with time by simply linking in a new record to the end of the list. This is not in general possible for the contiguous allocation, since the next block may already have been allocated.

Another technique for accessing a file is *random access*. Random access of a file and records within the file means that the time required for such access is independent of the location of the file or record relative to other files or records on the medium. Thus the order of retrieval of file information is unimportant and can be ignored.

Again, two possibilities exist when file access is random. These are contiguous allocation and indexed allocation. By knowing where the contiguous file begins, random accessing occurs in much the same fashion as element accessing occurs for a one-dimensional array. The limitation of the contiguous allocation remains the same, however: files cannot, in general, expand in length with time.

The use of an index into the file allows both random access and growth with time. Thus this method of allocation is preferred over contiguous allocation unless access time is important. Like linked-list allocation, indexed allocation requires that the location of the next record be fetched before the actual record may be accessed.

As a third alternative to the two access methods presented, an intermediate method may be used. This method, normally employed on disk and disk-like devices, allows a file to be accessed randomly while the file's data records may be accessed sequentially. This access method is called *indexed-sequential* and uses the indexed organization with more than one data record per block.

Indexed-sequential organization is well suited to those applications where it is necessary to access sets of records randomly but individual records of the set sequentially. A typical example of such an application would be a personnel records file where having found the records for a certain employee, it is necessary to update these employee records in a sequential fashion.

8.2.2. Directories

Having provided a file structure, and having specified its access method, the next problem is how the file is located by the system once stored away. One method that could be used is to keep track of the device addresses so that each file can be retrieved directly. The use of absolute addresses is not very acceptable, however, for much the same reasons that absolute addresses are avoided in symbolic programming. Instead, symbolic names must be associated with each file so that the files may be referred to by their *file names*.

To provide a connection between the file names and their device locations, a *file directory* or table of contents for each directoried file device must be part of the system. The file directory will contain not only the unique name of the file and its starting address on the device, but also its file structure, including, if necessary, a pointer to an index table. Figure 8-2 shows a directoried data access for a sequentially organized file that can be

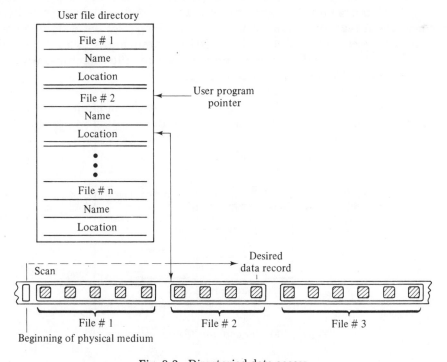

Fig. 8-2 Directoried data access.

randomly accessed. Devices such as tape cassettes and DECtapes have this capacity by which the transport may search to a known location before it begins processing the file.

When directoried data files are removable from the system, it is necessary to preserve the directory of files between uses. To do so requires that the directory be stored on the physical media, in a fixed location, along with the files it points to. As part of these directories, *bit maps* are maintained both to indicate which device blocks each file occupies and to show all occupied blocks.

File structures that employ a directory allow simpler and, in the long run, faster access to a file (e.g., the beginning of a file). This is a distinct advantage over those devices which do not use a directory and must therefore rely on a file's position relative to other files in order to locate it.

8.2.3. Multilevel Directories

When two or more people share the same device (such as the system disk) for storing files, problems may arise because of duplicate file names. Since both will have access to the same set of files, one user may accidently modify or destroy another's file by simply not knowing that the file name used was already assigned. The solution to this dilemma is to establish a separate user file directory for each system user. The separate directory will therefore allow each user to name a file without regard to the names chosen by others.

The basic mechanism for locating user files on a shared device requires a two-level file directory, as shown in Fig. 8-3. Each user has a unique code that must be provided whenever the LOGIN command is used. This code serves to identify a particular entry into the master file directory, which is actually a pointer to the user's file directory.

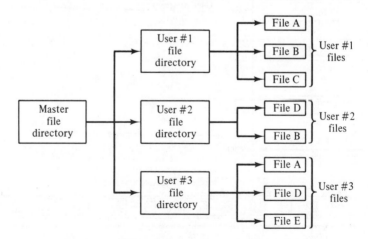

Fig. 8-3 Master and user file directories.

8.2.4. Problems of Control

Now that we have described an elaborate scheme to define the files within the system, it becomes obvious that one of the central functions of an operating system is control. For example, the file system represents one large facility that must be controlled in its allocation of peripheral device space and its storage and retrieval of file information on the peripheral devices. Fortunately, the function of the file system is precisely the minimization of the potential problem.

As far as the user is concerned, devices themselves are not of primary interest; the datasets of files that reside on them are. Thus a simple and useful extension may be made by broadening the concept of a file to encompass all information sets, including devices. In this manner it is easy to conceive of a paper tape reader as an information set (and hence a file) of a very special type. By *special type* is meant that the information set must be handled in only a very limited fashion (e.g., output not allowed to an input device). With suitable limitations, there is no reason why all devices cannot be conceived of as being file-like information sets. All that is necessary is to recognize and build into the system the fact that it is not possible to treat all files uniformly (e.g., not all files can be read from, written to, or rewound).

Both the system and the user can treat I/O devices uniformly as information sets. Within the system, however, there must be an interface between the system or user-created program and the external world of I/O devices. The purpose of the interface is to minimize I/O programming for the DOS user in the same way that the I/O programming system (IOPS) simplified I/O programming for the basic system user, as discussed in Chapter 6. In that chapter it was pointed out that the IOPS routines served to relieve the user of the burden of I/O service, file management, overlapping I/O considerations, and unnecessary device dependence. The last point, device independence, is especially important in a disk operating system, where an I/O service routine for a nonfile-structured device, such as the paper tape reader, must ignore (rather than declare as an error) a command to "seek a file" (which is required for all file-structured devices prior to issuing read commands).

Clearly, the central function of IOPS is to establish the information path between the system and the device. This requirement is met somewhat independently of the user, since one of the goals of IOPS is to minimize the user knowledge required. And since the user is to be spared the task of writing system software to perform I/O, standard system routines (called device handlers) must be a central part of IOPS. These routines perform the functions of

1. Driving the I/O devices.

2. Manipulating files on the devices.

3. Allocating/deallocating storage space on the devices.

4. Maintaining current records about user requests and device status.

5. Coordinating peripheral activities (such as buffering and blocking) as required by the I/O.

As pointed out in Chapter 7, system macros are the means of communication between user programs and I/O device handlers. These programmed I/O commands are also referred to as *requests*. Table 8-2 lists typical requests for the DOS-11 (PDP-11 DOS) system. Not all requests shown in the table actually perform I/O. Some, such as .OPEN and .CLOSE, merely serve to initialize a dataset or file for subsequent I/O processing. Others, such as .BIN2D, .RADPK, and .ALLOC, perform auxiliary operations on the data or the data file.

Table 8-2   Programmed requests.

Programmed Request	Function
.OPEN	Open a dataset.
.ALLOC	Allocate a sequential file.
.CLOSE	Close a dataset.
.DELET	Delete a file.
.LOOK	Search a directory for a file.
.READ	Read from a device.
.WRITE	Write on a device.
.WAIT	Wait for device completion.
.BIN2D	Convert binary to decimal ASCII.
.BIN2O	Convert binary to octal ASCII.
.D2BIN	Convert decimal ASCII to binary.
.O2BIN	Convert octal ASCII to binary.
.RADPK	Radix-50 ASCII pack.
.RADUP	Radix-50 ASCII unpack.

8.2.5. File Management Utility

Although program requests for file management provide the basic functions needed to utilize files, it is inconvenient to have to write a program every time one wishes to manipulate files. Thus most operating systems include a system software package for the transfer of data files from one I/O device to another, while performing simple editing and control functions as well. This package, known as PIP (*Peripheral Interchange Program*) on the PDP-11, handles all data and file formats found in DOS-11 so as to

1. Transfer a file or group of files from one device to another.

2. Merge files into a single file.

3. Delete, update, rename, or replace files.

4. Allocate file space and initialize whole devices.

5. Print listings of file directories.

6. Handle file protection.

In effect, the file utility package provides at the user level the same sort of services that IOPS provides at the program level. Users need only enter commands to the PIP program and it will decode the command and perform the desired function. For example, the user might wish to make a backup copy on DECtape of an existing disk file. To do so he would run the PIP program and then, in response to PIP's request for a command (indicated by a # sign), type in

```
#DT1:BACKUP.SRC<DC0:MYFILE.SRC
```

The new file, named BACKUP.SRC, would then be a copy of the original file, called MYFILE.SRC.

To examine the directory for a certain device, the command to PIP would be

```
#LP:<DC0:/DI
```

indicating that a *di*rectory listing of the contents of disk unit zero is to be produced on the *li*ne *p*rinter. This listing would appear as

```
DIRECTORY DC0: [   1,1   ]


25-NOV-73


        MONLIB.CIL    401C 09-SEP-73 <377>
        MACRO .OVR     28C 19-NOV-73 <233>
        LINK11.OVR     72C 19-NOV-73 <233>
        MACROP.LDA     97  19-NOV-73 <233>
        LINK  .LDA     56  19-NOV-73 <233>
        PIP   .LDA     36  19-NOV-73 <233>
        EDIT  .LDA     50  19-NOV-73 <233>
        LIBR  .LDA     30  19-NOV-73 <233>
        PIPOV0.OVR     18  19-NOV-73 <233>
        PIPOV1.OVR     14  19-NOV-73 <233>
        PIPOV2.OVR     18  19-NOV-73 <233>
        PIPOV3.OVR     12  19-NOV-73 <233>
        ODT   .OBJ     37  19-NOV-73 <233>
        TEST  .BAK      4  23-NOV-73 <000>
        TEST  .PAL      5  23-NOV-73 <000>


        TOTL BLKS:    878
        TOTL FILES:    15
```

where the fields indicate the file name, file size, file creation date, and file protection code. Also included are the total number of files and blocks in use for the "user identification code," [1,1].

It is important to bear in mind that a file management utility is a system software program in the same sense as were the programs in Chapter 7. The goal of such software programs is to provide routines that assist the user in solving his problems. As a consequence, these programs do not in and of themselves produce useful results but rather allow the user to utilize the hardware available to him effectively.

8.2.6. Device Independence

As the reader may recall, system macros are implemented using interrupt-generating instructions. For example, a write macro operation

```
        WRITE   LNKBLK, BUFHDR            ; WRITE DATASET
```

in DOS-11 is expanded into

```
        MOV     #BUFHDR, -(SP)            ; STACK
        MOV     #LNKBLK, -(SP)            ; MACRO ARGUMENTS
        EMT     2                         ; PERFORM EMULATOR TRAP
```

The two arguments of the macro call are called the *linkblock* and the *buffer header*. The buffer header serves to define the data buffer as described for IOX earlier in Chapter 6. The linkblock serves to establish the connection between the data file (logical device) and the physical device. A linkblock is defined as follows:

LNKBLK:	
	Error Return Address
	Link Pointer
	Name of File
	Unit Number
	Physical Device Name

The first two entries are used by the system for error processing and initializing the dataset. The next entry, the logical name of the dataset, is used to associate a logical file with a physical device. The function of the ASSIGN command is to fill in this entry. Finally, the last two entries serve to specify the standard name of the physical device associated with the file.

Ordinarily, a programmer specifies I/O devices as he writes the program. However, there are circumstances when he will want to change the device specifications when his program is run. For example:

1. A device that the user specified when he wrote his program is not in operation at run time, but an alternative device is available.

2. The programmer does not know the configuration of the system for which he is writing, or does not wish to specify it (i.e., he is writing a general-purpose package).

Through the use of the linkblock, the ASSIGN command, or by assuming the default condition, the programmer can write programs that are *device-independent*. From the user's point of view, such device independence results in very flexible programming.

8.2.7. Monitor

The user communicates with the system in two ways: (1) through keyboard instructions, which have been referred to as commands, and (2) through programmed macro instructions. In both cases the effect is to initiate a *control program* or routine which loads a file, makes a correspondence between a logical file and a physical device, opens a dataset, writes onto a device, etc.

Clearly, the control programs must work in mutual harmony if the system is to operate successfully. Although much of the system can be conceived as the sequencing of one program or *task*[†] after the other, it is possible to have two tasks operating in parallel (e.g., an I/O operation and a computation). Thus a master control program called the *monitor*, which can be responsible for the entire operating system and all of its component parts, is needed.

The monitor must be responsible for the initiation, maintenance, and termination of all other programs. It coordinates program-to-program and task-to-task transitions and processes the communications among the user, the system, and the many control programs. It also must act on monitor calls, validate and transmit I/O calls to device handlers, supervise data and file manipulations, and provide error diagnostics.

There are basically three sections of a monitor: (1) the permanently resident monitor, (2) the nonresident monitor, and (3) the system loader. The resident monitor remains in memory when system or user programs are

---

[†]A task is a well-defined unit of work that competes for the resources of the system (e.g., memory, files, I/O). Stated more simply, it is a program or routine with known inputs and outputs.

running and acts as the interface between the program and the system's facilities.

The user/operator may alter the structure of the resident monitor via commands to the nonresident monitor. The nonresident monitor allows the user to alter many key parts of the system, in order to set up the system for the next program. Normally, at the end of a particular program, the computer user or the program itself returns control to the nonresident monitor. At that point the user issues new commands to set up the system for the next program to be run.

The system loader builds the resident monitor according to prior commands to the nonresident monitor. It loads all system programs and all handlers for those system programs from the system disk, and these programs in turn allow the user to edit, assemble, load and link, perform file manipulations on, execute, debug, and so on, his programs. Since the purpose of the system loader is basically to set up the system (e.g., by loading system programs and setting them into execution), it is completely invisible to the user.

8.2.7.1. Monitor/User Interaction

The console teletypewriter is the primary user-system interface for DOS program control. This control is implemented by commands to the monitor which cause system and user programs to be loaded and executed (as described in Section 8.2), by commands that perform special services, and by control character commands that provide system control while running user or system programs.

Most of the monitor commands must be issued prior to loading programs and are interpreted by the nonresident monitor, since it is not, in general, necessary to keep the command recognizer in memory during system or user program execution. However, during program execution, a small set of keyboard commands must be available for general program control. These commands are interpreted by a portion of the teletypewriter's I/O device handler (which is part of the resident portion of the monitor) and are used to control program start and restart, dumping of memory, and reloading of the nonresident monitor.

Since the monitor and any program running under it must share the same console teletypewriter, the user must specify whether the given keyboard input is intended for the monitor or for the operating program. Consequently, the modes of operation are determined by the first character entered. All characters following a special control character (a CTRL/C for DOS-11) are interpreted as monitor commands and are passed to the monitor for execution. All other characters are assumed to be for the operating program, and the characters will be buffered until required by the program.

8.2.7.2. Monitor Organization

Figure 8-4 illustrates the data flow and general organization of the monitor. Although most of the functions of the various modules have already been described, several require further comment.

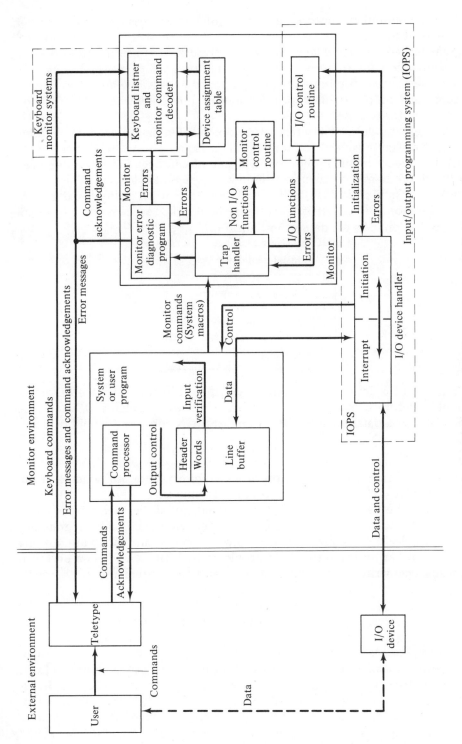

Fig. 8-4 Command, control, and data flow in monitor environment.

The first modules of interest are the command processor and the monitor command decoder. Both the user and the monitor share the same control program, called the *command string interpreter*. This routine preprocesses the specification for whatever user or system program it was called by. By having one routine for both the system and the user, one common format for input and output dataset specifications to a program is provided through a single monitor routine.

The next module of interest is the one labeled *device assignment table (DAT)*. This table is used to store the data from each ASSIGN entry, since device/file specification by console assignment can occur at any time, even before the program that requires the new assignment is loaded. The DAT is set up in a similar format to the linkblock (as shown below) and resides within the monitor so that its entry may be checked whenever the program under execution calls for dataset initialization.

Logical name of dataset
Physical device name
Unit number
File name

The use of a device assignment table can be illustrated by the following example. Before being run, a user program wishes to assign a DECtape file FREQ.BIN to a dataset called FRQ. The ASSIGN command would be used:

$$\text{ASSIGN, DT:FREQ. BIN, FRQ}$$

where the commas act as separators and the colon separates the name of the physical device (DT for DECtape) from the file name.

At first, the use of the ASSIGN command, the device assignment table, and the linkblock may seem strange. However, the FORTRAN programmer should be able to recognize that these new commands and tables are nothing more than a new solution to an old problem. In FORTRAN, when performing reads and writes, the programmer must write statements of the form

$$\text{READ} \quad (u,f) \quad \text{I/O list}$$
$$\text{WRITE} \quad (u,f) \quad \text{I/O list}$$

where u represents a unit and f a FORMAT statement label. Usually there are default values for u, and reading a data card is performed on unit 5 [e.g., READ (5,10) A,B,C] while printing a line occurs on unit 6 [e.g., WRITE (6,20) A,B,C]. However, when file-oriented devices such as tapes are used, some form of an assign command (or control card) must be used to equate the unit numbers to their particular devices. This, of course, associates all the files on the device media with the unit number, and it is up to the user to separate out the various files.

Going one step further, it would be very nice to be able to associate a particular file on a particular device with a unit number. As long as the device has a directory associated with it, this is a relatively simple process. For example, a programmer could issue the command

ASSIGN, DISK:MYFILE, 6

to assign the file, MYFILE, on DISK1 to unit 6. Alternatively, instead of using unit numbers, dataset names may be used, so the command becomes

ASSIGN, DISK1:MYFILE, MYDATA

allowing the user's program to refer to the file by its dataset name, MYDATA, rather than by a unit number.

Returning to Fig. 8-4, the last module to be explained is the one labeled *trap handler*. Both at the user level and internally within the monitor, the standard method by which a monitor routine is accessed is through a trap or monitor calling instruction. For the PDP-11, the EMT instruction is useful because its lower byte is not considered in the hardware decoding operation; it can therefore be used for a software code to identify the module required and avoids the use of a second word (e.g., as shown, a call for an I/O .WRITE is EMT 2 or 104002). By using the stack to pass arguments, the monitor call though the EMT ensures that the called module has complete freedom in its use of registers and that the necessary handler for this instruction has the opportunity to control all communication paths throughout the system (e.g., EMT is an interrupt-generating instruction). This control facility is a particular advantage to the small computer operating system which must *swap* monitor routines in and out of memory and maintain complete control of user and system programs, all without the aid of any special hardware.

8.2.7.3. *Monitor Residency Table*

An important part of the trap handler is the *monitor residency table (MRT)*, which supplies two types of information for the trap handler:

1. It shows which monitor routines are resident in memory, either permanently or for the duration of a program run, and where they are loaded currently.

2. It acts as a directory to the remaining routines as stored within the monitor library on the system device, to enable immediate access when one of these routines must be brought into memory.

For DOS-11, the table is a set of one-word codes and is ordered in the sequence of those codes starting at ∅.

The format of each word in the table (see Fig. 8-5) shows the current location of the monitor routine it represents, using the fact that for a valid PDP-11 address for execution access, bit ∅ must be ∅ (i.e., a word boundary).

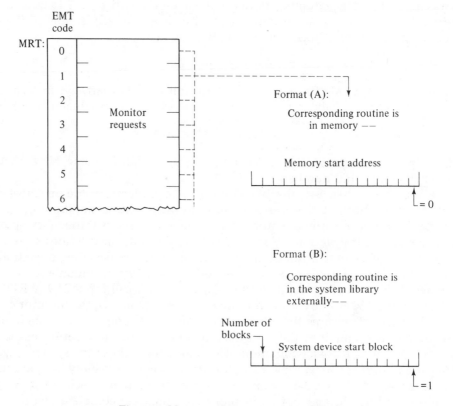

Fig. 8-5 Monitor residency table format.

The state of the table depends on which routines must remain within the computer memory at all times, because they control the system generally, and which routines may reside upon the system device, because they perform ephemeral tasks. By using the system loader, nonresident routines may be loaded when required and can later be removed when their purpose is served. In this way, available memory space need not be used by the system (e.g., the monitor) but may be made available to the user. Clearly, this is a necessary requirement for the small computer user who has a machine with somewhat limited memory space.

8.2.7.4. *Monitor Memory Organization*

From the previous sections it is clear that certain monitor routines/modules must be resident in memory at all times. These routines determine the minimum allocation of the computer's memory, as shown in Fig. 8-6. The modular structure of the monitor allows the user to determine which modules are to be resident and which modules are to be swapped from the disk. In the latter case, it should be noted that a temporarily loaded routine occupies a reserved area within the monitor (the swap area) and does not require that a part of a program be swapped out first. This means that no restrictions need be placed upon the activities of a program as might be the case if part of its area were potentially removable.

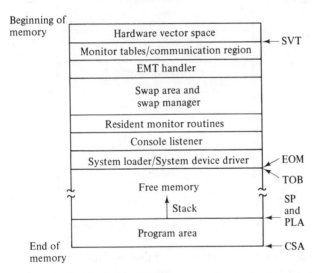

Fig. 8-6   Memory allocation.

Despite the fact that swapping can be accomplished fairly quickly from the disk, it still takes a finite time, and the user who has memory to spare may prefer to make use of it. Modularity of the monitor routines again helps, in that

1. If a particular module is required so frequently by the user(s) of the system, that module can be added to the list of those already part of the permanently resident monitor; or

2. If a module is particularly appropriate to one application, the routine can be loaded with the program concerned so that the routine is resident for the duration of the run.

8.2.7.5. Dynamic Memory Management

Another feature of the monitor as shown in Fig. 8-6 is its dynamic buffer allocation scheme for free memory management. This scheme postpones the allocation of memory for the purpose of I/O service until a running program actually requires it. Only then are the buffers allocated and the I/O drivers loaded, and when they are no longer required, their memory space is released. The allocation and deallocation of memory, being dynamic, means that the basic memory map varies with time. A typical memory map during program execution would appear as shown in Fig. 8-7.

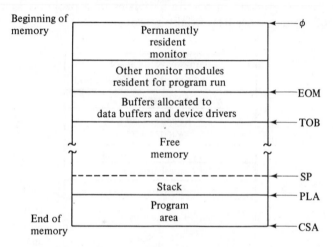

Fig. 8-7   Memory during program run.

Another consequence of dynamic memory allocation is that all the modules that take advantage of this feature must be independent of the positions they occupy. Position-independent coding presents no problems for a computer such as the PDP-11, but allowing independent modules to intercommunicate does. What is needed is a *system vector table (SVT)*, which provides a common area for the storage of information on the state of the system at any time. In particular, the SVT must contain pointers to the other parts of the system which provide such information as the end of the monitor, the start of the monitor residency table, the name of the loaded program, and so on, as shown below in Fig. 8-8. These pointers were previously indicated on Figs. 8-6 and 8-7, allowing the reader to go back and interpret their use.

8.2.8.   Use of Operating Systems

Having discovered something about the internals of a typical disk-based operating system, it is worthwhile to examine how an operating system meets the more general needs of its users. As might be expected, the needs tend to be rather diverse, and since it is clearly impossible to write operating

	Symbol	Meaning	Purpose
SVT:	EOM	End of monitor	Dynamic origin for free-core buffer space
	TOB	Top of buffers	Dynamic end of allocated buffer space
	CSA	Core size available	Set an initialization to highest memory address
	PLA	Program load address	Set only when a program is in core (lowest point loaded)
	SCW	System configuration	Reserved for bit switches to indicate available facilities
	BAT	Beginning of D.A.T.	Set only if a device assignment table is established
	MUS	Monitor/user switch	Low byte: 1 = program loaded; − 1 = program stopped High byte: 1 = program running; − 1 = program waiting
	PSA	Program start address	Set if program in core to address in source .END (or 1 if none)
	RSA	Restart address	Set by program for RESTART at console keyboard
	PGN	Program name	6-character value associated with source program
	MRT	MRT start address	Used for access to the monitor residency table
	DDL	DDL start address	Likewise for the device driver list
	MSB	MSB start address	Used for access to the main swap buffer

Fig. 8-8   System vector table contents.

systems tailored to each user's application, operating system designers generate systems that meet the needs of particular application areas. These areas and their operating environment may be broadly classified as one of the following:

1. Batch and time-sharing systems.

2. Real-time control systems.

3. Data-based systems.

4. Computer communications systems.

Batch processing and time-sharing systems are familiar operating environments for most computer system users. These general-purpose programming systems are best suited for the programmer who wishes to develop and execute his programs. From the standpoint of the small computer disk operating system, these systems represent add-on capabilities to the basic DOS environment.

Real-time control systems are designed for operating environments where many tasks must be maintained and controlled as events occur that are external to the computer. These systems must be capable of scheduling the real-time programs (called *tasks*) performing the input or output of necessary task information, communicating to the human operator what is happening, and performing such other functions as required for a real-time, multiprogrammed operation. A typical example might be found in a process control application.

The distinguishing feature of the data-based system is clearly the enormous amounts of information that must be managed. This information must be readily available to the user who queries the system, and must be well protected against accidental loss or unauthorized intrusion. Like the real-time system, emphasis is placed on program use rather than program development or testing.

Computer communications systems are often likened to electrical power utilities and natural gas networks. In both cases the system presents itself as a vast web of interconnected units capable of almost indefinite growth so that as the customer load increases, the system can be expanded without limit both by adding extra units and by connecting with other utilities to draw on their unused capacity. Such systems require well-defined interfaces and interconnection structures.

What follows in this chapter is an examination in more detail of each of these operating systems. Since the subject of this book is the small computer, emphasis will be on what types of small computer operating systems have been developed, and what function they serve.

8.3. BATCH AND TIME-SHARING SYSTEMS

Given the capabilities of the small computer plus the added flexibility of the disk-based operating system, it is not too difficult to develop a *batch processing system*. The batch processor is actually an additional control program within the monitor which allows user commands to come from the same device as the user programs. By placing user commands and programs together to form *jobs*, the system is capable of running many jobs consecutively without requiring operator intervention.

Special monitor commands (in addition to nonbatch commands) are used to

1. Enter batch mode.

2. Define and separate jobs.

3. Indicate that data follow.

4. Indicate the end of the job.

5. Terminate batch mode.

These commands form what is called a *job control language*, and if the batch input device is a card reader, they are punched into *job control cards*.

Besides the batch system, it is not uncommon to find *time-sharing systems* on small computers. Rather generally defined, a time-sharing system is one that provides many users with simultaneous access to a central computing facility.

A time-sharing system is, in fact, a *multiprogrammed* computer which allows its multiple users to share system resources in such a fashion that each user thinks that he is getting individual attention. The system is multiprogrammed in that several user programs will be simultaneously resident in memory at any given time. Each program receives a quantum of computer time, called a *time slice*, during which it may perform computations. Should it use up its time slice, or reach a point where further computation is not possible (e.g., some I/O information is needed), the CPU will be turned over to another program. This transfer of control is handled rapidly since the next program to gain the CPU will already be in memory.

The time-shared operation of a computer implies sharing the computer's time and space resources on a dynamic, and hence temporary, basis. Several (or all) user programs may be memory resident, while others may be in the process of being loaded from or to auxiliary mass storage. Indeed, if memory is not large enough to hold all the user programs and data, it will be necessary to swap user information in and out from the auxiliary storage upon demand.

The time-sharing operating system (TSOS) requires a sophisticated set of control programs to handle the sharing of system resources, the time slicing, the storage allocation and program relocation, and the basic servicing of users, besides the types of operations normally associated with a disk operating system. One of these control programs, the *scheduler*, has primary responsibility for both the basic servicing of the users and the optimal uses of the system resources. Each time the monitor gains control, it utilizes the scheduler to determine which program is to be put into execution next and what user swapping must occur if it is to keep the system busy and the users satisfied.

Because of heavy demands placed on the computer, it is often necessary to limit the flexibility of the TSOS. The most flexible TSOS is an *open, conversational system* that gives the user direct access to all the facilities (including I/O devices) of the operating system. *Closed, conversational systems* usually limit the user to specific languages and systems. *Remote program entry systems* are the most restricted form of time sharing, in that the user is capable of preparing and submitting programs from remote terminals, but he may not interact with the running program and he must wait for the program to run to completion before accessing the generated results.

The closed, conversation TSOS is the most common form of a small computer time-sharing system. Usually eight-to-sixteen users are able to program in a higher-level language, taking advantage of most of the system resources. Generally speaking, it is not the computer power which greatly limits the number of users but the amount of memory that is available to the system.

8.4. REAL-TIME CONTROL SYSTEMS

Real-time control systems are designed for handling data in a time that is consistent with the response time demanded by the process that generated the information. Such systems operate in a multiprogrammed environment with the real-time monitor controlling and supervising a large number of memory- or disk-resident programs and tasks. This control and supervision allows the tasks to share memory and disk space, I/O device handlers, and resource allocation and use.

The execution of the many tasks is determined by software priorities, hardware interrupts, timing algorithms, and requests from other tasks. Additionally, the user of the real-time system can install new tasks on-line, establish their software priority, and request their activation at any time with an automatic reactivation at a periodic interval of time thereafter.

The actual system response time for a task request depends mainly on whether or not another task is running at a higher-priority level. To prevent high-priority tasks from executing too long, a *watchdog timer* is often used to guarantee that all tasks are serviced. This timer is set at the start of each task with the maximum duration that a task may run, at a particular priority level, before being suspended or dropped.

The real-time monitor controls and executes all input and output operations. This is one of the areas of direct concern to the real-time user, since most real-time applications are characterized by a large amount of I/O. Indeed, tasks are initiated or suspended by the occurrence of some I/O operation.

8.4.1. Real-Time Programming

Programming for real-time control is generally performed in either assembly language or a higher-level language, usually FORTRAN, with extensions to allow real-time monitor calls. Program development can be done on-line with the real-time monitor, although the amount of memory available or the sophistication of the system may require off-line development.

Real-time programs rely heavily on system macro calls to schedule, queue, run, suspend, synchronize, and so on, tasks within the system. Often the data that are collected by the task is simply stored to be analyzed later under a general-purpose programming environment.

8.5. DATA-BASED SYSTEMS

Operating as a text-oriented information utility, the data-based system allows a large number of users to access a common data base. Problems such as order entry systems, automated medical records, seat reservations, information directories, and catalog searching represent prime candidates for implementation of data-based systems.

The conversational environment in which such systems are designed to operate typically demands little computer processing power, but tends to demand large storage facilities. When data are entered, the system must check its legality, decide where to file it, and select an appropriate response to be given to the user. None of these actions requires large amounts of processing.

When data are fetched and reports are generated, there will be a manipulation of information and/or the accessing of data from peripheral storage devices, in order to assemble the required data. Still, only a small amount of processing is necessary to actually format and produce the report. As a consequence of the small demand for the central processor, such system can be time-shared between a large number of users.

Although most of the data within the system may be potentially accessed at any time, large volumes of data need be available only for low-level, low-frequency usage. Thus the important aspect of these systems is the availability of large-capacity peripheral storage devices such as disks, drums, and data cells. Further, an effective data management system must use the storage effectively, minimizing the amount of storage utilized and providing fast and efficient data retrieval.

8.5.1. Effective Data Management

Features and techniques used to provide effective data management include:

1. Storing data in a hierarchical tree structure so that the most frequently accessed material can be optimally located in the structure.

2. Simultaneously updating and retrieving information.

3. Allowing dynamic restructuring of a structure during use.

4. Allocating space within the system as required rather than on a static basis.

5. Optimally mapping a data structure onto a peripheral device and retrieving it or rewriting it only as needed.

6. Making the system device-independent to avoid reprogramming.

7. Operating the system in a reentrant manner so that one copy may be shared by all users.

8. Keeping most of the system and user tasks resident in memory to minimize swapping.

One of the most time-consuming aspects of developing information system programs involves the optimal interfacing of the user and the system within a particular application area. Much attention must be given to human engineering and to the modification and revision of the techniques available to the user for the storage and retrieval of system data. In addition, the protection and security of the information itself must be guaranteed.

8.5.2. Storage, Manipulation, and Access of Data

The complexity, validity, security, and variety of the data that must be handled in a data-based information system impose a number of requirements on the system. A considerable amount of information will be input in the form of text strings of variable length. In processing these data, the system will often be required to check their syntax and even determine, where possible, their semantic content against some established limits.

When the information is accessed and possibly manipulated, the system must check to see if the user has been given such privileges. Consequently, each system user must have some capability/clearance list which can be compared with the list attached to the data he wishes to access and which will prevent unauthorized access or transformation. The security and privacy so gained will often be selective and data-dependent.

One way to aid the system in protecting itself is to make it a closed, conversational time-sharing system. Users may only make responses to pre-defined system requests, and may not write, test, or debug general-purpose programs. Additionally, the terminals for such systems may be designed so as to require push-button responses to "canned" messages displayed by the system. Alternatively, higher-level languages may be used to construct more complex search patterns or data structuring, but such languages should be executed interpretively so that system integrity may be preserved.

8.6. COMPUTER COMMUNICATION SYSTEM

The computer communication system operates as an interconnected network of independent computer elements which communicate with each other and share resources. As a component of these networks, the small computer generally serves as a dependent system that acts either as a data communicator or a data concentrator.

As a data communicator, the small computer serves as one of the following:

1. A device for the storing and subsequent forwarding operation of network messages.

2. A message translator and formator.

3. A controller for a large machine which it interfaces to the network.

4. A data entry system for providing remote job entry to a processing facility.

As a data concentrator, the small computer serves as

1. A multiplier that processes many low-speed terminals locally, concentrating the data into one medium-speed communications line to a larger system.

2. A message buffer, communications line control, and character-to-message assembler/disassembler for low-speed devices connected to it.

In both applications, the small computer offers a powerful, low-cost alternative to hard-wired communications controllers on the front end of large computer systems. And since these small computers are general-purpose machines with character-handling instructions and powerful interrupt structures, they may be programmed to

1. Route messages.

2. Provide code and speed conversions.

3. Handle line and error control.

4. Compress data and format messages.

5. Automatically identify terminals and their characteristics.

6. Provide time and date stamping of messages.

7. Establish communications automatically.

8. Preanalyze messages before transmission.

9. Provide editing, tabulation, and other formating services.

8.6.1. Communications Software

Manufacturer-supplied software comes in two forms: complete systems, often referred to as *turn-key systems*, which may be installed and placed in operation immediately, and *modular systems*, which consist of both hardware (including the computer and special communications hardware) and special-application software programs, such as device drivers and communication executives.

Turn-key systems do not require the user to program the computer. Indeed, some of these systems are supplied with read-only memories, which cannot be accidentally destroyed and which have been specifically programmed to perform a fixed sequence of instructions. On the other hand, modular systems are used as a base on which the user can build special-purpose systems tailored to his needs.

Within the modular systems there will be interrupt service routines, terminal applications programs, and system control/interface packages. Utilizing these routines, the user tailors his system to his specific application, thereby minimizing the amount of hardware and software required.

REFERENCES

Many good books on the subject of operating systems can be found. However, most of them, like Watson (1970), Katzan (1973), Donovan (1972), and Organick (1972), are concerned with the features and structure of particular systems (e.g., OS/360, Multics, and XDS-940). The notable exceptions are Hansen (1973), Cohen (1970), and Denning and Coffman (1973). Unfortunately, the latter three books tend to be more mathematical and theoretical in nature and may not be as useful as those geared to specific implementations. For a general treatment of modern operating systems, the reader should peruse Denning's (1971) survey article.

9 AN APPLICATIONS ENVIRONMENT

A computing system with the ability to incorporate user-defined programs as one of its tasks is essential in environments for scientific and laboratory experiments, process control, and real-time systems where continuous, long-term monitoring of a number of variables is required. Particular applications might include the monitoring of laboratory animals who have been trained to perform certain tasks, the control of refining plants where the flow of volatile fluids must be accurately regulated, and the processing of messages between one central computer and the multitude of remotely located terminal devices.

Although seemingly diverse, all these applications can be well served by the small computer system. Because of its low cost and yet sophisticated capability, the small computer can be programmed to provide task scheduling, I/O control, operator communication, and other functions as required by the particular application. Indeed, most small-computer manufacturers provide some form of real-time software package that can readily be adapted to the user's environment.

To gain some insight into what these systems do, this chapter is devoted to the development of a modest multiprogramming system, MMS, which can be used to execute, concurrently, several tasks on a PDP-11 computer. MMS itself is very unsophisticated, but it performs its function well and utilizes a minimum of memory and processor time to accomplish its task. Of particular importance is the fact that MMS has been set up as an open-ended system, so that once its basic functions have been understood, it can easily be expanded (see Section 9.5 and the Exercises at the end of the chapter).

9.1. OVERALL VIEW OF MMS

Since the cost of an operating system is measured in terms of both the resources it requires (and uses) and the amount of time required to process a user's task (e.g., the *overhead* associated with executing the system's programs), a primary goal of such a system is to use a minimum amount of memory. The minimum amount of memory for MMS is approximately 200 words because of its unsophisticated nature. This small amount of memory required occurs because each user must provide his own I/O routines, and there is no operator communication facility built in.

The purpose of the system is to perform three kinds of operations:

1. Upon a call from a task, switch the state of this task from "running" to "pending" and place the task on a queue according to its priority.

2. Examine the queue of tasks that are pending, and, having selected the task with the highest priority, unchain the task from the queue and switch its state from "pending" to "running."

3. Assign the CPU to the task now in the "running" state.

The general nature of such a system means that no special hardware is required, and any user-defined interfaces may be incorporated within it. The user need only define his tasks, written as PDP-11 programs, and integrate them into the base system by

1. Adding them somewhere between the end of one routine and the start of another.

2. Creating the proper entries in the various queues, tables, and PSECTs, as defined in the next section.

9.2. STRUCTURE OF THE QUEUES, TABLES, AND PSECTS

When a user places a task in the system, he must specify one of four levels of priority (0 through 3) for his task. These three software or user levels are all below the four system levels of priority that are entered due to an I/O or instruction trap interrupt. However, the three software (user) interrupt levels are true priority levels and do set the processor status word accordingly. For instance, it an interrupt occurs, indicating that it is time for a new task to begin, and the new task is of higher priority than the task interrupted, the lower-priority task is suspended and the higher-level task is activated. When the higher-level task gets suspended, the lower-level task is continued until the higher-level task can resume operation.

9.2.1. CPU Queue

The CPU Queue, CPUQ, is the data structure in which the information about which tasks are waiting to gain control of the CPU is kept. The queue is a vector of 8 bytes, divided into four entries, each entry corresponding to one of the four software priority levels allowed for tasks making use of the system. Consequently, each entry is 2 bytes long, with the high-order byte containing the identification (ID) of the first task on a linked list (Section 9.2.2) waiting to be served, and the lower-order byte containing the ID of the last task on that list. The 2 bytes thus serve as the head and tail pointers for the set of tasks (which are linked together) with a given priority level.

If no tasks exist at a certain priority level, the corresponding entry in the CPUQ will be zero. This means that no tasks making use of the system are allowed to have an ID equal to zero, because a zero in any entry of the CPUQ means "no tasks waiting at this priority level." Alternatively, if only one task is waiting to be served at a certain priority level, both bytes of the CPUQ for that level will contain the ID of the waiting task, because in this particular case the task is both the "first" and "last" task waiting on the queue. From what has been said it should be obvious that every task must have a unique ID. This ID is assigned by the user when it defines a PSECT (Section 9.2.4) for a task.

The structure of the CPUQ is shown in Fig. 9-1. For this example we have shown that

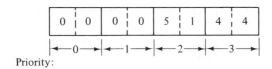

Priority:

Fig. 9-1 Structure of the CPUQ.

1. There are no tasks with priorities 0 or 1 waiting to be served.

2. There is a list of tasks waiting to be served at priority level 2. The task with ID = 5 is the first task on the list and the task with ID = 1 is the last.

3. There is only one task waiting to be served at priority level 3. Its ID is 4.

The serving of tasks proceeds from highest priority level to lowest. Thus the task with ID = 4 would be served first.

9.2.2. CPU Queue Table

The CPU queue table, CPUQTB, is a vector that will have as many entries (words) as there are tasks in the system. (Actually, it has as many entries as the number of tasks plus one, because entry zero is not used, for reasons which will become clear shortly.) The CPUQTB is a linked list of task IDs such that all tasks at the same priority level will be linked on the same list. Since there are four priority levels, four linked lists may exist on the CPUQTB at a time.

Assuming there are N tasks within the system (N = 255), the structure of the CPUQTB can be drawn as shown in Fig. 9-2. As stated before, each task has an identification number or ID which was assigned to it when its PSECT was created. These ID numbers run in numerical order from 1 up to the number of tasks that will be using the system, with a maximum of 255. Thus if three tasks are to be defined, IDs assigned to them would be 1, 2, and 3. (We remember that an ID of zero is illegal because zero is taken by the supervisor as the "nonexistence of a task" at a given priority level.)

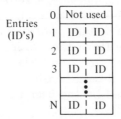

Entries (ID's)

Fig. 9-2 Structure of the CPU queue table.

As shown, each entry in the CPUQTB corresponds to the ID of a task waiting to be served. For example, entry 1 corresponds to the task with ID = 1, entry 2 corresponds to the task with ID = 2, and so on. (Of course, entry 0 is wasted because there can exist no tasks with ID = 0.) Looking at the contents of each entry, we see that the words are divided into two bytes with each byte storing pointers for the linked list. These pointers are not addresses, however; they are the IDs of the tasks in the linked list.

To clarify this last point, let us give an example. Suppose that there are four tasks with IDs 5, 2, 3, and 1, all with priority 2 waiting in the CPUQTB to be served. Further, there is a task with ID = 4 at level 3, also waiting to be served. Figure 9-1 shows the CPUQ for these five tasks and Fig. 9-3 shows the CPUQTB. As shown in Fig. 9-1, the first task at priority level 2 is the task with ID = 5; the last task in the list is the task with ID = 1.

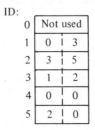

ID:

Fig. 9-3 Example of the entries in the CPUQTB.

As shown in Fig. 9-3, the entry for task with ID = 5 is divided into two bytes. The high-order byte contains an ID = 2 meaning: "task with ID = 2 follows task with ID = 5 on this linked list." The low-order byte contains a zero, meaning: "no task precedes this task with ID = 5," or "the task with ID = 5 is the head of the list." Going on, entry 2 of the CPUQTB corresponds to the task with ID = 2, and the following information is found in this entry: high-order byte = 3, low-order byte = 5, meaning: "task with ID = 5 precedes and task with ID = 3 follows this task with ID = 2." Finally, entry 1 of the CPUQTB is for the task with ID = 1, and it contains a 0 and a 3 in the high- and low-order bytes, meaning: "the task with ID = 3 precedes and no tasks follows this task with ID = 1," so task with ID = 1 is the last task on the list.

Reexamining the CPUQTB for the task with ID = 4, the reader will find both bytes zero for this entry. The entry contains zeros because the task with ID = 4 is not preceded or followed by any other on the queue (e.g., this task is the only task waiting for the CPU at priority 3).

9.2.3. PSECT Table

A PSECT (Section 9.2.3) is a vector, 11 words long, which is created for each task by the user. Information found in the PSECT of each task is used by the supervisor in task-switching operations. Before describing the PSECT, however, we shall examine the structure of the PSECT Table, PSECTB.

The PSECTB is a table that contains one entry for each PSECT. As each task must necessarily have one PSECT, the PSECTB will have as many entries as there are tasks. However, entry 0 of the PSECTB is not used, so in reality the PSECTB, like the CPUQTB, will have as many entries as the number of tasks plus one.

Each entry in the PSECTB corresponds to the ID of the task for which that entry will store information. The information stored in these entries is the address for the PSECT of the corresponding task. An example of the structure of this table is given in Fig. 9-4. As shown, entry 0 contains no information because there cannot exist a task with ID = 0. The remaining five entries correspond to tasks with IDs 1 through 5 for which the addresses of the PSECTs are defined symbolically as PSECT 1 through PSECT 5, respectively.

ID:

0	Not used
1	Psect 1
2	Psect 2
3	Psect 3
4	Psect 4
5	Psect 5

Fig. 9-4   Example of the entries in the PSECTB.

At this point the reader should recognize the value of the PSECT table and the use of IDs instead of actual addresses for the many tasks within the system. By not using address but rather indices (or IDs) for the various tables, less space is consumed (e.g., a byte rather than a word) for the various entries, thereby compressing the amount of memory required by the system. At the same time, processing of these tables is simplified because only linear lists in the form of one-dimensional tables or vectors are used, and accessing an entry requires only two steps: (1) shifting the index value left once to convert a byte offset into a word offset, and (2) adding in the base of the table to produce the actual table entry. For example, if the task ID is already in R0, the code to find the entry in the PSECTB is

```
ASL     R0                  ;CONVERT INDEX TO WORD OFFSET
ADD     #PSECTB,R0          ;ADD IN TABLE BASE ADDRESS
```

9.2.4. PSECT

The 11 words in the PSECT vector are reserved by the user at assembly time, one PSECT for each task. The vector is identified by the address of its first word, and this address is placed in the appropriate entry of the PSECTB. The PSECT contains information unique to the task, including a private stack where the contents of the task's registers will be saved while the task is waiting on a queue.

The structure of the PSECT is shown in Fig. 9-5. The first word of the PSECT is split into 2 bytes. The low-order byte contains the ID number assigned to the task. The high-order byte contains the state task. A task can be in one of two states: a "running" state, in which it has control of the CPU, and a "pending" state, in which the task is waiting on a queue. Other states could be defined, either by utilizing the individual bits to represent different states (up to 8), or by coding the state as a numerical value (up to 256), but for this simple system the two states are: running = 1 and pending = 2.

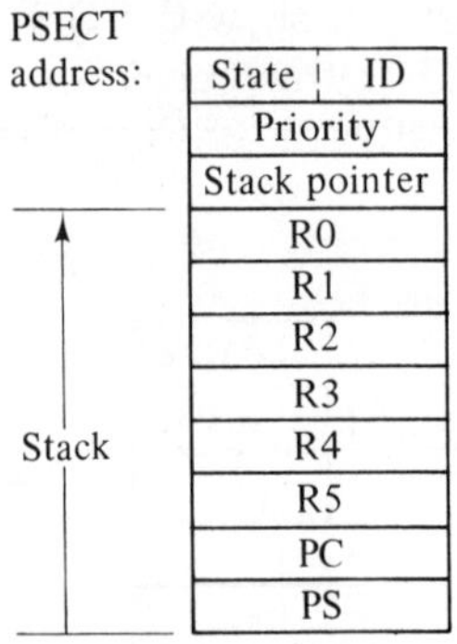

PSECT
address:

State	ID
Priority	
Stack pointer	
R0	
R1	
R2	
R3	
R4	
R5	
PC	
PS	

Stack

Fig. 9-5 Structure of a PSECT.

The second word of the PSECT will contain the priority level of the task. As stated earlier, a task can be in any one of four priority levels (0, 1, 2, and 3). The priority bits are set according to the structure of the processor status word, that is, bits 5, 6, and 7 form the priority, so if a task is to run at priority level 2, the second word of the PSECT should be set to 100 (octal).

The third word of the PSECT will be used to save the stack pointer for that task. The rest of the PSECT (8 words) is then used as a private stack where the contents of the registers PC and PS will be saved when the task is switched from the running to the pending state. The code to define a PSECT, therefore, appear as

```
PSECT1:  .BYTE    1, 1           ; STATE & ID BYTES
         .WORD    100            ; PRIORITY WORD, LEVEL 2
         .WORD     +2            ; STACK AREA POINTER
         =. +14                  ; STACK AREA
         .WORD    TASK1          ; PC FOR TASK 1
         .WORD    100            ; PS FOR TASK 1
```

Since the user's stack is defined to be in the PSECT area, there are certain restrictions on its use. First, if the user wishes to use his stack while running, no more than nine entries may be pushed into the stack. Second, at the time the task relinquishes the processor, the stack pointer, register 6, must be restored to its original value of #PSECT+26 (e.g., the top of the stack value), and no entries may be left in the stack during the time that the task is in a pending state. Of course, these restrictions can be removed, but this is left as an exercise for the reader (see Exercise 2 at the end of the chapter).

9.3. MMS SUPERVISOR

The heart of the MMS system is the supervisor, which may be called by any running task upon issue of a QUEUE supervisor call. *QUEUE* is an emulator trap instruction (QUEUE=104000) which will trap to a two-word vector starting at location 30 (octal). The first word of this vector contains the address of the first of a series of supervisor routines that will be executed in order to carry on the queue request. The second word of this vector contains the priority at which the supervisor routines will be executed.

The five routines that make up the supervisor are, in order of execution:

1. SCHEDL: the scheduling routine.

2. SAVE: the register save routine.

3. INSLAS: the insert last in queue routine.

4. DISPCH: the dispatch and register restore routine.

5. UNCHN: the unqueue routine.

Each of these routines is described in the following sections.

9.3.1. Schedule Routine

Control passes to the schedule routine, SCHEDL, as the result of a QUEUE supervisor call (e.g., an SVC). This call on the supervisor requires that the first of the two-word trap vector contain the address of SCHEDL.

As a result of the execution of a QUEUE SVC, the processor status and the program counter are "automatically" pushed into the private stack for the task issuing the SVC. Then, the first action of SCHEDL is to save (upon a call to the SAVE routine) the contents of all registers, that is, to push them also into the user's private stack.

Next, using the PSECT for the task issuing the SVC, SCHEDL gets the priority for the task and finds the correct entry to the CPUQ. The task is then inserted (upon a call to the INSLAS routine) at the end of the queue (CPUQTB), its state is switched from running to pending, and a new task is selected to be given control of the CPU (upon a call to the DISPCH routine).

9.3.2. Register Save Routine

The SAVE subroutine is called from the SCHEDL routine. Since R5 is already pushed into the stack by the JSR instruction, only the remaining registers R4 through R1 need be saved. At this point the user's stack pointer is saved, and the address of the active PSECT is placed in register 5. Finally, the system is switched to supervisor state, by making SUPSTK the new available stack, and control is given back to the calling routine.

In returning from this subroutine, the program must not execute an RTS instruction, since the new stack pointed to does not contain the return address. Instead, a jump instruction is used, utilizing the return address held in register 5. The jump instruction has the added advantage of not popping the stack, since this would contravene one of the purposes of the SAVE subroutine.

9.3.3. Insert Routine

SCHEDL calls the INSLAS routine after it calculates the entry address in the CPUQ of the calling task. INSLAS's purpose is to take the task that issued a SVC and place it in its appropriate waiting list. The steps that INSLAS goes through are explained as follows.

First, INSLAS gets the tasks ID from the task's PSECT, and with this ID it finds the appropriate entry in the CPUQTB. Since this task is going to be the most recent task placed on the queue, it means that the high-order byte of the CPUQTB entry is going to be zero (e.g., no other task follows this one on the waiting list). INSLAS knows the priority of this task, so it checks the appropriate entry of the CPUQ to see whether the queue is empty or not. If the queue is empty (e.g., the entry contains zeros), it means that this is going to be the only task on the queue, and INSLAS clears (zeros) the CPUQTB entry. It then goes on to store the ID for this task in both bytes of the CPUQ entry.

If the queue is not empty (e.g., the entry in the CPUQ is not zero), it means that there is a task (or several tasks) already waiting at that priority level, and INSLAS must insert this new task into the various queues. In this case INSLAS performs the following steps:

1. Get the contents of the low-order byte of CPUQ entry. This byte stores the ID of the last task, at that priority, waiting on the queue.

2. Get the entry for this ID in the CPUQTB. The high-order byte of this entry is zero, because this is the last task waiting on the queue.

3. Place the ID of the task being inserted in the queue into the high-order byte of the CPUQTB entry.

4. Place the ID of the inserted task in the low-order byte of the CPUQ entry. The old contents of the low-order byte of the CPUQ entry are saved.

5. Get the CPUQTB entry for the task being inserted.

6. Place the old contents of the low-order byte of the CPUQ entry in the low-order byte of the CPUQTB entry for the newly inserted task.

7. Clear the low-order byte of the CPUQTB for the newly inserted task.

Figure 9-6 illustrates the action of the insert routine for a task whose ID is 4 and whose priority level is 2. In the first case [Fig. 9-6(a) and (b)], we

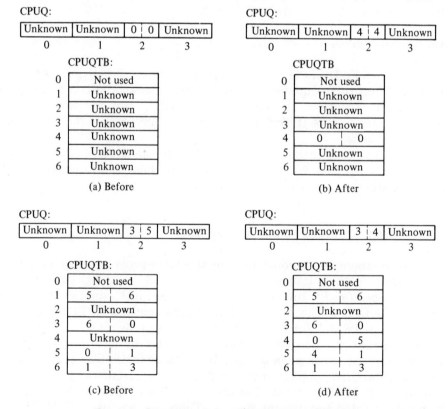

Fig. 9-6 Structure of the CPUQ and the CPUQTB before and after an INSLAS operation.

assume that no other task with priority 2 is waiting on the queue. In the second case [Fig. 9-6(c) and (d)], we assume there are four tasks at priority level 2 waiting on the queue. These tasks, in order, have IDs of 3, 6, 1, and 5.

9.3.4. Dispatch Routine

After a task is inserted into a waiting queue, its status is set to pending, and a new task is selected as a candidate for execution. The routine that selects this new task is the DISPCH routine called from SCHEDL. DISPCH performs its function by searching the CPUQ, from highest priority level to lowest, for any tasks that can be activated. If DISPCH finds such a task, it calls the unchain routine, UNCHN, in order to delink the selected task from its queue.

After the waiting task is unchained from the queue, the ACTIVE pointer is updated to reflect the PSECT for the newly selected task, the task's PSECT is set to indicate that it is in the running state, and the stack pointer for this task is loaded into the SP register. Finally, the contents of the task's registers are restored, and, as its final action, DISPCH issues an RTI (return from interrupt), which restores the contents of the PC and PS for this task. At this point the task takes control of the CPU.

9.3.5. Unchain Routine

When called by DISPCH, the unchain subroutine, UNCHN, takes the first waiting task out of the queue and updates the entries in both the CPUQ and the CPUQTB. In effect, the action of UNCHN is just the reverse of the INSLAS routine in that it performs a "remove first" rather than an "insert last" on the queue.

Besides updating entries, UNCHN also gets the address of the PSECT for the unchained task from the PSECTB. It then returns control to the DISPCH routine.

9.4. WRITING PROGRAMS TO RUN UNDER MMS

Although there is no constraint on the form programs may take while running under MMS, initializing this system properly is vital to get it to work correctly. Specifically, this means that the user must establish the correct entries in the CPU queue, the CPU queue table, and the PSECT table, plus defining a new PSECT for each task to be run (see Section 9.2.4). Having done so, the user can then set the system in motion by setting up the processor status and the user's stack pointer, by defining the PSECT pointer to the active task, and then jumping to the first task to be executed.

A listing of MMS is included at the end of this chapter to show the code for an implemented and running system. There are two tasks, "TASK1" and

"TASK2," included to show how MMS might be used. The tasks are nearly identical and have a logical structure, as shown in Fig. 9-7. The tasks perform their own I/O but do so without using interrupts. Thus they test the status of a device, and if it is not ready, the task queues itself, thereby relinquishing the CPU.

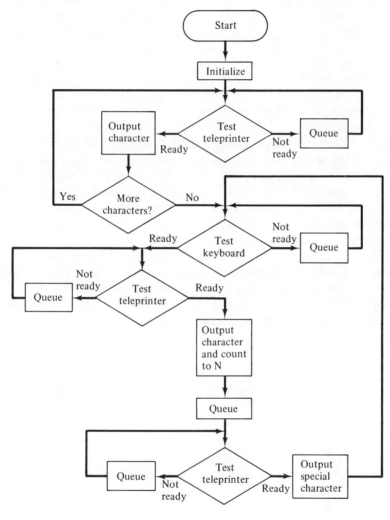

Fig. 9-7

9.5. EXPANDED SYSTEM

As shown, the system has the ability to interpret only one type of command, a QUEUE supervisor call, which places the task issuing the SVC at the end of a pending list and removes the task at the head of this list, assigning the CPU to it. Other supervisor calls could be implemented with little extra work, and an obvious candidate would be a "WAIT" SVC, which would place the task issuing it at the end of a "waiting state" list. Tasks on this list would not be placed on the pending list (e.g., made eligible for use of the CPU) until an external event, such as receipt of an interrupt signal, occurred.

The implementation of the WAIT SVC would speed up operations utilizing I/O devices, because a task requesting input or output would not regain control of the CPU until the I/O was actually ready or available. In the present system, any task at the head of the pending state list will gain control of the CPU and will have to test and possibly requeue if the I/O device is not ready. In those cases where a mix of I/O- and CPU-bound tasks were being executed, taking control away from the CPU-bound task before the I/O-bound task can proceed is clearly wasteful.

Three other features commonly found in small multiprogrammed operating systems are an I/O Control System (IOCS), a command language interpreter, and an error processor. The ideas behind an IOCS have already been discussed in Chapter 6, and these could be readily incorporated into MMS. A small and efficient command language interpreter would be useful in allowing the user to load and run tasks from a terminal device rather than by "programming them into" the system itself. Particularly useful might be commands that allow the terminal user to examine and change the contents of memory. Finally, error-diagnosis routines are necessary if the system is to be able to continue either after an error has occurred and some system (or user) action is required, or because an unexpected or unanticipated condition requires immediate attention.

9.6. LISTING OF MMS

```
1                   ;         M M S  -  - A MODEST MULTIPROGRAMMING SYSTEM
2                   ;         WRITTEN BY ED MACHADO AND MODIFIED BY R.  ECKHOUSE
3                   ;         1-NOVEMBER-1973
4                   ;
5        001000             =1000
6                   ;
7                   ;         R E G I S T E R   D E F I N I T I O N S
8                   ;
9        000000            R0=%0
10       000001            R1=%1
11       000002            R2=%2
12       000003            R3=%3
13       000004            R4=%4
14       000005            R5=%5
15       000006            SP=%6                ; STACK POINTER
16       000007            PC=%7                ; PROGRAM COUNTER
17                   ;
18                   ;         D A T A   D E F I N I T I O N S
19                   ;
20       104000            QUEUE=104000         ; SUPERVISOR CALL TRAP
21       000001            RUNBIT=1             ; RUN STATE BIT
22       000002            PENBIT=2             ; PENDING STATE BIT
23       000001            TKSTAT=1             ; TASK STATE OFFSET
24       000002            PRIO=2               ; PRIORITY OFFSET
25       000004            TKSP=4               ; STACK POINTER OFFSET
26       000017            STATMK=17            ; STATE MASK
27       000340            IOF=340              ; TO TURN OFF INTERRUPT
28       177400            HBM=177400           ; HIGH BIT MASK
29       177776            PSW=177776           ; PROCESSOR STATUS WORD
30       001554            USERST=TASK1         ; STARTING ADDRESS OF USER TASK
31                   ;
32                   ;         D E V I C E   D E F I N I T I O N S
33                   ;
34       177560            TKS1=177560          ; KEYBOARD 1 STATUS REG
35       177562            TKB1=TKS1+2          ; KEYBOARD 1 BUFFER
36       177564            TPS1=TKS1+4          ; TELEPRINTER 1 STATUS REG
37       177566            TPB1=TKS1+6          ; TELEPRINTER 1 BUFFER
38       176500            TKS2=176500          ; KEYBOARD 2 STATUS REG
39       176502            TKB2=TKS2+2          ; KEYBOARD 2 BUFFER
40       176504            TPS2=TKS2+4          ; TELEPRINTER 2 STATUS REG
41       176506            TPB2=TKS2+6          ; TELEPRINTER 2 BUFFER
```

```
 1
 2               ;
 3               ;      C P U    Q U E U E    D E F I N I T I O N
 4               ;
 5               ;   THERE ARE FOUR ENTRIES (EIGHT BYTES) IN
 6               ;   WHICH ENTRY 2 (PRIORITY 2) HAS THE ID
 7               ;   FOR THE ONLY TASK (TASK2) WAITING ON THE QUEUE
 8
 9 001000    000 CPUQ:    BYTE    0,0,0,0,2,2,0,0
   001001    000
   001002    000
   001003    000
   001004    002
   001005    002
   001006    000
   001007    000
10               ;
11               ;      C P U    Q U E U E    T A B L E    D E F I N I T I O N
12               ;
13               ;   ENTRY 2 IS THE ONLY ENTRY STORING RELEVANT
14               ;   INFORMATION.  IT CONTAINS ZEROS BECAUSE THE
15               ;   TASK WITH ID=2 (TASK2) IS NOT PRECEEDED OR
16               ;   FOLLOWED BY ANY OTHER TASK ON THE QUEUE, E.G.
17               ;   TASK WITH ID=2 IS THE ONLY TASK WAITING FOR
18               ;   THE CPU
19               ;
20 01010     000 CPUQTB:  BYTE    0,0,0,0,0,0,0,0,0,0
   01011     000
   01012     000
   01013     000
   01014     000
   01015     000
   01016     000
   01017     000
   01020     000
   01021     000
21               ;
22               ;      P S E C T    T A B L E    D E F I N I T I O N
23               ;
24               ;   THE PSECTB IS INITIALIZED WITH THE ADDRESS OF
25               ;   THE PSECT'S (PSECT1 AND PSECT2) DEFINED FOR
26               ;   THE TASKS WITHIN THE SYSTEM (TASK1 AND TASK2)
27               ;
28 01022  000000 PSECTB:  WORD    0,PSECT1,PSECT2,0,0
   01024  001110
   01026  001136
   01030  000000
   01032  000000
```

```
1                   ;
2                   ;      P O I N T E R S     A N D     T E M P O R I E S
3                   ;
4                   ;      ACTIVE HAS (IS INITIALIZED WITH) THE ADDRESS OF
5                   ;      THE PSECT FOR THE FIRST TASK TO GAIN CONTROL OF
6                   ;      THE CPU
7                   ;
8  001034 001110 ACTIVE: .WORD    PSECT1
9                   ;
10                  ;      SUPSTK IS THE STACK USED BY THE SUPERVISOR
11                  ;      WHILE IN CONTROL.
12                  ;
13        001106            .=.+50
14 01106 000000 SUPSTK: .WORD    0          ; STACK'S TOP CELL
15                  ;
16
17                  ;
18                  ;      P S E C T    D E F I N I T I O N S
19                  ;
20 01110    001 PSECT1: .BYTE    1,1        ; STATE AND ID RESP.
   01111    001
21 01112 000100          .WORD    100        ; PRIORITY OF 2
22 01114 001116          .WORD    .+2        ; STACK POINTER
23        001132          .=.+14             ; STACK AREA
24 01132 001554          .WORD    TASK1      ; PC FOR TASK1
25 01134 000000          .WORD    0          ; TOP OF STACK FOR PSECT1
26                  ;
27 01136    002 PSECT2: .BYTE    2,2        ; STATE AND ID RESP.
   01137    002
28 01140 000100          .WORD    100        ; PRIORITY OF 2
29 01142 001144          .WORD    .+2        ; STACK POINTER
30        001160          .=.+14             ; STACK AREA
31 01160 001710          .WORD    TASK2      ; PC FOR TASK2
32 01162 000000          .WORD    0          ; TOP OF STACK FOR PSECT2
```

```
 1                      ;
 2                      ;       INITIALIZE THE SYSTEM
 3                      ;
 4 001164 005000 START:  CLR     R0                      ; INITIALIZE ALL
 5 001166 010020 ST1:    MOV     R0,(R0)+                ; INTERRUPT VECTORS
 6 001170 005020         CLR     (R0)+                   ; TO HAVE THE PC
 7 001172 022700         CMP     #400,R0                 ; POINT TO THE NEXT LOCATION
          000400
 8 001176 001373         BNE     ST1                     ; WHICH IS A HALT INSTRUCTION
 9                      ;
10                      ;       SET UP THE INTERRUPT VECTORS
11                      ;
12 01200 012767          MOV     #SCHEDL,30              ; FOR SVC TRAP
         001236
         176622
13 01206 012767          MOV     #IOF,32                 ; WITH PRIORITY 7
         000340
         176616
14                      ;
15                      ;       SET UP PSW AND STACK, THEN BEGIN
16                      ;
17 01214 005067          CLR     PSW                     ; SET UP PROCESSOR STATUS
         176556
18 01220 012706          MOV     #PSECT1+26,SP           ; SET UP STACK POINTER
         001136
19 01224 012767          MOV     #PSECT1,ACTIVE          ; DEFINE THE ACTIVE TASK
         001110
         177602
20 01232 000167          JMP     USERST                  ; USER'S STARTING ADDRESS
         000316
```

```
 1
 2                    ;
 3                    ;     T H E     S C H E D U L E     R O U T I N E
 4              .      ;
 5                    ;                "S C H E D L"
 6                    ;
 7                    ;     THIS IS THE SUPERVISOR ROUTINE CALLED BY A
 8                    ;     TRAP THROUGH LOCATION 30 (OCTAL), IN RESPONSE
 9                    ;     TO AN SVC OR QUEUE CALL.
10                    ;
11 01236 004567 SCHEDL: JSR      R5, SAVE         ; SAVE ALL REGISTERS
         000044
12 01242 016500      MOV      PRIO(R5), R0     ; GET PRIORITY
         000002
13 01246 006200      ASR      R0               ; SHIFT
14 01250 006200      ASR      R0               ;   RIGHT TO
15 01252 006200      ASR      R0               ;     GET CORRECT
16 01254 006200      ASR      R0               ;        ENTRY IN CPUQ
17 01256 062700      ADD      #CPUQ, R0        ; ADD IN BASE OF QUEUE
         001000
18 01262 004767      JSR      PC, INSLAS       ; INSERT TASK IN QUEUE
         000056
19 01266 142765      BICB     #STATMK, TKSTAT(R5)     ; CLEAR TASK STATE
         000017
         000001
20 01274 152765      BISB     #PENBIT, TKSTAT(R5)     ; SET IT TO PENDING STATE
         000002
         000001
21 01302 000167      JMP      DISPCH           ; HEAD OF WAITING LIST
         000114
```

```
 1                    ;
 2                    ;          T H E    S A V E    R O U T I N E
 3                    ;
 4                    ;               "S A V E"
 5                    ;
 6                    ;     SUPERVISOR SUBROUTINE CALLED FROM SCHEDL WHICH
 7                    ;     PUSHES THE CONTENTS OF THE USER'S REGISTERS INTO
 8                    ;     THE PSECT STACK AND SWITCHES THE SYSTEM TO
 9                    ;     SUPERVISOR STATE (THE SYSTEM IS IN THE SUPERVISOR
10                    ;     STATE WHEN IT IS USING THE SUPERVISOR STACK).
11                    ;
12 01306 010446 SAVE:     MOV    R4,-(SP)         ;PUSH
13 01310 010346           MOV    R3,-(SP)         ;  REMAINING
14 01312 010246           MOV    R2,-(SP)         ;    REGISTERS
15 01314 010146           MOV    R1,-(SP)         ;      INTO
16 01316 010046           MOV    R0,-(SP)         ;       STACK
17 01320 010567           MOV    R5,RETADR        ;SET UP RETURN ADDR
         000016
18 01324 016705           MOV    ACTIVE,R5        ;ADDRESS OF ACTIVE PSECT
         177504
19 01330 010665           MOV    SP,TKSP(R5)      ;SAVE STACK PTR
         000004
20 01334 012706           MOV    #SUPSTK,SP       ;SUPERVISOR STATE/STACK
         001106
21 01340 000137           JMP    @#0              ;RETURN
         000000
22       001342           RETADR= -2             ;2ND WORD OF JMP INSTR
```

```
 1                ;
 2                ;     T H E     I N S E R T     R O U T I N E
 3                ;
 4                ;              "I N S L A S"
 5                ;
 6                ;     SUPERVISOR SUBROUTINE CALLED FROM SCHEDL TO
 7                ;     INSERT THE TASK THAT ISSUED AN SVC AT
 8                ;     THE END OF A WAITING LIST ("CPUQTB")
 9                ;
10  01344 111502 INSLAS: MOVB    @R5,R2          ;GET TASK'S ID
11  01346 042702         BIC     #HBM,R2         ;CLEAR THE HIGH BYTE
          177400
12  01352 006302         ASL     R2              ;MULTIPLY BY TWO
13  01354 062702         ADD     #CPUQTB,R2      ;GET CORRECT ENTRY
          001010
14  01360 005012         CLR     @R2             ;CLEAR THIS ENTRY
15  01362 111001         MOVB    @R0,R1          ;GET ID FOR LAST TASK
16  01364 001412         BEQ     EMPTYQ          ;IS IT ZERO?
17  01366 042701         BIC     #HBM,R1         ;NO, CLEAR HIGH BYTE OF ID WORD
          177400
18  01372 006301         ASL     R1              ;MULTIPLY BY TWO
19  01374 062701         ADD     #CPUQTB,R1      ;ADD IN BASE OF TABLE
          001010
20  01400 111012         MOVB    @R0,@R2         ;OLD LAST TASK IS PRECEEDING TAS
21  01402 111510         MOVB    @R5,@R0         ;NEW TASK IS LAST TASK
22  01404 111561         MOVB    @R5,1(R1)       ;PUT NEW TASK IN CPUQTB
          000001
23  01410 000207         RTS     PC              ;RETURN
24  01412 111510 EMPTYQ: MOVB    @R5,@R0         ;TASK ID INTO LOW BYTE
25  01414 111560         MOVB    @R5,1(R0)       ;AND HIGH BYTE OF CPUQ ENTRY
          000001
26  01420 000207         RTS     PC              ;RETURN
```

```
 1                    ;
 2                    ;        T H E     D I S P A T C H     R O U T I N E
 3                    ;
 4                    ;              "D I S P C H"
 5                    ;
 6                    ;        SUPERVISOR ROUTINE TO UNCHAIN A TASK FROM THE
 7                    ;        WAITING LIST AND ASSIGN THE CPU TO IT
 8                    ;
 9 001422 012700 DISPCH:  MOV     #CPUQ+10,R0        ; TRY HIGHEST PRIORITY
          001010
10 01426 005740 LOOP:     TST     -(R0)             ; ANYTHING TO DO?
11 01430 001776           BEQ     LOOP              ; NO, TRY THE NEXT LEVEL
12 01432 004767           JSR     PC,UNCHN          ; YES, UNCHAIN
          000042
13 01436 010567           MOV     R5,ACTIVE                 ; MAKE NEW TASK ACTIVE
          177372
14 01442 142765           BICB    #STATMK,TKSTAT(R5)        ; CLEAR TASK STATE
          000017
          000001
15 01450 152765           BISB    #RUNBIT,TKSTAT(R5)        ; SET STATE TO RUN
          000001
          000001
16 01456 016506           MOV     TKSP(R5),SP       ; GET TASK'S STACK POINTER
          000004
17 01462 012600           MOV     (SP)+,R0          ; RESTORE
18 01464 012601           MOV     (SP)+,R1          ;  CONTENTS
19 01466 012602           MOV     (SP)+,R2          ;   OF
20 01470 012603           MOV     (SP)+,R3          ;    REGISTERS
21 01472 012604           MOV     (SP)+,R4          ;     PREVIOUSLY
22 01474 012605           MOV     (SP)+,R5          ;      SAVED
23 01476 000002           RTI                       ; RETURN FROM INTERRUPT
```

```
 1
 2                   ;
 3                   ;      T H E    U N C H A I N    R O U T I N E
 4                   ;
 5                   ;              "U N C H N"
 6                   ;
 7                   ;      SUPERVISOR SUBROUTINE CALLED FROM THE DISPCH ROUTINE
 8                   ;      WHOSE ACTION IS TO TAKE THE FIRST TASK OUT OF A
 9                   ;      WAITING LIST AND UPDATE THE ENTRIES BOTH IN CPUQ AND
10                   ;      CPUQTB.
11                   ;
12 01500 011001 UNCHN:  MOV    @R0,R1              ; ID OF FIRST TASK ON QUEUE
13 01502 000301         SWAB   R1                  ; SWAP ID'S
14 01504 042701         BIC    #HBM,R1             ; CLEAR HIGH BYTE
         177400
15 01510 006301         ASL    R1                  ; MULTIPLY BY TWO
16 01512 116160         MOVB   CPUQTB+1(R1),1(R0)      ; NEW FIRST TASK
         001011
         000001
17 01520 001002         BNE    ANTKS               ; THERE IS ANOTHER TASK
18 01522 005010         CLR    @R0                 ; NO MORE TASKS-ZERO OUT ENTRY
19 01524 000406         BR     ARND                ; SKIP NEXT INSRTS
20 01526 111000 ANTKS:  MOVB   @R0,R0              ; NEW "FIRST TASK" ON QUEUE
21 01530 042700         BIC    #HBM,R0             ; CLEAR HIGH BYTE
         177400
22 01534 006300         ASL    R0                  ; MULTIPLY BY TWO
23 01536 105060         CLRB   CPUQTB(R0)          ; NO TASK PROCEEDS
         001010
24 01542 005061 ARND:   CLR    CPUQTB(R1)          ; CLEAR THIS ENTRY
         001010
25 01546 016105         MOV    PSECTB(R1),R5       ; GET PSECT'S ADDRESS
         001022
26 01552 000207         RTS    PC                  ; RETURN
```

```
 1                      ;
 2                      ;      "T A S K  1"
 3                      ;
 4                      ;      SIMPLE LITTLE TASK TO READ AND TYPE A CHARACTER,
 5                      ;      COUNT TO 100 (OCTAL), AND THEN INSERT A SPACE.
 6                      ;      AFTER EACH STEP, A QUEUE IS PERFORMED
 7                      ;
 8 001554 016705 TASK1:  MOV      BLANK,R5              ;PUT A BLANK IN R5
          000120
 9 001560 012701         MOV      #6,R1                 ;LETTER COUNT
          000006
10 01564 012702          MOV      #RDY,R2               ;BUFR POINTER
          001702
11 01570 105767 TA1:     TSTB     TPS1                  ;TIME TO PRINT?
          175770
12 01574 100402          BMI      PR1                   ;YES
13 01576 104000          QUEUE                          ;NO, GIVE UP CPU
14 01600 000773          BR       TA1                   ;TRY AGAIN
15 01602 112267 PR1:     MOVB     (R2)+,TPB1            ;PUT OUT CHARACTER
          175760
16 01606 005301          DEC      R1                    ;DECR LETTER COUNT
17 01610 001367          BNE      TA1                   ;MORE TO DO
18 01612 105767 AGN1:    TSTB     TKS1                  ;ANYTHING THERE?
          175742
19 01616 100402          BMI      YES1                  ;YES, DON'T QUEUE
20 01620 104000          QUEUE                          ;GIVE UP CPU
21 01622 000773          BR       AGN1                  ;TRY AGAIN
22 01624 105767 YES1:    TSTB     TPS1                  ;CAN WE PRINT?
          175734
23 01630 100402          BMI      YES2                  ;YES, DON'T QUEUE
24 01632 104000          QUEUE                          ;GIVE UP CPU
25 01634 000773          BR       YES1                  ;TRY AGAIN
26 01636 116767 YES2:    MOVB     TKB1,TPB1             ;PUT OUT CHARACTER
          175720
          175722
27 01644 012700          MOV      #100,R0               ;LOOP COUNT
          000100
28 01650 005300 T2:      DEC      R0                    ;DECR COUNT
29 01652 001376          BNE      T2                    ;LOOP UNTIL ZERO
30 01654 104000          QUEUE                          ;TIME TO GIVE UP CPU
31 01656 105767 T3:      TSTB     TPS1                  ;CAN WE SPACE?
          175702
32 01662 100402          BMI      YES3                  ;YES, GO AHEAD
33 01664 104000          QUEUE                          ;GIVE UP CPU
34 01666 000773          BR       T3                    ;TRY AGAIN
35 01670 110567 YES3:    MOVB     R5,TPB1               ;MOVE SPACE TO BUFFER
          175672
36 01674 104000          QUEUE                          ;GIVE UP CPU
37 01676 000745          BR       AGN1                  ;REPEAT THE WHOLE THING
38 01700    040 BLANK:   .ASCII   / /                   ;SOME BLANKS
   01701    040
39 01702    122 RDY:     .ASCII   /READY!/              ;READY MESSAGE
   01703    105
   01704    101
   01705    104
   01706    131
   01707    041
```

```
 1                    ;
 2                    ;      "T A S K  2"
 3                    ;
 4                    ;      THIS IS THE SAME AS TASK 1 WHICH SHOWS THAT
 5                    ;      THE TWO TASKS CAN RUN CONCURRENTLY WITHOUT
 6                    ;      USING INTERRUPTS AND WITHOUT THE LOSS OF INFORMATION.
 7                    ;
 8 001710 016705 TASK2:   MOV      DASH,R5           ;DIFFERENT SEPARATOR
        000120
 9 001714 012701         MOV      #7,R1             ;CHARACTER COUNT
        000007
10 01720 012702          MOV      #PRO,R2           ;BUFR POINTER
        002036
11 01724 105767 TA2:     TSTB     TPS2              ;TIME TO PRINT?
        174554
12 01730 100402          BMI      PR2               ;YES
13 01732 104000          QUEUE                      ;NO
14 01734 000773          BR       TA2               ;TRY AGAIN
15 01736 112267 PR2:     MOVB     (R2)+,TPB2        ;PUT OUT CHARACTER
        174544
16 01742 005301          DEC      R1                ;DECR CHAR COUNT
17 01744 001367          BNE      TA2               ;KEEP GOING
18 01746 105767 AGN2:    TSTB     TKS2              ;ANYTHING THERE?
        174526
19 01752 100402          BMI      YES4              ;YES, DON'T QUEUE
20 01754 104000          QUEUE                      ;GIVE UP CPU
21 01756 000773          BR       AGN2              ;TRY AGAIN
22 01760 105767 YES4:    TSTB     TPS2              ;CAN WE PRINT?
        174520
23 01764 100402          BMI      YES5              ;YES, DON'T QUEUE
24 01766 104000          QUEUE                      ;GIVE UP CPU
25 01770 000773          BR       YES4              ;TRY AGAIN
26 01772 116767 YES5:    MOVB     TKB2,TPB2         ;PUT OUT CHARACTER
        174504
        174506
27 02000 012701          MOV      #200,R1           ;LOOP COUNT
        000200
28 02004 005301 T4:      DEC      R1                ;DECR COUNT
29 02006 001376          BNE      T4                ;LOOP UNITL ZERO
30 02010 104000          QUEUE                      ;GIVE UP CPU
31 02012 105767 T5:      TSTB     TPS2              ;CAN WE DASH?
        174466
32 02016 100402          BMI      YES6              ;YES, GO AHEAD
33 02020 104000          QUEUE                      ;GIVE UP CPU
34 02022 000773          BR       T5                          ;TRY AGAIN
35 02024 110567 YES6:    MOVB     R5,TPB2           ;MOVE DASH TO BUFFER
        174456
36 02030 104000          QUEUE                      ;GIVE UP CPU
37 02032 000745          BR       AGN2      ;REPEAT
38 02034    055 DASH:    .ASCII   /--/              ;SOME DASHES
   02035    055
39 02036    120 PRO:     .ASCII   /PROCEED/         ;DIFF MESSAGE
   02037    122
   02040    117
   02041    103
   02042    105
   02043    105
   02044    104
40      001164'          END      START             ;END OF ASSEMBLY
```

EXERCISES

1. One of the problems with MMS is that there are insufficient states to handle tasks at various priority levels properly. Thus, if one job is at level 3 and one at level 7, the level 3 program can never pass the CPU to the level 7 program because the level 3 program is always chosen from the CPU queue of pending tasks. How could MMS be changed to overcome this limitation?

2. Instead of requiring the user to restore his stack, suggest an alternative whereby the system maintains the PSECT stack within the "system area."

3. If a system such as MMS can be written to operate without interrupts, what advantage do interrupts provide over polling or "scout's honor" programming (i.e., programming where each program guarantees to relinquish the CPU via an SVC within a given time interval).

4. How could an interrupting clock be added to MMS so that tasks would be forced to relinquish the CPU after a given time interval? Would such time slicing help or hinder the user? Would he need to know that it existed?

5. As suggested in Section 9.5, a WAIT SVC would be quite useful. How could it be integrated into MMS? What other SVCs could be added?

6. Design an IOCS for MMS. What type of SVCs would have to be added to MMS? How would the user call IOCS?

7. What type of commands would you implement in MMS? What new systems, besides IOCS, could be integrated into MMS (e.g., a loader, a text editor) requiring some form of command language interpretation?

8. MMS has no way to perform memory management. One technique is to form a chain of all unallocated words of memory into a chain of "free blocks." The first word of each block contains the size of the block; the link is maintained in the second word. When a request for memory is made, the chain is followed until a block, large enough to satisfy the request, is found. If such a block cannot be found, the system fails. When the block is found, the amount requested is removed from the end of the block and the block size is adjusted. Note that at least two words are necessary to maintain a block on the chain. If the block to be split exactly equals the requested size $+1$, the entire block is allocated.

   Deallocation operations are combined with maintenance operations. Each time a block is relinquished to the deallocator, the chain is searched for block contiguities. This is done in two steps. In the first, the chain is scanned to find a block that immediately follows the block being returned (tail contiguity). If such a block is found, it is unlinked from the chain and concatenated with the block being returned. This new block is then the subject of a head contiguity scan. If contiguity is detected, the block being returned is appended to the block on the chain and the size of the block is adjusted correspondingly.

   Integrate this memory management system into MMS.

9. What type of error-diagnosis routines should be implemented in MMS? Must these routines reside in memory.

10. Design and implement a file system for MMS.

A PRIMER OF NUMBER SYSTEMS

The concept of writing numbers, counting, and performing the basic operations of addition, subtraction, multiplication, and division has been directly developed by man. Every person is introduced to these concepts during his formal education. One of the most important factors in scientific development was the invention of the decimal numbering system. The system of counting in units of tens probably developed because man has 10 fingers. The use of the number 10 as the base of our number system is not of prime importance; any standard unit would do as well. The main use of a number system in early times was measuring quantities and keeping records, not performing mathematical calculations. As the sciences developed, old numbering systems became more and more outdated. The lack of an adequate numerical system greatly hampered the scientific development of early civilizations.

Two basic concepts simplified the operations needed to manipulate numbers; the concept of position, and the numeral zero. The concept of position consists of assigning to a number a value that depends both on the symbol and on its position in the whole number. For example, the digit 5 has a different value in each of the three numbers 135, 152, and 504. In the first number, the digit 5 has its original value 5; in the second, it has the value of 50; and in the last number, it has the value of 500, or 5 times 10 times 10.

Sometimes a position in a number does not have a value between 1 and 9. If this position were simply left out, there would be no difference in notation between 709 and 79. This is where the numeral zero fills the gap. In the number 709, there are 7 hundreds, 0 tens, and 9 units. Thus by using the concept of position and the numeral 0, arithmetic becomes quite easy.

A few basic definitions are needed before we proceed to see how these concepts apply to digital computers.

1. *Unit:* the standard utilized in counting separate items is the unit.

2. *Quantity:* the absolute or physical amount of units.

3. *Number:* a number is a symbol used to represent a quantity.

4. *Number system:* A number system is a means of representing quantities using a set of numbers. All modern number systems use the zero to indicate no units, and other symbols to indicate quantities. The *base* or *radix* of a number system is the number of symbols it contains, including zero. For example, the decimal number system is base or radix 10, because it contains 10 different symbols (0, 1, 2, 3, 4, 5, 6, 7, 8, and 9).

A.1. BINARY NUMBER SYSTEM

The fundamental requirement of a computer is the ability to represent numbers physically and to perform operations on the numbers thus represented. Although computers that are based on other number systems have been built, modern digital computers are all based on the binary (base 2) system. To represent 10 different numbers (0, 1, 2, . . ., 9) the computer must possess 10 different states with which to associate a digit value. However, most physical quantities have only two states: a light bulb is on or off; switches are on or off; holes in paper tape or cards are punched or not punched; current is positive or negative; material is magnetized or demagnetized; and so on. Because it can be represented by only two such physical states, the binary number system is used in computers.

To understand the binary number system upon which the digital computer operates, an analysis of the concepts underlying the decimal number system is beneficial.

A.1.1. Positional Coefficient

Although the decimal number system is familiar to us all, what we read and write as decimal numbers are not true mathematical quantities, but *symbolic representations.* These representations are sufficient for our use because they imply a *positional notation* which is well accepted. For example, 347 is the symbolic representation of

$$3 \times 10^2 + 4 \times 10' + 7 \times 10^0$$

Each numeral has a value that depends upon its position. The value of a position is called the *positional coefficient*, the digit-position weighting value, or simply the *weight.* The weights for each position are

$$\cdots \quad 10^3 \quad 10^2 \quad 10^1 \quad 10^0 \quad 10^{-1} \quad \cdots$$

Weighting values appear to serve no useful purpose in our familiar decimal numbering system, but their purpose becomes apparent when we consider the binary or base 2 numbering system. In binary we have only two digits, 0 and 1. In order to represent the numbers 1 to 10, we must utilize a count-and-carry principle familiar to us from the decimal system (so familiar we are not always aware that we use it). To count from 0 to 10 in decimal, we count as follows:

$$
\begin{array}{l}
0 \\
1 \\
2 \\
3 \\
4 \\
5 \\
6 \\
7 \\
8 \\
9 \\
10 \quad \text{with a carry to the } 10^1 \text{ column}
\end{array}
$$

Continuing the counting, when we reach 0 in the units column again, we carry another 1 to the tens column. This process is continued until the tens column becomes 0 and a 1 is carried into the hundreds column:

0	10	90
1	11	91
2	12	92
3	13	93
4	14	94
5	15	95
6	16	96
7	17	97
8	18	98
9	19	99
10 one carry	20 one carry	100 two carries

A.1.2. Counting in Binary Numbers

In the binary number system, the carry principle is used with only two digit symbols, 0 and 1. Thus the numbers used in the binary number system to count up to a decimal value of 10 are the following:

Binary	Decimal	Binary	Decimal
0	(0)	110	(6)
1	(1)	111	(7)
10	(2)	1000	(8)
11	(3)	1001	(9)
100	(4)	1010	(10)
101	(5)		

When using more than one number system, it is customary to subscript numbers with the applicable base (e.g., $101_2 = 5_{10}$).

A weighting table is used to convert binary numbers to the more familiar decimal system:

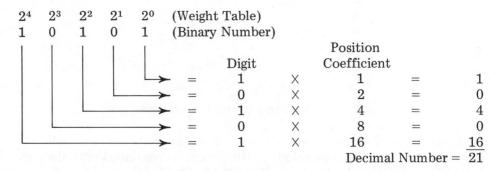

	Digit		Position Coefficient		
=	1	X	1	=	1
=	0	X	2	=	0
=	1	X	4	=	4
=	0	X	8	=	0
=	1	X	16	=	16

Decimal Number = 21

It should be obvious that the binary weighting table can be extended, like the decimal table, as far as desired. In general, to find the value of a binary number, multiply each digit by its position coefficient and then add all the products.

A.1.3. Arrangement of Values

By convention, weighting values are always arranged in the same manner, the highest on the extreme left and the lowest on the extreme right. Therefore, the position coefficient begins at 1 and increases from right to left. This convention has two very practical advantages. The first advantage is that it allows the elimination of the weighting table, as such. It is not necessary to label each binary number with weighting values, as the digit on the extreme right is always multiplied by 1, the digit to its left is always multiplied by 2, the next by 4, and so on. The second advantage is the elimination of some of the 0s. Whether a 0 is to the right or left, it will never add to the value of the binary number. Some 0s are required, however, as any 0s to the right of the highest-valued 1 are utilized as spaces or place keepers, to keep the 1s in their correct positions. The 0s to the left, however, provide no information about the number and may be discarded; thus the number 0001010111 = 1010111.

A.1.4. Significant Digits

The "leftmost" 1 in a binary number is called the *most significant digit (MSD)*. It is called the "most significant" in that it is multiplied by the highest position coefficient. The *least significant digit (LSD)* is the extreme right digit. It may be a 1 or 0 and has the lowest weighting value, 1. The terms LSD and MSD have the same meaning in the decimal system as in the binary system:

A.1.5. Conversion of Decimal to Binary

There are two commonly used methods for converting decimal numbers to binary equivalents. The reader may choose whichever method he finds easier to use.

1. *Subtraction-of-powers method:* to convert any decimal number to its binary equivalent by the subtraction-of-powers method, proceed as follows: Subtract the highest possible power of 2 from the decimal number and place a 1 in the appropriate weighting position of the partially completed binary number. Continue this procedure until the decimal number is reduced to 0. If, after the first subtraction, the next lower power of 2 cannot be subtracted, place a 0 in the appropriate weighting position. Example:

$$42_{10} \quad = \text{? binary}$$

42	10	2
-32	-8	-2
10	2	0

2^5	2^4	2^3	2^2	2^1	2^0	Power
32	16	8	4	2	1	Value
1	0	1	0	1	0	Binary

Therefore, $42_{10} = 101010_2$.

2. *Division method:* to convert a decimal number to binary by the synthetic division method, proceed as follows. Divide the decimal number by 2. If there is a remainder, put a 1 in the LSD of the partially formed

binary number; if there is no remainder, put a 0 in the LSD of the binary number. Divide the quotient from the first division by 2, and repeat the process. If there is a remainder, record a 1; if there is no remainder, record a 0. Continue until the quotient has been reduced to 0. Example:

$47_{10} = ?$ binary

Therefore, $47_{10} = 101111_2$.

A.2. OCTAL NUMBER SYSTEM

It is probably quite evident at this time that the binary number system, although quite nice for computers, is a little cumbersome for human usage. It is very easy for humans to make errors in reading and writing quantities of large binary numbers. The octal or base 8 numbering system helps to alleviate this problem. The base 8 or octal number system utilizes the digits 0 through 7 in forming numbers. The count-and-carry method mentioned earlier applies here also. Table A-1 shows the octal numbers with their binary equivalents.

Table A-1   Decimal–octal–binary equivalents.

Decimal	Octal	Binary	Decimal	Octal	Binary
0	0	0	7	7	111
1	1	1	8	10	1000
2	2	10	9	11	1001
3	3	11	10	12	1010
4	4	100	11	13	1011
5	5	101	12	14	1100
6	6	110	13	15	1101

The octal number system eliminates many of the problems involved in handling the binary number system used by a computer. To convert from binary numbers to octal numbers, the binary digits are separated into 3-bit groups. These 3-bit groups can be represented by one octal digit using the previous table of equivalents. A binary number,

$$11010111101$$

is separated into 3-bit groups by starting with the LSD end of the number and supplying leading zeros if necessary:

$$011\ 010\ 111\ 101$$

The binary groups are then replaced by their octal equivalents:

$$011_2 = 3_8$$
$$010_2 = 2_8$$
$$111_2 = 7_8$$
$$101_2 = 5_8$$

and the binary number is converted to its octal equivalent:

$$3\quad 2\quad 7\quad 5.$$

Conversely, an octal number can be expanded to a binary number using the same table of equivalents.

$$5307_8 = 101\ 011\ 000\ 111_2$$

A.2.1. Hexadecimal Number System

Another convenient number system is the *hexadecimal* or *base 16* number system. Like octal, hexadecimal is used to represent binary numbers in a more convenient fashion. Since it is base 16, there are 16 characters needed to represent the 16 digits in this number system. The decimal–hexadecimal–binary equivalents are shown in Table A-2.

Table A-2　Decimal–hexadecimal–binary equivalents.

Dec	Hex	Bin	Dec	Hex	Bin	Dec	Hex	Bin	Dec	Hex	Bin
0	0	0000	4	4	0100	8	8	1000	12	C	1100
1	1	0001	5	5	0101	9	9	1001	13	D	1101
2	2	0010	6	6	0110	10	A	1010	14	E	1110
3	3	0011	7	7	0111	11	B	1011	15	F	1111

In a fashion similar to the method for converting binary to octal, binary may be converted to hexadecimal by separating the binary digits into 4-bit groups. These 4-bit groups may be represented by one hexadecimal digit using Table A-2 as follows. The binary number

$$11010111101$$

is separated into 4-bit groups (supplying leading zeros, if necessary):

$$0110 \ 1011 \ 1101$$

and then the groups are replaced by their hexadecimal equivalents:

$$6 \qquad B \qquad D$$

That is,

$$6BD_{16} = 0110 \ 1011 \ 1101_2$$

A.2.2. Octal-to-Decimal Conversion

Octal numbers may be converted to decimal by multiplying each digit by its weight or position coefficient and then adding the resulting products. The position coefficients in this case are powers of 8, which is the base of the octal number system. Example:

$$2167_8 = ? \ \text{decimal}$$

$$
\begin{aligned}
2167_8 = \quad & 7 \times 8^0 = 7 \times 1 = 7 \\
+ & 6 \times 8^1 = 6 \times 8 = 48 \\
+ & 1 \times 8^2 = 1 \times 64 = 64 \\
+ & 2 \times 8^3 = 2 \times 512 = \underline{+1024} \\
& 1143
\end{aligned}
$$

Therefore, $2167_8 = 1143_{10}$.

A.2.3. Decimal-to-Octal Conversion

There are two commonly used methods for converting decimal numbers to their octal equivalents. The reader may choose the method that he prefers.

Subtraction-of-powers method. The following procedure is followed to convert a decimal number to its octal equivalent. Subtract from the decimal number the highest possible value of the form $a8^n$, where a is a number between 1 and 7 and n is an integer. Record the value of a. Continue to subtract decreasing powers of 8 (recording the value of a each time) until the decimal number is reduced to zero. Record a value of $a = 0$ for all powers of 8 that could not be subtracted. Table A-3 may be used to convert any number that can be represented by 12-bits (4095_{10} or less). Appendix G contains a similar table for converting larger numbers. Example:

$$2591_{10} = ? \text{ octal}$$

$$
\begin{array}{l}
2591 \\
-2560 = 5 \times 8^3 = 5 \times 512 \qquad\qquad 5 \quad 0 \quad 3 \quad 7 \\
\quad\ 31 \\
-\quad\ 0 = 0 \times 8^2 = 0 \times\ \ 64 \\
\quad\ 31 \\
-\quad 24 = 3 \times 8^1 = 3 \times\quad 8 \\
\quad\ \ 7 \\
-\quad\ \ 7 = 7 \times 8^0 = 7 \times\quad 1 \\
\quad\ \ 0
\end{array}
$$

Therefore, $2591_{10} = 5037_8$.

Table A-3　Octal–decimal conversion.

Octal-Digit Position/	Position Coefficients (Multipliers)							
8^n	0	1	2	3	4	5	6	7
1st (8^0)	0	1	2	3	4	5	6	7
2nd (8^1)	0	8	16	24	32	40	48	56
3rd (8^2)	0	64	128	192	256	320	384	448
4th (8^3)	0	512	1024	1536	2048	2560	3072	3584

Division method. A second method for converting a decimal number to its octal equivalent is by successive division by 8. Divide the decimal number by 8 and record the remainder as the least significant digit of the octal equivalent. Continue dividing by 8, recording the remainders as the successively higher significant digits until the quotient is reduced to zero. Example:

$$1376_{10} = ? \text{ octal}$$

	Quotient	Remainder
$8\,\overline{)\,1376}$	172	0
$8\,\overline{)\,172}$	21	4
$8\,\overline{)\,21}$	2	5
$8\,\overline{)\,2}$	0	2

$$2 \quad 5 \quad 4 \quad 0$$

Therefore, $1376_{10} = 2540_8$.

Using the division method to convert from one base to another is fine as long as one remembers that the arithmetic used must be in the base that one is converting from. Thus if we wish to convert 2540 in base 8 to its decimal equivalent, the example would appear as

	Quotient	Remainder
$12\,\overline{)\,2540}$	211	6
$12\,\overline{)\,211}$	15	7
$12\,\overline{)\,15}$	1	3
$12\,\overline{)\,1}$	0	1

$$1 \quad 3 \quad 7 \quad 6$$

Therefore, as expected from the results of the last example, $2540_8 = 1376_{10}$. Note that 10_{10} is 12_8 and all the arithmetic is base 8!

A.3. ARITHMETIC OPERATIONS WITH BINARY AND OCTAL NUMBERS

Now that the reader understands the conversion techniques between the familiar decimal number system and the binary and octal number systems, arithmetic operations with binary and octal numbers will be described. The reader should remember that the binary numbers are used in the computer and that the octal numbers are used as a means of representing the binary numbers conveniently.

A.3.1. Binary Addition

Addition of binary numbers follows the same rules as decimal or other bases. In adding decimal $1 + 8$, we have the sum of 9. This is the highest-value digit. Adding one more requires the least significant digit to become a 0 with a carry of 1 to the next place in the number. Similarly, adding binary $0 + 1$ we reach the highest value a single digit can have in the binary system, and adding one more $(1 + 1)$ requires a carry to the next higher power $(1 + 1 = 10)$. Take the binary numbers $101 + 10(5 + 2)$:

$$
\begin{array}{rcl}
101 &=& 5_{10} \\
+\ 010 &=& 2_{10} \\
\hline
111 &=& 7_{10}
\end{array}
$$

$0 + 1 = 1$, $1 + 0 = 1$, and $0 + 1 = 1$ with no carries required. The answer is 111, which is 7. Suppose that we add 111 to 101:

$$
\begin{array}{rcl}
11 &\leftarrow& \text{carries} \\
111 &=& 7_{10} \\
+\ 101 &=& 5_{10} \\
\hline
1100 &=& 12_{10}
\end{array}
$$

Now $1 + 1 = 0$ plus a carry of 1. In the second column, 1 plus the carry $1 = 0$, plus another carry. The third column is $1 + 1 = 0$ with a carry, plus the previous carry, or $1 + 1 + 1 = 11$. Our answer, 1100, is equal to $1 \times 2^3 + 1 \times 2^2$ or $8 + 4 = 12$, which is the correct solution for $7 + 5$.

A.3.2. Octal Addition

Addition for octal numbers should be no problem if we keep in mind the following basic rules for addition.

1. If the sum of any column is equal to or greater than the base of the system being used, the base must be subtracted from the sum to obtain the final result of the column.

2. If the sum of any column is equal to or greater than the base, there will be a carry to the next column equal to the number of times the base was subtracted.

3. If the result of any column is less than the base, the base is not

subtracted and no carry will be generated. Examples:

$$\begin{array}{rcl} & & 1 \\ 5_8 & = & 5_{10} \\ + 3_8 & = & 3_{10} \\ \hline 8 & & \\ - 8 & & \\ \hline 10_8 & = & 8_{10} \end{array}$$

$$\begin{array}{rcl} 3 \quad 5_8 & = & 29_{10} \\ 6 \quad 3_8 & = & 51_{10} \\ \hline 10 \quad 8 & & \\ - 8 - 8 & & \\ \hline 1 \quad 2 \quad 0_8 & = & 80_{10} \end{array}$$

A.4. NEGATIVE NUMBERS AND SUBTRACTION

Up to this point only positive numbers have been considered. Negative numbers and subtraction can be handled in the binary system in either of three ways: direct binary subtraction, by the two's-complement method, or by the one's-complement method.

A.4.1. Binary Subtraction (Direct)

Binary numbers may be directly subtracted in a manner similar to decimal subtraction. The essential difference is that if a borrow is required, it is equal to the base of the system, 2:

$$\begin{array}{rcl} 110 & = & 6_{10} \\ - 101 & = & 5_{10} \\ \hline 001 & = & 1_{10} \end{array}$$

To subtract 1 from 0 in the first column, a borrow of 1 was made from the second column which effectively added 2 to the first column. After the borrow, $2 - 1 = 1$ in the first column; in the second column $0 - 0 = 0$; and in the third column $1 - 1 = 0$.

The method of representation for direct binary subtraction is to show both the *sign* and the *magnitude* of the numbers being subtracted (the lack of a sign being taken to mean that the number is positive). In the example above, a smaller number was subtracted from a larger number so that the result was positive. If the problem had been stated as

$$\begin{array}{rcl} 101 & = & 5_{10} \\ - 110 & = & 6_{10} \\ \hline - 001 & = & - 1_{10} \end{array}$$

then the technique given for subtraction would not have worked. The technique requires us to always subtract the smaller number from the larger one and adjust the sign of the result if necessary.

As stated, the technique for subtracting binary *sign-magnitude* numbers on a computer is just too complicated. What is needed is a better, more uniform method which does not specify side conditions. What is used is *two's-complement arithmetic* because of its inherent simplicity for the computer.

A.4.2. Two's-Complement Arithmetic

To see how negative numbers are handled in the computer, consider a mechanical register, such as a car mileage indicator, being rotated backward. A five-digit register approaching and passing through zero would read the following:

$$
\begin{array}{c}
00005 \\
00004 \\
00003 \\
00002 \\
00001 \\
00000 \\
99999 \\
99998 \\
\text{etc.}
\end{array}
$$

It should be clear that the number 99998 corresponds to -2. Further, if we add

$$
\begin{array}{r}
00005 \\
99998 \\
\hline
\end{array}
$$

carry out of MSB 1   00003

and ignore the carry to the left, we have effectively performed the operation of subtracting

$$
5 - 2 = 3
$$

The number 99998 in this example is described as the *ten's-complement* of 2. Thus in the decimal number system, subtraction may be performed by adding the ten's complement of the number to be subtracted.

If a system of complements were to be used for representing negative numbers, the minus sign could be omitted in negative numbers. Thus all

numbers could be represented with five digits; 2 represented as 00002 and
−2 represented as 99998. Using such a system requires that a convention be
established as to what is and is not a negative number. For example, if the
mileage indicator is turned back to 48732, is it a negative 51268, or a positive 48732? With an ability to represent a total of 100,000 different numbers (0 to 99999), it would seem reasonable to use half for positive numbers
and half for negative numbers. In this situation, 0 to 49999 would be
regarded as positive, and 50000 to 99999 would be regarded as negative.

In this same manner, the two's complement of binary numbers are used
to represent negative numbers and to carry out binary subtraction. In octal
notation, numbers from 0000 to 3777 are regarded as positive and the
numbers from 4000 to 7777 are regarded as negative.

The two's complement of a number is defined as that number which
when added to the original number will result in a sum of zero. The binary
number 110110110110 has a two's complement equal to 001001001010,
as shown in the following addition:

$$
\begin{array}{c}
110\ 110\ 110\ 110 \\
001\ 001\ 001\ 010 \\
\hline
1\quad 000\ 000\ 000\ 000
\end{array}
$$

The easiest method of finding a two's complement is to first obtain the one's
complement, which is formed by setting each bit to the opposite value:

101 000 110 111	number
010 111 001 000	one's complement of the number

The two's complement of the number is then obtained by adding 1 to the
one's complement:

110 001 110 010	number
001 110 001 101	one's complement of the number
+1	add 1
001 110 001 110	two's complement of the number

Subtraction may be performed using the two's complement method.
That is, to subtract A from B, A must be expressed as its two's complement,
and then the value of B is added to it. Example:

010 010 010 111	A
101 101 101 001	two's complement of A
011 001 100 010	B
1 000 111 001 011	$B - A$

(carry is ignored)

A.4.3. One's-Complement Arithmetic

In generating the two's-complement form of a binary number, we first obtain the one's-complement form. This form may also be used to perform subtraction, as follows:

$$
\begin{array}{lll}
& 010\ 010\ 010\ 111 & A \\
& 101\ 101\ 101\ 000 & \text{one's complement of } A \\
& 011\ 001\ 100\ 010 & B \\
\hline
1\quad & 000\ 111\ 001\ 010 & B - A \\
& \quad\longrightarrow 1 & \text{carry is added in} \\
\hline
& 000\ 111\ 001\ 011 & \text{true result}
\end{array}
$$

The difference between one's- and two's-complement arithmetic is that in the first case the carry is not ignored (e.g., it is added back in), whereas in the second case it is.

A.4.4. Octal Subtraction

Subtraction is performed in the octal number system in three ways which are directly related to the subtractions in the binary system. Subtraction may be performed directly or by the radix (base) complement method.

A.4.4.1. Octal Subtraction (Direct)

Octal subtraction can be performed directly as illustrated in the following examples.

$$
\begin{array}{cc}
3567 - 2533 = ? & 2022 - 1234 = ? \\[4pt]
\begin{array}{r} 3567 \\ -\ 2533 \\ \hline 1034 \end{array}
&
\begin{array}{r} 2022 \\ -\ 1234 \\ \hline 0566 \end{array}
\end{array}
$$

Whenever a borrow is needed in octal subtraction, an 8 is borrowed, as in the second example above. In the first column, an 8 is borrowed which is added to the 2 already in the first column and the 4 is subtracted from the resulting 10. In the second column, an 8 is borrowed and added to the 1 which is already in the column (after the previous borrow) and the 3 is subtracted from the resulting 9. In the third column the 2 is subtracted from a borrowed 1 (originally a borrowed 8), and in the last column $1 - 1 = 0$.

A.4.4.2. Eight's-Complement Arithmetic

Octal subtraction may be performed by adding the eight's-complement of the subtrahend to the minuend. The eight's complement is obtained in the following manner.

3042   number
4735   seven's complement of the number
+1   add 1 to seven's complement to obtain
─────
4736   eight's complement

The seven's complement of the number is obtained by setting each digit of the complement to the value of 7 minus the digit of the number, as seen above. The eight's complement of the number is then obtained by adding 1 to the seven's complement. To prove that the complement is in fact a complement, the number is added to the complement and a result of zero and an overflow of 1 is obtained:

$$3042$$
$$+\ 4736$$
$$\overline{}$$
$$1\quad 0000$$

The following example uses the eight's complement to subtract a number:

3567 − 2533 = ?
2533   number
5244   seven's complement
+ 1   .
─────
5245   eight's complement

3567   minuend
+ 5245 eight's complement of subtrahend
─────
1   1034   difference

(carry is ignored)

A.4.4.3. Seven's-Complement Arithmetic

Analogous to the one's complement form for binary subtraction, there is the seven's-complement form for octal subtraction. Using the previous example, the seven's-complement arithmetic looks as follows:

3567 − 2533 = ?
2533   number
5244   seven's complement

3567   minuend
5244   seven's complement of subtrahend
─────
1   1033
     1   carry is added back in
─────
1034   true result

A.5. MULTIPLICATION AND DIVISION IN BINARY AND OCTAL NUMBERS

Though multiplication in computers is usually achieved by means other than formal multiplication, a formal method will be demonstrated as a teaching vehicle.

A.5.1. Binary Multiplication

In binary multiplication, the partial product is moved one position to the left as each successive multiplier is used. This is done in the same manner as in decimal multiplication. If the multiplier is a 0, the partial product can be a series of 0s, as in Example 2; or the next partial product can be moved two places to the left, as in Example 3; or three places, as in Example 4.

Example 1

$$
\begin{array}{ll}
462_{10} & \text{multiplicand} \\
127_{10} & \text{multiplier} \\
\hline
3234 & \text{first partial product} \\
924 & \text{second partial product} \\
462 & \text{third partial product} \\
\hline
58674 & \text{product}
\end{array}
$$

Example 2

$$
\begin{array}{r}
1110110_2 \\
1011_2 \\
\hline
1110110 \\
1110110 \\
0000000 \\
1110110 \\
\hline
10100010010_2
\end{array}
$$

Example 3

$$
\begin{array}{r}
1110110_2 \\
1011_2 \\
\hline
1110110 \\
1110110 \\
1110110 \\
\hline
10100010010_2
\end{array}
$$

Example 4

$$11001110_2$$
$$11001_2$$

$$11001110$$
$$11001110$$
$$11001110$$

$$1010000011110_2$$

Because of the difficult binary additions resulting from multiplications such as the previous examples, octal multiplication of the octal equivalents of binary numbers is often substituted.

A.5.2. Octal Multiplication

Multiplication of octal numbers is the same as multiplication of decimal numbers as long as the result is less than 10_8. Obviously this could be a problem if it were not for the fact that an octal multiplication table can be set up, similar to the decimal multiplication table, to make the job of multiplication of octal numbers quite simple. Table A-4 is a partially completed octal multiplication table that will be quite useful once you have filled in the blank squares.

Using the completed octal multiplication table, the following problems may be solved:

$$226_8 \times 12_8 = ?$$
$$226_8$$
$$\times 12_8$$

$$454$$
$$226$$

$$2734_8$$

$$1247_8 \times 305_8 = ?$$
$$1247_8$$
$$\times 305_8$$

$$6503$$
$$0000$$
$$3765$$

$$405203$$

Table A-4   Octal multiplication table.

	0	1	2	3	4	5	6	7
0	0	0	0	0	0	0	0	0
1	0	1	2	3	4	5	6	7
2	0	2	4	6	10			
3	0	3	6	11	14			
4								
5								
6								
7	0	7	16	25				

A.5.3. Binary Division

Once the reader has mastered binary subtraction and multiplication, binary division is easily learned. The following problem solutions illustrate binary division.

Divide $\dfrac{10010_2}{10_2}$

$$
\begin{array}{r}
1001 \\
10\,\overline{)\,10010} \\
\underline{10} \\
00 \\
\underline{00} \\
01 \\
\underline{00} \\
10 \\
\underline{10} \\
0
\end{array}
\qquad
\frac{10010_2}{10_2} = \frac{18_{10}}{2_{10}} = 1001_2 = 9_{10}
$$

Divide $\dfrac{1110_2}{100_2} = \dfrac{14_{10}}{4_{10}} = 3.5_{10}$

$$
\begin{array}{r}
11.1 \\
100\,\overline{)\,1110.0} \\
\underline{100} \\
110 \\
\underline{100} \\
100 \\
\underline{100} \\
0
\end{array}
\qquad
11.1_2 = 3.5_{10}
$$

A.5.4. Octal Division

Octal division uses the same principles as decimal division. All multiplication and subtraction must, however, be done in octal. (Refer to Table A-4.) The following problem solutions illustrate octal division.

$$\frac{62_8}{2_8} = \frac{50_{10}}{2_{10}} \qquad\qquad \frac{1714_8}{22_8}$$

$$
\begin{array}{r}
31 \\
2\,)\overline{62} \\
\underline{6} \\
02 \\
\underline{2} \\
0
\end{array}
= 31_8 = 25_{10}
\qquad\qquad
\begin{array}{r}
66 \\
22\,)\overline{1714} \\
\underline{154} \\
154 \\
\underline{154} \\
0
\end{array}
$$

EXERCISES

1. (a) Decimal-to-binary conversion: Convert the following decimal numbers to their binary equivalents:

1. 15_{10}	11. 4095_{10}
2. 18_{10}	12. 1502_{10}
3. 42_{10}	13. 377_{10}
4. 100_{10}	14. 501_{10}
5. 235_{10}	15. 828_{10}
6. 1_{10}	16. 907_{10}
7. 294_{10}	17. 4000_{10}
8. 117_{10}	18. 3456_{10}
9. 86_{10}	19. 2278_{10}
10. 4090_{10}	20. 1967_{10}

(b) Binary-to-decimal conversion: Convert the following binary numbers to their decimal equivalents:

1. 110_2	9. 11011011101_2
2. 101_2	10. 1110001110001_2
3. 1110110_2	11. 111010110100_2
4. 1011110_2	12. 111111110111_2
5. 0110110_2	13. 101011010101_2
6. 11111_2	14. 111111_2
7. 1010_2	15. 000101001_2
8. 110111_2	16. 111111111111_2

2. (a) Convert the following binary numbers to their octal equivalents:

1. 1110	9. 10111111
2. 0110	10. 111111111111
3. 111	11. 010110101011
4. 101111101	12. 111110110100
5. 110111110	13. 010100001011
6. 100000	14. 000010101101
7. 11000111	15. 110100100100
8. 011000	16. 010011111010

(b) Convert the following octal numbers to their binary equivalents:

1. 354	9. 70
2. 736	10. 64
3. 15	11. 7777
4. 10	12. 7765
5. 7	13. 3214
6. 5424	14. 4532
7. 307	15. 7033
8. 1101	16. 1243

(c) Convert the following decimal numbers to their octal equivalents:

1. 796	7. 1080
2. 32	8. 1344
3. 4037	9. 1512
4. 580	10. 3077
5. 1000	11. 4056
6. 3	12. 4095

(d) Convert the decimal numbers in (c) to their hexadecimal equivalents.

(e) Convert the following octal numbers to their decimal equivalents:

1. 17	7. 7773
2. 37	8. 7777
3. 734	9. 3257
4. 1000	10. 4577
5. 1200	11. 0012
6. 742	12. 0256

3. Perform the following binary additions:

1. 10110	2. 100	3. 11011
+ 101	+ 10	+ 0010

4. 10110111
   +   1
   ─────────

7. 1110
   100
   + 11
   ────

10. 100111
     111001
   + 101101
   ─────────

5. 1101
   101
   + 11
   ────

8. 1111
    101
   + 1000
   ──────

11. 11011001
     10010011
   + 11100011
   ──────────

6. 101
     1
   + 110
   ─────

9. 110111
    100100
   + 110001
   ────────

12. 11011011
     10111011
     00101011
     01010111
   + 01111101
   ──────────

4. Find the one's complement and the two's complement of the following numbers:

1. 011 100 110 010
2. 010 111 011 111
3. 011 110 000 000
4. 000 000 000 000
5. 000 000 000 001
6. 000 100 100 100

7. 000 000 000 111
8. 100 000 000 000
9. 100 000 010 010
10. 100 001 100 110
11. 111 111 111 110
12. 111 111 111 111

5. Subtract the following binary numbers directly:

1.   101000001
   − 010111101
   ──────────

3.   101011010111
   − 011111111101
   ─────────────

2.   1010111010
   − 0101110101
   ───────────

4.   101111100111
   − 010101110010
   ─────────────

6. Perform the following subtractions by the two's-complement method. Check your work by direct subtraction. Show all work.

1. 011 011 011 011 − 001 111 010 110
2. 000 111 111 111 − 000 001 001 101
3. 011 111 111 101 − 010 101 100 011
4. 001 101 111 110 − 001 100 101 011
5. 011 111 111 111 − 010 101 101 101

7. Multiply the following binary numbers:

1. 11011
   × 110
   ─────

2. 1011101
   × 101
   ───────

3. 101011101011
        × 10000
   ─────────────

8. Divide the following binary numbers:

1. 100
   ───
   10

2. 10000
   ─────
   100

3. 1100100
   ───────
   10100

9. Add the following octal numbers:

1.	42	4.	127	7.	777
	+ 53		256		543
			+ 724		+ 612

2.	45	5.	77	8.	437
	+ 23		+ 11		426
3.	34	6.	3357		772
	+ 76		+ 562		747
					+ 575

10. Subtract the following octal numbers directly:

1.	42	4.	53	7.	2743
	− 23		− 44		− 2174

2.	76	5.	7474	8.	7500
	− 34		− 4777		− 6373

3.	77	6.	7000
	− 11		− 6573

11. Perform the following octal subtractions by the eight's-complement method. Check your work by subtracting directly. Show all work.

    1. 0377 − 0233   5. 2311 − 2277
    2. 2345 − 1456   6. 0044 − 0017
    3. 1144 − 1046   7. 3234 − 2777
    4. 3000 − 0011   8. 1111 − 0777

12. Multiply the following octal numbers:

1.	65	3.	77	5.	425
	× 4		× 65		× 377

2.	14	4.	716	6.	571
	× 13		× 472		× 246

13. Prove the answers to the problems in Exercise 12 by division, as follows:

    multiplicand   multiplicand
    × multiplier   multiplier) product
    _____
    product

14. What two's-complement forms exist for base 5? For base r?

B PRIMER OF LOGIC OPERATIONS

Computers use logic operations in addition to arithmetic operations to solve problems. The logic operations have a direct relationship with the algebraic system and allow for the representation of logic statements in a special algebra of logic. In logic two basic connectives are used to express the relationship between two statements. These are the AND and the OR.

B.1. THE AND OPERATION

The following simple circuit with two switches illustrates the *AND operation*. If current is allowed to flow through a switch, the switch is said to have a value of 1. If the switch is open and current cannot flow, the switch has a value of 0. If the whole circuit is considered, it will have a value of 1 (i.e., current may flow through it) whenever *both* A and B are 1. This is the AND operation.

The AND operation is often stated $A \cdot B = F$. The multiplication symbol ($\cdot$) is used to represent the AND connective. The relationship between the variables and the resulting value of F is summarized in the following table.

A	B	F
0	0	0
0	1	0
1	0	0
1	1	1

When the AND operation is applied to binary numbers, a binary 1 will appear in the result if a binary 1 appeared in the corresponding position of the two numbers.

The AND operation can be used to *mask* out a portion of a 12-bit number:

To Be Masked Out	To Be Retained for Subsequent Operation	
010 101	010 101	(12-bit number)
000 000	111 111	(mask)
000 000	010 101	(result)

B.2. THE OR OPERATION

A second logic operation is the *OR* (sometimes called the *inclusive OR*). Statements that are combined using the OR connective are illustrated by the following circuit diagram:

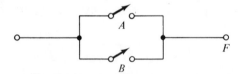

In this diagram current may flow whenever *either* A or B (or both) is closed ($F = 1$ if $A = 1$, or $B = 1$, or $A = 1$ and $B = 1$). This operation is expressed by the plus (+) sign; thus $A + B = F$. The following table shows the resulting value of F for changing values of A and B.

A	B	F
0	0	0
0	1	1
1	0	1
1	1	1

Thus, if A and B are the 12-bit numbers given here, $A + B$ is evaluated as follows:

$$A = 011\ 010\ 011\ 111$$

$$B = 100\ 110\ 010\ 011$$

$$A + B = 111\ 110\ 011\ 111$$

Remember that the "+" in the above example means "inclusive OR," not "add."

B.3. THE EXCLUSIVE-OR OPERATION

The third and last logic operation is the *exclusive-OR*. The exclusive-OR is similar to the inclusive-OR with the exception that one set of conditions for A and B are *excluded*. This exclusion can be symbolized in the circuit diagram by connecting the two switches together mechanically. This connection makes it impossible for the switches to be closed simultaneously, although they may be open simultaneously or individually.

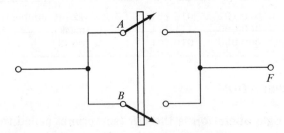

Thus the circuit is completed when $A = 1$ and $B = 0$, and when $A = 0$ and $B = 1$. This operation is expressed by the plus in a circle ($\oplus$) sign; thus $A \oplus B = F$. The results of the exclusive-OR operation are summarized in a table:

A	B	F
0	0	0
0	1	1
1	0	1
1	1	0

The exclusive-OR of two 12-bit numbers is evaluated and labeled F in the following operation:

$$A = 011\ 010\ 011\ 111$$
$$B = 100\ 110\ 010\ 011$$
$$F = 111\ 100\ 001\ 100$$

B.4. BOOLEAN ALGEBRA

Although we have considered only the three logical functions $\cdot$, $+$, and $\oplus$, there are others that we could have presented. These functions may be developed by considering all possible resulting values of F for changing values of A and B. The table of As, Bs, and Fs is as follows:

A	B	F_0	F_1	F_2	F_3	F_4	F_5	F_6	F_7	F_8	F_9	F_{10}	F_{11}	F_{12}	F_{13}	F_{14}	F_{15}
0	0	0	0	0	0	0	0	0	0	1	1	1	1	1	1	1	1
0	1	0	0	0	0	1	1	1	1	0	0	0	0	1	1	1	1
1	0	0	0	1	1	0	0	1	1	0	0	1	1	0	0	1	1
1	1	0	1	0	1	0	1	0	1	0	1	0	1	0	1	0	1

There are 16 different F's corresponding to two things (A and B) with two states (0 and 1) taken two at a time ($16 = 2^{2^2}$).

We may recognize that F_1 is the AND operation, F_2 the OR operation, and F_6 the exclusive-OR operation. In fact, all Fs have been named and represent such operations as $A(F_3)$, NOT $B(F_{10})$, and A AND NOT $B(F_2)$. From this set of 16 functions it is possible to form an algebra, called *Boolean algebra*, by choosing a set of functions (AND, OR, and NOT) different from the first three functions considered (e.g., AND, OR, and exclusive-OR), from which all other functions may be generated.

The term "algebra" refers to a mathematical system in which certain rules (called *postulates*) are defined and which relate how quantities in a certain domain may be manipulated. Boolean algebra is the product of George Boole, a nineteenth-century English mathematician, who wished to devise a mathematical formalism in which to express the concepts of symbolic logic. By developing a new algebra he hoped to be able to use the deductive properties of the system to deduce (prove) theorems from the given postulates.

The basic postulates in Boolean algebra are:

1. Commutativity:

$$A + B = B + A$$
$$A \cdot B = B \cdot A$$

2. Associativity:

$$A + (B + C) = (A + B) + C$$
$$A \cdot (B \cdot C) = (A \cdot B) \cdot C$$

3. Distributivity:

$$A \cdot (B + C) = (A \cdot B) + (A \cdot C)$$
$$A + B \cdot C = (A + B) \cdot (A + C)$$

4. Idempotence:

$$A + A = A$$
$$A \cdot A = A$$

5. Operation on 0 and 1:

$$0 + A = A$$
$$1 + A = 1$$
$$0 \cdot A = 0$$
$$1 \cdot A = A$$

6. Complementarity:

$$A \cdot \neg A = 0$$
$$A + \neg A = 1 \quad \text{where } \neg A \equiv \text{NOT } A$$

plus the laws of dualization, referred to as *DeMorgan's laws*:

7.

$$\neg(A \cdot B) = \neg A + \neg B$$
$$\neg(A + B) = \neg A \cdot \neg B$$

These postulates are actually more than sufficient, and it is easy to demonstrate that one postulate may be proved by utilizing the others.

For example, to prove

$$(A + B) \cdot (A + C) = A + B \cdot C$$

we show the following steps:

$$(A + B) \cdot (A + C) = (A \cdot A) + (A \cdot B) + (A \cdot C) + (B \cdot C)$$

But

$$(A \cdot A) = A = (A \cdot 1)$$
$$(A \cdot B) + (A \cdot C) = A \cdot (B + C)$$

so

$$(A + B) \cdot (A + C) = (A \cdot 1) + A \cdot (B + C) + (B \cdot C)$$

Now by applying the steps

$$(A \cdot 1) + A \cdot (B + C) = A \cdot (1 + B + C)$$
$$(1 + B + C) = 1 + (B + C) = 1$$

the result is

$$(A + B) \cdot (A + C) = A \cdot 1 + (B \cdot C)$$
$$= A + (B \cdot C)$$

Another means of proving such a deduction is through the use of a truth table. A truth table is nothing more than the table used to show the results of $A + B = F$ or $A \cdot B = F$, and so on. Each vertical column in the table represents a step toward the generation of the final desired result, which is equality of the functions on the right- and left-hand sides of the given equation. If the column result for the right-hand side agrees with the column result for the left-hand side, then equality is assumed to have been demonstrated.

For example, we may show that the equation

$$A \cdot B = \neg(\neg A + \neg B)$$

is true by constructing a truth table:

A	B	$\neg A$	$\neg B$	$(\neg A + \neg B)$	$\neg(\neg A + \neg B)$	$A \cdot B$
0	0	1	1	1	0	0
0	1	1	0	1	0	0
1	0	0	1	1	0	0
1	1	0	0	0	1	1

Since the last two columns are equal, the truth of the equation has been demonstrated.

Besides demonstrating the truth-table method, this example also points out that it is possible to construct the Boolean functions from each other. Thus given OR and NOT, AND can be constructed along with the other 13 Boolean functions. Interestingly enough, two of the functions (labeled F_8 and F_{14} and called NOR and NAND, respectively) are universal functions in that from just the one function all other functions may be constructed.

EXERCISES

1. Prove that $A \cdot B = \neg(\neg A + \neg B)$ by use of the postulates of Boolean algebra.

2. Prove that $(A + B) \cdot (A + C) = A + B \cdot C$ by use of the truth-table method.

3. Show how to construct the AND function given only the NOR function.

C ASCII AND RADIX-50 CHARACTER SETS

C.1. ASCII CHARACTER SET

Even-Parity Bit	7-Bit Octal Code	Character	Remarks
Ø	ØØØ	NUL	NULL, TAPE FEED, CONTROL/SHIFT/P.
1	ØØ1	SOH	START OF HEADING: ALSO SOM, START OF MESSAGE, CONTROL/A.
1	ØØ2	STX	START OF TEXT; ALSO EOA, END OF ADDRESS, CONTROL/B.
Ø	ØØ3	ETX	END OF TEXT; ALSO EOM, END OF MESSAGE, CONTROL/C.
1	ØØ4	EOT	END OF TRANSMISSION (END); SHUTS OFF TWX MACHINES, CONTROL/D.
Ø	ØØ5	ENQ	ENQUIRY (ENQRY); ALSO WRU, CONTROL/E.
Ø	ØØ6	ACK	ACKNOWLEDGE; ALSO RU, CONTROL/F.
1	ØØ7	BEL	RINGS THE BELL. CONTROL/G.
1	Ø1Ø	BS	BACKSPACE; ALSO FEO, FORMAT EFFECTOR. BACKSPACES SOME MACHINES, CONTROL/H.
Ø	Ø11	HT	HORIZONTAL TAB. CONTROL/I.
Ø	Ø12	LF	LINE FEED OR LINE SPACE (NEW LINE); ADVANCES PAPER TO NEXT LINE, DUPLICATED BY CONTROL/J.
1	Ø13	VT	VERTICAL TAB (VTAB). CONTROL/K.
Ø	Ø14	FF	FORM FEED TO TOP OF NEXT PAGE (PAGE). CONTROL/L.
1	Ø15	CR	CARRIAGE RETURN TO BEGINNING OF LINE. DUPLICATED BY CONTROL/M.
1	Ø16	SO	SHIFT OUT; CHANGES RIBBON COLOR TO RED. CONTROL/N.

Even-Parity Bit	7-Bit Octal Code	Character	Remarks
Ø	Ø17	SI	SHIFT IN; CHANGES RIBBON COLOR TO BLACK. CONTROL/O.
1	Ø2Ø	DLE	DATA LINE ESCAPE. CONTROL/P (DCØ).
Ø	Ø21	DC1	DEVICE CONTROL 1, TURNS TRANSMITTER (READER) ON, CONTROL/Q (X ON).
Ø	Ø22	DC2	DEVICE CONTROL 2, TURNS PUNCH OR AUXILIARY ON. CONTROL/R (TAPE, AUX ON).
1	Ø23	DC3	DEVICE CONTROL 3, TURNS TRANSMITTER (READER) OFF, CONTROL/S (X OFF).
Ø	Ø24	DC4	DEVICE CONTROL 4, TURNS PUNCH OR AUXILIARY OFF. CONTROL/T (AUX OFF).
1	Ø25	NAK	NEGATIVE ACKNOWLEDGE; ALSO ERR, ERROR. CONTROL/U.
1	Ø26	SYN	SYNCHRONOUS FILE (SYNC). CONTROL/V.
Ø	Ø27	ETB	END OF TRANSMISSION BLOCK; ALSO LEM, LOGICAL END OF MEDIUM. CONTROL/W.
Ø	Ø3Ø	CAN	CANCEL (CANCL). CONTROL/X.
1	Ø31	EM	END OF MEDIUM. CONTROL/Y.
1	Ø32	SUB	SUBSTITUTE. CONTROL/Z.
Ø	Ø33	ESC	ESCAPE. CONTROL/SHIFT/K.
1	Ø34	FS	FILE SEPARATOR. CONTROL/SHIFT/L.
Ø	Ø35	GS	GROUP SEPARATOR. CONTROL/SHIFT/M.
Ø	Ø36	RS	RECORD SEPARATOR. CONTROL/SHIFT/N.
1	Ø37	US	UNIT SEPARATOR. CONTROL/SHIFT/O.
1	Ø4Ø	SP	SPACE.
Ø	Ø41	!	
Ø	Ø42	"	
1	Ø43	#	
Ø	Ø44	$	
1	Ø45	%	
1	Ø46	&	
Ø	Ø47	'	ACCENT ACUTE OR ASPOSTROPHE.
Ø	Ø5Ø	(	
1	Ø51	)	
1	Ø52	*	
Ø	Ø53	+	
1	Ø54	'	
Ø	Ø55	—	
Ø	Ø56	.	
1	Ø57	/	
Ø	Ø6Ø	Ø	
1	Ø61	1	
1	Ø62	2	
Ø	Ø63	3	
1	Ø64	4	
Ø	Ø65	5	
Ø	Ø66	6	
1	Ø67	7	

Even-Parity Bit	7-Bit Octal Code	Character	Remarks
1	070	8	
0	071	9	
0	072	:	
1	073	;	
0	074	<	
1	075	=	
1	076	>	
0	077	?	
1	100	@	
0	101	A	
0	102	B	
1	103	C	
0	104	D	
1	105	E	
1	106	F	
0	107	G	
0	110	H	
1	111	I	
1	112	J	
0	113	K	
1	114	L	
0	115	M	
0	116	N	
1	117	O	
0	120	P	
1	121	Q	
1	122	R	
0	123	S	
1	124	T	
0	125	U	
0	126	V	
1	127	W	
1	130	X	
0	131	Y	
0	132	Z	
1	133	[	SHIFT/K.
0	134	\	SHIFT/L.
1	135	]	SHIFT/M.
1	136	↑	†
0	137	←	††
0	140	'	ACCENT GRAVE.
1	141	a	
1	142	b	

† The character ↑ appears as ^ on some machines.

†† The character appears as _ (underscore) on some machines.

Even-Parity Bit	7-Bit Octal Code	Character	Remarks
Ø	143	c	
1	144	d	
Ø	145	e	
Ø	146	f	
1	147	g	
1	15Ø	h	
Ø	151	i	
Ø	152	j	
1	153	k	
Ø	154	l	
1	155	m	
1	156	n	
Ø	157	o	
1	16Ø	p	
Ø	161	q	
Ø	162	r	
1	163	s	
Ø	164	t	
1	165	u	
1	166	v	
Ø	167	w	
Ø	17Ø	x	
1	171	y	
1	172	z	
Ø	173	{	
1	174	|	
Ø	175	}	THIS CODE GENERATED BY ALT MODE.
Ø	176	~	THIS CODE GENERATED BY PREFIX KEY (IF PRESENT)
1	177	DEL	DELETE, RUB OUT.

C.2. RADIX-50 CHARACTER SET

Character	ASCII Octal Equivalent	Radix-50 Equivalent
Space	4Ø	Ø
A–Z	1Ø1–132	1–32
$	44	33
	56	34
Unused		35
Ø–9	60–71	36–47

The maximum Radix-5Ø value is, thus,

$$47 * 50^2 + 47 * 50 + 47 = 174777$$

The following table provides a convenient means of translating between the ASCII character set and its Radix-50 equivalents. For example, given the ASCII string X2B, the Radix-50 equivalent is (arithmetic is performed in octal):

$$X = 113000$$
$$2 = 002400$$
$$B = 000002$$
$$\overline{}$$
$$X2B = 115402$$

Single Character or First Character		Second Character		Third Character	
A	003100	A	000050	A	000001
B	006200	B	000120	B	000002
C	011300	C	000170	C	000003
D	014400	D	000240	D	000004
E	017500	E	000310	E	000005
F	022600	F	000360	F	000006
G	025700	G	000430	G	000007
H	031000	H	000500	H	000010
I	034100	I	000550	I	000011
J	037200	J	000620	J	000012
K	042300	K	000670	K	000013
L	045400	L	000740	L	000014
M	050500	M	001010	M	000015
N	053600	N	001060	N	000016
O	056700	O	001130	O	000017
P	062000	P	001200	P	000020
Q	065100	Q	001250	Q	000021
R	070200	R	001320	R	000022
S	073300	S	001370	S	000023
T	076400	T	001440	T	000024
U	101500	U	001510	U	000025
V	104600	V	001560	V	000026
W	107700	W	001630	W	000027
X	113000	X	001700	X	000030
Y	116100	Y	001750	Y	000031
Z	121200	Z	002020	Z	000032
$	124300	$	002070	$	000033
.	127400	.	002140	.	000034
unused	132500	unused	002210	unused	000035
0	135600	0	002260	0	000036
1	140700	1	002330	1	000037
2	144000	2	002400	2	000040
3	147100	3	002450	3	000041
4	152200	4	002520	4	000042
5	155300	5	002570	5	000043
6	160400	6	002640	6	000044
7	163500	7	002710	7	000045
8	166600	8	002760	8	000046
9	171700	9	003030	9	000047

INSTRUCTION REPERTOIRE OF THE PDP-11

D

Mnemonic	Instruction Operation	Op Code	Condition Codes ZNCV
DOUBLE OPERAND GROUP: OPR scr, dst			
MOV(B)	MOVe (Byte (src) → (dst)	.1SSDD	√√−0
CMP(B)	CoMPare (Byte) (src) − (dst)	.2SSDD	√√√√
BIT(B)	Bit Test (Byte) (src) · (dst)	.3SSDD	√√−0
BIC(B)	Bit Clear (Byte) ¬ (src) · (dst) → (dst)	.4SSDD	√√−0
BIS(B)	Bit Set (Byte) (src) + (dst) → (dst)	.5SSDD	√√−0
ADD	ADD (src) + (dst) → (dst)	06SSDD	√√√√
SUB	SUBtract (dst) − (src) → (dst)	16SSDD	√√√√
CONDITIONAL BRANCHES: Bxx loc			
BR	BRanch (unconditionally) loc → (PC)	0004XX	−−
BNE	Branch if Not Equal (Zero) loc → (PC) if Z = 0	0010XX	−−
BEQ	Branch if Equal (Zero) loc → (PC) if Z = 1	0014XX	−−
BGE	Branch if Greater or Equal (Zero) loc → (PC) if N ⊕ V = 0	0020XX	−−

Mnemonic	Instruction Operation	Op Code	Condition Codes ZNCV
BLT	Branch if Less Than (Zero) loc → (PC) if N ⊕ V = 1	0024XX	— —
BGT	Branch if Greater Than (Zero) loc → (PC) if Z + (N ⊕ V = 0)	0030XX	— —
BLE	Branch if Less Than or Equal (Zero) loc → (PC) if Z + (N ⊕ V) = 1	0034XX	— —
BPL	Branch if Plus loc → (PC) if N = 0	1000XX	— —
BMI	Branch if Minus loc → (PC) if N = 1	1004XX	— —
BHI	Branch if Higher loc → (PC) if C + V = 0	1010XX	— —
BLOS	Branch if LOwer or Same loc → (PC) if C + V = 1	1014XX	— —
BVC	Branch if oVerflow Clear loc → (PC) if V = 0	1020XX	— —
BVS	Branch if oVerflow Set loc → (PC) if V = 1	1024XX	— —
BCC (or BHIS)	Branch if Carry Clear) loc → (PC) if C = 0	1030XX	— —
BCS (or BLO)	Branch if Carry Set loc → (PC) if C = 1	1034XX	— —

SUBROUTINE CALL: JSR reg, dst

Mnemonic	Instruction Operation	Op Code	Condition Codes ZNCV
JSR	Jump to SubRoutine (dst) → (tmp), (reg)↓ (PC) → (reg), (tmp) → (PC)	004RDD	— —

SUBROUTINE RETURN: RTS reg

Mnemonic	Instruction Operation	Op Code	Condition Codes ZNCV
RTS	ReTurn from Subroutine (reg) → (PC), ↑(reg)	00020R	— —

SINGLE OPERAND GROUP: OPR dst

Mnemonic	Instruction Operation	Op Code	Condition Codes ZNCV
CLR(B)	CLeaR (Byte) 0 → (dst)	.050DD	1000
COM(B)	COMplement (Byte) ¬(dst) → (dst)	.051DD	√√00
INC(B)	INCrement (Byte) (dst) + 1 → (dst)	.052DD	√√-√
DEC(B)	DECrement (Byte) (dst) − 1 → (dst)	.053DD	√√-√
NEG(B)	NEGate (Byte) ¬(dst) + 1 → (dst)	.054DD	√√√√
ADC(B)	ADd Carry (Byte) (dst) + (c) → (dst)	.055DD	√√√√

Mnemonic	Instruction Operation	Op Code	Condition Codes ZNCV
SBC(B)	SuBtract Carry (Byte) (dst) − (C) → (dst)	.056DD	√√√√
TST(B)	TeST (Byte) 0 − (dst)	.057DD	√√00
ROR(B)	ROtate Right (Byte) rotate right 1 place with C	.060DD	√√√√
ROL(B)	ROtate Left (Byte) rotate left 1 place with C	.061DD	√√√√
ASR(B)	Arithmetic Shift Right (Byte) shift right with sign extension	.062DD	√√√√
ASL(B)	Arithmetic Shift Left (Byte) shift left with lo-order zero	.063DD	√√√√
JMP	JuMP (dst) → (PC)	0001DD	— —
SWAB	SWAp Bytes bytes of a word are exchanged	0003DD	√√00

CONDITION CODE OPERATORS: OPR

Condition code operators set or clear combinations of condition code bits. Selected bits are set if $S = 1$ and cleared otherwise. Condition code bits corresponding to bits set as marked in the following word are set or cleared:

condition code operators:

0			0			0		2		4	S	N	Z	V	C

Thus SEC = 000261 sets the C-bit and has no effect on the other condition code bits (CLC = 000241 clears the C-bit).

OPERATE GROUP OPR

HALT	HALT processor stops; (R∅) and the HALT address in lights	000000	— —
WAIT	WAIT processor releases bus, waits for interrupt	000001	— —
RTI	ReTurn from Interrupt ↑ (PC), ↑ (PS	000002	√√√√
IOT	Input/Output Trap (PS)↓, (PC)↓, (20) → (PC), (22) → (PS)	000004	√√√√
RESET	RESET an INIT pulse is issued by the CP	000005	— —
EMT	EMulator Trap (PS)↓, (PC)↓, (30) → (PC), (32) → (PS)	104000-104377	√√√√
TRAP	TRAP (PS)↓, (PC)↓, (34) → (PC), (36) → (PS)	104400-104777	√√√√

NOTATION:

1. For order codes:

.	word/byte bit, set for byte (+100000)
SS	source field
DD	destination field
XX	offset (8-bit)

2. For operations:

·	and
+	or
¬	not
( )	contents of
⊕	XOR
↓	"is pushed onto the processor stack"
↑	"the contents of the top of the processor stack is popped and becomes"
→	"becomes"

3. For condition codes:

√	set conditionally
—	not affected
0	cleared
1	set

E THE OPERATOR'S CONSOLE

The PDP-11 Operator's Console allows the operator to achieve convenient control of the system. Through switches and keys on the console, programs or information can be manually inserted or modified. Moreover, indicator lamps on the console face display the status of the machine, the contents of the Bus Address Register, and the data at the output of the data paths. Although there are differences in the console among the members of the PDP-11 family, these differences can be ignored in this appendix and the 11/40's console can be explained as a fairly representative Operator's Console. The console is shown in Figure E-1.

Fig. E-1 PDP-11 Operators Console.

E.1. CONSOLE ELEMENTS

The console has the following indicators and switches:

1. A bank of six indicators, indicating the following conditions or operations: Run, Processor, Bus, Console, User, and Virtual.

2. An 18-bit Address Register display.

3. A 16-bit Data display.

4. An 18-bit Switch Register.

5. Control Switches:

   a. LOAD ADRS (Load Address)
   b. EXAM (Examine)
   c. CONT (Continue)
   d. ENABLE/HALT
   e. START
   f. DEP (Deposit)

E.1.1. Indicator Lights

The indicators signify specific machine functions, operations, or states. Each is defined below:

1. Run: lights when the processor clock is running. It is off when the processor is waiting for an asynchronous peripheral data response, or during a RESET instruction. It is on during a WAIT or HALT instruction.

2. Processor: lights when the processor has control of the bus.

3. Bus: lights when the UNIBUS is being used.

4. Console: lights when in console mode (manual operation). Machine is stopped and is not executing the stored program.

5. User: lights when the CPU is executing program instructions in User mode.

6. Virtual: lights when the ADDRESS Register display shows the 16-bit Virtual Address.

E.1.2. Register Displays

The Operator's Console has an 18-bit Address Register display and a 16-bit Data display. The Address Register display is tied directly to the output of an 18-bit flip-flop register called the Bus Address Register. This register displays the address of data examined or deposited.

The 16-bit data register is divided on the face of the console, by a line, into two 8-bit bytes. This register is tied to the output of the processor data paths and will reflect the output of the processor adder. After execution of a HALT instruction, the Data display will show the content of the R∅ register. It also will show data either examined or deposited when doing these control functions.

E.1.3. Switch Register

The PDP-11/10 and the PDP-11/20 can reference 2^{16} byte addresses, while the PDP-11/40 and PDP-11/45 can, using the memory management unit, reference 2^{18} byte addresses. Thus, the UNIBUS was designed with an expansion capability for full 18-bit addressing. In order that the console can access the entire 18-bit address scheme, the switch register is 18 bits wide. These bits are assigned as 0 through 17. The highest two are used only as addresses. A switch in the "up" position is considered to have a "1" value and in the "down" position to have a "0" value. The condition of the 18 switches can be loaded into the Bus Address Register or any memory location by using the appropriate control switches which are described below.

E.1.4. Control Switches

The switches listed in item 5 of the "Console Elements" have these specified control functions:

1. LOAD ADDR: transfers the contents of the 18-bit switch register into the bus address register.

2. EXAM: displays the contents of the location specified by the bus address register.

3. CONT: allows the machine to continue without initialization from whatever state it was in when halted, provided no other key operations have been performed.

4. ENABLE/HALT: allows or prevents running of programs. For a program to run, the switch must be in the ENABLE position (up). Placing the switch in the HALT position (down) will halt the system.

5. START: starts executing a program when the ENABLE/HALT switch is in the ENABLE position. When the START switch is depressed, it asserts a system initialization signal; the system actually starts when the switch is released. The processor will start executing at the address which was last loaded by the LOAD ADDR key, provided no other key operations have been performed. In HALT mode, depressing START effectively resets the entire system, thus acting as a manual I/O reset.

6. DEP: deposits the contents of the low 16 bits of the switch register into the address then displayed in the address register. (This switch is actuated by raising it.)

When the system is running a program, the LOAD ADDR, EXAM, and DEPOSIT functions are disabled to prevent disrupting the program. When the machine is to be halted, the ENABLE/HALT switch is thrown to the halt position. The machine will halt at the end of the current instruction.

E.2. OPERATING THE CONTROL SWITCHES

When the PDP-11 has been halted, it is possible to examine and update bus locations. To examine a specific location, the operator sets the switches of the switch register to correspond to the location's address. The operator then presses LOAD ADDRS, which will transfer the contents of the switch register into the bus address register. The location of the address to be examined is then displayed in the address register display. The operator then depresses EXAM. The data in that location will appear in the data register display.

If the operator then depresses EXAM again, the bus address register will be incremented by 2 to the next word address and the new location will be examined. In the PDP-11, the bus address register will always be pointing to the data currently displayed in the data register. The incrementation occurs when the EXAM switch is depressed, and then the location is examined.

The examine function has been designed so that if LOAD ADDR and then EXAM are depressed, the address register will not be incremented. In this case, the location reflected in the address register display is examined directly. However, on the second (and successive) depressings of EXAM, the bus address register is incremented. This will continue for successive depressings as long as another control switch is not depressed.

If the operator finds an incorrect entry in the data register, he can enter new data by putting it in the switch register and raising the DEP key. The address register will not increment when this data is deposited. Therefore, when the operator presses the EXAM key, he can examine the data he just deposited. However, when he pressed EXAM again, the system will increment.

If the operator attempts to examine data from, or deposit data into, a non-existent memory location, the "time out" feature will cause an error flag. The data register will then reflect location 4, the trap location, for references to nonexistent locations. To verify this condition, the operator should try to deposit some number other than four in the location causing the error; if four is still indicated, this would imply that either nothing is assigned to that location, or that whatever is assigned to that location is not working properly.

When doing consecutive examines or consecutive deposits, the address will increment by 2, to successive word locations. However, if the programmer is examining the fast registers (the "scratch pad" memory), the system only increments by 1. The reason for this is that once the switch register is set properly, the programmer can then use the four least significant bits of the switch register in examining fast memory registers from the front panel.

To start a PDP-11 program, the programmer loads the starting address of the program in the switch register, depresses LOAD ADDR, and after ensuring that the ENABLE/HALT switch is in the ENABLE position, depresses START. The program will start to run as soon as the START switch is released.

The Run indicator lamp is driven off the flip-flop that controls the clock. Normally, when the system is running, not only will this light be on, but the other lights (RUN, PROCESSOR, BUS, CONSOLE, USER, the Address lights, and the Address and Data registers) will be flickering. If the run light is on, and none of the other indicators are flickering, the system could be executing a "wait" instruction which waits for an interrupt. In this case, a "1" will appear in the data display.

While in the halt mode, if the operator wishes to do a single instruction, he simply depresses CONT. When CONT is depressed, the console momentarily passes control to the processor, allowing the machine to execute one instruction before regaining control. Each time the CONT switch is depressed, the machine will execute one instruction. The Bus Address Register will then show the last address referenced by the instruction (not necessarily the address of the instruction itself) and the Data display will reflect the data acted upon at that address.

To start the machine running its program again, the operator places the ENABLE/HALT switch in the ENABLE position, and depresses the CONT switch.

Appendix

F THE PDP-11 FAMILY OF COMPUTERS

The PDP-11 family of computers includes several processors, a large number of peripheral devices and options, and a broad range of software systems. All PDP-11 machines are architecturally similar, so that both hardware and software are upward compatible even though each machine has some of its own characteristics. Because of the UNIBUS characteristics, peripheral devices may be moved from one machine to another, so that if more processing power is needed, the user need only replace his processor, not his entire configuration. The major characteristics of the PDP-11 family of computers are summarized in Table F-1.

F.1. FAMILY DIFFERENCES

Probably the three most important differences between the members of the PDP-11 family are (1) processor operational mode, (2) the number of general-purpose registers, and (3) the memory management unit. The first feature, processor mode, is found in the expanded use of the processor status word shown in Fig. F-1.

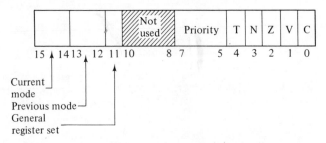

Fig. F-1 Processor status word.

Table F-1

	PDP-11 Family Computers			
	PDP-11/10	PDP-11/20	PDP-11/40	PDP-11/45
Central processor	KD11B	KA11	KD11A	KB11
General-purpose registers	8	8	8/9	16
Instructions	Basic set	Basic set	Extended set	Extended set
Segmentation hardware	No	No	Optional	Optional
Hardware stacks	Yes	Yes	Yes	Yes
Stack overflow detection	Fixed	Fixed	Variable option	Variable
Automatic priority interrupts	Single-line Multilevel	Multiline Multilevel	Multiline Multilevel	Multiline Multilevel
Processor modes	1	1	2	3
Overlapped instructions	No	No	No	Yes
Extended arithmetic	Option	Option	Option	Standard
Floating point	Software	Software	Option	Internal to CPU
Basic memory	Core	Core	Core	Core, MOS, or bipolar

On the 11/40 there are two modes of operation, kernel and user mode; on the 11/45 there is a third mode, called *supervisor mode*. These modes permit a fully protected environment for the multiprogramming system by providing the user with two (or three) distinct sets of processor stacks and memory management registers for memory mapping. In addition, certain instructions may not be executed in all modes and the processor will trap out if an inhibited instruction is executed.

The general registers found on the 11/40 and 11/45 are shown in Fig. F-2.

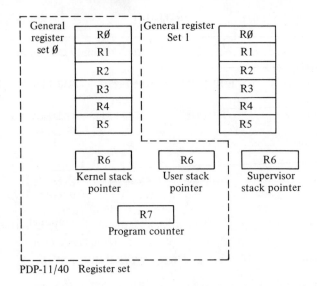

PDP-11/40   Register set

Fig. F-2   General registers.

The PDP-11/45 has two sets of general registers R0–R5, and there is a corresponding bit in the processor status word to show which set is in use. The two sets of registers can be used to increase the speed of real-time data handling or to facilitate multiprogramming. The six registers in general register set 0 can each be used as accumulator and/or index registers for a real-time task or device, or as general registers for a kernel or supervisor mode program. General register set 1 could be used by the remaining programs or user mode programs. The supervisor can, therefore, protect its general registers and stack from user programs, or other parts of the supervisor. Also, time can be saved by not having to save and restore registers when switching modes.

The last distinguishing characteristic of the top-of-the-line PDP-11s is the memory management unit. This unit provides the hardware facilities necessary for both memory management and protection. It is designed to be a facility for systems where the memory size is greater than 28K words, or for multiuser, multiprogramming systems where memory protection and relocation facilities are necessary.

The features of the memory management unit include

1. Separate pages for each mode of operation.

2. Varying page lengths, from 32 to 4096 words.

3. Protection and relocation on a per-page basis.

4. Fully transparent operation.

5. Memory expansion to 124K words.

F.2. VIRTUAL ADDRESSING

The addresses generated by all PDP-11 processors are 18-bit direct byte addresses. Although the PDP-11 word length and operational logic is all 16-bit length, the UNIBUS and CPU addressing logic actually is 18-bit length. Thus, while the PDP-11 word can only contain address references up to 32K words, the CPU and UNIBUS can reference addresses up to 128K words. These extra two bits of addressing logic provide the basic framework for expanded memory paging.

When the PDP-11 memory management unit is operating, the normal 16-bit direct byte address is no longer interpreted as a direct physical address (PA) but as a virtual address (VA), containing information to be used in constructing a new 18-bit physical address. The information contained in the VA is combined with relocation and description information contained in the active page register (APR) to yield an 18-bit PA (Fig. F-3). Memory can be dynamically allocated in pages each composed of from 1 to 128 blocks of 32 words.

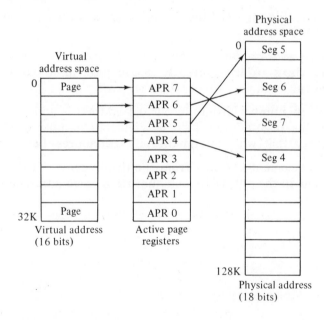

Fig. F-3 Virtual address mapping into physical address.

The starting address for each page is an integral multiple of 32 words and has a maximum size of 4096 words. Pages may be located anywhere within the 128K physical address space. The determination of which set of 8-page registers is used to form a PA is made by the current mode of operation of the CPU (i.e., kernel or user mode).

The formation of the physical address is illustrated in Fig. F-4.

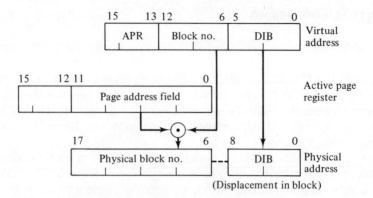

Fig. F-4 Construction of a physical address.

The logical sequence involved in constructing a PA is as follows:

1. Select a set of active page registers depending on current mode.

2. The active page field of the virtual address is used to select an active page register (APRØ–APR7).

3. The page address field of the selected active page register contains the starting address of the currently active page as a block number in physical memory.

4. The block number from the virtual address is added to the block number from the page address field to yield the number of the block in physical memory that will contain the physical address being constructed.

5. The displacement in block from the displacement field of the virtual address is joined to the physical block number to yield a true 18-bit physical address.

Appendix

CONVERSION TABLES

G.1. OCTAL-DECIMAL INTEGER CONVERSIONS

0000 to 0777 (Octal) = 0000 to 0511 (Decimal)

Octal	Decimal
10000	4096
20000	8192
30000	12288
40000	16384
50000	20480
60000	24576
70000	28672

	0	1	2	3	4	5	6	7
0000	0000	0001	0002	0003	0004	0005	0006	0007
0010	0008	0009	0010	0011	0012	0013	0014	0015
0020	0016	0017	0018	0019	0020	0021	0022	0023
0030	0024	0025	0026	0027	0028	0029	0030	0031
0040	0032	0033	0034	0035	0036	0037	0038	0039
0050	0040	0041	0042	0043	0044	0045	0046	0047
0060	0048	0049	0050	0051	0052	0053	0054	0055
0070	0056	0057	0058	0059	0060	0061	0062	0063
0100	0064	0065	0066	0067	0068	0069	0070	0071
0110	0072	0073	0074	0075	0076	0077	0078	0079
0120	0080	0081	0082	0083	0084	0085	0086	0087
0130	0088	0089	0090	0091	0092	0093	0094	0095
0140	0096	0097	0098	0099	0100	0101	0102	0103
0150	0104	0105	0106	0107	0108	0109	0110	0111
0160	0112	0113	0114	0115	0116	0117	0118	0119
0170	0120	0121	0122	0123	0124	0125	0126	0127
0200	0128	0129	0130	0131	0132	0133	0134	0135
0210	0136	0137	0138	0139	0140	0141	0142	0143
0220	0144	0145	0146	0147	0148	0149	0150	0151
0230	0152	0153	0154	0155	0156	0157	0158	0159
0240	0160	0161	0162	0163	0164	0165	0166	0167
0250	0168	0169	0170	0171	0172	0173	0174	0175
0260	0176	0177	0178	0179	0180	0181	0182	0183
0270	0184	0185	0186	0187	0188	0189	0190	0191
0300	0192	0193	0194	0195	0196	0197	0198	0199
0310	0200	0201	0202	0203	0204	0205	0206	0207
0320	0208	0209	0210	0211	0212	0213	0214	0215
0330	0216	0217	0218	0219	0220	0221	0222	0223
0340	0224	0225	0226	0227	0228	0229	0230	0231
0350	0232	0233	0234	0235	0236	0237	0238	0239
0360	0240	0241	0242	0243	0244	0245	0246	0247
0370	0248	0249	0250	0251	0252	0253	0254	0255

	0	1	2	3	4	5	6	7
0400	0256	0257	0258	0259	0260	0261	0262	0263
0410	0264	0265	0266	0267	0268	0269	0270	0271
0420	0272	0273	0274	0275	0276	0277	0278	0279
0430	0280	0281	0282	0283	0284	0285	0286	0287
0440	0288	0289	0290	0291	0292	0293	0294	0295
0450	0296	0297	0298	0299	0300	0301	0302	0303
0460	0304	0305	0306	0307	0308	0309	0310	0311
0470	0312	0313	0314	0315	0316	0317	0318	0319
0500	0320	0321	0322	0323	0324	0325	0326	0327
0510	0328	0329	0330	0331	0332	0333	0334	0335
0520	0336	0337	0338	0339	0340	0341	0342	0343
0530	0344	0345	0346	0347	0348	0349	0350	0351
0540	0352	0353	0354	0355	0356	0357	0358	0359
0550	0360	0361	0362	0363	0364	0365	0366	0367
0560	0368	0369	0370	0371	0372	0373	0374	0375
0570	0376	0377	0378	0379	0380	0381	0382	0383
0600	0384	0385	0386	0387	0388	0389	0390	0391
0610	0392	0393	0394	0395	0396	0397	0398	0399
0620	0400	0401	0402	0403	0404	0405	0406	0407
0630	0408	0409	0410	0411	0412	0413	0414	0415
0640	0416	0417	0418	0419	0420	0421	0422	0423
0650	0424	0425	0426	0427	0428	0429	0430	0431
0660	0432	0433	0434	0435	0436	0437	0438	0439
0670	0440	0441	0442	0443	0444	0445	0446	0447
0700	0448	0449	0450	0451	0452	0453	0454	0455
0710	0456	0457	0458	0459	0460	0461	0462	0463
0720	0464	0465	0466	0467	0468	0469	0470	0471
0730	0472	0473	0474	0475	0476	0477	0478	0479
0740	0480	0481	0482	0483	0484	0485	0486	0487
0750	0488	0489	0490	0491	0492	0493	0494	0495
0760	0496	0497	0498	0499	0500	0501	0502	0503
0770	0504	0505	0506	0507	0508	0509	0510	0511

			0	1	2	3	4	5	6	7		0	1	2	3	4	5	6	7
1000	0512	1000	0512	0513	0514	0515	0516	0517	0518	0519	1400	0768	0769	0770	0771	0772	0773	0774	0775
to	to	1010	0520	0521	0522	0523	0524	0525	0526	0527	1410	0776	0777	0778	0779	0780	0781	0782	0783
1777	1023	1020	0528	0529	0530	0531	0532	0533	0534	0535	1420	0784	0785	0786	0787	0788	0789	0790	0791
(Octal)	(Decimal)	1030	0536	0537	0538	0539	0540	0541	0542	0543	1430	0792	0793	0794	0795	0796	0797	0798	0799
		1040	0544	0545	0546	0547	0548	0549	0550	0551	1440	0800	0801	0802	0803	0804	0805	0806	0807
		1050	0552	0553	0554	0555	0556	0557	0558	0559	1450	0808	0809	0810	0811	0812	0813	0814	0815
		1060	0560	0561	0562	0563	0564	0565	0566	0567	1460	0816	0817	0818	0819	0820	0821	0822	0823
		1070	0568	0569	0570	0571	0572	0573	0574	0575	1470	0824	0825	0826	0827	0828	0829	0830	0831
		1100	0576	0577	0578	0579	0580	0581	0582	0583	1500	0832	0833	0834	0835	0836	0837	0838	0839
		1110	0584	0585	0586	0587	0588	0589	0590	0591	1510	0840	0841	0842	0843	0844	0845	0846	0847
		1120	0592	0593	0594	0595	0596	0597	0598	0599	1520	0848	0849	0850	0851	0852	0853	0854	0855
		1130	0600	0601	0602	0603	0604	0605	0606	0607	1530	0856	0857	0858	0859	0860	0861	0862	0863
		1140	0608	0609	0610	0611	0612	0613	0614	0615	1540	0864	0865	0866	0867	0868	0869	0870	0871
		1150	0616	0617	0618	0619	0620	0621	0622	0623	1550	0872	0873	0874	0875	0876	0877	0878	0879
		1160	0624	0625	0626	0627	0628	0629	0630	0631	1560	0880	0881	0882	0883	0884	0885	0886	0887
		1170	0632	0633	0634	0635	0636	0637	0638	0639	1570	0888	0889	0890	0891	0892	0893	0894	0895
		1200	0640	0641	0642	0643	0644	0645	0646	0647	1600	0896	0897	0898	0899	0900	0901	0902	0903
		1210	0648	0649	0650	0651	0652	0653	0654	0655	1610	0904	0905	0906	0907	0908	0909	0910	0911
		1220	0656	0657	0658	0659	0660	0661	0662	0663	1620	0912	0913	0914	0915	0916	0917	0918	0919
		1230	0664	0665	0666	0667	0668	0669	0670	0671	1630	0920	0921	0922	0923	0924	0925	0926	0927
		1240	0672	0673	0674	0675	0676	0677	0678	0679	1640	0928	0929	0930	0931	0932	0933	0934	0935
		1250	0680	0681	0682	0683	0684	0685	0686	0687	1650	0936	0937	0938	0939	0940	0941	0942	0943
		1260	0688	0689	0690	0691	0692	0693	0694	0695	1660	0944	0945	0946	0947	0948	0949	0950	0951
		1270	0696	0697	0698	0699	0700	0701	0702	0703	1670	0952	0953	0954	0955	0956	0957	0958	0959
		1300	0704	0705	0706	0707	0708	0709	0710	0711	1700	0960	0961	0962	0963	0964	0965	0966	0967
		1310	0712	0713	0714	0715	0716	0717	0718	0719	1710	0968	0969	0970	0971	0972	0973	0974	0975
		1320	0720	0721	0722	0723	0724	0725	0726	0727	1720	0976	0977	0978	0979	0980	0981	0982	0983
		1330	0728	0729	0730	0731	0732	0733	0734	0735	1730	0984	0985	0986	0987	0988	0989	0990	0991
		1340	0736	0737	0738	0739	0740	0741	0742	0743	1740	0992	0993	0994	0995	0996	0997	0998	0999
		1350	0744	0745	0746	0747	0748	0749	0750	0751	1750	1000	1001	1002	1003	1004	1005	1006	1007
		1360	0752	0753	0754	0755	0756	0757	0758	0759	1760	1008	1009	1010	1011	1012	1013	1014	1015
		1370	0760	0761	0762	0763	0764	0765	0766	0767	1770	1016	1017	1018	1019	1020	1021	1022	1023

	0	1	2	3	4	5	6	7		0	1	2	3	4	5	6	7
2000	1024	1025	1026	1027	1028	1029	1030	1031	2400	1280	1281	1282	1283	1284	1285	1286	1287
2010	1032	1033	1034	1035	1036	1037	1038	1039	2410	1288	1289	1290	1291	1292	1293	1294	1295
2020	1040	1041	1042	1043	1044	1045	1046	1047	2420	1296	1297	1298	1299	1300	1301	1302	1303
2030	1048	1049	1050	1051	1052	1053	1054	1055	2430	1304	1305	1306	1307	1308	1309	1310	1311
2040	1056	1057	1058	1059	1060	1061	1062	1063	2440	1312	1313	1314	1315	1316	1317	1318	1319
2050	1064	1065	1066	1067	1068	1069	1070	1071	2450	1320	1321	1322	1323	1324	1325	1326	1327
2060	1072	1073	1074	1075	1076	1077	1078	1079	2460	1328	1329	1330	1331	1332	1333	1334	1335
2070	1080	1081	1082	1083	1084	1085	1086	1087	2470	1336	1337	1338	1339	1340	1341	1342	1343
2100	1088	1089	1090	1091	1092	1093	1094	1095	2500	1344	1345	1346	1347	1348	1349	1350	1351
2110	1096	1097	1098	1099	1100	1101	1102	1103	2510	1352	1353	1354	1355	1356	1357	1358	1359
2120	1104	1105	1106	1107	1108	1109	1110	1111	2520	1360	1361	1362	1363	1364	1365	1366	1367
2130	1112	1113	1114	1115	1116	1117	1118	1119	2530	1368	1369	1370	1371	1372	1373	1374	1375
2140	1120	1121	1122	1123	1124	1125	1126	1127	2540	1376	1377	1378	1379	1380	1381	1382	1383
2150	1128	1129	1130	1131	1132	1133	1134	1135	2550	1384	1385	1386	1387	1388	1389	1390	1391
2160	1136	1137	1138	1139	1140	1141	1142	1143	2560	1392	1393	1394	1395	1396	1397	1398	1399
2170	1144	1145	1146	1147	1148	1149	1150	1151	2570	1400	1401	1402	1403	1404	1405	1406	1407
2200	1152	1153	1154	1155	1156	1157	1158	1159	2600	1408	1409	1410	1411	1412	1413	1414	1415
2210	1160	1161	1162	1163	1164	1165	1166	1167	2610	1416	1417	1418	1419	1420	1421	1422	1423
2220	1168	1169	1170	1171	1172	1173	1174	1175	2620	1424	1425	1426	1427	1428	1429	1430	1431
2230	1176	1177	1178	1179	1180	1181	1182	1183	2630	1432	1433	1434	1435	1436	1437	1438	1439
2240	1184	1185	1186	1187	1188	1189	1190	1191	2640	1440	1441	1442	1443	1444	1445	1446	1447
2250	1192	1193	1194	1195	1196	1197	1198	1199	2650	1448	1449	1450	1451	1452	1453	1454	1455
2260	1200	1201	1202	1203	1204	1205	1206	1207	2660	1456	1457	1458	1459	1460	1461	1462	1463
2270	1208	1209	1210	1211	1212	1213	1214	1215	2670	1464	1465	1466	1467	1468	1469	1470	1471
2300	1216	1217	1218	1219	1220	1221	1222	1223	2700	1472	1473	1474	1475	1476	1477	1478	1479
2310	1224	1225	1226	1227	1228	1229	1230	1231	2710	1480	1481	1482	1483	1484	1485	1486	1487
2320	1232	1233	1234	1235	1236	1237	1238	1239	2720	1488	1489	1490	1491	1492	1493	1494	1495
2330	1240	1241	1242	1243	1244	1245	1246	1247	2730	1496	1497	1498	1499	1500	1501	1502	1503
2340	1248	1249	1250	1251	1252	1253	1254	1255	2740	1504	1505	1506	1507	1508	1509	1510	1511
2350	1256	1257	1258	1259	1260	1261	1262	1263	2750	1512	1513	1514	1515	1516	1517	1518	1519
2360	1264	1265	1266	1267	1268	1269	1270	1271	2760	1520	1521	1522	1523	1524	1525	1526	1527
2370	1272	1273	1274	1275	1276	1277	1278	1279	2770	1528	1529	1530	1531	1532	1533	1534	1535

Left index:

2000	1024
to	to
2777	1535
(Octal)	(Decimal)

Octal	Decimal
10000	4096
20000	8192
30000	12288
40000	16384
50000	20480
60000	24576
70000	28672

		0	1	2	3	4	5	6	7		0	1	2	3	4	5	6	7
3000	1536	3000	1536 1537 1538 1539 1540 1541 1542 1543								3400	1792 1793 1794 1795 1796 1797 1798 1799							
to	to	3010	1544 1545 1546 1547 1548 1549 1550 1551								3410	1800 1801 1802 1803 1804 1805 1806 1807							
3777	2047	3020	1552 1553 1554 1555 1556 1557 1558 1559								3420	1808 1809 1810 1811 1812 1813 1814 1815							
(Octal)	(Decimal)	3030	1560 1561 1562 1563 1564 1565 1566 1567								3430	1816 1817 1818 1819 1820 1821 1822 1823							
		3040	1568 1569 1570 1571 1572 1573 1574 1575								3440	1824 1825 1826 1827 1828 1829 1830 1831							
		3050	1576 1577 1578 1579 1580 1581 1582 1583								3450	1832 1833 1834 1835 1836 1837 1838 1839							
		3060	1584 1585 1586 1587 1588 1589 1590 1591								3460	1840 1841 1842 1843 1844 1845 1846 1847							
		3070	1592 1593 1594 1595 1596 1597 1598 1599								3470	1848 1849 1850 1851 1852 1853 1854 1855							
		3100	1600 1601 1602 1603 1604 1605 1606 1607								3500	1856 1857 1858 1859 1860 1861 1862 1863							
		3110	1608 1609 1610 1611 1612 1613 1614 1615								3510	1864 1865 1866 1867 1868 1869 1870 1871							
		3120	1616 1617 1618 1619 1620 1621 1622 1623								3520	1872 1873 1874 1875 1876 1877 1878 1879							
		3130	1624 1625 1626 1627 1628 1629 1630 1631								3530	1880 1881 1882 1883 1884 1885 1886 1887							
		3140	1632 1633 1634 1635 1636 1637 1638 1639								3540	1888 1889 1890 1891 1892 1893 1894 1895							
		3150	1640 1641 1642 1643 1644 1645 1646 1647								3550	1896 1897 1898 1899 1900 1901 1902 1903							
		3160	1648 1649 1650 1651 1652 1653 1654 1655								3560	1904 1905 1906 1907 1908 1909 1910 1911							
		3170	1656 1657 1658 1659 1660 1661 1662 1663								3570	1912 1913 1914 1915 1916 1917 1918 1919							
		3200	1664 1665 1666 1667 1668 1669 1670 1671								3600	1920 1921 1922 1923 1924 1925 1926 1927							
		3210	1672 1673 1674 1675 1676 1677 1678 1679								3610	1928 1929 1930 1931 1932 1933 1934 1935							
		3220	1680 1681 1682 1683 1684 1685 1686 1687								3620	1936 1937 1938 1939 1940 1941 1942 1943							
		3230	1688 1689 1690 1691 1692 1693 1694 1695								3630	1944 1945 1946 1947 1948 1949 1950 1951							
		3240	1696 1697 1698 1699 1700 1701 1702 1703								3640	1952 1953 1954 1955 1956 1957 1958 1959							
		3250	1704 1705 1706 1707 1708 1709 1710 1711								3650	1960 1961 1962 1963 1964 1965 1966 1967							
		3260	1712 1713 1714 1715 1716 1717 1718 1719								3660	1968 1969 1970 1971 1972 1973 1974 1975							
		3270	1720 1721 1722 1723 1724 1725 1726 1727								3670	1976 1977 1978 1979 1980 1981 1982 1983							
		3300	1728 1729 1730 1731 1732 1733 1734 1735								3700	1984 1985 1986 1987 1988 1989 1990 1991							
		3310	1736 1737 1738 1739 1740 1741 1742 1743								3710	1992 1993 1994 1995 1996 1997 1998 1999							
		3320	1744 1745 1746 1747 1748 1749 1750 1751								3720	2000 2001 2002 2003 2004 2005 2006 2007							
		3330	1752 1753 1754 1755 1756 1757 1758 1759								3730	2008 2009 2010 2011 2012 2013 2014 2015							
		3340	1760 1761 1762 1763 1764 1765 1766 1767								3740	2016 2017 2018 2019 2020 2021 2022 2023							
		3350	1768 1769 1770 1771 1772 1773 1774 1775								3750	2024 2025 2026 2027 2028 2029 2030 2031							
		3360	1776 1777 1778 1779 1780 1781 1782 1783								3760	2032 2033 2034 2035 2036 2037 2038 2039							
		3370	1784 1785 1786 1787 1788 1789 1790 1791								3770	2040 2041 2042 2043 2044 2045 2046 2047							

		0	1	2	3	4	5	6	7		0	1	2	3	4	5	6	7
4000	2048	4000	2048	2049	2050	2051	2052	2053	2054	2055	4400	2304	2305	2306	2307	2308	2309	2310	2311
to	to	4010	2056	2057	2058	2059	2060	2061	2062	2063	4410	2312	2313	2314	2315	2316	2317	2318	2319
4777	2559	4020	2064	2065	2066	2067	2068	2069	2070	2071	4420	2320	2321	2322	2323	2324	2325	2326	2327
(Octal)	(Decimal)	4030	2072	2073	2074	2075	2076	2077	2078	2079	4430	2328	2329	2330	2331	2332	2333	2334	2335
		4040	2080	2081	2082	2083	2084	2085	2086	2087	4440	2336	2337	2338	2339	2340	2341	2342	2343
		4050	2088	2089	2090	2091	2092	2093	2094	2095	4450	2344	2345	2346	2347	2348	2349	2350	2351
Octal	Decimal	4060	2096	2097	2098	2099	2100	2101	2102	2103	4460	2352	2353	2354	2355	2356	2357	2358	2359
10000	4096	4070	2104	2105	2106	2107	2108	2109	2110	2111	4470	2360	2361	2362	2363	2364	2365	2366	2367
20000	8192																		
30000	12288	4100	2112	2113	2114	2115	2116	2117	2118	2119	4500	2368	2369	2370	2371	2372	2373	2374	2375
40000	16384	4110	2120	2121	2122	2123	2124	2125	2126	2127	4510	2376	2377	2378	2379	2380	2381	2382	2383
50000	20480	4120	2128	2129	2130	2131	2132	2133	2134	2135	4520	2384	2385	2386	2387	2388	2389	2390	2391
60000	24576	4130	2136	2137	2138	2139	2140	2141	2142	2143	4530	2392	2393	2394	2395	2396	2397	2398	2399
70000	28672	4140	2144	2145	2146	2147	2148	2149	2150	2151	4540	2400	2401	2402	2403	2404	2405	2406	2407
		4150	2152	2153	2154	2155	2156	2157	2158	2159	4550	2408	2409	2410	2411	2412	2413	2414	2415
		4160	2160	2161	2162	2163	2164	2165	2166	2167	4560	2416	2417	2418	2419	2.20	2421	2422	2423
		4170	2168	2169	2170	2171	2172	2173	2174	2175	4570	2424	2425	2426	2427	2428	2429	2430	2431
		4200	2176	2177	2178	2179	2180	2181	2182	2183	4600	2432	2433	2434	2435	2436	2437	2438	2439
		4210	2184	2185	2186	2187	2188	2189	2190	2191	4610	2440	2441	2442	2443	2444	2445	2446	2447
		4220	2192	2193	2194	2195	2196	2197	2198	2199	4620	2448	2449	2450	2451	2452	2453	2454	2455
		4230	2200	2201	2202	2203	2204	2205	2206	2207	4630	2456	2457	2458	2459	2460	2461	2462	2463
		4240	2208	2209	2210	2211	2212	2213	2214	2215	4640	2464	2465	2466	2467	2468	2469	2470	2471
		4250	2216	2217	2218	2219	2220	2221	2222	2223	4650	2472	2473	2474	2475	2476	2477	2478	2479
		4260	2224	2225	2226	2227	2228	2229	2230	2231	4660	2480	2481	2482	2483	2484	2485	2486	2487
		4270	2232	2233	2234	2235	2236	2237	2238	2239	4670	2488	2489	2490	2491	2492	2493	2494	2495
		4300	2240	2241	2242	2243	2244	2245	2246	2247	4700	2496	2497	2498	2499	2500	2501	2502	2503
		4310	2248	2249	2250	2251	2252	2253	2254	2255	4710	2504	2505	2506	2507	2508	2509	2510	2511
		4320	2256	2257	2258	2259	2260	2261	2262	2263	4720	2512	2513	2514	2515	2516	2517	2518	2519
		4330	2264	2265	2266	2267	2268	2269	2270	2271	4730	2520	2521	2522	2523	2524	2525	2526	2527
		4340	2272	2273	2274	2275	2276	2277	2278	2279	4740	2528	2529	2530	2531	2532	2533	2534	2535
		4350	2280	2281	2282	2283	2284	2285	2286	2287	4750	2536	2537	2538	2539	2540	2541	2542	2543
		4360	2288	2289	2290	2291	2292	2293	2294	2295	4760	2544	2545	2546	2547	2548	2549	2550	2551
		4370	2296	2297	2298	2299	2300	2301	2302	2303	4770	2552	2553	2554	2555	2556	2557	2558	2559

	0	1	2	3	4	5	6	7			0	1	2	3	4	5	6	7
5000	2560	2561	2562	2563	2564	2565	2566	2567		5400	2816	2817	2818	2819	2820	2821	2822	2823
5010	2568	2569	2570	2571	2572	2573	2574	2575		5410	2824	2825	2826	2827	2828	2829	2830	2831
5020	2576	2577	2578	2579	2580	2581	2582	2583		5420	2832	2833	2834	2835	2836	2837	2838	2839
5030	2584	2585	2586	2587	2588	2589	2590	2591		5430	2840	2841	2842	2843	2844	2845	2846	2847
5040	2592	2593	2594	2595	2596	2597	2598	2599		5440	2848	2849	2850	2851	2852	2853	2854	2855
5050	2600	2601	2602	2603	2604	2605	2606	2607		5450	2856	2857	2858	2859	2860	2861	2862	2863
5060	2608	2609	2610	2611	2612	2613	2614	2615		5460	2864	2865	2866	2867	2868	2869	2870	2871
5070	2616	2617	2618	2619	2620	2621	2622	2623		5470	2872	2873	2874	2875	2876	2877	2878	2879
5100	2624	2625	2626	2627	2628	2629	2630	2631		5500	2880	2881	2882	2883	2884	2885	2886	2887
5110	2632	2633	2634	2635	2636	2637	2638	2639		5510	2888	2889	2890	2891	2892	2893	2894	2895
5120	2640	2641	2642	2643	2644	2645	2646	2647		5520	2896	2897	2898	2899	2900	2901	2902	2903
5130	2648	2649	2650	2651	2652	2653	2654	2655		5530	2904	2905	2906	2907	2908	2909	2910	2911
5140	2656	2657	2658	2659	2660	2661	2662	2663		5540	2912	2913	2914	2915	2916	2917	2918	2919
5150	2664	2665	2666	2667	2668	2669	2670	2671		5550	2920	2921	2922	2923	2924	2925	2926	2927
5160	2672	2673	2674	2675	2676	2677	2678	2679		5560	2928	2929	2930	2931	2932	2933	2934	2935
5170	2680	2681	2682	2683	2684	2685	2686	2687		5570	2936	2937	2938	2939	2940	2941	2942	2943
5200	2688	2689	2690	2691	2692	2693	2694	2695		5600	2944	2945	2946	2947	2948	2949	2950	2951
5210	2696	2697	2698	2699	2700	2701	2702	2703		5610	2952	2953	2954	2955	2956	2957	2958	2959
5220	2704	2705	2706	2707	2708	2709	2710	2711		5620	2960	2961	2962	2963	2964	2965	2966	2967
5230	2712	2713	2714	2715	2716	2717	2718	2719		5630	2968	2969	2970	2971	2972	2973	2974	2975
5240	2720	2721	2722	2723	2724	2725	2726	2727		5640	2976	2977	2978	2979	2980	2981	2982	2983
5250	2728	2729	2730	2731	2732	2733	2734	2735		5650	2984	2985	2986	2987	2988	2989	2990	2991
5260	2736	2737	2738	2739	2740	2741	2742	2743		5660	2992	2993	2994	2995	2996	2997	2998	2999
5270	2744	2745	2746	2747	2748	2749	2750	2751		5670	3000	3001	3002	3003	3004	3005	3006	3007
5300	2752	2753	2754	2755	2756	2757	2758	2759		5700	3008	3009	3010	3011	3012	3013	3014	3015
5310	2760	2761	2762	2763	2764	2765	2766	2767		5710	3016	3017	3018	3019	3020	3021	3022	3023
5320	2768	2769	2770	2771	2772	2773	2774	2775		5720	3024	3025	3026	3027	3028	3029	3030	3031
5330	2776	2777	2778	2779	2780	2781	2782	2783		5730	3032	3033	3034	3035	3036	3037	3038	3039
5340	2784	2785	2786	2787	2788	2789	2790	2791		5740	3040	3041	3042	3043	3044	3045	3046	3047
5350	2792	2793	2794	2795	2796	2797	2798	2799		5750	3048	3049	3050	3051	3052	3053	3054	3055
5360	2800	2801	2802	2803	2804	2805	2806	2807		5760	3056	3057	3058	3059	3060	3061	3062	3063
5370	2808	2809	2810	2811	2812	2813	2814	2815		5770	3064	3065	3066	3067	3068	3069	3070	3071

5000   2560
to   to
5777   3071
(Octal)   (Decimal)

	0	1	2	3	4	5	6	7		0	1	2	3	4	5	6	7
6000	3072	3073	3074	3075	3076	3077	3078	3079	6400	3328	3329	3330	3331	3332	3333	3334	3335
6010	3080	3081	3082	3083	3084	3085	3086	3087	6410	3336	3337	3338	3339	3340	3341	3342	3343
6020	3088	3089	3090	3091	3092	3093	3094	3095	6420	3344	3345	3346	3347	3348	3349	3350	3351
6030	3096	3097	3098	3099	3100	3101	3102	3103	6430	3352	3353	3354	3355	3356	3357	3358	3359
6040	3104	3105	3106	3107	3108	3109	3110	3111	6440	3360	3361	3362	3363	3364	3365	3366	3367
6050	3112	3113	3114	3115	3116	3117	3118	3119	6450	3368	3369	3370	3371	3372	3373	3374	3375
6060	3120	3121	3122	3123	3124	3125	3126	3127	6460	3376	3377	3378	3379	3380	3381	3382	3383
6070	3128	3129	3130	3131	3132	3133	3134	3135	6470	3384	3385	3386	3387	3388	3389	3390	3391
6100	3136	3137	3138	3139	3140	3141	3142	3143	6500	3392	3393	3394	3395	3396	3397	3398	3399
6110	3144	3145	3146	3147	3148	3149	3150	3151	6510	3400	3401	3402	3403	3404	3405	3406	3407
6120	3152	3153	3154	3155	3156	3157	3158	3159	6520	3408	3409	3410	3411	3412	3413	3414	3415
6130	3160	3161	3162	3163	3164	3165	3166	3167	6530	3416	3417	3418	3419	3420	3421	3422	3423
6140	3168	3169	3170	3171	3172	3173	3174	3175	6540	3424	3425	3426	3427	3428	3429	3430	3431
6150	3176	3177	3178	3179	3180	3181	3182	3183	6550	3432	3433	3434	3435	3436	3437	3438	3439
6160	3184	3185	3186	3187	3188	3189	3190	3191	6560	3440	3441	3442	3443	3444	3445	3446	3447
6170	3192	3193	3194	3195	3196	3197	3198	3199	6570	3448	3449	3450	3451	3452	3453	3454	3455
6200	3200	3201	3202	3203	3204	3205	3206	3207	6600	3456	3457	3458	3459	3460	3461	3462	3463
6210	3208	3209	3210	3211	3212	3213	3214	3215	6610	3464	3465	3466	3467	3468	3469	3470	3471
6220	3216	3217	3218	3219	3220	3221	3222	3223	6620	3472	3473	3474	3475	3476	3477	3478	3479
6230	3224	3225	3226	3227	3228	3229	3230	3231	6630	3480	3481	3482	3483	3484	3485	3486	3487
6240	3232	3233	3234	3235	3236	3237	3238	3239	6640	3488	3489	3490	3491	3492	3493	3494	3495
6250	3240	3241	3242	3243	3244	3245	3246	3247	6650	3496	3497	3498	3499	3500	3501	3502	3503
6260	3248	3249	3250	3251	3252	3253	3254	3255	6660	3504	3505	3506	3507	3508	3509	3510	3511
6270	3256	3257	3258	3259	3260	3261	3262	3263	6670	3512	3513	3514	3515	3516	3517	3518	3519
6300	3264	3265	3266	3267	3268	3269	3270	3271	6700	3520	3521	3522	3523	3524	3525	3526	3527
6310	3272	3273	3274	3275	3276	3277	3278	3279	6710	3528	3529	3530	3531	3532	3533	3534	3535
6320	3280	3281	3282	3283	3284	3285	3286	3287	6720	3536	3537	3538	3539	3540	3541	3542	3543
6330	3288	3289	3290	3291	3292	3293	3294	3295	6730	3544	3545	3546	3547	3548	3549	3550	3551
6340	3296	3297	3298	3299	3300	3301	3302	3303	6740	3552	3553	3554	3555	3556	3557	3558	3559
6350	3304	3305	3306	3307	3308	3309	3310	3311	6750	3560	3561	3562	3563	3564	3565	3566	3567
6360	3312	3313	3314	3315	3316	3317	3318	3319	6760	3568	3569	3570	3571	3572	3573	3574	3575
6370	3320	3321	3322	3323	3324	3325	3326	3327	6770	3576	3577	3578	3579	3580	3581	3582	3583

6000 — 3072
to — to
6777 — 3583
(Octal) — (Decimal)

Octal	Decimal
10000	4096
20000	8192
30000	12288
40000	16384
50000	20480
60000	24576
70000	28672

	0	1	2	3	4	5	6	7		0	1	2	3	4	5	6	7
7000	3584 3585 3586 3587 3588 3589 3590 3591								7400	3840 3841 3842 3843 3844 3845 3846 3847							
7010	3592 3593 3594 3595 3596 3597 3598 3599								7410	3848 3849 3850 3851 3852 3853 3854 3855							
7020	3600 3601 3602 3603 3604 3605 3606 3607								7420	3856 3857 3858 3859 3860 3861 3862 3863							
7030	3608 3609 3610 3611 3612 3613 3614 3615								7430	3864 3865 3866 3867 3868 3869 3870 3871							
7040	3616 3617 3618 3619 3620 3621 3622 3623								7440	3872 3873 3874 3875 3876 3877 3878 3879							
7050	3624 3625 3626 3627 3628 3629 3630 3631								7450	3880 3881 3882 3883 3884 3885 3886 3887							
7060	3632 3633 3634 3635 3636 3637 3638 3639								7460	3888 3889 3890 3891 3892 3893 3894 3895							
7070	3640 3641 3642 3643 3644 3645 3646 3647								7470	3896 3897 3898 3899 3900 3901 3902 3903							
7100	3648 3649 3650 3651 3652 3653 3654 3655								7500	3904 3905 3906 3907 3908 3909 3910 3911							
7110	3656 3657 3658 3659 3660 3661 3662 3663								7510	3912 3913 3914 3915 3916 3917 3918 3919							
7120	3664 3665 3666 3667 3668 3669 3670 3671								7520	3920 3921 3922 3923 3924 3925 3926 3927							
7130	3672 3673 3674 3675 3676 3677 3678 3679								7530	3928 3929 3930 3931 3932 3933 3934 3935							
7140	3680 3681 3682 3683 3684 3685 3686 3687								7540	3936 3937 3938 3939 3940 3941 3942 3943							
7150	3688 3689 3690 3691 3692 3693 3694 3695								7550	3944 3945 3946 3947 3948 3949 3950 3951							
7160	3696 3697 3698 3699 3700 3701 3702 3703								7560	3952 3953 3954 3955 3956 3957 3958 3959							
7170	3704 3705 3706 3707 3708 3709 3710 3711								7570	3960 3961 3962 3963 3964 3965 3966 3967							
7200	3712 3713 3714 3715 3716 3717 3718 3719								7600	3968 3969 3970 3971 3972 3973 3974 3975							
7210	3720 3721 3722 3723 3724 3725 3726 3727								7610	3976 3977 3978 3979 3980 3981 3982 3983							
7220	3728 3729 3730 3731 3732 3733 3734 3735								7620	3984 3985 3986 3987 3988 3989 3990 3991							
7230	3736 3737 3738 3739 3740 3741 3742 3743								7630	3992 3993 3994 3995 3996 3997 3998 3999							
7240	3744 3745 3746 3747 3748 3749 3750 3751								7640	4000 4001 4002 4003 4004 4005 4006 4007							
7250	3752 3753 3754 3755 3756 3757 3758 3759								7650	4008 4009 4010 4011 4012 4013 4014 4015							
7260	3760 3761 3762 3763 3764 3765 3766 3767								7660	4016 4017 4018 4019 4020 4021 4022 4023							
7270	3768 3769 3770 3771 3772 3773 3774 3775								7670	4024 4025 4026 4027 4028 4029 4030 4031							
7300	3776 3777 3778 3779 3780 3781 3782 3783								7700	4032 4033 4034 4035 4036 4037 4038 4039							
7310	3784 3785 3786 3787 3788 3789 3790 3791								7710	4040 4041 4042 4043 4044 4045 4046 4047							
7320	3792 3793 3794 3795 3796 3797 3798 3799								7720	4048 4049 4050 4051 4052 4053 4054 4055							
7330	3800 3801 3802 3803 3804 3805 3806 3807								7730	4056 4057 4058 4059 4060 4061 4062 4063							
7340	3808 3809 3810 3811 3812 3813 3814 3815								7740	4064 4065 4066 4067 4068 4069 4070 4071							
7350	3816 3817 3818 3819 3820 3821 3822 3823								7750	4072 4073 4074 4075 4076 4077 4078 4079							
7360	3824 3825 3826 3827 3828 3829 3830 3831								7760	4080 4081 4082 4083 4084 4085 4086 4087							
7370	3832 3833 3834 3835 3836 3837 3838 3839								7770	4088 4089 4090 4091 4092 4093 4094 4095							

7000   3584
to   to
7777   4095
(Octal)   (Decimal)

G.2. POWERS OF TWO

2^n	n	2^{-n}
1	0	1.0
2	1	0.5
4	2	0.25
8	3	0.125
16	4	0.062 5
32	5	0.031 25
64	6	0.015 625
128	7	0.007 812 5
256	8	0.003 906 25
512	9	0.001 953 125
1 024	10	0.000 976 562 5
2 048	11	0.000 488 281 25
4 096	12	0.000 244 140 625
8 192	13	0.000 122 070 312 5
16 384	14	0.000 061 035 156 25
32 768	15	0.000 030 517 578 125
65 536	16	0.000 015 258 789 062 5
131 072	17	0.000 007 629 394 531 25
262 144	18	0.000 003 814 697 265 625
524 288	19	0.000 001 907 348 632 812 5
1 048 576	20	0.000 000 953 674 316 406 25
2 097 152	21	0.000 000 476 837 158 203 125
4 194 304	22	0.000 000 238 418 579 101 562 5
8 388 608	23	0.000 000 119 209 289 550 781 25
16 777 216	24	0.000 000 059 604 644 775 390 625
33 554 432	25	0.000 000 029 802 322 387 695 312 5
67 108 864	26	0.000 000 014 901 161 193 847 656 25
134 217 728	27	0.000 000 007 450 580 596 923 828 125
268 435 456	28	0.000 000 003 725 290 298 461 914 062 5
536 870 912	29	0.000 000 001 862 645 149 230 957 031 25
1 073 741 824	30	0.000 000 000 931 322 574 615 478 515 625
2 147 483 648	31	0.000 000 000 465 661 287 307 739 257 812 5
4 294 967 296	32	0.000 000 000 232 830 643 653 869 628 906 25
8 589 934 592	33	0.000 000 000 116 415 321 826 934 814 453 125
17 179 869 184	34	0.000 000 000 058 207 660 913 467 407 226 562 5
34 359 738 368	35	0.000 000 000 029 103 830 456 733 703 613 281 25
68 719 476 736	36	0.000 000 000 014 551 915 228 366 851 806 640 625
137 438 953 472	37	0.000 000 000 007 275 957 614 183 425 903 320 312 5
274 877 906 944	38	0.000 000 000 003 637 978 807 091 712 951 660 156 25
549 755 813 888	39	0.000 000 000 001 818 989 403 545 856 475 830 078 125
1 099 511 627 776	40	0.000 000 000 000 909 494 701 772 928 237 915 039 062 5
2 199 023 255 552	41	0.000 000 000 000 454 747 350 886 464 118 957 519 531 25
4 398 046 511 104	42	0.000 000 000 000 227 373 675 443 232 059 478 759 765 625
8 796 093 022 208	43	0.000 000 000 000 113 686 837 721 616 029 739 379 882 812 5
17 592 186 044 416	44	0.000 000 000 000 056 843 418 860 808 014 869 689 941 406 25
35 184 372 088 832	45	0.000 000 000 000 028 421 709 430 404 007 434 844 970 703 125
70 368 744 177 664	46	0.000 000 000 000 014 210 854 715 202 003 717 422 485 351 562 5
140 737 488 355 328	47	0.000 000 000 000 007 105 427 357 601 001 858 711 242 675 781 25
281 474 976 710 656	48	0.000 000 000 000 003 552 713 678 800 500 929 355 621 337 890 625
562 949 953 421 312	49	0.000 000 000 000 001 776 356 839 400 250 464 677 810 668 945 312 5
1 125 899 906 842 634	50	0.000 000 000 000 000 888 178 419 700 125 232 338 905 334 472 656 25

G.3. SCALES OF NOTATION

G.3.1. 2^x in Decimal

x	2^x	x	2^x	x	2^x
0.001	1.00069 33874 62581	0.01	1.00695 55500 56719	0.1	1.07177 34625 36293
0.002	1.00138 72557 11335	0.02	1.01395 94797 90029	0.2	1.14869 83549 97035
0.003	1.00208 16050 79633	0.03	1.02101 21257 07193	0.3	1.23114 44133 44916
0.004	1.00277 64359 01078	0.04	1.02811 38266 56067	0.4	1.31950 79107 72894
0.005	1.00347 17485 09503	0.05	1.03526 49238 41377	0.5	1.41421 35623 73095
0.006	1.00416 75432 38973	0.06	1.04246 57608 41121	0.6	1.51571 65665 10398
0.007	1.00486 38204 23785	0.07	1.04971 66836 23067	0.7	1.62450 47927 12471
0.008	1.00556 05803 98468	0.08	1.05701 80405 61380	0.8	1.74110 11265 92248
0.009	1.00625 78234 97782	0.09	1.06437 01824 53360	0.9	1.86606 59830 73615

G.3.2. $10^{\pm n}$ in Octal

10^n	n	10^{-n}
1	0	1.000 000 000 000 000 000 00
12	1	0.063 146 314 631 463 146 31
144	2	0.005 075 341 217 270 243 66
1 750	3	0.000 406 111 564 570 651 77
23 420	4	0.000 032 155 613 530 704 15
303 240	5	0.000 002 476 132 610 706 64
3 641 100	6	0.000 000 206 157 364 055 37
46 113 200	7	0.000 000 015 327 745 152 75
575 360 400	8	0.000 000 001 257 143 561 06
7 346 545 000	9	0.000 000 000 104 560 276 41
112 402 762 000	10	0.000 000 000 006 676 337 66
1 351 035 564 000	11	0.000 000 000 000 537 657 77
16 432 451 210 000	12	0.000 000 000 000 043 136 32
221 411 634 520 000	13	0.000 000 000 000 003 411 35
2 657 142 036 440 000	14	0.000 000 000 000 000 264 11
34 327 724 461 500 000	15	0.000 000 000 000 000 022 01
434 157 115 760 200 000	16	0.000 000 000 000 000 001 63
5 432 127 413 542 400 000	17	0.000 000 000 000 000 000 14
67 405 553 164 731 000 000	18	0.000 000 000 000 000 000 01

G.3.3. $n \log 2$ and 10 in Decimal

n	$n \log_{10} 2$	$n \log_2 10$	n	$n \log_{10} 2$	$n \log_2 10$
1	0.30102 99957	3.32192 80949	6	1.80617 99740	19.93156 85693
2	0.60205 99913	6.64385 61898	7	2.10720 99696	23.25349 66642
3	0.90308 99870	9.96578 42847	8	2.40823 99653	26.57542 47591
4	1.20411 99827	13.28771 23795	9	2.70926 99610	29.89735 28540
5	1.50514 99783	16.60964 04744	10	3.01029 99566	33.21928 09489

G.3.4. Addition and Multiplication, Binary and Octal

Addition	Multiplication

Binary Scale

$$0 + 0 = \ 0$$
$$0 + 1 = 1 + 0 = \ 1$$
$$1 + 1 = 10$$

$$0 \times 0 = 0$$
$$0 \times 1 = 1 \times 0 = 0$$
$$1 \times 1 = 1$$

Octal Scale

0	01	02	03	04	05	06	07
1	02	03	04	05	06	07	10
2	03	04	05	06	07	10	11
3	04	05	06	07	10	11	12
4	05	06	07	10	11	12	13
5	06	07	10	11	12	13	14
6	07	10	11	12	13	14	15
7	10	11	12	13	14	15	16

1	02	03	04	05	06	07
2	04	06	10	12	14	16
3	06	11	14	17	22	25
4	10	14	20	24	30	34
5	12	17	24	31	36	43
6	14	22	30	36	44	52
7	16	25	34	43	52	61

G.3.5. Mathematical Constants in Octal

$$\pi = 3.11037\ 552421_8 \qquad e = 2.55760\ 521305_8$$
$$\pi^{-1} = 0.24276\ 301556_8 \qquad e^{-1} = 0.27426\ 530661_8$$
$$\sqrt{\pi} = 1.61337\ 611067_8 \qquad \sqrt{e} = 1.51411\ 230704_8$$
$$\ln \pi = 1.11206\ 404435_8 \qquad \log_{10} e = 0.33626\ 754251_8$$
$$\log_2 \pi = 1.51544\ 163223_8 \qquad \log_2 e = 1.34252\ 166245_8$$
$$\sqrt{10} = 3.12305\ 407267_8 \qquad \log_2 10 = 3.24464\ 741136_8$$

$$\gamma = \ \ \ 0.44742\ 147707_8$$
$$\ln \gamma = -0.43127\ 233602_8$$
$$\log_2 \gamma = -0.62573\ 030645_8$$
$$\sqrt{2} = \ \ \ 1.32404\ 746320_8$$
$$\ln 2 = \ \ \ 0.54271\ 027760_8$$
$$\ln 10 = \ \ \ 2.23273\ 067355_8$$

BIBLIOGRAPHY

Abrams, M. D., and P. G. Stein, *Computer Hardware and Software: An Interdisciplinary Introduction*, Addison-Wesley, Reading, Mass., 1973.

Bell, C. G., and A. Newell, *Computer Structures: Readings and Examples*, McGraw-Hill, New York, 1971.

Berztiss, A. T., *Data Structures—Theory and Practice*, Academic Press, New York, 1971.

Brillinger, P. C., and D. J. Cohen, *Introduction to Data Structures and Nonnumeric Computations*, Prentice-Hall, Englewood Cliffs, N.J., 1972.

Brinch Hansen, P., *Operating System Principles*, Prentice-Hall, Englewood Cliffs, N.J., 1973.

Cohen, L. J., *Operating Systems Analysis and Design*, Spartan Books, New York, 1970.

Denning, P. J., "Third Generation Computer Systems," *Computing Surveys*, Vol. 3, No. 4, 1971.

Denning, P. J., and E. G. Coffman, *Operating-Systems Theory*, Prentice-Hall, Englewood Cliffs, N.J., 1973.

Donovan, J. J., *Systems Programming*, McGraw-Hill, New York, 1972.

Flores, I., *Computer Programming*, Prentice-Hall, Englewood Cliffs, N.J., 1966.

Flores, I., *Computer Organization*, Prentice-Hall, Englewood Cliffs, N.J., 1969.

Flores, I., *Data Structure and Management*, Prentice-Hall, Englewood Cliffs, N.J., 1970.

Foster, C. C., *Computer Architecture*, Van Nostrand Reinhold, New York, 1970.

Gear, C. W., *Computer Organization and Programming*, 2nd ed., McGraw-Hill, New York, 1974.

Hellerman, H., *Digital Computer System Principles*, 2nd ed., McGraw-Hill, New York, 1973.

Husson, S. S., *Microprogramming: Principles and Practices*, McGraw-Hill, New York, 1970.

Johnson, L. R., *System Structure in Data, Programs, and Computers*, Prentice-Hall, Englewood Cliffs, N.J., 1970

Katzan, H., *Computer Organization and the System/370*, Van Nostrand Reinhold, New York, 1971.

Katzan, H., Jr., *Operating Systems—A Pragmatic Approach*, Van Nostrand Reinhold, New York, 1973.

Kent, W., "Assembler-Language Macroprogramming," *Computing Surveys*, Vol. 1, No. 4, 1969.

Knuth, D. E., *The Art of Computer Programming*, Vol. 1, *Fundamental Algorithms*, Addison-Wesley, Reading, Mass., 1968

Mauer, W. D., *Programming: An Introduction to Computer Languages and Techniques*, Holden-Day, San Francisco, 1968.

Organick, E.I., *The Multics System: An Examination of Its Structure*, MIT Press, Cambridge, Mass., 1972.

Phister, M., *Logical Design of Digital Computers*, Wiley, New York, 1959.

Presser, L., and J. R. White, "Linkers and Loaders," *Computing Surveys*, Vol. 4, No. 3, 1972.

Ralston, A., *Introduction to Programming and Computer Science*, McGraw-Hill, New York, 1971.

Rosin, R. F., "Contemporary Concepts of Microprogramming and Emulation," *Computing Surveys*, Vol. 1, No. 4, 1969.

Stone, H. S., *Introduction to Computer Organization and Data Structures*, McGraw-Hill, New York, 1972.

Van Dam, A., and D. E. Rice, "On-Line Text Editing: A Survey," *Computing Surveys*, Vol. 3, No. 3, 1971.

Walker, T. M., *Introduction to Computer Science: An Interdisciplinary Approach*, Allyn and Bacon, Boston, 1972.

Watson, R. W., *Timesharing System Design Concepts*, McGraw-Hill, New York, 1970.

Wegner, P., *Programming Languages, Information Structures, and Machine Organization*, McGraw-Hill, New York, 1968.

Edit-11 Text Editor, Digital Equipment Corp., Maynard, Mass., 1972.

Link-11 Linker and Libr-11 Librarian, Digital Equipment Corp., Maynard, Mass., 1972.

Macro-11 Assembler, Digital Equipment Corp., Maynard, Mass., 1972.

ODT-11R Debugging Program, Digital Equipment Corp., Maynard, Mass., 1972.

PDP-11 Paper Tape Software Programming Handbook, Digital Equipment Corp., Maynard, Mass., 1973.

PDP-11 Peripherals and Interfacing Handbook, Digital Equipment Corp., Maynard, Mass., 1972.

PDP-11 Processor Handbook, Digital Equipment Corp., Maynard, Mass., 1972.

INDEX